The Search for Government Efficiency

The Search For Government Efficiency

From Hubris to Helplessness

George W. Downs
University of California

Patrick D. Larkey
Carnegie-Mellon University

RANDOM HOUSE   New York

To the many hard-working and surprisingly efficient
government employees in the United States

First Edition
987654
Copyright © 1986 by George W. Downs and Patrick D. Larkey

Library of Congress Cataloging-in-Publication Data

Downs, George W.
  The search for government efficiency.

  Bibliography: p.
  Includes index.
  1. Public administration.   2. Industrial management.
3. Organizational effectiveness.   I. Larkey, Patrick D.,
1943–   .   II. Title.
JF1411.D66   1986   350.007'5   85-24371
ISBN 0-394-35213-0 (pbk.)

Manufactured in the United States of America

PERMISSIONS: Pages 11, 17: Paul A. Taylor, *Civil Service at 100: Cliches and Contradictions.* Copy-right © 1983 by The Washington Post. Page 55: Joseph H. Engel, *Operations Research.* Copyright © 1969 by Operations Research Society of America. Reprinted by permission. Page 250: Herbert A. Simon, *The Science of the Artificial.* Copyright © 1969 by MIT Press.

PREFACE

If you are like most Americans, you believe that governments are inherently inefficient and that if all the waste in government were eliminated, taxes could be low-
ered substantially. You believe that government employees have extremely secure
jobs with high wages and retirement benefits and that these jobs require them to
do very little work. You believe that the life of an employee is much harder in
private business where the drive for profits leads to a high degree of insecurity,
low wages, and extreme pressure to perform. You believe that there should be less
government and that what remains should be run as if it were a business. Almost
certainly you believe that if you were in charge, the government would not pay
$90 for screws that cost 3 cents at any local hardware store, $1,000 for wrenches
that cost $9 at the same store, and $6,000 for coffee makers that are not very different from those available for $35 or $40.

If this book succeeds, it will force you to confront and complicate these beliefs.
You will be asked to think about what evidence you actually have on the efficiency
of government, and you will learn why some evidence like the much ballyhooed
$90 screws, $1,000 wrenches and $6,000 coffee pots are instances that may or may
not be symptomatic of more general efficiency problems. You will learn that business may not be all that it cracks itself up to be in terms of efficiency. You will
learn that over the past two hundred years several of the currently popular reform
strategies have been tried more than once with no success. Most importantly, you
will learn that the problem of government efficiency is not nearly as simple as it
has been made to appear.

It is important to understand what this book does and does not argue. It does
argue that governments are more efficient and businesses less efficient than popularly believed. It does argue that it is very difficult to know just how efficient any
particular government agency or business firm is and virtually impossible to fairly
compare the relative efficiency of these two types of organizations. It *does not* argue that governments are efficient and that there are no problems. The book does
argue that many reform strategies have been tried again and again with no success
and that there are more promising lines of reform. It *does not* offer a simple, sure-
fire method of improving government efficiency, such as "run it like a business."
Indeed, the book argues that all such methods are inherently foolish and that they
enjoy periodic popularity mainly because they pander to widespread prejudices
and to the American penchant for simple, quick solutions to complex problems.

The book is not a partisan tract. Democrats and Republicans alike have embraced foolish, ineffective reforms. If it appears that conservative Republicans are
criticized more than other groups, it is merely because they have spent more time
excoriating government for its supposed inefficiency and congratulating private enterprise for its supposed efficiency. We are not in favor of more government and

less private enterprise. We are in favor of a more balanced and thoughtful approach to the problem of inefficiency as this country sorts out the appropriate roles of business and government.

We have benefited from the comments of many people. Bob Atkins, Bill Cobb, Greg Fischer, and Hal Hovey read early versions and made helpful suggestions. Tom Anton, Bob Coulam, Jim Hudak, Steve Klepper, Larry Mohr, Richard Smith, Ken Oye and four anonymous reviewers provided exceptionally extensive and useful comments on earlier versions. We have not accepted all of their advice, but the book is certainly better as a result of their efforts. The manuscript at various stages over the past three years has been used in classes at Carnegie-Mellon University and the University of California at Davis. The student feedback has been useful both in sharpening the exposition and in sustaining our morale when it seemed that the writing and revisions would never end.

The manuscript took an interminably long time to prepare and outlasted one publisher, three computer systems, and four secretaries. We are extremely grateful to F. Dorothea Marsh for her efforts in text editing, formatting, and copying the manuscript over the last three years of the preparation odyssey.

One last point: should readers detect any remaining errors and find a particular argument inadequate, they should not hesitate to draw them to the attention of one of the authors. Experience has shown that it is invariably the author not present who is responsible.

George W. Downs
DAVIS, CALIFORNIA

Patrick D. Larkey
PITTSBURGH, PENNSYLVANIA

CONTENTS

The Search for Government Efficiency

CHAPTER 1

The Perpetual Problem of Government Performance: If You're So Rich and Powerful, Why Aren't You Smart?

Too bad that all of the people who know how to run the country are busy driving taxicabs and cutting hair.

GEORGE BURNS

Government in the United States is perpetually a target for reform. Most people believe government is doing things that it should not do and not doing things that it should do. Almost everyone believes that government bureaucracies are inefficient and ineffective. The disagreements about what government should do are inevitable and not particularly bothersome. Indeed, they are the foundation of politics. Agreement about waste and mismanagement in government is more disturbing, because these problems seem more amenable to solution and because each succeeding national, state, and municipal administration has vowed to improve government performance.

Yet, despite the promises, the history of attempts to make government more efficient and effective seems largely one of futility. In the wake of campaign after campaign, reform after reform, the incidents of bureaucratic stupidity and waste seem only to multiply. Consider the following examples from contemporary, much-reformed U.S. governments.

The state of Pennsylvania pays out $492,000 in subsidies to the Pittsburgh and Lake Erie Railroad, which is used by an average of 250 commuters a day. At this rate the state could afford to buy each rider a new Toyota every three years.

A new federal program designed to determine how well the nation's meat inspectors protect consumers found that 32 percent of the meat packing plants rated satisfactory by inspectors failed to meet minimum Department of Agriculture standards.

A funeral director had to spend $200 to replace a sign at his funeral home because a state inspector noticed that the lettering was only 2 ¾ inches high. A 3-inch height is required by law.

A 67-year-old crippled newspaper vendor in Charlottesville, Va., lost her Medicaid benefits when it was discovered that she had saved and invested $1,000 in a certificate to pay for her funeral.

Investigators for the House Appropriations Committee have charged that the Defense Department is needlessly wasting millions of dollars in "excess procurement costs"

1

because it refuses to get competitive bids on spare parts for major weapons systems. Staffers cite a 10-foot aluminum ladder used by mechanics to service the A-10 attack plane. In 1980 the Air Force bought 71 such ladders at a cost of $1,167 each. Comparable models sell in hardware stores for $160.

The Labor and Industry Department of one state refused to grant an operating permit to a McDonald's restaurant because it had no ramp to aid handicapped people trying to enter the basement. This was done over the manager's protest that there was no reason for customers—whether handicapped or not—to enter the basement.

Investigators of the Jersey City Redevelopment Agency discovered an "extraordinary array of improper fiscal practices," which ran the gamut from the outright theft of $100,000 to the spending of $2.5 million without adequate budgets, record keeping, or fiscal controls. "The agency's check-writing machine and blank checks were sitting on a windowsill, but the toilet paper was locked up . . . . . "

Despite the fact that accountants estimate that $10 million a year in operating costs could be saved by moving the small staff assigned there a few miles up the road to a more modern facility, Fort Monroe (Va.) remains an active army post. Characterized as an afterthought of the War of 1812, it is, in fact, the only post left with a moat around it.

In order to symbolize his commitment to eliminating red tape for small businesses, a recent governor of Pennsylvania sent out thousands of spools of the bothersome stuff. The stunt cost $30,500.

Secretary of Commerce Malcolm Baldrige spent close to $120,000 in 1981 replacing office carpeting that was only eight months old, expanding his official dining room, modernizing his private bathroom, and buying color-coordinated sport coats for his security guards.

Initial projections estimated that the F-15 fighter would require 11 maintenance man-hours for every hour of flight time and a mean time between system failures of 5.6 hours. To date, the plane has required an average of 27 man-hours of maintenance per hour aloft and has had a mean time between failures of only 1.2 hours—a "shockingly low" figure.

Mr. Gerald L. Lichty received a notice of overdue personal property taxes from Prince William County (Va.). The notice told Lichty to pay promptly or legal action would begin on August 14. The amount in question was 1 cent.

Over a five-year period Colonel Bob Dilger managed to save the Air Force over $124 million that had been allocated for a weapons project. He was subsequently passed over by the Air Force for promotion and resigned in disgust.

Such accounts of government behavior are common and frustrating. The majority of government employees are reasonably intelligent, honest, and well-meaning people who should be able to avoid such incidents. What's wrong?

This book examines the problem of government performance and the prospects for improving it. The central questions are: Why do citizens believe that governments are so badly mismanaged? How inefficient are governments? What reforms have been tried and how successful were they? Why do so many reforms fail? What reforms are worth undertaking in the future?

In the course of examining these questions, several interrelated themes are developed. *First, governments are probably not as poorly managed and businesses are certainly not as well managed as is generally believed.* Popular conceptions of government performance are not founded on careful analysis but on an amalgam of ideology, anecdotal evidence, and invidious comparison. Images of U.S. private sector performance ignore a remarkably undistinguished record of productivity growth relative to other industrialized nations as well as countless individual instances of business inefficiency comparable to those of the worst government bureaucracies. The vast majority of supposedly rigorous comparisons of performance in the public and private sectors tend to be flawed or inconclusive and not particularly useful in devising reforms.

Second, regardless of how many times and how loudly those who have not tried it assert the contrary, running a government bureaucracy is not the same as running a business. The frequently (and piously) cited experience of "meeting a payroll" is largely irrelevant to managing a governmental agency; success in meeting payrolls in business does not qualify one as an expert in government management, any more than success in playing point guard in the National Basketball Association qualifies one to play defensive tackle in the National Football League or experience playing the role of a doctor in a television series qualifies one to practice medicine. There are substantially more limitations on executive authority in government than in business. The time horizon for accomplishing programs is often shorter. Perhaps most importantly, the goals in government are different in kind as well as content. Government bureaucracies are not only often expected to achieve conflicting goals but are also frequently assigned tasks that no one inside or outside of government knows how to accomplish. In government, unlike the private sector, the feasibility and expected rate of return of a project are of less concern than its general praiseworthiness and appeal to the electorate. Government goals aren't chosen on the basis of what *can* be done but on what *should* be done. Health care costs should be reduced, cancer should be cured, illegal immigration should be checked, energy independence should be achieved, and crime should be reduced. In areas where there is no reliable technology, expecting organizations to function as efficiently and effectively as firms that manufacture beer or aspirin is expecting too much.

Third, attempts to reform government are almost never informed sufficiently by past attempts at reform. The same strategies, usually renamed, are tried again and again with limited success. Rarely do proponents ask why previous efforts achieved only modest success and what this implies for their proposals. The result is that the ideals of government efficiency and effectiveness are being pursued very inefficiently and ineffectively. Those who seek to reform government must realize both that some otherwise commendable schemes enjoy only a miniscule chance of successful implementation and that simple-minded solutions to complex problems are capable of doing as much harm as good. For example, if all that was needed to improve the performance of government was to give control to a group of hard-charging, tough-minded business executives committed to remaking government in the image of the private sector, government's problems would have been solved when this strategy was first attempted some 100 years ago in city governments. A recent grandiose reform attempt, the President's Private Sector Survey on Cost Control (PPSS)—also known as the Grace Commission—is the archetype of the ineffectual, uninformed reform initiative that would bring business methods to government.

Fourth, there are probably inherent limitations on how efficiently any large organization can operate. Most man-made physical systems (e.g., engines) achieve, at best, 20 to 30 percent efficiency in converting energy from one form to another. Plants are only 2 to 8 percent efficient in converting the potential energy of light into fuel. Knowledge of this relatively modest performance disciplines the expectations of both engineers and agronomists. There are doubtless similar if much more ambiguous limitations on the maximum efficiency of human systems like government and other large-scale organizations. These limitations should discipline the expectations of voters and reformers. Some proportion of the output of these organizations will almost certainly be flawed or produced at something less than the maximum imaginable efficiency.

Fifth, politics and administration are inextricably intertwined. While we are more concerned here with the administrative issues surrounding the design of government programs than with the political issues of which programs are undertaken, the two are not easily separated. For governments, the binding limits on efficiency and effectiveness stem partly from the need to pursue conflicting objectives simultaneously. In many cases, these conflicting objectives directly reflect conflicting special interests. For example, the federal government has substantial price support programs for tobacco farmers; simultaneously, it publicizes the harmful effects of smoking, sponsors research to mitigate these ill effects, and pays much of the health care cost for smoking-related diseases. Politically justifiable—but inherently inefficient—decisions about which programs to operate and what constraints the programs must satisfy are often a more important source of poor performance than bad management.

Sixth, performance appraisal is a treacherous business. Researchers and government officials alike have an excessive faith in the management value of productivity data. When dealing with an undeveloped and poorly understood technology (e.g., crime prevention, health planning) or an area that is affected by the uncertain impact of uncontrollable and frequently unknown external factors (e.g., foreign affairs, managing the growth of the money supply), the possession of accurate, quantitative indicators of goal accomplishment can still leave decision makers in the dark about how well government agencies are doing and what to do next. Success at balancing your checkbook and completing your income tax return does not guarantee that you will achieve your goal of becoming a millionaire.

Seventh, grandiose strategies for improving government efficiency—such as the program, planning, and budgeting system; zero-base budgeting; management by objectives; and sunset legislation—contain the seeds of their own destruction. The prospective benefits of the reform strategies must be greatly overstated at the outset in order to "sell" the strategy to the politicians. The reform strategies assume a considerable willingness on the part of politicians to follow the dictates of analysis—a willingness that rarely exists; and implementation of such strategies requires analytic and personnel resources far in excess of what is usually available. As a result, these strategies leave in their wake a cynicism that makes it more difficult to implement more "tactical" reforms that promise to achieve genuine—if more modest—results.

The picture of government operations and reform attempts presented in this book is more complicated than that reflected in the media and political rhetoric. There it is assumed that one must favor either increasing or decreasing the size and role of government in the economy and society. This dichotomy—and the attention it gets—is regrettable. It distracts us from the complexity of many important questions concerning the functions that government can and should perform and how agencies can best perform the tasks assigned them. The focus on the pros and cons of government growth is also unfortunate because it means that Republican politicians have to spend a lot of time explaining why they nonetheless cast so many votes to sustain or increase government activities, while Democrats must continually explain how they can simultaneously favor government and free enterprise.

Although there are many complaints about "big government" and many contemporary reforms seek primarily to reduce the size of government, the complaints and reforms usually stem from dissatisfactions with particular government activities rather than from objections to mere size. Even its most ardent critics want government to do more in some areas and less in others. Ronald Reagan and his conservative allies in Congress increased defense expenditures while cutting the growth in social programs.

There is a story that St. Peter was once asked by some new arrivals about the difference between heaven and hell. He responded that the real differences are not so great as commonly imagined and turn on who performs what functions. In heaven, the French are the cooks, the British are the police, the Swiss are the administrators, the Italians are the lovers, and the Germans are the mechanics. In hell, the English are the cooks, the Germans are the police, the Italians are the administrators, the Swiss are the lovers, and the French are the mechanics. The problem in hell is not the number of cooks, the number of English, or hell's total population. Similarly, the problem with government is not simply its size or its rate of growth but what it is doing and how it is doing it.

BASIC CONCEPTS

You should never confuse efficiency with a liver condition.
MARY POPPINS

Before we can think seriously about government performance, it is essential to understand some basic terms. Popular discussions of "efficiency," "effectiveness," and "productivity" tend to be confused and confusing. Although there is an important distinction between efficiency and effectiveness, these terms are often used synonymously. Another important source of confusion is the strong tendency to describe programs whose goals you do not share, even well-managed programs, as inefficient and ineffective. The purpose of this section is to introduce and define the basic concepts.

There are two important types of efficiency: managerial (or engineering) efficiency and economic efficiency. Managerial efficiency is a ratio measure relating outputs to inputs. Inputs are the human, material, and other resources used to produce a good or service. For example, a municipal street cleaning operation uses the inputs of personnel, vehicles, gasoline, maintenance services, various materials and supplies, and building space (office, storage, etc.) in producing its service. All these inputs have some associated cost that can be summed for a total service cost. Outputs are units of goods or services produced from inputs. For the street cleaning operation, the measure might be the number of lane-miles cleaned. The managerial efficiency measure, then, is cost per unit of output or, in the example, cost per lane mile cleaned.

For all practical purposes, managerial efficiency is a relative measure based on previous performance levels or performance levels of other government agencies. If the cost of street cleaning has decreased from \$13.73 to \$10.16 per lane-mile from last year to this year, it is common to assume that the service is more efficient. The improvement might be due to an improved maintenance program that made more sweepers usable on average, fewer coffee breaks and other down time for drivers, better enforcement of parking ordinances prohibiting parking on streets to be swept, and the like. We say "assume" because the apparent improvement may also result from falsified records; crews resweeping the same streets again and again to maximize mileage; or new, more reliable equipment whose cost reflects in capital accounts but not in the efficiency measure. Similarly, if it costs Cleveland \$13.09 and Pittsburgh \$15.47 to sweep a lane-mile in the same year, the difference may be a difference in relative efficiency, or it may be attributable to a host of other factors such as physical differences between the cities, labor market differences, quality differences in the service provided, or accounting practices. One production system is more managerially efficient than another if it has a lower cost per unit of output or higher output per unit of cost and the systems are identical in all other relevant respects.

It is possible to think idly about absolute managerial efficiency where we would know *all* of the ways a given objective (set of outputs) might be attained and how much each would cost. We would then know how our current way compares to all other alternatives; if properly motivated, we would choose the least-cost (most efficient) alternative. It is, however, difficult to convince yourself in any real, non-trivial situation that you really know all of the alternatives and their costs. We are stuck with relative managerial efficiency measures.

Managerial efficiency takes the output you intend to produce as given; it does not question the output's benefit. Thus the Air Force can talk about the efficiency associated with different bomb delivery systems in terms of cost per kiloton of explosives on target without having to introduce data about the relative utility of tactical versus strategic weapons or defense versus domestic programs. The most efficient delivery system is simply the one that puts a given amount of explosives on target at the lowest cost or the most explosives on target for a given cost. Yet the fact that managerial efficiency is insensitive to the ultimate value of the output does not mean that it holds no implications for the general welfare. Designing a weapons system that accomplishes the same mission as an earlier system for much less money leaves that much more available to further improve defense, increase social security, or pursue cancer research.

Economic efficiency is a much more abstract concept than managerial efficiency. The criterion of efficiency widely preferred, at least conceptually, by economists is the Pareto criterion: An economic state (a given set of organizational, allocational, and distributional arrangements) is economically efficient if it is not possible to change the state and have someone better off and no one worse off. One practical problem with this criterion is that it is extremely difficult to invent or discover new policies that do not make someone worse off. Another practical problem is in making the concept concrete. Applying the criterion in any real circumstance requires accurate forecasts of all of the relevant effects of a proposed policy change; these are usually numerous and complicated, often unmanageably so.

The more widely cited criterion of efficiency, at least in benefit–cost analysis, is the Kaldor-Hicks criterion: A state is economically efficient if it is not possible to change it so that those who are better off *could* compensate those worse off. This criterion implies that projects with positive net benefits (or a ratio of benefits to costs greater than 1) are desirable. It does not require that winners compensate losers but only that such compensation be feasible. Not surprisingly, there are few instances of actual compensation to losers, although there are exceptions. One prominent recent example of such compensation is the federal aid to industries and employees who are affected by tariff reductions under the General Agreement on Tariffs and Trade (GATT).

The primary uses of the criteria of economic efficiency are conceptual. They raise important questions about organizational arrangements, particularly market organizations versus nonmarket organizations: What functions should government perform and which ones should be left to the private sector? To what extent should government regulate business? And so on. In addition, the Kaldor-Hicks criterion provides a loose rationale for the criterion of maximizing net present value in benefit–cost analysis—an analytic reform strategy considered in Chapter 4.

Because the economic efficiency criteria are defined with respect to individuals, they do not suffer from the same potential moral insensitivity as the managerial efficiency criterion. It would obviously be very difficult to justify as economically efficient any bomb delivery system if the interests of target populations are considered; the target populations would be "worse off." But the economic efficiency criteria do presume that the prevailing distribution of benefits and costs prior to the contemplation of change is reasonable if not optimal. The criteria endorse the status quo regardless of its moral standing.

Effectiveness is a measure of attainment. It is a ratio measure relating observed (actual) output (θ_t) to the planned (or desired) output ($\hat{\theta}_t$) for some time period (t). When multiplied by 100, the measure $\theta_t/\hat{\theta}_t$ is a statement of percentage effectiveness. For example, if our street cleaning operation planned to clean 2,500 lane-miles in the second quarter and managed to clean only 2,250, the operation would be only 90 percent effective. If the operation planned to clean 2,500 lane-miles and cleaned 7,500, it would be 300 percent effective. Note that a very effective organization need not be efficient. The operation cleaning 7,500 lane-miles for 300 percent effectiveness may be doing so at four times the cost per lane-mile of other comparable operations.

The usefulness of an effectiveness measure depends directly on the usefulness of the planned output. If the planned output is a meaningful target—that is, we value the output and the level of planned output places reasonable demands on producers (i.e., it requires them to do their best but not more)—then the effectiveness measure can be a useful managerial tool.

Effectiveness measures raise all the problems of government goals. Who should establish them? Organized special interests? Citizens, who pay for governments but who are disorganized and usually ignorant about public services? Employees, who might want to reduce levels of planned output in order to reduce their personal work loads? Government managers, who often lack clear incentives to maximize effectiveness (and efficiency)? Politicians, who are perpetually running for reelection and representing special interests? Analysts, on the basis of economic calculations of benefits and costs? All of the above? There are no easy answers.

Disagreement on goals and therefore on desired outputs and on what constitutes "effectiveness" is endemic to U.S. governments. We each bring a personal vision, however rough, of what levels of various governments' outputs are acceptable, and that vision changes with roles, experience, and what we are attending to at the moment. Because practical measures of effectiveness require specificity and can often be achieved only by arbitrary simplification, this means that effectiveness measures are, at best, problematic.

Still another way to gauge performance is by measuring productivity. Productivity measures are most closely related to managerial efficiency measures. The most common productivity measure relates a single input factor, labor, to output. These "single factor" productivity measures tell us how many person-years, person-months, person-days, or person-minutes it takes to produce an automobile or refrigerator. They are often used to compare productivity changes over time (e.g., it took x person-hours to produce a refrigerator in 1940 and it takes y—where y is less than x—person-hours today) or across locales (e.g., the average Japanese compact car uses 19.7 hours of labor while the comparable American car uses 49.3 hours). Although widely cited, such measures are less useful than they appear because of the difficulties in relating particular inputs to particular outputs. Once we leave the world of the assembly line, we find that labor often contributes to multiple outputs, and it is hard to apportion the effort among them. Perhaps the most extreme example of this difficulty is the problem of apportioning the efforts of a chief executive officer (CEO) of a multiproduct firm to the firm's products. Many of the CEO's activities involve more than one product, and there is no unequivocal way to decide what proportion of his or her effort is associated with a given product; there are only arbitrary ways (e.g., the cost of the CEO times each product's sales as a proportion of gross revenues).

A second serious problem with single-factor productivity measures is joint output. Multiple inputs determine outputs jointly. Single-factor comparisons are meaningless unless we somehow control for other relevant factors that play a role in determining output. A single-factor comparison in 1982 of a corn farmer in

Kentucky who is farming a few acres on a hardscrabble hillside using a mule and a plow forged in 1900 with a corn farmer in Indiana who is farming several hundred acres of prime bottom land with the advantages of modern farm machinery and new high-yield strains of corn from genetic research will show that the Indiana farmer uses much less labor input per bushel than the Kentucky farmer. Few of us would be tempted to make the inference commonly made from other productivity comparisons (e.g., Japanese and American steel workers) that the Indiana farmer is working harder than the Kentucky farmer. Other inputs, in this example land and capital, determine production simultaneously with labor. Single-factor productivity comparisons do not control for these other factors and are apt to be misleading. Dissatisfaction with single-factor productivity measures has led economists to devise total-factor productivity (TFP) measures that relate output to all inputs. TFP measures are essentially efficiency measures. We will examine productivity measures and the ways in which they have been used (and misused) later.

Although the basic concepts are simple enough in the abstract, the world is a messy, complex place and there remains a substantial gap between clear, concise definitions of efficiency, effectiveness, and productivity concepts like those just given and an ability to use the concepts in practical situations. This is true both in trying to understand how efficient or effective a government is and in trying to improve its efficiency and effectiveness. This gap has been apparent throughout the history of attempting to reform government.

BELIEFS ABOUT GOVERNMENT PERFORMANCE

Nobody notices when things go right.
ZIMMERMAN'S LAW OF COMPLAINTS

Although certain political leaders and public programs have been able, at times, to achieve some measure of popularity, this popularity has almost never carried over to "government" as an institution. Historically, most governments have been perceived as inefficient, ineffective, and venal. Contemporary U.S. governments are not exceptions to this general rule and the situation is worsening. The results of periodic surveys summarized in Table 1.1 show a clear trend of declining support for government in all five questions. The trend in question 3 about the wastefulness of government, the most directly relevant question here, is striking; 76 percent of the sample in 1976 believed that "people in government waste a lot of money we pay in taxes," compared with only 45 percent in 1958. More than half of those surveyed in 1976 believed that many of those running the government don't know what they are doing.

Few beliefs are more widely and persistently held in the United States than the belief that government employees are overpaid and underworked. Results like those from a recent survey on federal government employees reported in Tables 1.2 and 1.3 are the norm. Government employees are the butt of many jokes and cartoons. Politicians from both major political parties and at all levels of govern-

Table 1.1   Trends in Trust in Government, 1958–1976 (Percentages)

Attitudes of Trust or Distrust	Response Categories	1958	1964	1968	1970	1972	1973	1974	1976
1. How much of the time do you think you can trust the government in Washington to do what is right?	Always	16	15	8	7	7	4	3	4
	Most of the time	59	63	55	43	47	30	35	31
	Some of the time	24	22	37	45	46	66	63	65
	Total	99	100	100	100	100	100	100	100
	Number of cases	1,711	1,423	1,310	1,539	1,286	1,383	2,413	2,272
2. Would you say the government is pretty much run by a few big interests looking out for themselves or that it is run for the benefit of all of the people?	For benefit of all	—	69	56	45	47	28	27	27
	Few big interests	—	31	44	55	53	72	73	73
	Total		100	100	100	100	100	100	100
	Number of cases		1,335	1,212	1,423	1,223	1,317	2,270	2,565
3. Do you think that people in the government waste a lot of money we pay in taxes, waste some of it, or don't waste very much of it?	Not much	11	7	4	4	3	3	1	3
	Some	44	45	35	27	28	22	23	21
	A lot	45	48	61	69	69	75	76	76
	Total	100	100	100	100	100	100	100	100
	Number of cases	1,704	1,413	1,309	1,555	1,303	1,394	2,458	2,772
4. Do you feel that almost all of the people running the government are smart people who usually know what they are doing, or do you think that quite a few of them don't seem to know what they are doing?	Know what they are doing	61	72	61	54	56	53	52	47
	Don't know what they are doing	39	28	39	46	44	47	48	53
	Total	100	100	100	100	100	100	100	100
	Number of cases	1,681	1,386	1,280	1,508	1,262	1,348	2,378	2,660
5. Do you think that quite a few of the people running the government are a little crooked, not very many are, or do you think hardly any of them are crooked at all?	Hardly any	28	19	20	17	17	12	10	14
	Not very many	46	51	54	50	48	35	43	42
	Quite a few	26	30	26	33	36	53	47	44
	Total	1,670	1,383	1,283	1,517	1,284	1,373	2,412	2,684

Source: SRC/CPS election studies of 1958, 1964, 1968, 1970, 1972, 1973, 1974, and 1976 in Asher (1980, p. 9).

Table 1.2 **Who Works Harder?**

Q. OVERALL, WHO DO YOU THINK WORKS HARDER—PEOPLE IN FEDERAL GOVERNMENT JOBS
OR PEOPLE IN SIMILAR JOBS OUTSIDE THE GOVERNMENT?

Government Workers	14%
Nongovernment Workers	60%
No Difference	17%
No Opinion	9%

Source: Paul Taylor, "Civil Service at 100: Cliches and Contradictions," *Washington Post*, January 16, 1983.

ment run for office as critics of bureaucracy (i.e., the faceless collection of government employees). Once in office, many politicians discover that the bureaucracy serves them as a convenient scapegoat in explaining to their constituents why things have gone wrong or why they cannot accomplish anything.[1]

Where do these beliefs come from? Are they based on an unbiased analysis of a carefully selected sample of government agencies or activities? We doubt it. Most citizens have very limited knowledge about government and how it operates. The inattention of voters to candidates and issues is legendary: a mule, Boston Curtis, was elected Republican precinct committeeman from Milton, Washington, in 1938. Although this sort of behavior (assuming that Boston Curtis was not the most qualified candidate) is hardly the norm, many people cannot name key elected and appointed officials at the federal, state, and local levels or describe their stated policy preferences or responsibilities. Citizens also have a very limited knowledge of how the local taxes they pay are apportioned among governments and which governments provide which services. Many California voters, for example, thought that Proposition 13, which established property tax limitations on local government, would cut welfare expenditures. They were surprised to learn that local government's financial involvement in welfare was virtually nonexistent and that what they had done was to reduce the capacity of local governments to finance education, police and fire departments, parks, and other "basic" services.

Of course, the fact that citizens often have no more than a superficial knowledge of government and its actual level of performance is not solely attributable to disinterest and inattention. It is very difficult, as much research demonstrates, for

Table 1.3 **Who Is Paid More?**

Q. DO YOU BELIEVE THAT FEDERAL EMPLOYEES ARE PAID MORE, LESS, OR ABOUT THE SAME
AS PEOPLE IN SIMILAR JOBS OUTSIDE THE GOVERNMENT?

	January 1983	*September 1978*
PAID MORE	55%	56%
PAID LESS	10%	8%
PAID ABOUT THE SAME	22%	24%
NO OPINION	13%	12%

Source: Paul Taylor, "Civil Service at 100: Cliches and Contradictions," *Washington Post*, January 16, 1983.

even the most concerned and knowledgeable analyst to gauge performance. The size and complexity of government is one obstacle. In 1802 there were more criminals being held in federal prisons than the combined personnel in the armed services and federal bureaucracy. Twenty-seven years later, in 1829, the situation was still much the same: 95 percent of those employed by the government were either in the armed forces or collecting taxes, and there were more people in Congress than in the entire federal law enforcement establishment (Young, 1966, pp. 28–30). Needless to say, times have changed. By 1977 there were over 80,000 units of government in the United States with a combined work force constituting nearly 20 percent of the working population. The size and complexity of the federal government, in particular, has become awesome and incomprehensible. Just how much is a trillion dollars?

If most citizens know relatively little about what government is and how it performs, why do such a substantial majority believe so fervently that it is inefficient and ineffective? There are several possible explanations.

One possibility is that the belief in governmental inefficiency and ineffectiveness is ingrained in most of us as we are socialized. Perhaps we don't so much learn through objective experience that government works poorly as gradually absorb this attitude through contact with family, the media, and the rhetoric of political campaigns. This would place the belief in poor government performance in the same category as attitudes about self-reliance, hard work, and the democratic process. They are simply part of our culture.

If these attitudes are imprinted through socialization, they will be difficult to overturn, regardless of individuals' objective experience or exposure to conflicting evidence. Social psychologists have produced an enormous amount of experimental evidence showing the limited ability of individuals to evaluate objectively new evidence that conflicts with deeply ingrained predispositions. If, for example, people support capital punishment because they believe that it deters crime, no amount of data indicating that states with and without capital punishment have the same murder rate is likely to change their minds. Similarly, those convinced that capital punishment does not have a deterrent effect respond with an equally closed mind to data contradicting their position. Indeed, many findings suggest that conflicting evidence often reinforces a preexisting bias (see Nisbett and Ross, 1980, p. 170).

If such results accurately characterize the way people assess fresh evidence, it is easy to see how a belief in government inefficiency, even if untrue, could thrive. People are exposed to the view that government is inefficient at an early age, gradually absorb it, and then unconsciously reinforce that belief as they grow older by selectively admitting information in agreement with it and discounting conflicting information. This is the process by which ideologies come to masquerade as informed opinions. The ideological character of attitudes about government performance combined with the chronic absence of anything resembling legitimate evidence makes us suspect that something like this process may be operating in the formation and maintenance of beliefs about government.

Another possible explanation for the persistence of the belief in government inefficiency and ineffectiveness that also has a strong ideological flavor and involves selective perception focuses on differences between individuals' values and the goals of government. If an individual believes that the business of government should lie primarily in providing services A and B but observes that it is also providing C and D, the temptation is to view this as frivolous and inefficient behavior. After all, if less time were spent on services C and D, there could be greater output of services A and B, hence greater efficiency.

> Popular dissatisfaction with government cannot, of course, be solely attributed to mismanagement or to failures of execution by the government's senior officials. Capable administration of federal programs such as a Quiet Communities Program or a program to assure a free, appropriate education for handicapped children will not mollify those critics who object as a matter of principle to the very existence of the programs. The careful rationing of scarce fiscal resources or the efficient redistribution of income from one group to another via taxes and transfer payments will hardly silence the complaints of those who perceive that they are losers in the process. (Lynn, 1981, p. 22)

The claim that differences about government priorities are partly behind claims of government inefficiency enjoys considerable circumstantial support. The next time you read a column on government waste by an author of well-known persuasions, carefully note the examples used. There is an uncanny tendency for the authors to draw examples from service areas that they do not hold in particularly high esteem. Conservatives discover flagrant inefficiency in regulatory and welfare programs; liberals find waste rampant in military procurement and environmentally insensitive capital projects. There appears to be an especially high correlation between belief in government inefficiency and a distaste for redistributive programs of many types: medicare, federal aid to education, food stamps, and so forth. While it is possible that the distaste for the programs stems from objective evidence that they are managed inefficiently, it is at least as likely that they—and the government responsible for delivering them—are considered inefficient partly because the programs are politically unpalatable.

From the perspective of those responsible for operating a government, this tendency to equate the pursuit of goals that differ from one's own with inefficient administration is particularly distressing because it makes the judgment of inefficiency inevitable. There is no conceivable pattern of government spending and service delivery that will be viewed as optimal by everyone. Each individual will always see it as possible for government workers to produce a different set of outputs that are more valuable and thus to become more efficient. To the extent that we judge the efficiency (and effectiveness) of government by the congruence between its goals and our own, it will always disappoint us.

In addition to the preconceptions and values that color our assessment of government performance, there are also problems with the available "evidence." How much confidence can we have that stories in the press and the seemingly endless list of charges by political candidates seeking to unseat incumbents present an accurate sample of government activity?

Consider the portrait of government performance to which the average American is exposed. On the effectiveness side, we have schools in 1980 that are incapable of teaching the basic skills that were taken for granted in 1960. We appear to have an Office of Safety and Health Administration that busies itself with harassing small businesses about the height of fire extinguishers and the availability of portable toilets out on the prairie, while local newspapers report the daily discovery of dangerous chemicals next to housing developments, playgrounds, and sources of drinking water. We have a military that is increasingly dependent on planes that can't stay in the air and tanks that can't stay out of maintenance shops. On the efficiency side, conditions seem even worse. The media give the impression that street cleaners make at least $33,000 a year and that police and firemen regularly get raises of 25 percent or more after going out on prolonged strikes. The cost of constructing highways appears to have increased twenty fold in the last ten years. Then, there is always the U.S. Postal Service, which seems forever imposing higher postage rates and more complicated zip codes while service deteriorates.

Regardless of how accurate the above observations are as individual descriptions, it is a mistake to view them as a set of random observations. Neither the prospective officeholders nor the media are in the business of providing us with an objective portrait of government performance. Aspiring officeholders have strong incentives to paint a grim picture and, if possible, blame their opponents. The task of the media is to direct the public's attention to issues that will interest and inform. Tales of corruption, waste, and poor judgment in government do both. Such tales sell newspapers, boost ratings, and purportedly help a democracy function. Stories about the efficient collection of sales taxes and the effective treatment of water are neither particularly interesting nor particularly informative. Such positive accounts might provide citizens with a more well-rounded portrait of government performance, but they hardly constitute the same call to arms as stories about graft-taking politicians or drug use in schools. Some bias in the sample of government activity presented to citizens by the media is inevitable.

The many horror tales about government inefficiency and ineffectiveness may not mean very much. Given the combined size of federal, state, and local government and the range of services provided, it would be possible to have a far more efficient and effective government than has ever been provided anywhere in the world and still have enough scandalous examples of government performance to fill daily newspapers, half-hour news programs, and campaign speeches forever.

Citizens also gather evidence on government performance directly through personal contacts; but again, there are biases. Citizens are, for example, more likely to come into contact with some agencies than others. In earlier times, for instance, there was more citizen contact with local governments than with the federal government. Here is a description of the situation that existed around the turn of the century.

> In peaceful times the national government is remote from the daily life of the average citizen. Its wastefulness does not come home to him. Its corrupting patronage and jobbery are unperceived by him. Errors in the financial policy of the government become plain to him, only when he experiences their ill effects. The post-office is the only function of the national government which concerns him intimately, and that function is really a simple business, and has always been a government monopoly; so that the average citizen who gets his mail with tolerable regularity, and has no experience of any other method of sending letters and newspapers generally, thinks that the post-office business is as well done by government as it could be by any agency. Munic-

ipal functions, on the other hand, touch the average citizen very nearly. It makes a great difference to him whether the city keeps good schools or bad, and clean streets or dirty, supplies him with good water or bad, and taxes him fairly or unfairly. Moreover, all critics of the working of the institutions of the United States during the last fifty years—whether friendly or hostile, whether foreign or native—agree that municipal government has been the field in which the least efficiency for good has been exhibited and the greatest positive evils have been developed. (Eliot, 1891, pp. 153–154.)

Needless to say, this situation has changed. The enormous expansion of federal redistributive and regulatory activities together with the move from relatively invisible sources of revenue such as tariffs and excise taxes to more highly visible sources such as the income and corporate taxes, have made the federal government much less remote. Nonetheless, it is still true that the average citizen has no direct contact with many, if not most, state and federal agencies. Ask a neighbor how he thinks the Marine Mammal Commission is doing, whether the Board of International Broadcasting is still shirking its responsibilities, or whether the Milk Marketing Board has changed its inefficient ways. Unless your neighbor is very different from most, bewilderment is a more likely response than informed evaluation.

A bigger source of bias in the evidence on government performance is that most of what government does tends to be ignored unless something goes wrong. When we turn on the water in the morning to brush our teeth and potable water flows from the tap immediately, how many of us think positively about the municipal water department or are prompted to call and thank them for doing a good job? How many of us even notice? If, on the other hand, the water does not flow or flows with a strange color or smell, the switchboard in City Hall and phones in the water department will be busy.

The same phenomenon is evident in every service area. The amount of credit assigned to government for smooth roads, safe air corridors, coherent traffic management, solvent small farmers, and effective flood control is usually zero. Should conditions in these areas get 20 percent better, the credit will still be close to zero. If, however, conditions were to deteriorate by 20 percent, the probability that the incidents associated with this declining performance would be noted is fairly high. Potholes, aircraft near-misses, traffic jams, farm bankruptcies, and floods are much more conspicuous in their presence than in their absence.

Matters are made still worse by the uncanny tendency of many people to formulate generalizations about government efficiency and effectiveness on the basis of isolated instances of poor performance. When a Social Security disability claim is delayed or a weapons system suffers from a large cost overrun, the typical reaction is to credit the problems to bureaucratic bungling by government—casually lumping the behavior of the Social Security Administration and that of a small-town public works department into one large, homogeneous entity. Contrast this with what occurs when an organization in the private sector performs poorly. When Firestone Rubber Company produces tires that disintegrate at high speeds; Ford Motor Company builds a car that incinerates its passengers in rear-end collisions; Douglas Aircraft Company builds a "jumbo jetliner" whose cargo doors open, causing crashes that kill a few hundred people; we learn that drug compa-

nies and food processors have been selling us carcinogens for years; we discover
that industries have, over decades, been placing lead and harmful chemicals in
our waterways; or we find that the house we have purchased was built over a
chemical or nuclear waste dump, we may not buy the same product (if that option
is available) or we may seek legal remedies, but we are not prone to generalize
about the inefficiency and ineffectiveness of the business sector. We may, in fact,
direct our criticism at the government's regulatory apparatus that we rely on to
protect us from the objectionable consequences of the perhaps profitable activities
of "efficient," profit-seeking entities. The toxic waste cleanups in Missouri and
California are not voluntary acts by the polluters.

To this point we have concerned ourselves with factors that distort the ability
to assess objectively the efficiency and effectiveness of government: (1) beliefs that
government performance acquired during socialization coupled with an inclination toward selective reporting and perception are likely to cause individuals to become increasingly convinced that government performs poorly regardless of how
well it is actually doing; (2) the tendency to ignore the priorities that emerge from
political processes in favor of one's own values can create a basis for judgment that
has nothing to do with what government is mandated to achieve; and (3) exposure
to an unrepresentative set of government activities provides a biased picture of the
true situation. These factors probably account for a substantial portion of the present discontent about government performance. Suppose, however, for the sake of
argument, that there were a small group of observers who were both scrupulously
objective and well informed. These imaginary individuals would be capable of
measuring government achievement with uncommon accuracy and have a representative sample at their fingertips. How dissatisfied would they be with the current levels of government performance?

The answer to this question hinges on the nature of their expectations and the
standard of comparison used to establish these expectations. The most obvious
source of such a standard for comparison involves the past behavior of the same
government or the current behavior of other, comparable governments. These are
almost invariably the grounds for comparison in the private sector. Indeed, the
results of such comparisons are paraded in front of the American public at least
quarterly. Great attention is paid to the profitability and productivity of the steel,
automobile, and other industries relative to what they were doing last quarter or
last year or relative to the performance of the same industries in countries with
which the U.S. competes. If the rate of productivity increases or profitability is
greater than that of both the past and rival economies, observers are generally
pleased. If rates fall below past values or what is being achieved by West Germany
or Japan, there is often great concern.

The use of past behavior and the achievements of competitors as a basis for
forming judgments about present performance has a number of attractive features.
It grounds the judgment in reality by employing standards that are known to be
within the realm of possibility and it provides an easily interpretable context for
judging changes in performance. Rarely, however, is the performance of public
sector organizations evaluated in terms of their past performance or that of comparable units in the United States and other countries. Such comparisons are cer-

tainly not the principal source of popular dissatisfaction with government performance captured by opinion polls.

Indeed, when such comparisons are made, the results often conflict dramatically with preconceptions. Consider the U.S. Postal Service, an agency frequently vilified for its inefficiency and ineffectiveness.

> The fact is the United States Postal Service delivers more mail, more efficiently, for less money than in any other nation on earth, and it is getting better.
>
> It moves 110 billion pieces of mail per year, or some 161,879 pieces per employee, a productivity-per-worker rate that is 44 percent above that of the closest competitor, Japan.
>
> The cost of mailing a first class letter in the United States is 12th lowest of 14 industrialized nations surveyed last summer, with only Belgium, at an equivalent of 19.9 cents per letter, and Switzerland, at 19.2 cents, below the Postal Service's 20 cents. Germany charges the equivalent of 33 cents.
>
> Rates here have been rising at a slower pace than inflation since 1974 and, in 1979 for the first time in four decades, the Postal Service operated in the black. It did it again last year, and it is now operating on a fee basis. There are no subsidies anymore from Uncle Sam.
>
> Speed-of-delivery is on the rise, too. In 1982, the Postal Service met its next-day-delivery standard for first class mail traveling within a metropolitan area 95.5 percent of the time. In the two-day category, performance was 88 percent and in three-day delivery, 90 percent.
>
> Are its window clerks surly? The postal system monitors transactions at postal windows with inspectors asking out-of-the-ordinary questions. How must a parcel be wrapped to qualify for a special rate? That sort of thing. The accuracy rate was 75 percent in one 1980 study, but the pattern of mistakes and inaccurate charges was interesting. It tended to be the clerk giving the customer the benefit of the doubt. (Taylor, 1983.)

It would be very difficult to construct comparisons for the U.S. steel or automobile or electronics industries that show them doing as well relative to themselves historically or to the Japanese or Germans as the U.S. Postal Service is doing against comparable benchmarks. The highly efficient and profitable United Parcel Service and other private delivery services that are often offered as pejorative benchmarks for the U.S. Postal Service are simply not comparable. They "skim the cream" off the delivery business and have no obligation to provide a public service in handling unprofitable deliveries.

Moreover, it is very easy to find stories about the performance of the governments of other nations or of U.S. governments at an earlier time that make the problems of U.S. contemporary governments pale in comparison. Consider the following.

On municipal government in earlier times:

> Typical of cities under the sway of political bossism, Boston had a government filled with party regulars whose performance was questionable and whose handsome salaries were proving to be a costly drain on the city's treasury.
>
> [The Finance Commission of 1907] pointed to the "excessive number" of clerical employees and day laborers as the main source of "waste and inefficiency" in the city government. In the years from 1895 to 1907 the population of Boston had increased

by 22.7 percent, while the number of clerks had increased by 75 percent. At the same time, salaries continued to rise and by 1907 they were being paid three times more than those employed for similar work by the state government and private companies . . . .

These conditions were more evident in the employment of day labor. Since 1895 the number of workers employed by the city had increased by 50 percent. By 1907 the efficiency of labor had declined to a point where the work done per man was half as much as it had been before 1895. (Schiesl, 1977, pp. 102–104.)

Regarding the state of early federal public works:

In extending the Union Pacific railroad westward, the directors of the company set up a subsidiary corporation known as Credit Mobilier and then awarded fantastically profitable construction contracts to it. The actual cost of building the road from Omaha, Nebraska, to Promontory Point, Utah, has been estimated at $44 million, but Credit Mobilier charged more than $94 million. Oakes Ames, a wealthy and enterprising congressman from Massachusetts, was one of the principal officers of the new "railroad milking" corporation. From his vantage point in Congress, he sought to ward off any government inquiry into the activities of the two related companies by distributing Credit Mobilier stock to selected congressmen and administrative officials ("where it would do most good," as he told his business colleagues) at a fraction of their value and in some cases free. Among the recipients were House Speaker James Blaine, Vice President Schuyler Colfax, and a future president of the United States, James Garfield, then a member of the House of Representatives. When the scheme was exposed, the House contented itself with censuring Ames and absolving the other members involved, stating that they had behaved without corrupt motives. This action, almost as shocking as the wrongdoing itself, was symptomatic of the moral climate of the era (as well as the traditional reluctance of Congress to take action against its own members). As Ames argued in his defense, he was merely following practices that for years had been condoned in business and political life. (Bollens and Schmandt, 1979, pp. 32–33.)

On the early (pre-civil service) personnel practices of the federal government:

Appointment of illiterate clerks as a reward for party services did not advance the competence of the public service. Charles W. Clement was a clerk in the naval storekeeper's office in Philadelphia Navy Yard, keeping books. He was asked if he was acquainted with business of that kind, and replied, "Not much." He was invited to spell "crucifix" but failed in the test: "My memory is poor, and it is a long time since I went to school. I do not suppose I could spell it." He was a bricklayer by trade.

Henry J. Alvord, a clerk in the Detroit post office, admitted under examination that he performed his official duties in about one hour a day. He was also a reporter for a Detroit newspaper. George W. Baker was a brother of the collector of the port of Philadelphia, and had the good fortune also to marry a niece of President Buchanan. He was appointed assistant disbursing clerk at $1,200 a year in the Philadelphia customhouse, but admitted he acted instead as a confidential clerk to his brother. The Covode Committee could discover no official work that he performed. He was editor of *The Pennsylvania*, Buchanan's state journal. (White, 1954, pp. 328–329.)

From abroad:

Historically, Italian bureaucrats have given special meaning to the old expression *dolce far niente* (it is pleasant to do nothing). Absenteeism was rampant, feigned illness a way of life. In many cases, civil servants who did show up for work arrived late and left early.

Enter an anonymous postal inspector who recently spot-checked the mail facilities at Rome's Fiumicino Airport, one of the more glacial arms of Italy's infamous postal service. The inspector found only four of the office's 49 workers on the job . . . .

Maria Ferraguto, 50, who had won bonuses for hard work on her climb to the job of a personnel director in a Rome post office . . . was charged with aggravated and continuous fraud against the state, a felony that carries a penalty of up to three years in jail and up to $318 in fines. Her alleged crime: consistently checking in to her office at 11 a.m. and leaving at 1 p.m., thus working only two of the six daily hours required. Alessandro Bigneri, 29, police claim, should have been handling baggage at Fiumicino Airport, instead of working in his own elegant hi-fi store in nearby Ostia, when the cops showed up to woof and tweet.

The arrests are just beginning. Ten other government employees in Rome have been put behind bars, and another 278 government employees have been informed that they are under investigation, as are 90 doctors who signed suspect medical certificates.

(*Time*, 1982.)

From abroad at an earlier time:

Standards of performance [of the British Civil Service] were mediocre and remained indifferent throughout the first half of the nineteenth century. The collection of the revenue was in arrears to the amount of nearly 400,000 Pounds in 1780. The exchequer clung obstinately to the use of the Latin language and Roman numerals; to add them it was necessary to transcribe the columns into Arabic numerals and then translate back again to Latin. Lord Nelson asserted that the Navy had been defrauded by the official victualers "in a most scandalous and infamous manner." (White, 1948, p. 469.)

Although hardly a random sample, these examples are fairly outrageous by contemporary standards of honesty and efficiency among U.S. governments. We did not even have to draw upon the better-known scandals such as the Tweed Ring or Teapot Dome, or foreign fiascoes such as the U.S.S.R.'s management of agriculture, Polish human rights, or British management of nationalized industries. Where is the balance in the treatment of contemporary U.S. governments? By some standards, aren't they doing "better"?

Is public transportation more efficient and effective in 1980 than it was in 1950? Are public health departments doing a better job now than ten years ago? Are social services more efficiently delivered in St. Louis or Paris? Has the efficiency of federal agencies like the Securities and Exchange Commission, Institutes of Health, and Department of Labor increased or declined during the past five years? How much more (or less) effective are state insurance regulation agencies or state mental health agencies than they were a decade ago? Despite the fact that they set the background for virtually every discussion of performance in the private sector, such questions are so infrequently asked about government performance that they sound strange.

There is almost always a movement afoot that aspires to make such information on comparative performance available on a regular basis, but it never seems to exist.[2] Time-series and comparative data may be eminently sensible standards for assessing government performance, but they are not the ones generally used.

Still another source for standards of comparison are normative models. Here the observer pictures an optimally functioning agency and judges the performance of real government agencies in comparison to that ideal. For example, if the observer is an economist with conservative inclinations, that model will be grounded in the functioning of a well-disciplined market. Inefficiency will be charged wherever government fails to take advantage of the benefits that the creation or maintenance of such a market could purportedly provide. This judgment is not established empirically by examining the benefits and costs of the alternatives. It is reached analytically by a sort of syllogism:

a. Market systems allow individuals to choose freely and the invisible hand ensures societal efficiency.
b. Service X (education, pollution control, etc.) is bureaucratically supplied in a manner that is unresponsive to market forces.
c. Service X is being inefficiently supplied.

Much of the average American's conviction that private organizations are far more efficient than public bureaucracies rests on an unshakable faith in the virtues of a free market economy. It is a faith that has endured recessions, depressions, inflation, social unrest, recalls, and price-fixing scandals. Such markets emphasize individual freedom and, according to several generations of economists, produce an economy that efficiently responds to consumer demands. In the ideal market, associations are voluntary, power is diffused, and coordination is automatic. Suppliers are free to make those products or provide those services that they believe will make money. If they succeed in satisfying consumer tastes on quality and price, they will survive and perhaps, thrive. If not, they will be eliminated through "natural selection." Consumers are free to buy those products and services that they find most valuable, constrained only by the level of their resources.

The business executive's version of this creed turns on these proclaimed differences in the pressures on private versus government organizations to be efficient.

> Private sector management is driven by the need to ensure the enterprise's continued economic survival. This is a precondition for profit or any other measure of success and the satisfaction of this precondition requires constant attention to managerial efficiency and the effective use of resources in a competitive arena. The unforgiving tests of both the balance sheet and the marketplace must be met. Failure to meet the demands of either will, in time, bring the enterprise to an end, with the attendant consequences not only to management but to the investors, employees, suppliers, customers and the community as well. In short, the private sector cannot operate with a continuing and growing deficit. Failure to operate efficiently and to ensure a satisfactory return to investors will cause the private sector enterprise to fail, with devastating effects on all its components—particularly its employees.
>
> Government has no such incentive to survive, let alone succeed, nor any such test to meet. The Government, unlike private sector enterprise, is not normally managed as if it were subject to the consequences of prolonged managerial inefficiency or persistent failure to control costs. Such consequences have historically been avoided in the public sector — or, more accurately, postponed — by Government's propensity to in-

crease tax revenues, engage in deficit spending, and spend yet more money on failed programs with the result of masking their ineffectiveness. (PPSS, sec. VI, p. 2)

From this rendition of an increasingly popular refrain, it is clear that the only possible solution for the efficiency problems of governments is to provide them with a test equal to that faced by private-sector organizations as well as the management tools that firms use to pass their test.

If our observer is not a conservative economist or a business executive impressed with the extreme difficulty of what he or she does for a living, the model employed to generate a standard by which to gauge government performance will be much less formal. Often, it will be nothing more than a highly personal vision of the way things ought to be. One doesn't have to be an economic theorist or captain of industry to know that something is wrong if garbage is piling up in city streets and city buses are all 45 minutes late. But intuitions about what government should be able to do will carry us only so far. In many situations it is much more difficult to assess the level of efficiency and effectiveness relative to what could and should be achieved. For instance, it is not at all clear that city governments could or should be providing much better water services or fire protection, at least when the costs of doing so are considered. Nor on the federal level is it obvious that the Forest Service or Internal Revenue Service could easily double its effectiveness at half the price.

When intuitions about what constitutes efficient and effective government are overwhelmed by complex assessment problems, most people begin to evaluate government agencies not so much by the services they provide but by how they operate as organizations. In doing so, they usually adopt what they imagine the behavior of private corporations to be as their standard of comparison. To the extent that agencies operate like "bureaucracies" and not like corporations such as IBM or Mobil, they are judged to be performing poorly and to be in need of reform. At least two important assumptions lie behind such a judgment: (1) corporations are not bureaucracies and are run more efficiently than bureaucracies and (2) if government agencies behaved like corporations, they would become more efficient. As we shall see in the next chapter, both assumptions are questionable.

NOTES

1. Like the critical beliefs about Congress, the beliefs about the bureaucracy apply to the collective and are usually inconsistent with beliefs about specific individuals and the believer's direct experience with government. When asked about Congress as an institution, a high proportion of citizen respondents are very critical. But when asked about their own representative in Congress, a high proportion of respondents are highly complimentary (Fenno, 1978). Similarly, when the same respondents who believe that federal government workers are overpaid and underworked were asked about their levels of satisfaction with the conduct of government workers with whom they had some dealing in the past year, 14 percent were very pleased, 57 percent were pleased, 14 percent were

displeased, 4 percent were very displeased, and 11 percent had no opinion (Taylor, 1983). We have no data but expect that critics of government with a neighbor or relative who is a government employee often wonder how that individual can be so good when most government employees are obviously awful.

2. Indeed, the first movement we can discover was in the 1890s when the Census Bureau designed and collected municipal performance statistics for a few years. The effort died because of controversy about the interpretation of the numbers and because of budget problems in the Census Bureau.

REFERENCES

Asher, Herbert B. *Presidential Elections and American Politics: Voters, Candidates and Campaigns since 1952.* Homewood, Illinois: The Dorsey Press, 1980.

Bollens, John C., and Schmandt, Henry J. "Understanding Political Corruption." In *Political Corruption: Power, Money and Sex,* edited by J. C. Bollens and H. J. Schmandt. Pacific Palisades, Calif.: Palisades Publishers, 1979, pp. 32–33.

Eliot, Charles. "One Remedy for Municipal Misgovernment." *Forum* 12 (September 1891):153–154.

Fenno, Richard F. *Home Style: House Members in Their Districts.* Boston: Little, Brown, 1978.

Lynn, Lawrence. *Managing the Public's Business: The Job of the Government Executive.* New York: Basic Books, 1981.

Nisbett, Richard E., and Ross, Lee. *Human Inference: Strategies and Shortcomings of Social Judgment.* Englewood Cliffs, N.J.: Prentice-Hall, 1980.

President's Private Sector Survey on Cost Control: A Report to the President (PPSS), Committee for consideration at its meeting on January 15, 1984, processed.

Schiesl, Martin J. "The Politics of Efficiency," *Municipal Administration and Reform in America 1880–1920.* Berkeley, Calif.: University of California Press, 1977.

Taylor, Paul. "Civil Service at 100: Cliches and Contradictions," *Washington Post,* January 16, 1983.

Time, March 1, 1982.

White, Leonard D. *The Federalists.* New York: Macmillan, 1948.

White, Leonard D. "Government and the Public Economy," *The Jacksonians, 1829–1861.* New York: Macmillan, 1954.

Young, James S. *The Washington Community, 1800–1828.* New York: Harcourt, Brace & World, 1966.

CHAPTER 2

Business Versus Government: An Invidious Comparison?

> The problem is one we do not like to face. American government
> may be bureaucratic and inefficient, but American industry is just
> as bureaucratic and inefficient.
>
> LESTER THUROW

Throughout the past 100 years one major motivation for government reform has been to remold government agencies in the image of private firms.

> There is no reason why our city governments should be considered failures, and they would not be so considered if the majority of the people who live in cities desired their affairs to be conducted on the simple lines of common-sense and prudence which are followed in every branch of private enterprise, and had the energy to enforce their wishes; but the lamentable truth is that such is *not* the case. The whole question of more efficient city government will be solved when politics are permitted to have no more place in the management of our cities than in individual or corporate enterprise . . . . (Davidson, 1891, pp. 587–588.)

Virtually every well-known reform from accounting principles to PPBS and MBO has deep roots in popular conceptions of "good business practices." At the beginning of every new administration, limousine loads of prominent business executives are brought to Washington to reduce bureaucratic waste and inefficiency. It doesn't make much difference whether the administration is Republican or Democratic; the executives, the techniques they bring, and the disappointing results are surprisingly interchangeable.

There are two principal reasons why private-sector reforms and the executives brought in to implement them fail to transform government agencies into precision instruments of administrative control. The first reason is that neither the reforms nor the executives are the powerful instruments of efficiency and effectiveness they are imagined to be. Our picture of the private sector and those who control it is as unjustifiably romantic as our picture of the public sector is unjustifiably cynical. This idealized vision continually leads us to overestimate the potential contribution of private-sector techniques and sets the stage for frustration and disappointment. The second reason these reforms fail is that the public sector differs in some fundamental ways from the private sector—ways that cannot, and probably should not, be changed at the drop of a presidential or gubernatorial memo. History has shown that those who think that managing the Department of

23

Health and Human Services is pretty much the same as managing General Electric are in for a rude awakening and, perhaps, short terms of office.

If the same sorts of anecdotes used to judge public-sector organizations are used in evaluating private-sector organizations, those in the private sector are not doing nearly as well as the popular ideology holds. In fact, many business firms appear to be behaving in a manner not substantially different from that of the most despicable government bureaucracy. Take the matter of executive compensation. There is a prevalent belief that government employees are generally overcompensated and that their salaries have grown at an exorbitant rate. People in jobs that require little skill or training are paid wages that seem too high, and top-level civil servants in reputedly inefficient organizations such as the Postal Service and the Department of Health and Human Services take home \$40,000 to \$50,000 for doing heaven knows what. This stands in stark contrast, it is commonly believed, to the situation that exists in the private sector, where the ruthless discipline of the market ensures that a person gets paid only what he or she is worth.

Consider, however, the following observation from a recent article in *Fortune* magazine entitled "The Madness of Executive Compensation."

> In the upper reaches of corporate America, the market frequently does not seem to work. In a totally rational world, top executives would get paid handsomely for first-class performance, and would lose out when they flopped. But to an extraordinary extent, those who flop still get paid handsomely. (Loomis, 1982, p. 42.)

This conclusion was based on an examination of the relationship between the rate of return on stockholder equity (a measure of corporate performance) and the amount of compensation paid the chief executive in 140 companies representing ten industries. Only in the petroleum refining and steel industries did there appear to be even the slightest relationship between compensation and performance, and in both of these cases the linkage was weak. More characteristic were multi-industry companies (i.e., conglomerates). The president of ITT received a 1981 salary of \$1,150,000 for guiding the corporation to a performance record described as "dismal," while the president of Raytheon received a mere \$635,000 (anything less than \$800,000 in this league means that you are being exploited) despite the fact that his company had compiled a far better record than ITT over the preceding five years. The author could have pointed to the even more dramatic example of the notoriously inefficient International Harvester Corporation, which hurtled down the road to bankruptcy under the supervision of a chief executive making over \$600,000 a year. This same CEO was loaned \$1.8 million in 1977 to buy company stock, a loan that was forgiven three years later on the basis of "spectacular performance" (*Fortune*, 1982, p. 7). Policies of executive compensation in the private sector may not offer as positive an example to government as many devotees of free enterprise may suppose.

Once we leave the world of systematic studies—regardless of how informally conducted—and descend to the level of isolated anecdotes, the private sector provides as rich a source of examples of inefficiency and incompetence as could be desired by the most ardent socialist. It isn't even necessary to look beyond the Fortune 500. There is the case of the temporarily defunct Braniff Airlines, where "aggressive management" and "a willingness to take chances" turned a policy of breathtaking expansion following deregulation into equally breathtaking losses. There is the Chrysler Corporation, whose premature introduction of the Volare-Aspen in the mid 1970s led to a flood of recall notices that made GM's Corvair look well engineered. This was only the most visible of a series of management and engineering decisions that brought Chrysler to the verge of bankruptcy and, ironically, to the government trough, the launching pad for the company's spectacular resurrection.

For those who believe that the monumental cost overruns on high-technology programs are the sole province of the Defense Department and its bungling on weapons systems development, there is the example of General Dynamics attempting to enter the civilian jet transport market with the Convair 880 and 990. Over the two-year period from 1960 to 1962, General Dynamics managed to sustain the unprecedented loss of $425 million—a figure twice as great as that associated with Ford's Edsel debacle. It is impossible to detail in a paragraph or two all the mistakes in cost estimation and market forecasting that led to this disaster, but one anecdote helps provide the flavor of what transpired. Midway through the development of the Convair 880, an engineer in the purchasing department discovered that the cost of subcontracted components totaled more than the $4.25 million selling price of the plane. After paying its bills to subcontractors, General Dynamics wouldn't have enough money left to cover its costs, much less make a profit. The engineer concluded that General Dynamics should abandon the entire venture and write off the loss. When he pressed his case to upper-level executives (who had already made up their minds that the project was economically viable), the engineer was labeled a crank and fired (Smith, 1966, p. 90).[1]

If a loss of $425 million seems trivial by today's standards, there is what is affectionately known in some circles as the Westinghouse uranium fiasco. In the early 1970s Westinghouse sold uranium to purchasers of its reactors under a fixed-price contract. If a utility company would buy a reactor, Westinghouse, under a long-term contract at a fixed price, would commit itself to supplying the fuel. Although this arrangement left Westinghouse vulnerable to large fluctuations in the price of uranium, that vulnerability could be limited through a strategy of conservative pricing and uranium acquisition that would tie the price of the reactor to the spot price of uranium (and any recent trends in prices) and would involve the accumulation of uranium stockpiles at a rate determined by reactor sales.

Problems arose, however, when this conservative strategy was abandoned. For reasons that are not entirely clear, reactor sales and the stockpiling of uranium became disconnected in corporate decision making. More and more reactors were sold without increasing uranium stockpiles proportionately. In effect, Westinghouse began selling uranium short. This new policy would have worked fine if the price of uranium had dropped below the price figured into the price of the reactor; Westinghouse could then have used the extra cash for other purposes and purchased the uranium as necessary at the new, reduced price. Unfortunately, the price of uranium rose.

Westinghouse found itself committed to delivering uranium fuel that it would have to buy at dramatically higher prices than those anticipated at the time the reactor purchase contracts were negotiated. In 1971 uranium was selling at $5.95 a pound and Westinghouse had a modest inventory. In 1975 the price had risen to $35 a pound and Westinghouse was committed to delivering at least 40,000 tons (estimates vary) it didn't have. Since it had sold the uranium at $10 a pound, Westinghouse found itself in the position of having to pay for at least 40,000 *tons* of uranium with $25 *per pound* of its own money. Before the crisis was over, Westinghouse had developed a liability of between $1 and $2 billion—an impressive feat even by the inflated standards of the 1980s.[2]

Yet another example of business practices that would certainly not serve as a model for reforming government can be found in the automotive and steel industries. From a recent *Fortune* article by Steven Flax, "How Detroit is Reforming the Steelmakers," it appears that both the steel and auto industries were operating for many years with enormous inefficiencies in the production, provision, and use of steel for the manufacture of automobiles. The management innovation that exposed the inefficiencies of past practices and promises substantial efficiency gains is hardly novel: "General Motors, the U.S. Steel industry's largest customer, announced last year it would henceforth require steel suppliers to bid against one another for its orders" *(Fortune*, 1983, p. 126). Ford Motor Co. has apparently contributed to new practices by stressing steel quality.

Under past practices—which included steel production to specifications and tolerances set for the industry by the American Iron and Steel Industry and GM annually awarding steelmakers fixed percentages of the particular steels required for particular auto plants—some of the effects were as follows:

1. "Neither side paid scrupulous attention to quality. Thousands of tons of rejected steel piled up at many auto plants."
2. GM paid steel "suppliers' list prices even though it had the clout to bargain."
3. "Banking on the consumer's willingness to absorb price increases, the company chose to pass costs on rather than disrupt the comforts of doing business as usual."
4. Suggestions from steelmakers on how auto companies could cut costs and increase quality were not encouraged. "You make the steel. Don't tell us how to make a car."
5. There was little use of "statistical process control techniques to guarantee [steel] quality."
6. "One major steelmaker acknowledged, astoundingly, that it had not previously analyzed in detail the difference in cost between making 100 tons and 500 tons of certain products." *(Fortune*, 1983, p. 126.)

These are effects of business practices in place as recently as 1980, when the full extent of the Japanese and German competitive threats in steel and autos had been known for some time. Indeed, the practices postdate numerous requests by these industries for governments' intervention to protect them from "unfair foreign competition."

It is not at all clear what governments can constructively learn, from such business practices, about managing their own operations. It is not clear how much these inefficient practices have cost U.S. consumers in unnecessarily high automobile prices and U.S. workers in jobs now filled by Japanese and Germans in companies with superior management practices.

We could carry on in this vein for many more pages. We have not discussed Continental Illinois, W. T. Grant Co., Lockheed, Penn Central, Franklin National Bank, the forest industry, and so on. Bad judgment, inaccurate forecasts, corruption, the refusal to abandon obsolete technologies, Byzantine bureaucratic practices, and every conceivable inefficiency have at one time or another plagued many corporations. For every one of the seemingly countless number of executives profiled in the pages of *Business Week, Fortune,* and *Forbes* who save a corporation by "hard-driving," "farsighted," "fat-trimming" management, there was a corporation that needed saving. As often as not it must have been poor management that created the problems; otherwise, how could the new management take credit for the salvation?

Of course, contrary to what individuals of some political persuasions might argue, examples of waste and inefficiency in the private sector—no matter how egregious—do not necessarily imply that capitalism should be abandoned. Such anecdotes are a notoriously undependable source for formulating generalizations and provide no evidence that any alternative system would necessarily perform better. The point, of course, is that the same reasoning holds for anecdotal indictments of the public sector.

Measures of productivity provide a more systematic analysis of private-sector performance than anecdotes. As introduced in Chapter 1, productivity is a measure of how efficiently labor and capital are used to produce goods and services. Like efficiency, it is usually expressed as the ratio of the quantity of output to the quantity of input used in production. Its attractiveness as a summary measure of private-sector performance lies principally in its apparent simplicity and its clear relationship to a variety of corporate goals. If it took Ford 13 hours to produce one car in 1903 and it now takes less than a minute, productivity has grown (by the measure of cars produced per hour) 780-fold. If American farmers can now produce 20 percent more corn on 25 percent fewer acres than was possible in 1930, productivity has increased 60 percent. For firms operating within competitive markets, productivity, at least total factor productivity, measures both efficiency and effectiveness. A higher level of productivity (i.e., more efficiency) achieved by either increasing output or decreasing the level of inputs, produces both greater consumer satisfaction through lower prices and higher profits (i.e., effectiveness) for stockholders.

Figure 2.1 contains a graphic presentation of the productivity growth rates of major western industrial countries from 1950 to 1975. Because of the unavailability of hourly employment data for some of the countries, the productivity is described in terms of real gross domestic product per employed civilian. Obviously, the performance of the United States is unimpressive in either absolute or relative terms. Growth in U.S. productivity averaged less than 2 percent per year for the 25-year period covered; this figure is dramatically lower than those of Japan, Germany, and France. Moreover, the superior performance of those countries does not appear to be simply an artifact of their having to rebuild economies shattered by World War II. Both Figure 2.1 and Table 2.1 reveal that their rates of growth after 1965 were still dramatically greater than that of the United States. Since 1973 there has been a decline in the productivity growth of every leading industrial

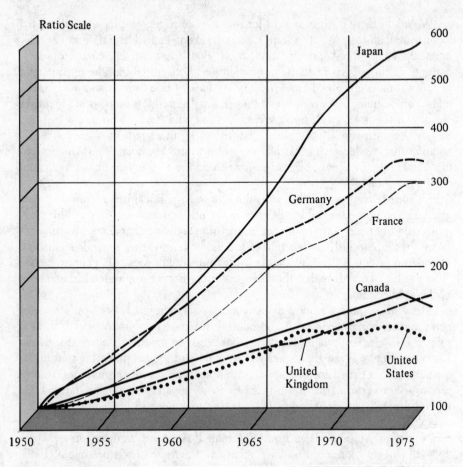

Figure 2.1   Real gross domestic product (GDP) per employed civilian in selected countries, 1950–75.
Source: U.S. Department of Labor, Bureau of Labor Statistics.

country, but the relative position of the United States remains the same—dead last.

These data suggest that the standard for improvement in efficiency set by the U.S. private sector is not particularly high. Unless productivity/efficiency is actually declining in the public sector at a marked rate—something that even the more strident critics of the public sector have yet to charge—the private sector does not possess the kind of advantage in this area that is generally assumed. In fact, it appears that an analysis of recent productivity performance on the part of the private sector may be more useful in understanding the nature of efficiency problems than in providing a model for the public sector to emulate.

Are these aggregate figures misleading? Perhaps the productivity-rate changes in most parts of the private sector are quite satisfactory, but the total figures are distorted by an area of the economy that is suffering extraordinary problems

Table 2.1 Annual Growth in Gross Domestic Product per Employed Worker in Leading Industrial Countries, 1965–1979 (percent change per year)

Country	1965–1973	1973–1979
United States	1.6	0.3
Belgium	4.3	2.7
Canada	2.4	0.4
France	4.5	2.9
Germany	4.3	3.1
Italy	5.8	1.7
Japan	9.1	3.4
Netherlands	4.6	2.6
United Kingdom	3.4	1.1

Source: U.S. Department of Labor, Bureau of Labor Statistics, unpublished data.

brought about, for example, by the continuing energy crisis or severely restrictive regulatory actions out of Washington. This doesn't seem to be the problem. The performance of individual sectors of the economy presented in Table 2.2 provides relatively little insight into what is wrong with U.S. productivity and certainly does not suggest that the aggregate productivity figures give a false impression. While high energy costs are partly responsible for the recent subpar performance of transportation and utilities and while government regulation has hurt productivity in mining, most other sectors are still doing relatively poorly by comparison with the growth rates of other countries.

Table 2.2 Rates of U.S. Productivity Growth by Industrial Sector

Industrial Sector	AVERAGE OF ANNUAL PRODUCTIVITY GROWTH RATES (PERCENT)		
	1949–1965	1966–1973	1974–1978
Agriculture, forestry, and fisheries	5.0	3.7	2.1
Mining	4.3	1.9	−4.8
Construction	3.4	−2.1	−1.0
Nondurable goods manufacturing	3.3	3.3	2.4
Durable goods manufacturing	2.8	2.2	1.2
Transportation	3.1	2.9	0.8
Communications	5.4	4.6	7.2
Electric, gas, and sanitary services	6.4	3.5	0.8
Wholesale trade	3.1	3.4	−0.5
Retail trade	2.7	2.1	1.1
Finance, insurance, and real estate	2.0	0.2	1.8
Services	1.2	1.7	0.3
Total	3.3	2.2	1.2

Source: Congressional Budget Office calculations based on data from the U.S. Department of Commerce and the U.S. Department of Labor, Bureau of Labor Statistics.

DIRECT COMPARISONS

If fifty million people say a foolish thing it is still a foolish thing.
ANATOLE FRANCE

The rates of productivity growth for the entire private sector and some of its key components indicate serious problems relative to other advanced industrial countries. The rates are so disappointing that it is difficult to believe that the public sector could have done much worse. Nonetheless, the preoccupation with productivity growth rather than absolute levels of productivity may be producing a portrait of private-sector productivity that is seriously distorted. If the absolute level of productivity in the private sector is two or three times greater than in the public sector, the similarity in their growth rates is largely irrelevant. The profits of a corner grocery store may have grown at the same rate as those of IBM or Shearson/American Express during the past five years, but if they are still several thousands times smaller, it doesn't make much sense to speak of these enterprises as being equally profitable. Unfortunately, the difficulties associated with assigning dollar values to many government outputs make it impossible to estimate absolute levels of public-sector productivity. Another approach to comparing public- and private-sector performance is to find an activity common to both sectors and then to compare the relative efficiency or effectiveness in performing the activity.

Of course, such direct comparisons have their own problems. For a comparison to be believable, it must establish that the performance level revealed in the study is broadly representative of that normally achieved in a given sector. There is no way, short of working with a random sample of activities from both sectors, to ensure that this is the case; but a positive step in this direction is to think about whether the set of activities being examined is representative of those performed. No economist or stock analyst would suggest evaluating the relative efficiency of a U.S. and Japanese steel manufacturer by closely scrutinizing the performance of their cafeterias. These activities are too peripheral to the primary goods and services produced by these firms to be representative of general levels of performance in any meaningful sense. The same would be true of a comparison of General Motors and IBM that was based on the relative efficiency of their motor pools or management information systems. Here the problem of representativeness is compounded by the fact that the activities analyzed are closer to one firm's basic product than the other. The operation of a motor pool is closer to the basic business of GM than that of IBM. The opposite is true in the case of management information systems. This may of course be wrong: GM may have superior management information systems and IBM may operate an extraordinarily efficient motor pool. Nonetheless, the choice of either as the sole basis for evaluating comparative efficiency would be hard to justify.

Another requirement is that the activities must be performed under identical conditions or that the effect of any difference must be statistically controlled. It makes no sense to praise home builders in the South and West for being more efficient than those in the Northeast if this performance gap is entirely attributable to differences in climate. In many instances the detection and control of these influences is fairly straightforward, but in others the technology in question may be so poorly understood that problems arise. A good rule of thumb in gauging the confidence to place in the results of any natural experiment is to see how much of the variance in performance within each group can be explained through the use of the control variables. When a high proportion of the variation can be explained, it is possible that the activity in question is understood deeply enough to infer accurately the role of private- versus public-sector control. When the proportion is low, it is quite possible that the effect attributed to the source of control might actually result from other variables whose influence and distribution are not understood.

If there is sufficient reason to believe that these limitations are being adequately handled, the prospect of conducting direct comparisons is intriguing. Not only are they less costly and more conceptually manageable than attempting to estimate and compare total public and private sector productivity, but they would appear to have a prescriptive potential that goes far beyond any macroscopic analysis. At best, a comparison of total public- and private-sector productivity can do little more than reveal which is the more productive. Suppose the private sector emerges victorious. What does this tell us about which specific methods utilized in the private sector should be adopted by the public sector? Should the defense department increase the salaries of its upper-level managers 350 percent? Should the civil service system be altered to permit more flexible personnel practices? Should the wages of blue-collar and service workers be cut? Would all these changes help? We won't know because aggregate productivity studies can't throw light on the critically important question of *why* the inefficient practices found in public agencies exist. Is efficiency, as some defenders of public administration have argued, traded off to achieve better quality? Is efficiency sacrificed to achieve a welfare goal such as providing a "just" wage as opposed to paying the market rate for some categories of workers? Do efficiency losses occur from efforts to maintain a deliberatively democratic administrative apparatus? Until the answers to such questions are known, the *costs* and ultimately the wisdom of reforming the public sector cannot be calculated.

Direct comparisons, on the other hand, should be a better approach to learning why the private or public sector is performing better and what reform strategies for improving performance are appropriate. If it is discovered that privately owned mass transit systems not only operate more efficiently than publicly owned systems but also possess more modern equipment and pay workers significantly lower salaries, this suggests how to improve public systems. While it is always possible that the real source of private-sector superiority in mass transit does not stem from either superior equipment or a more conservative wage policy, assuming that this may be the case is a sensible way to proceed in terms of more detailed analysis.[3]

When enough such studies have been completed that we can begin thinking of them as collectively representing a significant sample of private–public activities, we should be well on our way to having an empirically derived theory about the benefits and costs of public versus private enterprise.

Consider a hypothetical study of public and private schools that finds that private-school students achieve higher standardized test scores and that their per-pupil costs are less. Before admitting these results as evidence in the public–private productivity debate, we would want to determine that education represents a reasonable test case. We should be confident that what takes place in this area is somehow indicative of the basic processes that characterize the two sectors. Convinced of this, we would then have to examine our samples for comparability. In this case, this means ensuring that the student populations and the families they come from are roughly equivalent or that any differences are statistically controlled. If there is good reason to believe that the students in the private schools are more gifted or come from much wealthier and more education-conscious families, a simple comparison of their test scores will not mean very much.

After satisfying ourselves that the superiority shown by private schools was the result of some real differences in school performance, we could begin the challenging task of trying to account for the sources of this superiority. What are they doing that is different? Does their performance advantage appear to stem from more effective methods of student control and discipline? A more academically oriented curriculum? Better-trained teachers? There are obviously numerous possible explanations that have to be evaluated if the behavior of the private schools is to provide a useful model for reforming public schools.

The final step, rarely undertaken, is to account for why the differences exist and to determine what effect bringing public methods in line with those used in the private sector might have on other values that are considered important. Are the differences in curriculum (assuming that this is thought to be a source of private-school advantage) attributable to a greater emphasis on cultural enrichment courses (art, music) in public schools, and would a reform of public school curriculums necessitate the abandonment of these courses? Or assume that the basis of private school superiority is thought to lie in better discipline. Does the greater discipline found in private school classrooms stem from the use of a wider variety of disciplinary alternatives (corporal punishment, expulsion without possibility of readmission) than are usually permitted in public institutions? Would a change be justifiable? When such questions are not carefully considered, policy changes in education and elsewhere can be fraught with unintended consequences.

During the past 15 years, comparisons of the relative efficiency of public- and private-sector organizations have become increasingly popular among economists and a mainstay of certain academic journals, notably the *Journal of Political Economy*. There have now been studies of public and private utilities, urban transit systems, hospitals, nursing homes, fire departments, railroads, airlines, and a host of other services.[4] This literature is too large to review here in its entirety, but several of the major studies represent the methods of analysis and the kind of conclusions that have been reached.

Perhaps the most ambitious comparison of public- and private-sector delivery is Savas's study of refuse collection (1977). One of the study's strengths was the sample used. A set of 1,378 communities was carefully selected from a universe of 2,060 for preliminary analysis, and then 315 of these were studied intensively. This sample is noteworthy because there is a tendency in comparative studies to work with a group of organizations that hardly qualifies as a sample of anything in a statistical sense. Refuse collection may or may not be an archetypical service provided by public and private firms, but Savas was working with a fair sample of communities.

Savas divided his communities according to the nature of the arrangements under which refuse services were provided: municipal, contract, franchise, private, and self-service. Many municipalities provide the service themselves or contract directly for a private firm or other government to collect refuse. Under franchise collection, a private firm is granted the exclusive right to provide service in a given area. Under private collection arrangements, no monopoly rights are granted by the city; the citizens simply contract directly with the firm of their choice for service. Self-service simply refers to a system whereby households dispose of their refuse by taking it to a dump site.

Savas defined efficiency in terms of the cost of service per household. For municipal service, this might be paid through user charges or general revenue. For private suppliers, it was the price of service. The cheaper the service, it was reasoned, the more efficient the provider. Using this criterion, Savas obtained the results shown in Table 2.3. Contract service emerged as the least costly, followed by franchise and municipal arrangements. Private collection appears to be the most expensive. Differences in the nature of the service not captured in this table were that the frequency of collection was slightly higher in municipally served cities than in contract cities. There also tended to be more backyard service in municipally served cites.

More sophisticated analysis that controlled for the effect of variables such as the quantity of refuse generated per household, household density, frequency of collection, and the location of pickup point revealed a more complete and slightly different picture.

> No significant difference was found between municipal and contract collection for cities with less than 50,000. But for cities of more than 50,000, contract collection was slightly less expensive than municipal collection: the cost per household for municipal collection in such cities was found to be 29 percent (or 37 percent) greater than the corresponding cost of contract collection, on the basis of refuse data in terms of tons (or cubic yards). (Savas, 1977, p. 68.)

Savas proceeds to argue that if we reestimate efficiency for private firms not on the basis of the price they charge but on their actual costs, they are even more

Table 2.3 **Annual Cost per Household, by Service Arrangement**

	Mean	Maximum	Minimum	Ratio of Mean to Contract Mean	Number of Cities
Municipal	$32.08	$71.12	$13.96	1.15	102
Contract	27.82	89.00	11.73	1.00	68
Franchise	29.74	50.28	12.00	1.07	59
Private	44.67	92.04	22.14	1.61	86
Total	$34.16	$92.04	$11.73		315

efficient than these statistics indicate. Private firms have to make a profit and pay taxes. This means that their costs of production must be substantially lower than the price they charge for service, a condition that does not have to be met by municipal waste removal agencies.

There are a number of possible explanations for the higher level of municipal costs. Municipalities have higher employee absentee rates (12 percent versus 6.5 percent), employ larger crews (3.26 men versus 2.15), and spend more time servicing each household (4.35 man-hours per year versus 2.37). Unfortunately, we don't know whether these factors are really the reasons for the apparent inefficiency or simply incidental differences between types of service. It would have been helpful if Savas had shown that variation in these three factors could account for the superior performance of some contract or municipal agencies as opposed to others. It is also unclear whether these differences can be partly attributed to the differences in service levels already mentioned or to differences in technology (i.e., type of trucks). Backyard pickup and less efficient equipment might explain part of the variation in each of these three variables.

What does this research tell us about relative efficiency and the ultimately more important questions of how public agencies can successfully duplicate the methods used by private-sector firms and what the costs of doing so might be? First, there is the matter of representativeness. Can we assume that the operation of municipal and contract firms in the area of refuse collection is characteristic of performance found in both the public and private sectors? One possible source of difficulty is that a private firm under contract to a city government may well be regulated to a greater degree than would be the case if it had contracted directly with householders. A municipality may be more capable of ensuring that the provisions of the contract are carried out in good faith than the individual citizen would be, and perhaps capable of negotiating a better contract (one with fewer loopholes, etc.) in the first place.

With respect to ensuring that the firms operated under comparable conditions or controlling for differences that did exist, this study has done as well as can be expected. While it seems likely that private firms involve themselves in communities where collection problems are fewest (and the potential for profit is the greatest) and leave the difficult spots for the public agencies, there is no evidence to support the claim that the two samples are biased in this regard. Savas and fellow researchers have controlled for most of the obvious confounding factors and have qualitatively evaluated the potential effect of numerous others. The case they have made for greater relative efficiency of contract collection appears reasonably secure.

The case for why contract collection is more efficient is not as well made. Savas identifies some potential explanations but does little statistically to corroborate his argument. It is not clear what factors are important or what the relative importance is. Having digested the results of the research, we can't recommend a set of actions that is likely to improve the efficiency of publicly provided service. We can, of course, suggest that communities replace their municipal collection systems with contract service, but even this recommendation has a catch. *Although the average cost of contract collection is less, the variation in both municipal and contract collection costs is great enough that there are many otherwise comparable cities in which contract collection is more expensive.* In some cities, a change to contract collection might well increase costs, resulting in less efficient service. Because it is not known why contract services were more efficient on the average, there is no way of knowing when this will happen.

This study also leaves aspiring government reformers in the dark about the deeper question of why municipal refuse agencies possess the inefficient characteristics they do and what other consequences, apart from increased efficiency, might be associated with a wholesale shift to contract services or an attempt by municipal firms to behave like private firms. Savas points out that a devil's advocate could take the position that the price of greater efficiency is that private firms provide unreliable, incomplete, and unresponsive service. Such a position does seem extreme, but it would be helpful to have some information about what municipal firms are doing differently and the costs of change. For example, do their efficiency problems stem from public employee unions and are the solutions likely to necessitate departing from a uniform wage scale for all municipal workers? From an efficiency perspective, the research shows that something is probably wrong with many municipal firms and a somewhat smaller number of private firms. However, just what it is, how it can best be identified and corrected on a case-by-case basis, and what the cost of making the necessary adjustments will be are unknown.

In another frequently cited comparison of public and private performance, David G. Davies examined the relative efficiency of Australia's two interstate airlines: Trans Australian Airlines (TAA) and Ansett Australian National Airways (Ansett ANA). TAA is a government firm and Ansett ANA is a private corporation. The most striking characteristic of both firms' operations is the extent to which the government involves itself in virtually every major policy decision and the lengths to which it goes to preserve equality between them. For example, the Commonwealth of Australia estimates the freight-carrying capacity (in tons per mile) required to satisfy demand for a six-month period and then assigns each carrier the right to haul exactly half that amount. It also mandates that "the two airlines must choose aircraft . . . which are so close in work capacity that they generally must be of the same type" (Davies, 1971, p. 16). The government even forces the public firm (TAA) to pay an annual dividend into the treasury to ensure that both it and the private firm are facing comparable costs. Routes, frequency of stops, and fares are all similarly regulated.

Despite this atmosphere of regulated equality, Davies discovered that the relative efficiency of the two airlines was not the same. The private corporation was found to dominate the public line on each of the three single-factor productivity measures employed: tons of freight and mail carried per employee; number of paying passengers per employee; and revenue per employee. Ansett ANA's average freight and mail carried per employee was a little over twice that of TAA. The average number of passengers transported per employee was over 20 percent higher. And the average revenue per employee was $9,627 versus $8,428. This pattern remained quite stable over the ten-year period under consideration; the private airline appeared to be consistently more efficient.

Approaching this study with the same questions in mind that were asked of Savas's research, one is immediately struck by the calculated unrepresentativeness of the sample. Here is a private corporation operating in a regulated environment remarkably different from the environments in which most corporations function. Given that its behavior is so highly regulated, there is little reason to believe its actions to be characteristic of those of other corporations whose environment is dominated by free enterprise and competition. The potential for generalization appears small.

Davies was, in fact, delighted rather than dismayed by the unique character of his sample, because some economists believe that the principal distinction between the public and private sectors is not the traditional one that centers on the competitiveness of the markets in which they function but the nature of their ownership.[5] The ownership of public agencies is distributed equally across citizens within the particular jurisdictions and cannot be transferred from one citizen to another. In the private sector, ownership is narrowly concentrated in the hands of stockholders and can readily be transferred by stock transactions.

An understanding of these differences in property rights and their implications, it is argued, is critical to understanding differences in public and private firms. The property rights characteristics of the public sector assure that the benefits and costs of public agency decisions are diffused over a large population. A given citizen (owner) has little incentive to oversee carefully the behavior of government officials in general or to become a specialist in a given field because the benefits of doing so are not apt to be too great and the costs of failing to do so are borne by the rest of society. For example, from the perspective of a single taxpayer, the consequences of the U. S. Postal Service saving or wasting an extra $5 million are insignificant. Contrast this with the private sector. Here the transferability of property and exclusive rights to its earnings (or appreciation) make it possible for an individual to focus the benefits and costs of participation by buying a large amount of stock. Because the large stockholder has a greater incentive to monitor the efficiency of the private firm than the ordinary citizen has to monitor the efficiency of the public agency, it is hypothesized that management in the private sector will have to be more sensitive to the efficiency consequences of decisions.

One might object on the grounds that the degree to which ownership is concentrated in most large corporations is not substantial and that the complexity of their functions and financial dealings is so great as to prevent careful scrutiny by stockholders. Arguing that ownership is more concentrated in the private sector is one thing, arguing that it is concentrated enough to make a difference in managerial behavior is quite another. One of the principal points made by A. A. Berle and Gardiner Means in their classic *The Modern Corporation and Private Property* was that corporate control has steadily drifted into the hands of corporate managers at the expense of stockholders, who have little independent capacity to assess management's performance accurately. The response of the property-rights economists is to acknowledge that this may be true but to point out that a variety of mechanisms have been devised by stockholders to ensure that management will adopt a stockholder perspective and perform efficiently without informed oversight. These mechanisms include profit sharing, stock options, and appreciation rights. To the extent that management maximizes the value of these incentives, it also maximizes efficiency.

For Davies the Australian airlines case seemed to present a perfect opportunity to isolate the impact of property rights differences while controlling for a host of other variables. If the government was successful in its campaign to create identical decision environments for the two airlines, it would be reasonable to assume that whatever differences remained in their performance would be due to their property-rights characteristics. Thus Davies's main concern was not so much whether the two firms he examined were accurate archetypes of private and public enterprises but whether the differences existing between them reflected the impact of the variation in property rights.

Here, however, a problem arises. While the airlines case may present a golden opportunity to explore the consequences of property-rights variation, it would be overly optimistic to generalize too broadly from the results. Conclusions based on a nonrandom sample of two have their limitations. We have already seen how the results of the Savas study suggest that there is substantial variation in the performance of both public and private firms that appear to be operating in almost identical environments. There is no way of knowing whether the performance of the two airlines is "typical" of that to be expected from their respective sectors. What we have here is not a "test" of anything, but a provocative case study.

The value of Davies's research is also limited by inattention to other key questions. No effort was made to (1) account for why the private airline is performing more efficiently, (2) identify what changes the public airline would have to introduce to duplicate this level of performance, or (3) evaluate what the costs (if any) of making these changes would be. Nor was any attempt made to account for the curious fact that most of the performance disparity between the firms existed at the beginning of the time series, before any of the legislation designed to ensure comparability was passed. Since the legislation, the performance of the firms—variation in property rights notwithstanding—has been remarkably similar and the differences between them have actually declined. Why? Because both firms, the public and the private, are treated as black boxes, the study yields little detailed knowledge to support governmental reforms.

The final study considered is the work of Douglas Caves and Laurits Christensen in a 1980 article comparing two railroads: the Canadian National (a Crown Corporation) and the Canadian Pacific (privately owned). These two very large railroads have received the bulk of rail revenues in Canada for over 50 years. As the authors point out, previous studies have usually dealt with service industries that are heavily regulated. In this case, the two firms operated in a largely unregulated environment, competing with each other.

The measure of productive efficiency employed by Caves and Christensen is total factor productivity (TFP). Described in Chapter 1, this measure is based on an estimate of real output per unit of real resources expended and provides a more precise estimate of efficiency than that used in either the Savas or Davies studies. The output measures used were freight ton-miles and passenger miles. The inputs consisted of labor, structures, equipment, fuel, and materials.

Both the growth rate of TFP and the relative levels for each railroad were estimated for the period 1956–1975. The results of the comparison provide no evidence for the claim that government-operated enterprises are inherently less efficient than privately operated firms. In fact, Caves and Christensen found that Canadian National actually achieved larger rate gains than Canadian Pacific between 1956 and 1967. While in absolute terms the Canadian Pacific had a 10 percent higher level of productivity during the 1950s and early 1960s, this gap has subsequently been closed.

The explanation advanced by the authors for this similarity in performance is that the positive effects of competition on the public firm proved stronger than any negative effects associated with a difference in property rights. Such results imply, they believe, that public ownership is not inherently less efficient than private ownership. The inefficiency documented by previous studies stems from the isolation of public enterprises from effective competition. Under similar circumstances, the productivity of private firms might also decline.

In terms of describing the "typical" behavior of public and private organizations, this study presents a situation that is almost the opposite of that encountered in the Davies case. Here the private corporation is functioning in an unregulated environment that is more or less typical of the private sector. On the other hand, the public enterprise is operating in an environment that is strikingly different from that facing most public-sector organizations. The Canadian National Railroad is not only sheltered from competition but is actually encouraged to operate on a purely commercial basis (without government subsidy), with the government acting as stockholder rather than manager. As a result, Caves and Christensen make no effort to generalize about the behavior of government bureaucracies. Their interest is to evaluate the relative effects of competition and property rights in a context acknowledged to be unusual. If there are generalizations to be made, they relate to the property-rights/competition issue, not the relative efficiency of public firms as a group.

Another barrier to generalization is obviously the nature of the sample. As in the case of Davies's research, we have a nonrandom sample of two. Because we once again expect variation in the performance of both public and private firms that cannot be accounted for by any known statistical controls, we can't be sure that these results are truly representative of public and private performance in a competitive environment. Thus as in any case study, it is best to view the findings tentatively.

What makes the Caves and Christensen study particularly provocative is that property-rights theory has no way of explaining why the Canadian National can successfully compete with (be as efficient as) the Canadian Pacific. The Canadian Pacific must be relatively efficient in order to deliver to investors a rate of return comparable to that of other firms and sufficient to acquire further capital through the sale of stock. But what is the incentive for the managers of the public firm to be competitive? Who plays the role of stockholders and oversees the managers' performance? In theory, their behavior is ultimately evaluated by the Canadian electorate, but each member of that electorate possesses the usual nontransferable property rights that supposedly make oversight so unlikely.

The simplest explanation for the railroad results is that certain public-sector agencies, like modern corporations, have devised methods of dealing with the oversight problems posed by property rights. Mechanisms such as stock options and profit sharing are used by large corporations to overcome the problems caused by the dilution of stockholder control and to make managerial interests congruent with those of stockholders. Perhaps something similar is occurring in the public sector but remains ignored by researchers, whose understanding of public-sector control mechanisms is less sophisticated than their understanding of private-sector control mechanisms. Certainly it would be strange if individuals in their role as stockholders were capable of recognizing property-rights conflicts and devising ingenious methods of overcoming them but became naive and helpless in relation to similar conflicts in their roles as citizens.

The public sectors in the United States and other industrialized democratic regimes display rich variation in the institutions and mechanisms that link political behavior with bureaucratic control. Agency behavior is often closely regulated by elected officials, political appointees commonly occupy high bureaucratic offices, and legislatures frequently have a direct input into agency policymaking through oversight and budgetary control. Beyond this, bureaucratic behavior is constrained and influenced by a complex web of cultural, legal, and political mores. These institutions and mechanisms may have evolved partly to cope with property-rights difficulties.

Yet if mechanisms capable of overcoming property-rights problems are already in place in the public sector, why doesn't the public sector do better in these public–private comparisons? The performance of the public railroad in the Caves and Christensen study is unusual. Most comparative studies reveal the private firm to be at least marginally more efficient than its public counterpart. Perhaps there is something unusual about the information passed to elected officials through competition (as in the Caves and Christensen study) that permits these mechanisms to work better than is generally the case. Alternatively it may be that these mechanisms usually work quite well but that the values achieved are generally more complex than simple efficiency. From this standpoint, the exceptional component of the Canadian railroad example isn't the information provided to decision makers. Rather, it is the straightforward nature of the mandate given managers by the government: generate a profit. In other cases, public agencies may be pursuing their goals with comparable efficiency; but because their goals are more complex than those of private organizations, they frequently *appear* inefficient.

This issue of goal complexity is of more than passing interest because it can render straightforward performance comparisons worthless. If a company is spending $40 million in pursuit of a goal X while a bureaucracy is spending the same amount in pursuit of that goal and three additional goals, the bureaucracy will probably not attain as much X as will the company. If efficiency is estimated by dividing the annual increase in X by $40 million, it will appear less efficient. Does this imply that bureaucracy would achieve more X through the use of business methods if it must still attend to the three additional goals? Clearly not. The management of a public railroad that is told to generate a profit—but must also maintain services to a large number of communities regardless of profitability and must continue to subsidize rates for communities and large classes of shippers and passengers—is in quite a different position than the Canadian National Railroad's management; with these constraints reflecting complex public purposes, it would not be surprising to find a far inferior profit picture. The inferior profits (losses?) are not, however, evidence of inferior management and inefficiency.

The next section will take a closer look at the argument that goal complexity and other intrinsic differences between public and private organizations are responsible for performance differences.

MANAGING PUBLIC VERSUS PRIVATE ORGANIZATIONS: THE DIFFERENCES THERE ARE AND THE DIFFERENCES THEY MAKE

> The principles of management are the same, whether you're making chocolate chip cookies or incarcerating people.
>
> JOHN KING, DIRECTOR,
> LOUISIANA DEPARTMENT OF CORRECTION

Many of the scholars and managers closely connected with public-sector administration have little difficulty conceding, in spite of the meager research support for such a concession, that private firms are often more efficient than public agencies. They argue, however, that this superiority is largely a function of basic differences between the two sectors and is irrelevant to the critical issue of how to improve public-sector performance.[6] They believe that public and private organizations perform different tasks under markedly different conditions. The fact that private-sector management methods succeed admirably in private firms is no guarantee that they will not fail miserably in what amounts to a very different context. From this perspective, comparing a private firm with a public agency always involves a comparison of apples and oranges. To quote William Sayre's well known maxim: "Public and private organizations are alike in all unimportant respects."

The difference between public and private organizations that is most frequently held to have important implications for their relative performance concerns the incentive to be efficient and effective provided by a competitive market. According to the usual reasoning, if a business is inefficient and ineffective, it will probably not survive and will certainly not prosper. Other companies are always waiting in the wings to take away the market and profits. If, on the other hand, a government agency is ineffective and inefficient, it will almost certainly survive and might well prosper. The agency can simply request a larger budget and the legislature—somewhat less simply perhaps—can impose higher taxes.

A particularly forceful reiteration of this basic argument was recently made by J. Peter Grace, President of W. R. Grace Co. and head of President Reagan's Private Sector Survey on Cost Control (PPSS), in response to the age-old question "Why can't government be run like a business?"

Because there is no incentive to do so at all. They all come down to Washington, and the top people are probably here for two or three years, and they move out. There is no long-term responsibility put on anybody. At W. R. Grace, when I became president of it, at age 32, I knew that my life would depend on whether I ran it effectively or not. I gave 100 percent of my time, seven days a week to see that it was run properly. You don't see that kind of service down here. There is no continuous pressure put on people to make it efficient. Their whole attitude is that it is not going to hurt anybody if we are spending this much money. Who gets hurt? The taxpayer gets hurt.

On the surface, this line of argument is persuasive. The contention that the competitive pressures on Eastman Kodak or Avis are greater then those on the city of Detroit or the State Department would seem hard to contest. In 1982 alone, about 5,000 businesses, mostly new and small, failed every week, while the number of government agencies going out of business was negligible. True, there may be a kind of competition among bureaucratic agencies for additional funding that inspires good management, and a citizen dissatisfied with the extravagance of local officials can move to another city or vote for candidates that promise reform. However, the situation really isn't comparable to that faced by a firm whose inefficient practices force it to charge 50 percent more for cornflakes than its competitors in order to cover costs. It is obviously much easier for people to switch brands of cornflakes than it is for them to work for the election of cost-conscious officials or to move to another city.

One problem with the competitive pressure argument is that the relationship between pressure and the performance of individual workers is much more tenuous than proponents believe. Individual productivity is a function of a variety of factors that are not directly related to market competitiveness. A worker possessing a very rare and highly valued skill may, for example, have little incentive to work very hard regardless of how competitive the industry is, since he or she can easily get a job elsewhere. Alternatively, a member of a profession is often so socialized with respect to performance standards that the organizational context appears to be a relatively unimportant determinant of performance. In fact, the linkages between market competition constructed to reward efficiency and punish inefficiency have never been convincingly established empirically. Until the recent divestiture, were the production managers and engineers who worked for AT&T (a protected monopoly) significantly more inefficient than those who worked for Westinghouse? Are accountants who work for firms in competitive markets (e.g., retail sales) more productive than those who work for firms that are members of oligopolies (e.g., oil producers)? Are both more productive than accountants who work for city governments? We don't know, but we have our doubts.

We do know that there are countless instances in both the private and public sectors where organizations have established internal incentive systems that seem inconsistent with the degree of competition they face externally. On the private side, we have observed no tendency of firms in competitive markets to provide fewer paid country club memberships, limousine services, catered lunches, or elaborately appointed offices than their counterparts in less competitive markets. On the public side, Grace's work schedule of "100 percent of [his] time, seven days a week . . . " is common to a large number of top executives and their staffs in government, including many with the supposed comforts of civil service who are confident that their agencies will not go out of business. Grace should look in on the offices at the White House, the Office of Management and Budget, the National Security Council, the Pentagon's E and A rings, the State Department, the Central Intelligence Agency, or any city hall or police department on a Sunday afternoon—*any* Sunday afternoon. The number of executives and staff hard at work would surprise him. During peak periods before budget submission or during crises, many of these executives and staff may not get home at all for more than a shower, meal, and nap for days on end.

Grace's self-righteous attitude is typical of many executives with no experience in government and contrasts starkly with the comments of many businessmen who have worked in government. The comments of David Lehman, an executive who went from IBM to the Department of Transportation (DOT) and back to IBM, are characteristic of those with direct experience.

> I was very impressed with [the] intellectual ability and with the hard-driving nature of many people in the super grades [at DOT]. I gained a great deal of respect for these people and confidence in their ability to manage their agency, and I guess I had not held that viewpoint before. I used to feel that the ordinary bureaucrat was below average in capability.
>
> That was not the case. The super grades were largely filled with people who had grown up with the Agency. They were dedicated, they worked very hard, and I think I worked harder there than I ever did at IBM, every single day and weekend from October first to April first, with Christmas Eve and Christmas Day off. I got so involved, in fact, that I didn't do some of the social things I was looking forward to when I went to Washington. (Weiss, 1974.)

It would seem to be easier to sustain your prejudices about the virtues of business, the vices of government, and what motivates hard work if you avoid firsthand experience working in government.

Three other differences between public and private organizations are more likely to be responsible for making the former appear more efficient and effective. These are (1) the nature of public agency goals, (2) limitations on executive authority, and (3) shorter time horizons.

THE NATURE OF PUBLIC AGENCY GOALS

> When Columbus left on his famous voyage, he did not know where
> he was going; when he landed, he did not know where he was;
> and when he returned, he did not know where he had been. But
> he did it all on government money.
>
> ANONYMOUS

The potential importance of goal complexity in determining relative performance was discussed above in conjunction with the Caves and Christensen article. If government agencies tend to have more goals than private firms (even when they appear to be doing the same thing), it is only natural to assume that their resources will be less focused and their accomplishments in any given area will be less. If some of these additional goals conflict with each other, the perceived effectiveness and efficiency of the government agencies will decline still further.

Consider the mandate given to state and local health planning agencies to implement the 1974 National Health Planning and Resources Development Act (P.L. 93-641). The responsibilities assigned them include nothing less than to "restrain cost increases, improve the general health status of the population, and increase the accessibility, continuity, and quality of care." Even apart from the fact that no one knows how to reduce the cost of health care, this is an imposing set of goals. It would be difficult enough to make headway in accomplishing any single goal; to expect progress on all fronts within the confines of a very limited budget is to make a judgment of ineffectiveness and inefficiency inevitable. Planning agencies are hardly atypical in this respect. Public agencies are often general-purpose organizations designed to provide all things to all people at the lowest possible cost.

Goal complexity breeds contradiction. Trying to upgrade simultaneously the quality of health care while reducing its cost is no small challenge. Nor is simultaneously increasing the security and rehabilitative contribution of prisons, preserving wilderness while developing natural resources, or maximizing farm productivity while sustaining the family-owned farm. Yet these are some of the things that the Bureau of Prisons, Forest Service, and Department of Agriculture, respectively, are supposed to do. It is impossible for any organization inside or outside government to pursue all of these ends as efficiently or effectively as they might pursue one of them.

Another difference between the goals of public and private organizations is so obvious that it is often overlooked. It concerns the feasibility of the projects that are undertaken. Private firms are accustomed to working within the confines of technology. Should General Motors decide to develop a high-mileage six-passenger car for marketing in 1988, it will undoubtedly be powered by gasoline or diesel fuel rather than solar power. This is because regardless of how praiseworthy and marketable a solar-powered car might be, its development is not possible within the constraints of current technology. Everyone involved in making the decision would know this and realize that if they ignored this technological imperative and attempted to mass produce a solar car anyway, disaster (and considerable ineffectiveness and inefficiency) would result.

Public agencies do not always enjoy the luxury of being assigned projects that are possible to accomplish. The feasibility and expected rate of return of a public project are frequently less important to elected officials than the praiseworthiness and electoral appeal of the goals that the project is supposed to accomplish. Projects are not selected—as they are in the private sector—on the basis of what can be done but rather on what should be done. Health costs should be reduced, cancer should be cured, illegal immigration should be checked, energy independence should be achieved, and crime should be reduced. There is nothing wrong with government trying to deal with these matters, but to expect these organizations, which are operating in areas where there is no reliable technology, to appear as efficient and effective as firms that are utilizing tried and true technologies—to produce, for example, aluminum or shampoo—is wholly unreasonable.

There is also the matter of how well goal attainment and subordinate performance can be measured. One of the things that has long frustrated attempts to evaluate the performance of federal agencies such as the State Department, U.S. Information Service, and Department of Commerce is that it is extremely difficult to measure the extent to which they are accomplishing their goals. How does one quantify successful goal achievement for the State Department? The decrease in the number of diplomatic protests? The rate of retention of foreign service officers? The increase in pro-United States attitudes among foreign countries? The balance of trade? The absence of war? All of these? If so, how should they be weighted? The problem is classic and vexsome.

Problems in measuring goal attainment make agencies harder to manage as well as harder to evaluate. If an outsider cannot easily tell how well the State Department is doing its job, the chances are that it is none too easy for the secretary of state to tell how well his subordinates are doing their jobs. While it is true that he can devise numerous methods to help himself in this task, the precision of any of them is inevitably in doubt. Evaluating the competence of a foreign service officer by scrutinizing his or her written reports is more problematic than evaluating a sales representative by the number of sales made. And even evaluating the relative performance of salespersons may be complicated by the need to control for the difficulty of the "territory" they work and for other factors affecting their performance.

It is easy to carry this argument about the difficulty of public-sector work assessment too far. Assessing the work of many (if not most) individuals in a modern corporation is also difficult. The number of executives directly engaged in sales work and the number of blue-collar workers who are responsible for their own rate of output is small and diminishing every year. The precise contribution that a laboratory researcher, a corporate planner, an accountant, or a financial analyst makes to corporate profits is impossible to estimate. Nonetheless, this problem is usually more severe in the public sector, where a "technology" linking worker activity and "success" (e.g., lower health care costs or crime rates) is often totally absent.

To some extent the increasingly strident complaints of business about excessive government regulation reflect the growing complication of business goals as firms are required to attend to many other goals than narrow productivity and profit. A firm that is free to despoil the environment at no cost, to subject workers and consumers to safety and health hazards with no liability, to set prices collusively with its competition, to use bribes to secure contracts and market channels, to exploit labor, and to pay far less in taxes than it consumes in infrastructure may be very efficient in terms of the narrower firm goals of productivity and profitability. But how efficient would such a firm's behavior be for society?

As societal values have changed, the regulation of firms has increased to reflect the new values and expectations; voluntary compliance has never worked very well. Cleaner air and water, greater security for employees, and higher levels of worker and consumer safety are important examples of value changes. Improvements in these areas can only be achieved at the expense of other values, most often productivity and efficiency. The domestic steel industry could compete more effectively with the Japanese and German industries if all corporate and employee taxes were halved and all environmental and worker safety constraints were relaxed or removed. But it could also compete more effectively if the taxes and constraints were left in place while employee compensation was halved and capital investment was doubled. The political process is one mechanism that strikes and adjusts the balance among all these values.

For calculations of societal efficiency, multiple goals exist. Clean air has some value, just as a short ton of steel does. Business management can look forward to greater and greater goal complexity as new societal goals are discovered and expectations on existing goals are raised. On goal complexity, business management has come to look more and more like government management, with all of the attendant productivity and efficiency problems. The solution to these problems is in learning to cope better managerially with multiple, complex goals, not in yearning for a return to the world of simple goals in which 12-year-olds worked 12 hours a day, six days a week, in plants spewing smoke and poisonous waste, under unsafe and unhealthful working conditions and for starvation wages. There are good arguments for complex business goals and limits on managerial discretion even if lower *measurable* productivity and profitability are an implication.

LIMITATIONS ON EXECUTIVE AUTHORITY

Nothing is impossible for the man who doesn't have to do it himself.
WEILER'S LAW

Few public-sector executives possess the administrative discretion of their private-sector counterparts. Just as presidents are continually frustrated by having to share power with two houses of Congress and the judiciary, public administrators at every level find their powers strictly circumscribed.

> . . . one can describe public officials as outsiders who enter office with cherished policy objectives, accomplish little, and leave office with unfilled desires for structural reform; for, in order to accomplish important political objectives having to do with due process and responsiveness to the electorate, the United States has very nearly denied the public executive the tools of management. It is almost true that the business executive's enabling resources—structure and people—are the public executive's constraints. (Bower, 1977, p. 134.)

One problem is the legal framework within which they must act. Administrators must function within a web of rules and statutes whose primary purpose is not to achieve maximum efficiency but to ensure stability of service, accountability, and equality of treatment. Cecil Andrus, a former secretary of the interior, has commented that he did not do one thing of importance during his four-year term without having to defend the action in court. The complexities have been with us a long time and are imposing:

> In 1836, the House Ways and Means Committee investigated the Treasury Department's excruciating slowness in releasing public funds. If found that, to guard against embezzlement, five internal clearances were needed before any transaction could be made. More recently, when Rep. Patricia Shroeder (D-Colo.) asked the Pentagon to outline the procedures it follows before approving a contract, the outline required a sheet of paper 33 feet long. There is a plus side to this. Even with its periodic scandals, and the others that surely go undiscovered, the bureaucracy, by worldwide standards, is considered a center of integrity. (Taylor, 1983.)

Although such rules and statutes may appear unnecessary, even ludicrous, in retrospect, there were usually good reasons for their creation. In the examples given above, one need look no further for reasons than the record of abuse and fraud in the disbursement of public funds and in defense contracting over the life of the republic. Where a $6,000 coffeepot (only slightly different than one available for $29.95 at K-Mart) or a $111 bolt (exactly the same as one available for 19 cents at the local hardware store) is reported widely in the media, almost every such incident leads to more rules and perhaps new employees to guard the public purse.

A second source of limitations on authority is the overlapping responsibilities of other government institutions and agencies. Through the budgetary process and judicial review, legislative committees and courts often have a major input into the character of program design and operation. Moreover, a host of different agencies are often involved in the same area, which causes numerous problems of coordination. In their classic study of the problems associated with the implementation of government programs, Jeffrey Pressman and Aaron Wildavsky (1973) described how the Economic Development Administration found it necessary to coordinate with literally dozens of government agencies at various levels in trying to set up job development programs in Oakland, California.

Civil service and government personnel systems at the state and local levels further restrict the discretion of the government executive by making it far more difficult to hire, transfer, promote, or fire people than is true in the private sector. Unions may cause similar difficulties for business executives, but they usually fall far short of public personnel systems as a source of day-to-day constraints on executive behavior. One reason is that unions rarely include as large a percentage of workers. Former Secretary of the Treasury Michael Blumenthal's comments are characteristic: "Out of 120,000 people in the Treasury, I was able to select twenty-five, maybe. The other 119,975 are outside my control. And not only are they outside my control in terms of hiring and firing—they're also virtually outside my control in terms of transferring" (Nickel, 1979, p. 39).

Yet, we should not, while railing against the abuses of highly secure, well-paid positions by some civil servants, forget the abuses in the 100 years prior to the creation of the civil service that led to reforms. Under the spoils and patronage systems that prevailed before civil service, the levels of incompetent, inefficient employees were probably far greater that they have been since civil service. The only criteria that mattered for the selection, retention, and advancement of employees under the old system were political criteria; political allegiances, campaign contributions, and the like were much more important than one's ability to perform a function of direct value to citizens. It can and has been argued that, in excising the abuses with the series of civil service reforms beginning with the Pendleton Act of 1883, the reforms created a situation in which jobs are so secure that well-paid employees who do not perform cannot be fired or penalized except through long, arduous processes. However, the abuses after reform are, on balance, probably less than the abuses prior to reform in terms of both corruption and efficiency.

The net effect of these limitations on executive authority is a high level of frustration among government officials, particularly those like Blumenthal, who have entered the public service directly from the business community (he had been chief executive officer of the Bendix Corporation). As Lawrence Lynn observes, their tenure in public office is frequently not a happy one.

> A majority of business executives are uncomfortable and unsuccessful in the federal government's topmost political, policy making posts as department heads and assistant secretaries. They are unaccustomed to and sometime resentful of the interest of the legislative branch in administrative affairs. They are unfamiliar with the necessity of clearance and coordination with numerous other departments. They are irritated by public scrutiny of their actions and by rigid controls exercised over recruitment of personnel, budgeting of funds, and procurement of supplies and equipment (1981, p. 120).

SHORTER TIME HORIZONS

> In love affairs, it is a very different kind of efficiency if you want to achieve marriage or if you want to seduce someone for one night.
> MANFRED STANLEY

Despite the popular image of a government bureaucracy as an organization unconcerned with the deadlines that rule the business world, government managers often have time horizons that are shorter than those in private sector. Joseph Bower reminds us that it took IBM ten years to develop the highly successful 360 series computer and that George Romney spent at least seven years trying to convince American Motors to take a chance on marketing a compact car (Bower, 1977, p. 135). By contrast, upper-level appointed and career civil service officials frequently find themselves responsible for organizing programs to reduce drug abuse, achieve energy independence, or reduce automobile emissions in a terrifyingly short period of time.

The short tenure of most elected executives in the United States means that top public-sector managers must work quickly. Programs that develop slowly may be overturned by the next political administration. The treatment of Carter's environmental and consumer affairs programs by the Reagan administration is a good recent example of this. Another reason officials must act quickly is also "political" in nature. Only quick results can help solve the electoral problems of the officials who appoint these managers. Unless voters can be convinced that a new program has "generated results," it is useless as evidence for maintaining tenure in office.

Business and government certainly differ on dimensions other than these three. But these appear to be the most important differences in determining relative efficiency and effectiveness. As a defense of public-sector management practices and as an explanation for any relative inefficiency, the "public sector is different" argument has to be made very carefully. No one on the private side has ever contended that the two types of organizations were identical. Nor have they insisted that the job of the public executive is not harder. Indeed, the cumbersome organizational apparatus that often frustrates agency executives has often played a major role in their indictment of public-sector management. The difference between the attitudes of those who advocate the use of more private-sector management methods and those who doubt that such methods will be effective is that the first group believes that the unique attributes of public bureaucracies are nothing more than pathologies that can and should be eliminated. The second group believes that these attributes are somehow intrinsic to public management and that their efficiency inhibiting effects cannot be overcome by the introduction of "businesslike" techniques.

It is not enough for defenders of public management to demonstrate that public agencies are different. What they must do is convince us that these aspects of public organizations are (1) responsible for most of any relative inefficiency that exists compared to private-sector performance, (2) politically or constitutionally immutable, and/or (3) incompatible with the introduction of private-sector management methods.

Most writings in this area have addressed the second of these contentions. They have considered, for example, whether goal conflict and complexity are inevitable outgrowths of our political system or only characteristics of the poor management that takes place in the public sector. The arguments of Peter Drucker, a well-known commentator whose background and sympathies lie predominantly with the private sector, are fairly typical here and somewhat persuasive.

> A shoe manufacturer who has 22 percent of the market for work shoes may have a profitable business. If he succeeds in raising his market share to 30 percent, especially if the market for his kind of footwear is expanding, he is doing very well indeed. He need not concern himself too much with the 78 percent of the users of work shoes who buy from somebody else. And the customers for ladies' fashion shoes are of no concern to him at all. Contrast this with the situation of an institution on a budget. To obtain its budget, it needs the approval, or at least the acquiescence, of practically everybody who remotely could be considered a "constituent." Where a market share of 22 percent might be perfectly satisfactory to a business, a "rejection" by 78 percent of its "constituents"—or even by a much smaller proportion—would be fatal to a budget-based institution. And this means that the service institution finds it difficult to set priorities; it must instead try to placate everyone by doing a little bit of everything — which, in effect, means achieving nothing. (Drucker, 1973, p. 52.)

It is not the goal of this volume to prove conclusively that efficiency differences between the public and private sectors can be attributed to immutable differences in goal complexity, limitations on executive authority, time horizons, incentives for performance, and so forth. Even a preliminary attempt to address this question would constitute a massive study in itself. We will, however, argue that these special attributes of public agencies have had an important effect on attempts to introduce private-sector-inspired management reforms. As we shall see, they help explain why the record of such reforms has been so dismal and help suggest how future reforms might be more effective.

CONCLUSION

The hardest crossword puzzle to solve is the one in which we have
penciled in a wrong word and are too stubborn or fixated to erase it;
in much the same way, it is often easier to solve a problem when
you are merely ignorant than when you are wrong.

SIDNEY J. HARRIS

The beliefs that government is less efficient than business and that its performance could be improved through the incorporation of businesslike methods are part of a long-standing national ideology. The rhetoric that the beliefs inspire dominates discussions of government reform, fills newspaper editorials, and helps untold numbers of candidates get elected to office each year. Yet the quality of evidence that supports these beliefs is at best weak. Private-sector productivity data suggest that the standard for efficiency growth set by the business community is not particularly high and that we are now in the midst of what many commentators have described as a crisis in productivity.

Attempts to compare the performance of the two directly by examining the productivity of private and public firms engaged in the same activity have been inconclusive. The research, overall, provides some evidence that private firms are somewhat more efficient in the delivery of certain services. However, this finding is not universal, nor is the magnitude of the efficiency gap between them as large as popularly believed. For reasons as yet unknown (and likely to remain so unless the character of the analysis is changed significantly), some public agencies do as well as or better than their private counterparts.

Particularly disappointing for those who advocate the adoption of business methods by public bureaucracies is the fact that this literature provides few indications as to what these methods are. Nor, for that matter, is it of much help in identifying irreversible organizational pathologies in public-sector decision structures.[7] In study after study, researchers have declined to identify essential differences in the operation of private and public organizations in favor of attempting to decide which sector is most efficient from a nonrandom sample of two or three

organizations. As a result, little has been learned about which sector is most efficient and next to nothing has been learned about what differences exist and why.

From the comparative performance literature, we moved to a consideration of
claims that management in the public sector is fundamentally unlike private management and that performance comparisons are therefore largely a waste of time.
Three differences that are often thought to be of particular importance were discussed: (1) the nature of public agency goals; (2) the limitation on executive authority, and (3) shorter time horizons. In each case, the claims of public-sector
defenders appear to have a certain face validity. Agency goals often appear to be
more complex, unrealistic, and unmeasurable than corporate goals. Government
executives have considerably less discretion than their private-sector counterparts.
While governments are not subject to the same competitive pressures as businesses, pressure to accomplish the impossible instantaneously is a fact of life in
government.

These differences do not appear to be transient products of poor management
practices on the part of public-sector decision makers. There are fundamental institutional and political reasons why these public–private differences exist, and
they cannot be lightly dismissed or easily eliminated. Limitations on executive authority, for example, are nothing less than regulation *within* the public sector, and
such regulation is invoked for precisely the same reasons as regulation is imposed
on the private sector. While in theory some of these regulations could be eliminated in an attempt to make the public sector as administratively efficient as a
modern corporation, there would undoubtedly be costs in the form of reduced
due-process protections, less predictable decision outcomes, and less democratic
administration.

Do these differences account for most of government inefficiency and ineffectiveness? No one knows. Just as the comparative performance literature provides
no guidance as to the specific sources of private-sector superiority, works that focus
on the critical differences between the two sectors rarely contain any empirical justification for their claims. Yet, regardless of whether these differences are the principal sources of inefficiency, they nonetheless represent real constraints on reform.
As we shall see, they lie in the background of a number of largely unsuccessful
attempts to introduce business management practices directly into government.
These differences can also play a valuable role in evaluating the feasibility of new
proposals to increase the efficiency and effectiveness of government.

Thinking about the relative performances of the private and public sectors may
help put the problems of government performance in better perspective, but the
fact remains that there are many instances in which governments are needlessly
inept and wasteful. Knowing that all is not well in the private sector is unlikely to
placate residents of a street where potholes began appearing just six months after
resurfacing or city dwellers who have just been informed that their mass transit
system is going to cost three times as much and take twice as long to construct as
they were originally told. Differences in political philosophy notwithstanding,
there is plenty of room for improvement. The pressing question is how to bring
this about.

ADDENDUM: WHAT METHODS? WHOSE PROBLEMS?

The chief cause of problems is solutions.

SEVAREID'S LAW

To this point we have discussed the private sector (businesses) and the public sector (governments) and the differences between the two as if there were extensive, enduring similarities within each group. Business is business and government is government and each has more in common with its own kind than with the other kind. This was a useful, indeed necessary, simplification in laying out the general issues for this book. It is a simplification common to much of the popular discourse on reforming government and comparing business to government. But the reality is something else. We need to complicate matters before considering specific reforms and specific organizations.

It makes very little sense to generalize about "businesses" and "governments," because the differences within these groups are at least as great as the differences between the groups. For determining efficient and effective management practices, the differences in scale and function within each group are often just as important as differences in "publicness" and "privateness." The management practices appropriate for running a McDonald's franchise in Murfreesboro, Tennessee, are not apt to provide much guidance to the owner of the local Ford dealership or to the chairman of the board of General Motors. The differences in function and scale, respectively, are just too great. Similarly, successful management practices in running the Murfreesboro Water Department are not apt to transfer easily and usefully to the Murfreesboro Board of Education or the Department of Defense. Nor is it clear what practices any of these three private-sector organizations could conceivably give to their three public-sector counterparts to improve their efficiency and effectiveness.

The "useful" advice that the manager of the McDonald's franchise could give the director of the water department might be:

> Serve fresh buns and meat every day! Stay open long hours! Hire teenagers at minimum wage! Run newspaper coupon and radio spot campaigns! Sell discount glasses embossed with cartoon characters! Sing the company song! Give lottery tickets with each purchase! Have your counter people always smile and ask customers whether they want fries or an apple turnover before ringing up the purchase! Discharge all employees who violate company rules! Keep your customer service areas extremely clean!

Even if we translate this advice into more generic forms such as "Serve a high quality product," "Control costs," "Maximize customer convenience and satisfaction," and the like, the advice is still not terribly useful to the director of the water department or, for that matter, the Los Angeles school superintendent or the secretary of defense or the owners of the Murfreesboro Ford dealership or the chairman of General Motors.

Functional similarities and dissimilarities are important. Research labs in business and government have more in common with each other than with functionally different organizations within their own sectors. The same holds, of course, for transportation and other functionally specialized service organizations in each sector that have no obvious counterparts in the other sector; the private sector does very little legally sanctioned adjudication and the public sector does very little retailing for profit, for example. The more functionally dissimilar organizations are, the less likely it is that methods appropriate to one will be appropriate to the other. Communication, coordination, and control problems abound as an organization's scale increases in terms of people and tasks. Within or between sectors, large organizations probably have little useful advice for small organizations, and vice versa.

When we talk of bringing "business methods" to bear on the problems of governments, the first problem is to determine just what the "methods" are. There is considerable variety in the methods—including both managerial philosophies and specific techniques used by businesses, even by firms within the same industries and by the same firm over time. The differences that exist across firms, functional units, and time can be staggering. There are important differences in strategy, managerial style, employee relations, financing, organization, accounting practices, and virtually anything else that one might choose to call a "business method" or a "management practice." The aspiring government reformer's problem is complicated by the fact that, in business, almost all methods or practices, even those that are contradictory (e.g., "participative" versus "authoritarian" managerial decision making), work for some firms in some situations and not for others in ostensibly identical situations. Methods and practices that work for a while for a firm seem to lose effectiveness over time, requiring new methods and practices even when it is not clear how the situation has changed. For government reforms predicated on private experience, we ideally want methods that have a record of success in the private sector in situations comparable to those governments face.

Although there has been an enormous amount of empirical research on what factors distinguish successful companies from unsuccessful companies, this research is, at best, inconclusive. It suffers from many of the same problems as the research comparing public and private organizations reviewed above. The determinants of success are ambiguous and the research is not pointed enough to reveal specific, transportable techniques as determinants of success. The enduring principles of business—like "be in the right industry at the right time" and "buy low, sell high"—do not tell you "how" to do this and are largely irrelevant to government.

There is a very large popular (as opposed to scientific) literature on business methods and management practices. Some of this literature is evangelistic and panders to the insecurities and greed of businessmen in the same ways that the literatures on "How to meet girls (or boys) and get dates" or "How to find peace of mind" or "How to cure baldness" or "How to get rich quick" pander to more general insecurities and greed. Pandering is good business practice for publishers; it sells a lot of books.

There is a somewhat higher cut of this popular, evangelistic literature in the seemingly endless stream of panaceas for business ills: matrix organization, T-groups, experience curves, management by objectives, quality circles, or the latest hypothesis about why Japanese business is beating the socks off American business. The generic ideas behind these panaceas include such priceless gems as: "First, decide exactly what it is you want to do," "Care about your people, get them enthused about the organization's objectives, treat them like adults and they will be motivated to produce for you," and "Make use of what employees at all levels know about how operations could be improved." Good managers in business and government probably already know and behave in accordance with such advice and bad managers don't.

There is yet another higher cut of popular literature on business practices that uses a lot of observation and experience and a modicum of scientific method. A recent prominent example of such work is the book *In Search of Excellence: Lessons from America's Best-Run Companies* by Thomas J. Peters and Robert H. Waterman, Jr., of McKinsey & Co., management consultants. Peters and Waterman combined their extensive management consulting experience with a study of 62 large companies reputed to have excellent management. They used interviews and 25-year literature reviews[8] to study the companies. To further narrow their list and direct their interviewing attention, they imposed more objective performance criteria on the sample. They posited six measurable criteria, three each on "growth" (e.g., "the average ratio of market value to book value") and "return on capital and sales" (e.g., "average return on capital,") for the 1961–1980 period. To stay in the sample, "a company must have been in the top half of its industry in at least four out of six of these measures over the full twenty-year period. . . . " They also used "selected industry experts . . . to rate the companies' twenty-year record of innovation . . . . " The authors interviewed 21 of the 43 companies that met these criteria "in depth" and "conducted less extensive interviews in each of the remaining twenty-two." They also interviewed in 12 other companies that had "just barely missed" being "top performers" on all the criteria. Finally, the authors picked a group of 14 companies—Bechtel, Boeing, Caterpillar Tractor, Dana, Delta Airlines, Digital Equipment, Emerson Electric, Fluor, Hewlett-Packard, IBM, Johnson & Johnson, McDonald's, Procter & Gamble, and 3M—as "exemplars" that they use as the primary source of anecdotal information they offer in support of "the eight attributes that emerged to characterize most nearly the distinction of the excellent, innovative companies . . . . "

Peters and Waterman found that

> The excellent companies were, above all, brilliant on the basics. Tools didn't substitute for thinking. Intellect didn't overpower wisdom. Analysis didn't impede action. Rather, these companies worked hard to keep things simple in a complex world. They persisted. They insisted on top quality. They fawned on their customers. They listened to their employees and treated them like adults. They allowed their innovative product and service "champions" long tethers. They allowed some chaos in return for quick action and regular experimentation. (Peters and Waterman, 1962, p. 13.)

The authors went on to summarize eight attributes common to excellent companies:

1. A *bias for action*, for getting on with it.
2. *Closeness to the customer*. These companies learn from the people they serve.
3. *Autonomy and entrepreneurship*. The innovative companies foster many leaders and many innovators throughout the organization.

4. *Productivity through people.* The excellent companies treat the rank and file as the root source of quality and productivity gains.
5. *Hands-on, value-driven.* Thomas Watson, Jr., said that "the basic philosophy of an organization has far more to do with its achievements than do technological or economic resources, organizational structure, innovation, or timing."
6. *Stick to knitting.* The odds for excellent performance seem strongly to favor those companies that stay reasonably close to business they know. (Like business rather than government?)
7. *Simple form, lean staff.* The underlying structural forms and systems in the excellent companies are elegantly simple. Top-level staffs are lean; it is not uncommon to find a corporate staff of fewer than 100 people running multibillion-dollar enterprises.
8. *Simultaneous loose-tight properties.* The excellent companies are both centralized and decentralized. They are centralized in terms of their core values and decentralized organizationally.

In terms of scientific rigor, the Peters and Waterman study leaves a lot to be desired. Since they do not make strong use of comparison groups, (i.e., they fail to include bad as well as good companies) in identifying the factors contributing to success, it is not clear from their study if there are unsuccessful companies with all or some of the eight "attributes." They do not describe their interview procedures very satisfactorily, raising the possibility that they elicited just the results for which they were looking. They emphasize intangible, unmeasurable factors; it is hard to imagine how one would go about devising measurable variables for the eight attributes summarized above. Finally, the support the authors offer for their findings is largely anecdotal, an approach that increases the psychological impact of the findings on popular audiences but leaves the weight of evidence in scientific terms ambiguous.

Nonetheless, one cannot read the book without believing that the "eight basics" contain a lot of wisdom about how to manage a large business successfully or at least what some of the characteristics of companies are after they become successful. How one should take this wisdom and use it to improve the efficiency and effectiveness of U.S. Steel or the U.S. Congress is a more elusive matter.

What should governments learn from these successful businesses and their "basics," assuming that Peters and Waterman are right that these are causal determinants of success? How might these "methods" increase the efficiency and effectiveness of government? Do the eight basics suggest any specific government reforms? Government executives with *a bias for action* (basic no. 1) must still attend to the procedural niceties and different opinions or a resentful, rebellious legislature (or unsympathetic judiciary) is likely to leave them with just a bias and no action. Regulators and tax collectors are constantly trying to get close to and learn from the "people they serve" (basic no. 2), but their efforts are not generally appreciated. Leaders and innovators (basic no. 3) in many government organizations run afoul of those who would lead and innovate in the opposite direction and earn a living doing so. Rank-and-file government personnel are probably the best potential source of quality and productivity gains (basic no. 4), but they are often too demoralized and busy defending themselves from attacks asserting that they are the primary source of quality and productivity problems to realize any gains. The notion of a hands-on, value-driven government (basic no. 5) is a bit frightening; what would you do if you didn't happen to share the values? Love it or leave it? An important part of government is figuring out what its "knitting" should be (basic no. 6), and it is constantly given tasks ("businesses") that it does not know how to do but that are too important to ignore (e.g., reduce poverty, end discrimination). It would probably be possible and desirable to simplify the form of government and have leaner staffs (basic no. 7); the problem is to convince those whose interests are tied to existing structures, including those who would lose their jobs. Government already has "simultaneous" loose-tight properties (basic no. 8); it is decentralized in terms of core values and centralized organizationally. It is just not clear how to get everyone (or even a substantial majority) to agree on the same values and then truly delegate responsibility for achieving those values.

In inspiring reforms to improve the efficiency and effectiveness of governments, the main private-sector contributions have not been specific remedies for specific problems. It is surprisingly hard to identify instances in which businesses have had a problem, a brilliant solution to the problem was devised, someone noticed that governments have exactly the same problem, and the brilliant solution was successfully applied to the government's problems. Instead, the dominant private-sector contributions to attempts to reform government have included (1) the widespread belief that there must be problems with the efficiency and effectiveness of government because its methods are different, (2) the widespread belief that these problems can be solved by making government more like business, and (3) an enormous amount of folklore about the techniques that presumably make businesses efficient and effective.

Much of the folklore about successful business methods that governments should use to improve performance comes from managers in the private sector reflecting on why they have been so successful. Humans are notoriously bad at such attributions. They tend to attribute the success to their own characteristics or to a method that they invented or had the wisdom to adopt. They tend to rationalize the methods that led to the success, leaving out most of the more wandering and gory details. Like politicians, they almost never attribute their own success to luck; that explanation is reserved for their failures and for the successes of their enemies.

The danger in basing government reforms on such self-serving attributions is that the advice may be essentially for government to get "brains and personality," as Joseph H. Engel (1969)[9] described it in his little fable.

> Once upon a time, there were two little maggots. They were identical twins, born in the same litter. As soon as they'd hatched and opened their eyes (I think maggots have eyes), they both set out into the wide world to make their fortunes. After traveling for a few feet, one of them fell into a crack in the road in front of a gas station, and the other fell into a crack in the road in front of a stable . . . . Neither maggot was big enough to climb up out of the crack it had fallen into, so each decided to make the best of the situation in which it found itself.
>
> Pickings were very lean for the first maggot. Grease, gas, and oil dripped on him constantly. Seldom did any decent nourishment come his way. He grew thin and weak,

his skin was cracked and dull. But he hung on, as even maggots do, and did his best to make ends meet.

The second maggot, however, thrived. Horse droppings were plentiful. The maggot grew and grew. His coat took on a fine waxy gloss. He got big and fat and strong.

One day, a couple of weeks after they'd fallen into their cracks in the road, both maggots decided it was time to travel on. After all, two weeks is a long time in the life of a maggot, and it was probably time for them to find a suitable place to moult, or spin a cocoon, or do whatever it is that maggots do as they approach middle age. So the two maggots each climbed out of their cracks in the road and continued on their travels.

What do you think happened next? You're right. They met. They hadn't really gone very far from where they'd hatched to begin with and, hence, it wasn't too surprising that as they resumed their travels their paths crossed again.

The first little maggot, the one who had fallen in the crack near the gas station, saw the other maggot and recognized him as his twin. He rushed up to him and embraced him fondly. Picture, if you can, this touching scene. But the second maggot pushed his brother off, ashamed, perhaps, to be seen in public with such a scruffy character.

"I'm your brother," the first maggot cried. "Don't you know me?"

"Humph, indeed," said the second maggot, and on looking more closely, said "Yes, I suppose you are. I didn't recognize you at first. You look so seedy."

"That's true," said the first maggot. "I haven't been doing well at all, I've been sick, and I just can't seem to manage. But you look very well. Have you prospered?"

"Oh, yes," said the second maggot. "I'm doing quite nicely. I watch my investments and always have something put aside for a rainy day."

"Oh, how I envy you," said the first maggot. "I wish I could learn to be as successful as you are. Maybe it isn't too late. Tell me the secret of your success."

So, the second maggot, the one that had fallen into the crack in front of the stable, pleased by his brother's praise, puffed up his chest with pardonable pride and answered, "You want the secret of my success, eh? Well—in a nutshell—harumph—it is brains and personality."

At that moment the story came to a close as a crow swooped down and swallowed them both.

We argue above that the beliefs about the severity of government's problems, about the quality of the private sector's example, and about the power of "business methods" may be mistaken because of the ways in which the beliefs are constructed and sustained. We have noted some differences between the public and private sectors that might lead to problems in attempting to transport management and organizational practices from one sector to another. In this final section, we have argued that there may be more than a few problems in getting very widespread agreement within the business community on what constitutes good business methods. Such agreements seem to be achievable only on desired outcomes—make a profit or buy low, sell high—or by stating methods very vaguely and conditionally—stay close to the customer, achieve productivity through people, etc. We stopped short, just short, of arguing that the private sector's advice for the public sector is primarily "get brains and personality."

We now turn to some of the experience with reforming government to improve its efficiency and effectiveness.

NOTES

1. To General Dynamics' credit, the engineer was rehired two years later after he had been proved correct and the project was abandoned.
2. See Jaskow, 1977.
3. Even where the difficult analytic problems are solved and the reasons for inefficiency are known, it does not follow that changing matters to improve efficiency will be easy. In the mass transit example, modernizing the equipment may not be possible because the banks won't lend the money and the politicians won't raise taxes or sell bonds; the wage cuts may be successfully fought by the employees of the public transit system.
4. For a useful if partisan review of this literature, see Savas, 1982.
5. See Alchian and Demsetz, 1972; De Alessi, 1980; Borcherding, 1981.
6. For some representative articles dealing with public/private differences, see Allison, 1979; Bower, 1977; McCendy, 1978; Murphy, 1975; and Rainey, 1976.
7. The more we believe that private sector superiority stems from inherent differences in factors such as property rights, the less can be done to reform the public sector since private property rights can never be realized in agencies such as the judiciary or defense department.
8. "Literature" was annual reports and anything in the popular business literature about the companies that could be found.
9. *Operations Research*, September–October 1969, pp. 761–762.

REFERENCES

Alchian, A., and Demsetz, H. "Production, Information Costs, and Economic Organization." *American Economic Review* 62 (1972):777–795.

Allison, Graham T. *Essence of Decision: Explaining The Cuban Missile Crisis.* Boston: Little, Brown, 1979.

Borcherding, Thomas E. "Toward a Positive Theory of Public Sector Supply Arrangements." In *Public Enterprise in Canada*, edited by N. Prichard. Toronto: Butterworth, 1981.

Bower, Joseph L. "Effective Public Management." *Harvard Business Review* (March–April 1977):134.

Davidson, Robert C. "How to Improve Municipal Government." *North American Review* 153 (November 1891):587–588.

Davies, David G. "The Efficiency of Public versus Private Firms, The Case of Australia's Two Airlines." *Journal of Law and Economics* 14 (1971):149–165.

De Alessi, Louis. "The Economics of the Evidence." *Research in Law and Economics* 2 (1980):1–47.

Drucker, Peter F. "Management: Tasks, Responsibilities, Practices." New York: Harper & Row, 1973, p. 52.

Engel, Joseph H. *Operation Research*, September–October 1969, pp. 761–762.

Flax, Steven. "How Detroit is Reforming the Steelmakers." *Fortune*, May 16, 1983, p. 126.

Jaskow, Paul. "Commercial Impossibility, the Uranium Market and the Westinghouse Case." *Journal of Legal Studies* 6 (1977)1:119–176.

Loomis, Carol J. "The Madness of Executive Compensation." *Fortune*, July 12, 1982, p. 42.

Lynn, Laurence E., Jr. *Managing the Public's Business: The Job of the Government Executive*. New York: Basic Books, 1981, p. 120.

McCendy, Howard. "Selecting and Training Managers: Business Skills versus Public Administration." *Public Administration Review* 36 (November–December 1978)6:571–578.

Murphy, Michael. "Comparing Public and Private Management." *Public Administration Review* 35 (July–August 1975)4:364–371.

Nickel, Stephen J. "Effect of Unemployment and Related Benefits on the Duration of Unemployment." *Journal of Economics* 89 (1979):39.

Peters. Thomas J., and Waterman, Jr., Robert H. *In Search of Excellence: Lessons from America's Best-run Companies*. New York: Harper & Row, 1962, p. 51.

Rainey, Hal G., et al., "Comparing Public and Private Organizations." *Public Administration Review* 36 (March 1976):233–244.

Savas, E. S. "An Empirical Study of Competition in Municipal Service Delivery." *Public Administratin Review* 37 (November–December 1977):68.

Savas, E. S. *Privatizing the Public Sector*. New Jersey: Chatham House, 1982.

Smith, Richard A. *Corporations in Crisis*. Garden City, New York: Doubleday, 1966.

Tatom, John A. "The Productivity Problem." *Federal Reserve Bank of St. Louis Review* 61 (September 1979) 9:3–16.

Taylor, Paul. "Civil Service at 100: Cliches and Contradictions." *Washington Post*, January 16, 1983.

Weiss, Herman L. "Why Business & Government Exchange Executives." *Harvard Business Review*, July–August 1974.

CHAPTER 3

Systems for Measuring and Managing

> Public agencies are very keen on amassing statistics—they collect
> them, add them, raise them to the nth power, take the cube roots
> and prepare wonderful diagrams. But what you must never forget is
> that every one of those figures comes in the first instance from the
> village watchman, who just puts down what he damn pleases.
>
> SIR JOSIAH STAMP

Since the beginning of this century, the development of quantitative, summary measures of performance has been a centerpiece of most attempts to improve governmental performance. They lie at the core of the productivity movement in general and of specific reform attempts such as program, planning, and budgeting systems (PPBS) and management by objectives (MBO). Not surprisingly, the inspiration behind this approach is heavily rooted in the business method folklore and beliefs about superior efficiency of private as compared to public organizations. The folklore surrounds the role that performance measurement plays in good management. It tells us that in a well-run company managers are constantly informed and inspired by performance data ranging from simple productivity information about workers' output to the "bottom line" measures of profit, growth, and market share. Many of the public sector's problems, it is assumed, stem from the absence of comparable information in public bureaucracies. The Grace Commission was particularly forceful in attributing many of the managerial problems in federal government to a lack of information:

> The absence of the right information, at the right time, in the right amounts, to
> make the right decision, renders the Government incapable of effectively assessing its
> strengths and weaknesses and achieving any reasonable degree of managerial efficiency.
> Key information concerning budget, programmatic, managerial, administrative, and
> financial operations is frequently lacking or, when available, is outdated, incomplete,
> or inaccurate." (PPSS, sec. III, p. 16)

As a result of this lack of information in government, information purportedly widely available and used in business, there tend to be few internal standards of performance; meaningful oversight by the public and elected officials is virtually impossible. How can you fire a lazy worker when you can't define "lazy" and have no data on what the workers have done?

While the justification for the use of productivity measures is persuasive, this chapter explores why they are not a magical cure-all for the performance problems that might plague the public sector. Indeed, the difficulties associated with their creation and use are often so great that private firms employ them much less frequently than is popularly believed.[1] Yet because of the role that productivity measures have played in many government reform strategies and the insight that an understanding of their limitations provides into the overall problem of government efficiency and effectiveness, their study provides us with an excellent point of departure for what follows.

Further, government reform is increasingly plagued with an excessive number of "in principle" arguments at high levels of abstraction about the feasibility of accomplishing reforms and what the effects of reforms will be. Academics and business executives tout the relevance of their favorite methods to government in principle much more often than they roll up their sleeves and provide specific, practical demonstrations of their relevance.

Nowhere have these "in principle" arguments been more persuasive and perverse than those that encourage attempts to develop systems for measuring and managing. In principle, such systems are feasible and would have salutary effects. In practice, such systems are infeasible in many respects and have often had undesirable effects. The difficulties are clearer when dealing with concrete examples rather than abstract possibilities. Performance measurement and inference is necessarily a detailed, highly technical business. You cannot fully appreciate the potentials and weaknesses without dealing with the concrete details of creating and using measures such as "number of curb miles of streets cleaned per dollar" or "number of arrests per police employee." We provide concrete examples in two forms. First, we review the actual experience with measuring and managing systems in the federal government and state and local governments. Then, we present an extended hypothetical example of the difficulties in using a measuring and managing strategy to improve the efficiency and effectiveness of a restaurant inspection service.

PRODUCTIVITY MEASUREMENT IN THE FEDERAL GOVERNMENT

> Any argument worth making within the bureaucracy must be capable of being expressed in a single simple declarative sentence that is obviously true once stated.
>
> McNAUGHTON'S RULE

The relevant history of organizational productivity measurement in the federal government dates from the early years of the Great Depression. Partly in response to a widespread concern for the productivity and future of American industry that existed at that time, the Bureau of Labor Statistics undertook an experimental study of productivity in the U.S. Postal Service in 1932. It created a brief stir of interest among professional analysts, but that interest soon waned in the face of the larger problems posed by the state of the general economy.

During the next 40 years, other exploratory studies of agency productivity were periodically undertaken and forgotten. One of the most elaborate of these was conducted in 1964 by the Bureau of the Budget. BOB painstakingly examined output and productivity in five different agencies: the Division of Disbursement of the Bureau of Accounts in the Department of the Treasury, the Department of Insurance in the Veterans Administration, the Post Office, the Systems Maintenance Service of the Federal Aviation Agency, and the Bureau of Land Management. For each of the agencies a system of productivity data based on several indexes was developed. In the Treasury Department's Division of Disbursement, for example, which is responsible for issuing checks and savings bonds, output was defined by two indexes: number of checks and number of bonds issued. Inputs, in this case, were defined in three different ways: (1) paid man-years, (2) labor costs, and (3) total budget costs. Trends in the ratio of inputs to outputs, such as the numbers of bonds issued per man-year, were then calculated to reveal changes in productivity.

BOB was pleased with the results. While a final output measure could never be agreed upon for the Bureau of Land Management because of difficulties in measuring success in its range and recreation program, BOB was satisfied that meaningful and useful productivity measures had been created for the other four agencies. It concluded that productivity measurement was feasible in those federal agencies where the prospect for the quantitative description of outputs was reasonable. Just what percentage of the total number of agencies might fall into this category BOB didn't bother to speculate, but it obviously felt that the Bureau of Land Management was an exception. Perhaps the best news was that productivity measurement didn't have to be expensive. In every case, the basic data needed for determining the measures of output were already on hand in agency files.

The officials at BOB believed that productivity measurement was the wave of the future:

> The productivity data may be used to organize diverse management information to evaluate the net contribution to the productive efficiency of the organization as a whole of improvements made in parts of the organization. Accumulation of productivity measures will also provide a store of knowledge that may serve as a basis for appraising the short-term and the long-term sources of productivity improvements in a meaningful perspective. This knowledge may, in turn, sharpen the effectiveness of policies intended to raise Government productivity.
>
> Productivity data, where feasible, may be used effectively at the various stages of the budget process: by providing a vehicle for systematic projection of resource needs based on the end-product outputs, by providing better information on the unit cost trends of different alternative services, by making possible a rational selection of realistic improvement targets, and by providing a progress report on how these goals are being achieved. (BOB, 1964, p. 18.)

Yet despite the BOB's optimism and carefully prepared final report, the federal government's interest in productivity measurement could not be maintained. After a limited follow-up effort the next year, the project was terminated and the staff that had prepared the study was reassigned to more fashionable projects such as program planning and budgeting systems (PPBS). Productivity measurement, it appeared, could generate a great deal of initial excitement and high expectations but very little permanent funding. Another cycle of concern for government productivity began six years later in 1970, when Senator William Proxmire, chairman of the Joint Economic Committee, requested the comptroller general to evaluate the potential for measuring productivity in the federal sector.

Proxmire, like those who commissioned earlier pilot studies, had found it "distressing that we have no real measures of efficiency in government" (Morris et al., 1972, p. 754). A joint task force composed of representatives from the three central management agencies in the government (the Civil Service Commission, the Office of Management and Budget, and the General Accounting Office) was quickly organized, and by early 1971 the most elaborate productivity measurement project ever attempted was ready to begin.

The motivation behind Proxmire's request is not hard to imagine. The decline in U.S. productivity growth described in Chapter 2 was becoming a matter of increasing concern to both Congress and the executive branch. It was generally felt that any permanent solution to the problem would have to involve reforms in the public as well as the private sector. At about the same time Proxmire was making his request, a National Commission on Productivity created by President Nixon had begun moving in the same direction. In September 1971, the Commission issued its first policy statement and listed government productivity as one of the six targets of opportunity that should be emphasized in any general recovery attempt. The Commission provided the Joint Task Force with the very modest sum of $50,000 to support research aimed at developing and implementing productivity indexes wherever possible (Peterson, 1972, p. 40).

Over the next two years, the Joint Task Force studied productivity measurement in great detail. It began logically enough by trying to learn what, if anything, agencies were currently doing in the area. The Task Force found that productivity indexes were not widely used for a number of reasons. First, although it may have seemed simple conceptually, creating measures that were meaningful over time was often a problem. A number of agencies found themselves involved in a slightly different mix of tasks each year and had difficulty making the output measures commensurate over a significant period. This could be a problem even for agencies like the Treasury's Division of Disbursement. Keeping track of the number of checks issued seems like a straightforward measure of productivity to an outsider, but it turns out that one check is not really the same as any other. There are stencil-prepared checks, thermal-printed checks, manual-posted checks, typed checks, automatic-transfer-posted checks, and this is only the beginning. Because there are different cost and manpower requirements associated with printing each, an increase of 10,000 checks of one sort has different efficiency implications than an equivalent increase in another type. The technologies for check writing are changing constantly; new technologies with yet different efficiency implications become available. Reconciling the differences in outputs in order to estimate real changes in productivity accurately is not always easy. The interpretation of productivity data, even if output differences are resolved, may not be straightforward, because the possibilities in new technologies must always be considered.

A second reason for agency reluctance to employ productivity indexes was a general lack of appreciation of their potential. Managers acknowledged the necessity of reporting on their departments' activities to superiors but couldn't perceive the contribution that careful analysis of productivity trends might make to their own work. Possibly because of the exclusive reliance of PPBS on the prospective use of analytic techniques like benefit-cost analysis, systematic program evaluation rarely took place in most agencies.

Another explanation lies in the fear of misuse. Once gathered, productivity data are difficult to contain. The suspicion that superiors and the press may blame a manager for a drop in productivity over which he or she had no control is pervasive at every level. It is one thing to file an annual or quarterly productivity report with cautionary warnings against misinterpretation and quite another to have these warnings responsibly heeded in a political environment. This potential for abuse encourages the politically astute manager either to reveal productivity data selectively or to suppress their collection entirely.

Finally, there was the issue of faddism. Feeling themselves harassed by demanding superiors and inadequate resources, lower level managers were growing intolerant of managerial gadgets that required their time and attention. Many of these managers had already endured the "revolution" of programmed budgeting and were unenthusiastic about another proposal from a group of managerial technocrats for whom they often had little respect (Morris et al., 1972, p. 753).

Well aware of these problems, the Task Force proceeded to develop productivity indexes for a sample of activities in 17 different agencies. It soon discovered that federal agencies were not nearly as inefficient—at least when measured by productivity growth—as everyone seemed to assume. During the period covered (1967–1971), productivity growth in the sample was a respectable 7.7 percent, which averages out to a growth rate of about 1.9 percent per year. This may not seem especially dazzling, but when one considers that the private sector productivity growth rate during the same period was only 1.5 percent per year, it wasn't bad. More importantly, if this sort of respectable productivity growth was normal, think of the gains that might be possible through a coordinated campaign to boost government productivity.

In addition to measuring the productivity growth that had taken place, the Joint Task Force tried to account for the sources of particularly large gains and losses. Questionnaires were distributed and workshops conducted in an attempt to learn what factors the managers themselves believed to be responsible. Three categories of such factors were identified: human factors, management factors, and work-load factors. The first category included increased personnel efficiency, the acquisition of new skilled personnel, and improved motivation of personnel through job upgrading, redesign, etc. The second category, management factors, was by far the most commonly mentioned source of gains. It included improvement though capital acquisition (especially the purchase of computers) and organizational improvements such as a bank's decision to organize staff by type of loan rather than by geographic location. The third category, work-load factors, consisted of changes in the stability, amount, and complexity of tasks. This source was mentioned less frequently than the other two.

The causes of productivity declines were grouped in the same three categories. Some of the human factors responsible for declines included high turnover, loss of skilled employees, and, interestingly, increase in the time devoted to training. Management factors included downtime while phasing in new facilities and equipment, loss of productive effort during reorganization, and the use of outmoded facilities. Work-load factors mentioned were unmet data-processing requirements, decline in demand for certain types of support services (often attributed to the slow process of scaling down operations that supported military operations during the Vietnam War), and increases in task complexity that required additional training.

Of course, it is difficult to know how seriously to take these results. Government executives, like the rest of us, frequently choose explanations on the basis of their biases and preconceptions rather than on the basis of objective analysis. This is especially true in the case of productivity declines. If you discover that productivity has dropped in your unit by 15 percent, the temptation to attribute the loss to essential increased training rather than to a poor decision on your part can be very powerful. Nonetheless, the findings are provocative. For one thing, the variety of sources to which productivity improvements were attributed provide yet another caution against adopting the old assembly-line view of productivity. Working harder has an impact on productivity, but so, apparently, do other things. The importance of management factors is especially significant in this respect, because it suggests that a relationship between capital spending technology and productivity exists in the public sector as well as the private sector.

More novel is the implication that many of the factors involved in productivity gains can also contribute to declines. Computing, reorganization, and training can lead to dramatic increases in productivity in one context, but they can lead to equally dramatic decreases in another. Part of the problem may simply be the fact that the Joint Task Force's data are excessively time-bound and insensitive to the lag times connected with innovations. The adoption of new methods and techniques characteristically involves a short-term sacrifice in productivity in the same way that a blue-collar worker sacrifices output and income while attending school to become an engineer. Similarly, for an agency installing an elaborate management information system, a temporary loss of efficiency is an expected part of the system's "cost." Nonetheless, one suspects that the findings of the Task Force represent something more. It is impossible to spend very much time around organizations without noticing that computer systems do sometimes lessen rather than increase efficiency or that reorganizations frequently cause more confusion than anything else. Most techniques designed to increase efficiency have an effect that is highly variable and contingent on numerous factors, something that should be kept in mind whenever one is faced with arguments to adopt a "sure-fire" method of increasing productivity.

Since the Joint Task Force completed its final report in 1973, the federal productivity program has been kept alive, if not heavily funded, through a confusing administrative arrangement involving OMB, the Bureau of Labor Statistics, the Civil Service Commission, the General Service Administration, the Joint Financial Management Improvement Program, and, until it was terminated in 1978, the National Center for Productivity and Quality of Work Life. The intermittent character of the support for productivity efforts at the federal level was again evidenced by the administrative and funding problems that plagued the National Center from its inception in 1975. It took more than a year, for example, to select its board, and the Carter administration didn't bother to fill the positions that became empty when it took office.

This is not to suggest that nothing has been done for productivity improvement during the past years. In some sense productivity improvement programs emerged from the 1970s more fashionable than ever. Individual agencies such as the Government Accounting Office and Health and Human Services experimented with a number of productivity improvement approaches, including something called the total performance measurement system (TPMS), which attempted to integrate data on efficiency, effectiveness, and both citizen and employee attitudes (Kull, 1978, p. 6). Nonetheless, presidential and OMB leadership in the area has been far less than that associated with PPBS and zero-based budgeting (ZBB). (See Chapter 5 for a discussion of those reforms.)

Not surprisingly perhaps, given the support they have received, the aggregate impact of these recent productivity improvement efforts has not been great. The productivity growth figure for the federal government as a whole hasn't changed very much since it was first estimated. If anything, it has fallen slightly.

Moreover, it is beginning to appear that politicians and upper-level administrators do not pay nearly as much attention to productivity data as they claim and as advocates of this approach expected. It is hard to prove that this is the case. No one currently possesses reliable data on what factors such people consider before they make a policy decision, and it isn't clear how you would go about collecting such data. Very few of the men and women who are smart enough to get to the top of their profession are also dumb enough to state publicly that they don't view productivity data as being important. There are, however, several unobtrusive indicators of the role that productivity measures play in governmental decision making; none of them are very encouraging.

First, there is the minor role that productivity data play in the budgetary process. Although federal budget instructions explicitly call for the use of productivity figures in budgetary justifications (and have done so for many years), a substantial number of agencies provide none. A few agencies include careful discussions of long-term trends and the sources of productivity variation, but most do not. The impression given by the budgetary documents is corroborated by the legislative hearings. At least in the limited set of hearings examined, specific questions about productivity and the effect of alternative levels of funding on productivity rates were relatively rare.

Beyond this, there is the equally minor role that actual productivity data play in political campaigns and candidate platforms. It is not uncommon for candidates to speak eloquently of the need to increase federal productivity, but more specific charges or promises are usually absent. For the most part, it is obvious that candidates have little idea how productive various agencies are or how much more productive they could be.

As we shall see, the incomplete integration of productivity data into the budgetary and political process is no accident. The data are difficult to interpret, can easily be employed as a weapon by critics, and are often peripheral to the issues that generate the most political concern.

PRODUCTIVITY AT THE STATE AND LOCAL LEVELS

> However well-conceived and well-intentioned the program of city
> government may be, its value to the community will depend upon
> the frequency with which accomplishment is checked against
> standards of possible results, and misdirection of effort and other
> waste is detected and diverted into channels of needed activity.
>
> GEORGE J. WASHIN

The concern for productivity in state and local government is nothing new. From the standpoint of both theory development and actual accomplishments, the history of the productivity movement in state and local government is probably richer and more distinguished than at the federal level. Consider the following accomplishments that were cited in the same volume from which the quote above was drawn. The language and approaches have a strong air of contemporaneity, but the year is 1910.

> In Philadelphia, mothers of young infants in four wards are the target for a special program of education in infant care through home visits by trained nurses. This special program provides a comparison with a traditional advertising approach to educating mothers. The mortality rate for infants under one year of age was reduced 27.3 percent in the four experimental wards, compared with a reduction of 11.8 percent city-wide.
>
> In New York City, through reorganization as well as installation of improved methods and procedures, the Bureau of Water Registry has increased water fee revenue collections by 40 percent in two years. The Bureau of Sewers there has raised the efficiency of one sewer cleaning group in Manhattan by 275 percent. (Washin, 1980, p. 9.)

Fueled by the activities of professional associations made up of working city administrators and provided with intellectual legitimacy by the growing academic discipline of public administration, productivity improvement projects that emphasized the role of performance measurement enjoyed an increasing popularity during the 1920s and '30s at the local level. In 1928, the National Commission on Municipal Standards developed an assortment of effectiveness measures for local services, and in 1933, the International City Management Association produced a handbook to help enable city managers to assess service performance quantitatively. This early work appeared to have an impact. A few large cities such as New York, Chicago, and Milwaukee have employed at least some quantitative efficiency and effectiveness measures for almost half a century.

Productivity measurement at the state level lagged behind that of cities until after World War II largely because the role of states in service delivery and urban assistance was generally modest. However, as those responsibilities grew, so did interest in measuring efficiency and effectiveness. By the 1960s, a concern for productivity led states such as Arizona and Vermont to pass personnel legislation requiring supervisors to establish precise performance targets to be used in justification of pay increases (Crane, 1980, p. 57). During the early 1970s, when it was becoming painfully clear that the era of abundance in state and local government was ending, interest in productivity at the state level accelerated. Wisconsin instituted a program that required all state agencies to increase productivity at least 2.5 percent per year. Other states including Illinois, California, Hawaii, Colorado, and Washington have adopted major initiatives in the area.

Yet despite this flurry of activity, the majority of cities and states are probably not doing as much in this area as is often assumed. The results of a 1977 survey reported in the *Municipal Yearbook* are shown on Tables 3.1 and 3.2. Table 3.1 reports the percentage of cities that currently employ four different (but in some cases related) measures of performance.[2] It suggests that performance measurement

Table 3.1   **Productivity Improvement for State and Local Government***

		PERFORMANCE MEASURES USED			
Classification	*No. of Cities Reporting (A)*	*Work Load (% of A)*	*Unit Cost or Efficiency (% of A)*	*Effectiveness (% of A)*	*Goals and Objectives (% of A)*
Total, all cities	400	85	65	70	72
Population group					
Over 500,000	16	94	81	75	69
250,000–500,000	15	100	87	93	93
100,000–249,999	53	91	74	72	77
50,000–99,999	113	88	65	66	78
25,000–49,999	203	83	60	68	66
Geographic region					
Northeast	65	85	60	66	58
North central	112	84	66	68	71
South	103	88	64	69	70
West	120	88	67	73	83
Metro status					
Central	162	91	73	71	76
Suburban	193	84	61	70	71
Independent	45	78	51	62	62
Form of government					
Mayor-council	79	80	65	62	61
Council manager	308	89	66	72	76
Other	13	62	31	62	46

Source: Adapted from "Table 3/2, Performance Measures Used." *The Municipal Yearbook 1977.* ICMA, Washington, D.C.: International City Management Association 1977, p. 194.

*Totaled percentages exceed 100 percent because of multiple choices.

has made strong inroads in city governments. At least 65 percent of the nearly 400 cities participating in the survey employ each of the four types of performance measures; while a larger percentage of large cities tend to adopt the techniques than do small cities, the difference is not particularly great. On the basis of these figures, it is easy to conclude that the era of high-tech, administratively rational city government has arrived. The catch is that "using" a particular performance measure only means that it is used somewhere, sometime. If a city conducts a small survey about user satisfaction with operating hours in one library, it can be said to be employing effectiveness measures, regardless of what it is doing in other service areas. Obviously such a scoring procedure can easily lead to an inflated representation of how much performance measurement is actually taking place.

Table 3.2 **Productivity Measurement Systems and Their Implementation***

		PERFORMANCE MEASURES USED IN FUNCTIONAL AREAS			
Functional area	*No. of Cities Reporting (A)*	*Work Load (% of A)*	*Unit Cost or Efficiency (% of A)*	*Effectiveness (% of A)*	*Goals and Objectives (% of A)*
General administration	373	30	9	29	53
Personnel	365	41	7	29	47
Finance	375	39	16	26	50
Purchasing	361	41	23	27	43
Tax assessing/collecting	188	46	17	25	44
Planning/zoning	359	38	9	27	54
Social services	184	47	21	38	54
Health/hospitals	101	54	23	27	47
Housing	168	39	20	32	61
Inspections/code	375	66	20	33	46
enforcement	375	66	20	33	46
Public transit	120	51	43	39	51
Parks	350	54	29	39	53
Recreation	344	50	22	43	52
Libraries	226	58	24	39	46
Police	370	69	29	55	56
Criminal justice/courts	157	51	13	20	33
Fire prevention	345	55	20	40	52
Streets maintenance/construction	375	70	55	43	47
Solid-waste collection/disposal	274	70	55	43	47
Waste water/sewerage	292	61	39	38	47
Public works	368	61	35	37	51
Water supply	279	63	46	38	47
Gas/electric	52	62	42	25	42

Source: Adapted from "Table 3/3, Performance Measures Used in Functional Areas." *The Municipal Yearbook 1977.* Washington, D.C.: International City Management Association 1977, p. 195.

*Totaled percentages exceed 100 percent because of multiple choices.

A quick glance at Table 3.2 confirms this suspicion. Here we have a list of 24 functional areas and the percentage of cities that use performance measures in each area. For the most part the figures are dramatically lower than those depicted in Table 3.1 and indicate that there are some services, such as general administration and finance, in which performance measurement is far from commonplace. Interestingly, the steepest fall-off takes place in connection with the efficiency measures, those that come closest to measuring productivity. While 65 percent of all cities surveyed indicated that they were using some efficiency measures, less than 30 percent were doing so in most functional areas. Moreover, these figures are probably somewhat inflated, since the use of a single measure of efficiency in a particular area gives a city full credit for measuring efficiency even when several might be necessary to do an adequate job.[3]

What's going on here? The technology of productivity measurement for many urban services is relatively well developed. City administrations know about the existence of measurement techniques and already make limited use of them. Nonetheless, most cities do not measure productivity or effectiveness in most service areas. Why not? Why hasn't performance measurement caught on?

MEASURING PRODUCTIVITY IN CITY SERVICES: SOLID WASTE DISPOSAL AND LAW ENFORCEMENT

> Most men cannot hold themselves to their highest standard of efficiency unless they are constantly stimulated by the prospect of a rigid and impartial appraisal of their work. No one factor of efficient control is more commonly neglected in municipal management.
>
> JESSE D. BURKS, 1913

In order to understand why performance measurement isn't more widely employed, it is useful to look at an area in which it seems to be popular and compare it with another where it is less common. Waste removal (i.e., solid waste disposal) is a good example of an area where performance measurement appears to have been successful. Of the cities in the *Municipal Yearbook* survey, 70 percent measure work load in this area and 43 percent measure efficiency. More generally, whenever an advocate of productivity improvement programs begins to cite figures about the dramatic improvements that are possible through productivity measurement, the odds are high that the figures come from a waste-removal program. Not the most aesthetically appealing of city services perhaps, but in the world of performance measurement, this is where much of the action has taken place.

The amount of money that cities spend to remove refuse is significant, amounting to about 10 percent of a typical city's budget. Increasing waste removal productivity won't save New York City or Detroit from bankruptcy, but it can yield nontrivial savings. Reducing the size of a sanitation department's work force by just three people (or making the hiring of three additional people unnecessary) can easily lead to the saving of $100,000 or more in salary, fringe benefits, and over-head costs.

In the area of solid waste removal, productivity is generally estimated by what are called "intermediate efficiency measures." These are created by dividing work-load measures by either cost or labor input. The measures are intermediate because the output measured is not an authentic measure of effectiveness. For ex-ample, cost per ton of waste removed, one of the most common measures of pro-ductivity used in this area, shows how efficiently a department is handling its work load, but not how efficiently it is accomplishing its ultimate goals of creating a sanitary and aesthetically attractive environment. To measure efficiency accurately with respect to these latter goals would require data on environmental hazards (bacteria levels, etc.) and consumer satisfaction.[4] Obviously it would be possible for a waste removal unit to be very efficient at removing a ton of waste but very ineffective (and therefore unproductive in a broader sense) because it left an addi-tional 500 pounds of waste scattered in the street. Unfortunately, gathering au-thentic effectiveness data is often so time-consuming and expensive that a choice must be made between using intermediate measures or none at all. For the most part, the experience with intermediate efficiency/productivity measures in the area of waste removal has been good. The most widely employed measures are:

1. Cost per ton or cubic yard
2. Cost per household or business
3. Cost per capita
4. Number of curb miles of streets cleaned per dollar
5. Number of large items hauled away (e.g., refrigerators, abandoned autos) per dollar
6. Tons of waste collected per man-hour of labor
7. Households or businesses serviced per man-hour of labor

Once a decision is made as to which data need to be collected, it is necessary to devise procedures to obtain the information on a periodic basis and establish the baseline measures that can be used to estimate productivity gains and losses. In the area of solid waste disposal, both these tasks can be done fairly easily. Large cities tend to rely on the use of computer-based, automatic data recording systems to keep track of the tonnage of waste taken to dump sites. Drivers of trucks need only insert a plastic card and drive onto the scales. The computer ensures that the relevant information is recorded and prepares summaries of work-crew and depart-mental productivity. Smaller cities and towns must usually prepare records and reports manually, but the job is relatively simple and straightforward. It isn't even necessary to record the weight of every truck, since sampling procedures can easily be designed. Usually enough data are collected within a year to establish a reliable baseline level of productivity for the department. (More than a month or two of record keeping is necessary to avoid being misled by seasonal fluctuations.)

After the selection of the productivity measures and the establishment of base-line productivity rates, cities can begin to experiment with different methods to increase efficiency. One common productivity strategy is to experiment with dif-ferent routing patterns. Choices must be made about which dump sites will serve different parts of the community and how trucks will proceed to cover their routes.

Through the application of sophisticated operations research techniques or not-quite-so-sophisticated "principles" of route management (such as "Routes should start near the dispatching station" and "Routes where collection is from one side of the street should have as few left turns as possible"), significant savings can be achieved. A very useful article by Savas et al. (1981), from which many of the details included here are drawn, cites the example for Fort Worth, Texas; there, a 14.6 percent annual cost reduction was achieved by nothing more than routing.

Another area of waste removal where experimentation often takes place is in equipment. There are three basic types of loading configurations for trucks and numerous variations in load capacity, safety features, fuel consumption, etc. The right choice can make a noticeable difference in productivity. In low-density residential areas, where the amount of refuse picked up at any given stop is relatively small and the politics permit requiring residents to take their own refuse to the curb, side loaders with one-person crews can be much more efficient and economical than rear loaders with two- or three-person crews. Over 100 cities now make use of one-person systems and obtain cost savings of 25 to 50 percent (Savas et al., 1981, p. 609). Recently developed mechanized systems in which containers are mechanically lifted and emptied promise even greater efficiency. There are numerous other innovations in the waste disposal field—such as the use of incentive pay for workers, the use of plastic bags and special containers by householders, and more extensive use of private contracting—that are constantly being evaluated. Productivity measurement makes it possible for policymakers to choose intelligently among these innovations.

In the area of law enforcement, productivity measurement has not been nearly so successful, at least as measured by the frequency with which it has been implemented. Only 29 percent of the cities in the survey say that they keep track of police efficiency or productivity (see Table 3.2). Those unfamiliar with the past 25 years of research sponsored by the Law Enforcement Assistance Administration (LEAA) and similar agencies might think that most of the problem lies in the relative absence of output measures. Surprisingly, it does not. Actually, a wealth of intermediate and final output measures are available for tracking law enforcement productivity. A few sample measures are:

A. Intermediate productivity measures (workload/input)
   1. Number of service calls responded to per hour of police officer time, by type of call
   2. Number of investigations conducted per hour of police officer time, by type of case
   3. Number of arrests per police employee or per $1,000
   4. Administrative and processing costs per arrest, by type

B. Final productivity measures (effectiveness/input)
   1. Number of arrests surviving judicial screening per police employee-year or per $1,000
   2. Reduction in reported number of crimes—by type per police employee-year or per $1,000
   3. Percentage of households or businesses victimized per police employee-year or per $1,000

4. Arrests that have survived preliminary screening per police employee-year or per $1,000
5. Percentage of stolen property recovered per police employee-year or per $1,000

These and dozens of other productivity and effectiveness measures deal with virtually every aspect of law enforcement. Measures have been constructed that probe the extent of citizen satisfaction, police response time, police misbehavior, quality of crime prevention programs, patrol effectiveness, and even incidence of casualties among police, suspected criminals, and innocent bystanders. Of course, keeping track of all of the data necessary to maintain records of achievement on these measures is a more imposing problem than was the case in solid waste removal and requires that larger sums of money and manpower be appropriated to this task.

Once in place, a productivity measurement system can be used to evaluate a wide variety of law enforcement innovations. Such a system enabled officials in Scottsdale, Arizona, for example, to estimate that the use of civilian police assistants saved an estimated 9,000 patrol officer work days and $188,000 in salaries during the program's first four years of operation. A related program that used civilian help to issue warrants is reported to have helped save over 50 percent of previous costs in Palo Alto, California. Other innovations that have been evaluated using performance measurement systems include computer-designed patrol beats, compact versus full-sized public cars, and one-officer versus two-officer patrols.

Yet while two decades of research on criminal justice productivity have produced a broad array of performance measures and there appear to be a large number of law enforcement innovations waiting to be evaluated, most cities do not bother to measure law enforcement productivity. Why not? What makes the experience with productivity measurement in law enforcement—and areas like general administration, finance, personnel, and libraries—so much less successful (at least measured by frequency of use) than that in waste removal, street maintenance, or sewage?

The reflex response to this question—the one that is heard again and again—is that productivity measurement fails when outputs cannot be meaningfully quantified. Undoubtedly, this is a necessary prerequisite for productivity measurement. Historically, quantification problems have played a role in the failure of efforts to chart performance in federal agencies such as the State Department and Bureau of Land Management. But on the surface, at least, the ability to quantify outputs is not what distinguishes solid waste removal from law enforcement. Something else must be going on there.

The ability to quantify agency outputs — to define effectiveness criteria rigorously and measure their achievement—is not the only factor that influences the success of a productivity improvement program. In the case of waste removal versus law enforcement, the measurement advantages in the first area result less from the integrity and meaningfulness of the measures that are used than from the relative simplicity of a waste removal agency's goals. As a measure of output, "number of arrests cleared by initial court screening" (i.e., arrests that are not thrown out for lack of sufficient evidence) is not obviously inferior to tons of refuse. Accurate records can easily be maintained on arrest rates and, while it is an intermediate measure of efficiency based on work load rather than ultimate effectiveness, the same is true for tons of refuse. A more serious problem is that while one ton of waste is pretty much like any other ton of waste (at least for purposes of record keeping), the same is not true for arrests. Depending on your priorities, arrests for drunken driving may be more or less important than arrests for burglary or arson. Even if there is community agreement about the importance of a given crime (an improbable situation), trying to aggregate different offenses into a single "crime index" is a problem. Does one grand larceny equal two simple assaults?

A related difficulty is that arrest rates provide a more seriously incomplete picture of law enforcement activity than does tons of waste removed for sanitation activity. Before making any judgment about police productivity, one would also want to know something about changes in crime rate, response time to emergency calls, the presence or absence of corruption, and a variety of other things. Accurately summarizing the performance of police departments entails keeping track of many more measures than in waste removal, and there are going to be some hard choices in combining measures to summarize overall performance. What does it mean when arrests go up 20 percent for one crime and down 2 percent for another? Has the police department become more or less productive? If there are only three or four different areas, this doesn't constitute too great a problem. Analysts can simply present a page of statistics showing what happened in each area and let decision makers and citizens reach their own conclusions. The trouble is that there are more than a few different relevant measures. To capture accurately the performance of a police department in a large city might require 20 measures, perhaps more. This is far greater number than is needed to give a satisfactory portrait of sanitation department performance. The measures inevitably present problems that have less to do with measurement strictly defined than with interpretation.

To better appreciate the interpretative difficulties, assume that you are a member of a city council that has recently implemented a productivity measurement system in the police department. The council discovers that "the percentage of burglaries in which an arrest was made (and that survive preliminary screening) per $1,000" decreased over the past year by 4 percent. Armed with this figure that you have good reason to believe is accurate and discouraged by what seems to be firm evidence of declining productivity on the part of the police department, the city council calls in the police chief and confronts him with the discouraging news.

The police chief regretfully acknowledges the existence of the decline but assures you that the figures are misleading. First, he says, you have to realize that the decline in burglary arrests was an inevitable result of the increased departmental priority on reducing violent crime. The murder rate, he points out, increased less than it had during the previous year. Second, although the percentage of arrests surviving initial screening was down 10 percent, the absolute number of burglary arrests did not decline at all, and the percentage of arrests resulting in conviction has increased. The department is simply using much stricter internal screening procedures in response to some of the judges who are becoming increasingly preoccupied with offender rights. The department feels that it saves the city money if it doesn't bother booking suspects in cases where the evidence is not airtight. Third, the chief tells you that there has been a 17 percent increase in the number of attempted robberies and a 10 percent increase in the number of arsons during the past year. His officers are so busy preparing reports and conducting investigations in these areas that they don't have time to catch burglars. In conclusion, the chief adopts a world-weary expression of concern and says that no one is more disappointed than he. "The citizens certainly deserve better and that is the best argument for my requested budget increase of $400,000 next year."

What do you do now? How do you translate the information revealed by the productivity measurement system into intelligent action? Has productivity increased or declined? Do you cut the police department's budget or grant the increase? These questions are not easy to answer. But the questions are no harder than those that arise in fire protection, building inspection, health inspection, defense, and a host of other governmental service areas.

The best way to appreciate the complexities of performance measurement in government is to try to do it in a real setting. While we cannot offer that experience here, we can offer a detailed hypothetical example of what it might be like in a service area—restaurant inspection—that would seem to lend itself to quantitative performance measurement.

MEASURING AND MANAGING RESTAURANT INSPECTIONS

You can observe a lot just by watching.

YOGI BERRA

In larger U.S. cities, all public establishments that prepare and serve food on their premises are subject to inspection and licensing (and perhaps grading) by a city, county, or state health department.[5] The same department may also be inspecting or monitoring other food-handling operations (e.g., grocery stores), drinking water facilities, barbershops, sewage and waste disposal, rental housing, public lodgings, and public bathing facilities. But for this hypothetical example we will consider only the subfunction of inspecting and licensing public establishments such as restaurants, cafes, and lunch stands that prepare and serve food on their premises.

The avowed purpose of inspection and licensing is to prevent the spread of "food-borne illness" (defined broadly to include both infectious diseases like hepatitis, cholera, and typhoid and health incidents like ptomaine or salmonella poisoning). Our hypothetical department seeks to accomplish this objective by inspecting facilities and operations in great detail. The department has ten inspectors dedicated exclusively to this one type of inspection. When an establishment is opened, it is inspected and, if approved, licensed. After licensing, each establishment is supposed to be inspected two to four times a year. In our hypothetical city there have been about 2,200 licensed establishments on average over the five-year period. Each regular inspection is unannounced and consists of the inspector going through a checklist of 102 items (see Figure 3.1)[6] that range from appraising structural features of the building to ensuring the hollandaise sauce is made of fresh ingredients and discarded or used within three hours. If one or more violations are found on a regular inspection, a follow-up inspection is scheduled for the same inspector to see that violations have been corrected.

Each inspector can do one to four inspections per day depending on the difficulty of the inspection, the degree of care taken in the inspection, and the inspector's efficiency. Each inspector has approximately 250 days per year, on average, that can be devoted to inspection. The current work day also includes two hours in the office at the end of the day to receive the next day's assignments and to complete and file reports.

Table 3.3 shows the average annual costs per inspector. The direct costs include salary, fringe benefits, and the cost of a vehicle to transport the inspector to and from inspections. The salaries and benefits vary because of seniority. The other costs related to inspection in the division are summarized in Table 3.4.

Table 3.5 shows data on the number of inspections (regular, follow-up, and total) conducted by each inspector over the last five years. Inspector 1 conducted 743 inspections in year 1 (column 1, row 1); 539 of these inspections were regular and 204 were follow-up. Row 11 gives averages by year.

What can we say about the efficiency and effectiveness of our hypothetical inspection process and the productivity of the inspectors with the data given so far?[7] Not much. We note from Table 3.5 that there is a lot of variation among inspectors in the number of inspections they conduct and in the proportions of inspections that are regular and follow-up. Inspector 8 has averaged 746.9 inspections per year over the five-year period while Inspector 6 has averaged only 381.4 inspections per year. But we immediately note that Inspector 6 has the highest average proportion of follow-up inspections over the five-year period, while Inspector 8 has the lowest proportion. The difference in the number of inspections between the two is conceivably because Inspector 6 is more thorough than Inspector 8 in inspecting; almost every regular inspection that Inspector 6 conducts results in a finding of one or more violations and a follow-up inspection; while only about 10 percent, on average, of Inspector 8's inspections find violations. Another explanation for the variation in inspection rates may be that the assignment of establishments for inspection are not random. Inspector 8 may have been assigned a higher proportion of "easy" inspections (i.e., he may have inspected primarily small, clean establishments that take very little time to run through the checklist and that yield few violations).

Which inspector, 6 or 8, is more efficient? It is impossible to say, given what we know to this point, because inspections, our measure of inspector's output for the moment, may not be homogeneous and comparable. Differences in the output among inspectors may be attributed to nonrandom assignments and differences in the difficulty of the inspection task or, given random assignments, to the care (quality) of inspections. Differences in output are not directly and obviously attributable to differences in efficiency.

Of course, we still have not used all of the data. Table 3.6 shows the calculated average cost per inspection by inspector and by year. Again, there is a lot of

Figure 3.1 Inspection Checklist

STRUCTURE NUMBER

SUB NUMBER   DATE

ESTABLISHMENT NAME

304A-1 FLOORS

1	FLOORS NOT CLEAN	2
2	FLOOR CONSTRUCTION DOES NOT ALLOW EASY CLEANING; CARPETING NOT IN GOOD REPAIR	1
3	FLOORS NOT GRADED PROPERLY; ADEQUATE DRAINS NOT PROVIDED	2
4	MATS AND DUCKBOARDS NOT CLEANABLE, REMOVABLE AND CLEAN	2
5	FLOORS AND WALL JUNCTURES NOT PROPERLY CONSTRUCTED	2

304A-2 WALLS AND CEILINGS

6	WALLS, CEILINGS AND ATTACHED EQUIPMENT NOT CLEAN	2
7	WALLS AND CEILINGS NOT IN GOOD REPAIR, WITHOUT SMOOTH, WASHABLE SURFACE	1
8	FINISH OF WALLS AND CEILINGS NOT IN A LIGHT COLOR; NOT WASHABLE TO SPLASH LEVEL	2

304A-3 DOORS AND WINDOWS

9	OPENINGS INTO OUTER AIR NOT EFFECTIVELY SCREENED; NOT RODENT PROOF	2

304A-4 LIGHTING

10	LESS THAN 20-FOOT CANDLES OF LIGHT ON WORKING SURFACES	4
11	LESS THAN 10-FOOT CANDLES OF LIGHT ON FOOD EQUIPMENT, UTENSIL WASHING, HAND WASHING AREAS, AND TOILET ROOMS	2
12	LESS THAN 5-FOOT CANDLES OF LIGHT 30; FROM FLOOR IN ALL OTHER AREAS DURING CLEANING OPERATION	2
13	LIGHTING FIXTURE AND GUARD NOT OF AN APPROVED TYPE	2

304A-9 CONSTRUCTION OF UTENSILS AND EQUIPMENT

		NOT IN GOOD REPAIR	NOT EASILY CLEANED	UNAPPROVED MATERIAL	
32	FOOD-CONTACT SURFACES OF EQUIPMENT				2
33	UTENSILS				2
34	NON-FOOD-CONTACT SURFACES OF EQUIPMENT				2
35	EXISTING EQUIPMENT NOT CAPABLE OF BEING CLEANED, TOXIC AND NOT IN GOOD REPAIR				2

304A-10 CLEANING AND BACTERICIDAL TREATMENT OF UTENSILS AND EQUIPMENT

36	TABLEWARE NOT CLEAN TO SIGHT AND TOUCH	4
37	KITCHENWARE AND FOOD-CONTACT SURFACE NOT CLEAN TO SIGHT AND TOUCH	4
38	STOVES AND GRILLS NOT CLEANED DAILY	4
39	HOODS NOT CLEAN	2
40	NON-FOOD-CONTACT SURFACES OF EQUIPMENT NOT CLEAN	2
41	WIPING CLOTHS NOT CLEAN, USE NOT PROPERLY RESTRICTED	2
42	UTENSILS AND EQUIPMENT NOT PREFLUSHED, SCRAPED, OR SOAKED	2
43	TABLEWARE NOT SANITIZED AFTER EACH USE	4
44	KITCHENWARE AND FOOD-CONTACT SURFACES NOT SANITIZED	4
45	FACILITIES FOR WASHING AND SANITIZING EQUIPMENT AND UTENSILS NOT APPROVED, ADEQUATE, PROPERLY CONSTRUCTED, MAINTAINED, AND OPERATED	4
46	WASH AND SANITIZING WATER NOT CLEAN	2
47	WASH WATER NOT AT PROPER TEMPERATURE	2
48	APPROVED THERMOMETERS NOT PROVIDED AND USED	2

68	CONTAINERS OF FOOD STORED ON FLOOR	2
69	WET STORAGE OF PACKAGED FOOD	2
70	DISPLAY CASES, COUNTER PROTECTION DEVICES, OR CABINETS NOT OF APPROVED TYPE	2
71	SUGAR NOT IN CLOSED DISPENSER OR INDIVIDUAL PACKAGES	2
72	UNWRAPPED AND POTENTIALLY HAZARDOUS FOOD RESERVED	4
73	POISONOUS AND TOXIC MATERIALS IMPROPERLY IDENTIFIED, COLORED, STORED, OR USED	6
74	BACTERICIDES, CLEANING, AND OTHER COMPOUNDS, IMPROPERLY STORED AND TOXIC IN USE DILUTIONS	6
75	ANIMALS ALLOWED IN ROOMS WHERE FOOD IS PREPARED, STORED, OR SERVED	2

304A-14 WHOLESOMENESS OF FOOD AND DRINK

		FOOD	DRINK	FROZEN DESSERT	DAIRY PRODUCTS	SHELLFISH	
76	UNAPPROVED SOURCE						6
77	NOT WHOLESOME, ADULTERATED						6
78	NOT ORIGINAL CONTAINER; IMPROPERLY IDENTIFIED						2
79	UNAPPROVED DISPENSER						2
80	FLUID MILK AND FLUID MILK PRODUCTS NOT PASTEURIZED						4
81	FOOD NOT COOKED TO PROPER TEMPERATURE						6
82	FRUITS AND VEGETABLES NOT WASHED THOROUGHLY						2

304A-15 INSECT AND VECTOR CONTROL

83	PRESENCE OF RODENTS, FLIES, ROACHES	4
84	OUTER OPENINGS NOT PROTECTED AGAINST FLYING INSECTS AS REQUIRED; NOT RODENT PROOFED	2

304A-5 VENTILATION

No.	Item	Pts
14	ROOMS NOT REASONABLY FREE FROM STEAM, CONDENSATION, SMOKE, ETC.	2
15	ROOMS AND EQUIPMENT NOT VENTED TO OUTSIDE AS REQUIRED	2
16	HOODS NOT PROPERLY DESIGNED: FILTERS NOT REMOVABLE	2
17	INTAKE AIR DUCTS NOT PROPERLY DESIGNED AND MAINTAINED	1
18	SYSTEMS DO NOT COMPLY WITH FIRE PREVENTION REQUIREMENTS; NO NUISANCE CREATED	2

304A-6 TOILET FACILITIES

No.	Item	Pts
19	TOILET FACILITIES FOR EMPLOYEES INADEQUATE, INCONVENIENTLY LOCATED AND OR IMPROPERLY INSTALLED	6
20	TOILET ROOMS NOT COMPLETELY ENCLOSED, NOT EQUIPPED WITH SELF-CLOSING, TIGHT FITTING DOORS; DOORS NOT KEPT CLOSED	2
21	TOILET ROOMS FLOORS, WALLS, AND CEILING NOT IN GOOD REPAIR AND FREE FROM ODOR	2

304A-7 WATER SUPPLY

No.	Item	Pts
22	WATER SUPPLY INADEQUATE AND NOT OF A SAFE, SANITARY QUALITY	6
23	SUPPLY OF HOT AND COLD RUNNING WATER NOT ADEQUATE AT ALL TIMES	4
24	TRANSPORTED WATER NOT HANDLED, STORED OR DISPENSED IN A SANITARY MANNER	6
25	ICE FROM UNAPPROVED SOURCE; NOT MADE FROM POTABLE WATER	6
26	ICE MACHINES AND FACILITIES IMPROPERLY LOCATED, INSTALLED AND MAINTAINED	2
27	ICE CONTACT SURFACES NOT APPROVED; IMPROPER MATERIAL AND CONSTRUCTION	2

304A-8 HANDWASHING FACILITIES

No.	Item	Pts
28	ADEQUATE AND CONVENIENT HANDWASHING FACILITIES NOT PROVIDED, IMPROPERLY INSTALLED	6
29	HOT AND COLD RUNNING WATER NOT PROVIDED THROUGH PROPER FIXTURES	4
30	SOAP AND APPROVED HAND-DRYING DEVICE OR SANITARY TOWELS NOT PROVIDED	2
31	LAVATORY FACILITIES NOT CLEAN OR IN GOOD REPAIR	2

No.	Item	Pts
49	SUITABLE DISH BASKETS NOT PROVIDED	2
50	SINGLE SERVICE ARTICLES USED MORE THAN ONCE	6

304A-11 STORAGE AND HANDLING OF UTENSILS AND EQUIPMENT

No.	Item	Pts
51	CLEANED AND SANITIZED UTENSILS AND EQUIPMENT IMPROPERLY STORED AND HANDLED	2
52	SUITABLE FACILITIES AND AREAS NOT PROVIDED FOR STORING UTENSILS AND EQUIPMENT	2
53	SINGLE SERVICE ARTICLES IMPROPERLY STORED, DISPENSED, OR HANDLED	2
54	FROZEN DESSERT DIPPERS IMPROPERLY STORED	2
55	ICE HANDLING UTENSILS IMPROPERLY HANDLED AND STORED	2

304A-12 DISPOSAL OF WASTES

No.	Item	Pts
56	APPROVED CONTAINERS NOT PROVIDED	2
57	CONTAINERS NOT CLEANED WHEN EMPTY	2
58	CONTAINERS NOT COVERED WITH TIGHT FITTING LIDS; ACCESSIBLE TO VERMIN	2
59	STORAGE AREAS INADEQUATE, NOT CLEAN, NUISANCES; PROPER FACILITIES NOT PROVIDED	2
60	NOT DISPOSED OF IN AN APPROVED MANNER AT APPROVED FREQUENCY	2
61	FOOD WASTE GRINDERS AND INCINERATORS IMPROPERLY INSTALLED, CONSTRUCTED, AND OPERATED; INCINERATOR AREAS NOT CLEAN	2

304A-13 FOOD PROTECTION

No.	Item	Pts
62	SUITABLE THERMOMETERS IMPROPERLY LOCATED	2
63	PERISHABLE FOOD NOT AT PROPER TEMPERATURE	4
64	NOT PROTECTED FROM CONTAMINATION	6
65	POTENTIALLY HAZARDOUS FOOD BETWEEN 45°F OR 140°F	6
66	HANDLING OF FOOD NOT MINIMIZED BY USE OF SUITABLE UTENSILS	4
67	HOLLANDAISE SAUCE NOT OF FRESH INGREDIENTS, NOT DISCARDED AFTER THREE HOURS	2

No.	Item	Pts
85	HARBORAGE AND FEEDING OF VERMIN NOT PREVENTED	2

304A-16 CLEANLINESS OF EMPLOYEES

No.	Item	Pts
86	OUTER GARMENTS NOT CLEAN, HAIR RESTRAINTS NOT USED	2
87	HANDS NOT WASHED AND CLEAN	6
88	EMPLOYEES USE TOBACCO IN ROOMS IN WHICH FOOD IS PREPARED	2

304A-17 MISCELLANEOUS

No.	Item	Pts
89	PREMISES NOT KEPT CLEAN, NOT FREE OF LITTER	2
90	OPERATIONS CONDUCTED IN ROOM USED AS LIVING OR SLEEPING QUARTERS	1
91	ADEQUATE LOCKERS OR DRESSING ROOMS NOT PROVIDED	1
92	LOCKERS OR DRESSING ROOMS NOT KEPT CLEAN	2
93	NO CONTAINERS PROVIDED FOR SOILED LINENS, COATS, AND APRONS	1
94	LAUNDERED CLOTHES AND NAPKINS NOT STORED IN CLEAN PLACE	2

310 COMMUNICABLE DISEASE CONTROL

No.	Item	Pts
95	PERSONS WITH BOILS, INFECTED WOUNDS, RESPIRATORY INFECTIONS, OR OTHER COMMUNICABLE DISEASES NOT PROPERLY RESTRICTED	6
96	KNOWN OR SUSPECTED COMMUNICABLE DISEASE CASES NOT REPORTED TO THE DIRECTOR	6

PLUMBING

No.	Item	Pts
97	PLUMBING AND FIXTURES NOT PROPERLY CONNECTED, VENTED, OR MAINTAINED	2
98	NON-POTABLE WATER PIPING NOT IDENTIFIED	1
99	PLUMBING OR FIXTURES NOT PROPERLY DRAINED	2
100	CROSS CONNECTION	6
101	BACK SYPHONAGE POSSIBLE	6

SEWAGE DISPOSAL

No.	Item	Pts
102	NOT INTO PUBLIC SEWER, OR APPROVED PRIVATE FACILITIES	6

Table 3.3 Average Annual Costs per Inspector

Year	Salary	Fringe	Vehicle	Total
1	$18,000	$4,500	$3,200	$25,700
2	21,000	5,250	3,600	29,850
3	22,500	5,625	3,900	32,025
4	24,000	6,000	4,400	34,400
5	27,000	6,750	4,700	38,450

variation among inspectors; the average cost over the full five years for Inspector 6 was $83.76, almost twice the $43.39 average cost per inspection for Inspector 8. Unfortunately, the cost data do not help us in conclusively determining the relative efficiency of inspectors because differences are still possibly attributable to factors other than efficiency. Even if the costs for the inspectors differed (e.g., Inspector 6 was senior to Inspector 8 and earned a higher salary) we still could not determine relative efficiency unless we controlled for both the relative difficulty and quality of the inspections. We could get around the relative difficulty problem by assigning inspectors randomly to restaurants. This would mean losing out on any efficiency gains that come from assigning each inspector a territory (e.g., less travel, more familiarity with special problems, etc.), but it could be done. Controlling for the quality of the inspections is harder. It would probably require instituting a procedure for inspecting the inspectors where a supervisor reinspected a random sample of inspections and graded inspectors on quality. Such a system would have its own costs and, because of the nature of the inspection process, the system would probably be highly judgmental.

It is no easier to determine changes in the relative efficiency of the same inspector over time. For example, Inspector 1 has done fewer inspections in each successive year over the five-year period (Table 3.5) at greater cost (Table 3.6). Is Inspector 1 becoming less efficient (less productive)? We won't know until we control for the difficulty of the inspection tasks and for the quality of inspections. For that matter, the increases in average costs per inspection (Table 3.6) may reflect only inflation. In calculating costs for comparison over time, costs should be expressed in constant dollars. Using previous years as a standard raises another prob-

Table 3.4 Indirect Inspection Costs

Year	Supervisor's Salary	Fringe Benefits	Secretaries' Salaries	Fringe Benefits	Misc. (Supplies, Telephone, Rental)	Total
1	$23,000	$5,750	$20,000	$5,000	$ 3,000	$56,750
2	26,000	6,500	23,000	5,750	4,500	65,750
3	28,000	7,000	24,000	6,000	7,000	72,000
4	30,500	7,625	26,000	6,500	8,500	79,125
5	32,500	8,125	28,000	7,000	10,500	86,125

lem for gauging efficiency. What if an inspector has maintained a tradition over the whole five years of spending the first two hours every morning in a coffee shop reading the newspaper rather than inspecting? Such a temporally consistent source of inefficiency would not show up in the intertemporal comparisons.

Is the overall inspection system becoming more efficient? Again, it is difficult to say. The average number of inspections conducted annually (row 12, Table 3.5) appears relatively stable and the average annual costs per inspection are rising (bottom row, Table 3.6). But for the entire system we encounter the same difficulties in interpretation as we did in attempting to understand the relative efficiency of particular inspectors over time. We might look for another city with comparable characteristics in the inspection task and all other factors relevant to inspecting. However, such comparisons are extremely difficult to do primarily because there are so many relevant factors for which one must control. For example, we have not included the indirect costs of inspections (Table 3.4) in any of our calculations. There are often a large number of inconsistencies in measure construction, like which costs are included, that complicate comparisons of functions across governments.

Planning models are another possible source of a standard for appraising the efficiency of the inspection system. We could sit down and calculate, perhaps supported by rigorous experiment, how long an average inspection of given quality should take, how long it should take on average to get from one inspection site to another, how long it should take to write up report, and how many violations per inspection should be expected. We could then construct an expected day for inspectors and require them to justify days that deviate abnormally from the expectation. Unfortunately, such models are difficult to construct and apply for many reasons. Two of the most important reasons are:

1. There are costs associated with explaining these deviations because of the several competing causal explanations available in each case. An articulate but perhaps not diligent inspector will be able to explain away almost any deviation.
2. Conditions (e.g., the number and type of restaurants) change, putting the expectations out of date and requiring that you periodically replan.

What can we say about about the effectiveness (as opposed to the efficiency) of the system with the data given so far? Nothing, because no effectiveness standard has been provided. One form such a standard might take is the "number of inspections of given quality for a year" based on historical performance. A common example would be 110 percent of last year's level. So we did 5,718 inspections in year 1, which means that 6,290 inspections are planned for year 2. Unfortunately, only 5,448 inspections were accomplished in year 2, for an 87 percent level of effectiveness (output/planned output). But what does this really mean? Is the system really ineffective? What is the logic behind the 110 percent standard? Often there is none.

A slightly better approach to calculating effectiveness in this hypothetical case would be to calculate the number of planned inspections per year on the basis of the legally required inspections. If there are 2,200 licensed establishments in the city and each one is supposed to be inspected two to four times a year, a total of 4,400 to 8,800 inspections should be carried out each year. We could then take

Table 3.5 Inspection Data

		Year 1	2	3	4	5	Five-Year Averages	Percent Follow-up
Inspector 1.	Total	743	719	664	647	583	671.2	28.9%
	Regular	539	512	481	443	411	477.2	
	Follow-up	204	207	183	204	172	194	
Inspector 2.	Total	426	351	487	469	503	447.2	47.4%
	Regular	225	165	262	258	274	236.8	
	Follow-up	201	186	225	211	229	212	
Inspector 3.	Total	528	470	371	494	431	458.8	37.3%
	Regular	431	397	174	209	227	287.6	
	Follow-up	97	73	197	285	204	171.2	
Inspector 4.	Total	684	652	714	826	760	727.2	30.7%
	Regular	414	403	476	615	612	504	
	Follow-up	270	249	238	211	148	223.2	
Inspector 5.	Total	560	544	527	513	506	530	39.8%
	Regular	337	329	322	301	305	318.8	
	Follow-up	223	215	205	212	201	211.2	
Inspector 6.	Total	347	361	383	399	417	381.4	49.3%
	Regular	170	186	193	204	213	193.2	
	Follow-up	177	175	190	195	204	188.2	

Inspector 7.	Total	501	498	511	492	507	501.8	47.2%
	Regular	264	255	265	259	282	265	
	Follow-up	237	243	246	233	225	236.8	
Inspector 8.	Total	809	767	743	719	695	746.6	9.9%
	Regular	743	711	681	631	598	672.8	
	Follow-up	66	56	62	88	97	73.8	
Inspector 9.	Total	480	489	472	496	504	488.2	43.7%
	Regular	268	274	226	282	287	275	
	Follow-up	212	215	208	214	217	213.2	
Inspector 10.	Total	640	597	703	681	623	648.8	37.1%
	Regular	411	396	442	409	381	407.8	
	Follow-up	229	201	261	272	242	241	
Inspector 11.	All total	5718	5448	5575	5736	5529	5601.2	35.0%
	Regular	3802	3628	3560	3611	3590	3638.2	
	Follow-up	1916	1820	2015	2125	1939	1963	
Inspector 12.	Yearly averages	572	545	558	574	553		
		380	363	356	361	359		
		192	182	202	213	194		
Inspector 13.	Percent follow-up	33.6	33.4	36	37.1	35.1		

Table 3.6 Average Cost per Inspection

Inspector/Year	1	2	3	4	5	Average
1	$34.60	$41.52	$48.23	$53.17	$65.95	$48.68
2	60.33	85.04	65.76	73.35	76.44	72.18
3	48.76	63.51	86.32	69.35	89.21	71.41
4	37.57	45.78	44.85	41.65	50.59	44.09
5	45.89	54.87	60.77	67.06	75.99	60.92
6	74.06	82.69	83.62	86.21	92.21	83.76
7	51.30	59.94	62.67	69.92	75.83	63.93
8	31.77	38.92	43.10	47.84	55.32	43.39
9	53.54	61.04	67.85	69.35	76.29	65.61
10	40.16	50.00	45.55	50.51	61.71	49.59
Average annual cost	47.79	58.32	60.87	62.83	71.95	60.35

the number of inspections completed as a percentage of a planned number in that range. But this measure would not recognize that each establishment is supposed to be inspected at least twice and not on average; inspecting two establishments twice is not the same as inspecting one four times and another not at all. A solution would be to construct a measure like "percentage of all establishments inspected at least twice." The plan would be 100 percent or 4,400 regular inspections per year. Note from the data of row 11, Table 3.5, that we have done less than 4,000 regular inspections in each of the last five years and cannot, therefore, be meeting the minimum inspection standard unless a follow-up inspection on an establishment is the second inspection.[8] This is an interesting finding and may be grounds for hiring another inspector or two or for changing the minimum inspection standard.

Still there is a nagging problem: What does a measure like "percentage of all establishments inspected at least twice" really have to do with the goal of "averting food-borne illness"? Perhaps very little. We assume that more high-quality inspections improve conditions in establishments, eliminating conditions that might lead to food-borne illness, thus averting some food-borne illnesses. But this is all very "iffy." To have any real confidence that we understand the efficiency and effectiveness of the inspection system, we would like to construct measures further up the means–end chain toward the ultimate goal for the service of averting illness (see Figure 3.2).

Suppose we had data on the incidence of the various illnesses that are sometimes food-borne. Table 3.7 gives incidence data for five specific illnesses and a catchall category for our hypothetical five-year period. How could such data be used to understand the effect of the inspection process? It would be very difficult. We would first want to identify those incidents that were caused by the victims eating in public establishments. In our hypothetical example, 20 of the hepatitis cases in year 2 are traceable to a hepatitis carrier who worked as a dishwasher in a downtown restaurant. Six of the 20 food poisoning cases in year 4 resulted from

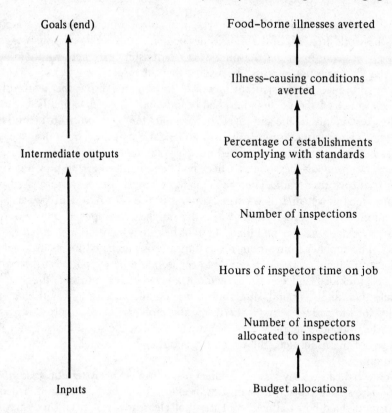

Goals (end)

Food-borne illnesses averted

Illness-causing conditions averted

Percentage of establishments complying with standards

Intermediate outputs

Number of inspections

Hours of inspector time on job

Number of inspectors allocated to inspections

Inputs

Budget allocations

Figure 3.2   Means–End Chain—Health Inspections

bad hollandaise sauce at another restaurant. And 3 of the 6 cases of salmonellosis in the same year occurred when yet another restaurant served crabmeat that had apparently been improperly stored. There will be other cases that are traceable to other causes. For example, all of the other food poisoning cases occurred immediately after the victims had eaten at home or in other private homes. The 29 salmonellosis cases in year 2 all stemmed from a bad turkey at a private country club Thanksgiving dinner. About 80 percent of the hepatitis cases occurred soon after the victims had had blood transfusions, which is probably the cause. And the one

Table 3.7 **Illness Frequencies**

Illness/Year	*1*	*2*	*3*	*4*	*5*
Food poisoning	13	17	1	20	14
Salmonellosis	0	29	0	6	0
Hepatitis	84	111	62	91	53
Cholera	0	0	1	0	0
Typhoid	0	0	0	0	0
Other	1	0	0	0	0

cholera case occurred with a victim who had just returned from a two-month round-the-world trip. All of the remaining incidents have unknown origins.

The next step is to try to determine what relationships exist between these incidents and the inspection process. To assume that the inspection system is to blame could be a mistake. The restaurant in which the hepatitic dishwasher worked had just been inspected and no violations had been found. The dishwasher had worked in other restaurants in the city over the previous ten years with no identifiable problems. The restaurant serving the bad hollandaise sauce had been inspected six months before and had had unrelated minor violations. The hollandaise sauce at fault had been handled exactly as sauces had been handled for 40 previous years at this exclusive restaurant. The problematic crabmeat had been purchased one morning, iced down, and then carried around in the back of a delivery van on a hot, humid day for several hours while the purchaser completed other errands. This was standard practice and the restaurant held that the supply must have been at fault. The supplier from whom the crabmeat was purchased insists that it must have been mishandled by the restaurant because the other 95 pounds in the same lot were purchased and consumed without any problems. Further, the supplier indicates that all 100 pounds of crabmeat was handled the same way it had been handled for the past 20 years; if there was any problem in the supply, it must be due to the supplier's supplier. You can imagine what the supplier's supplier had to say about the fishermen, the fishermen about crabs, the crabs about polluters, and so on.

Now what can we say about the effect of the inspection system on food-borne illness? The system, either the standards or enforcement of the standards, failed to eliminate all food-borne illness. But it is not clear how you would redesign the system so that it would have prevented the crabmeat, hollandaise, and hepatitis-carrier cases from happening. Even a system that placed, at astronomical expense, an inspector (or three to cover all hours of operation) in each of the 2,200 establishments might not have prevented the incidents.

In evaluating the effectiveness of the service, the incidents that did occur are less important than those that did not occur because of the inspection. An inspection system that prevents 450 food poisonings is more effective than one that prevents only 2. A table like Table 3.7 where the entries are the *incidents that would have occurred without the inspection system* is needed. How could we estimate such data? We might look back at the incidence of food-borne illness prior to the creation of the inspection system. But this is not very useful because inspections in some form have been done for about 100 years. Before inspection, the world was very different. There were iceboxes but no refrigeration. Foodstuffs were different. There was no widespread use of vaccines for cholera or typhoid and the incidence of these diseases, from a variety of causes, was much greater than now. Modern water treatment and sewage disposal were unknown; few restaurants had running water and flush toilets. Fecal material from horses on urban streets was an important source of unsanitary conditions and disease. This historical source of standards is hopeless.

We might look for a comparable city in which there is no inspection system. But there aren't any. All comparable cities have inspection systems. The few cities without effective inspection systems, largely in Third World countries, differ on more important dimensions than we can control; imagine attempting a systematic comparison between Calcutta and New York. We might use theories of the incidence of illness that incorporate inspection systems as part of their causal description to predict incidents without inspection systems. Unfortunately, there are no such theories and they are beyond our ability to develop in the foreseeable future.

The measures of input and intermediate outputs, rather than the more desirable final outputs, are pragmatic compromises. Managers are often under pressure to measure something so that they can "manage by objectives" and the like, and these sometimes highly unsatisfactory measures are the best that one can do at reasonable effort and expense. The problems of understanding the causal relationship between inspections and illnesses are very great, but they are not greater than the problems in understanding the causal relationships between:

1. Police activities and crime incidence.
2. Road maintenance and transportation costs.
3. Public transit services and commuting behavior.
4. Building codes and the quality of construction.
5. Welfare and work incentives.
6. Defense expenditures and the probability of war.
7. Recreation facilities and psychological well-being and life expectancy.
8. Taxes and work incentives.
9. Federal deficits and rates of inflation and interest rates.
10. Agricultural subsidies and levels of agricultural outputs and prices.
11. Housing subsidies and the supply and price of housing.
12. Fire protection and the loss of life and property due to fire.
13. Mental health treatments and the psychological condition of patients.

Our understanding of public service-production functions, causal linkages between government activities and societal effects, is very sketchy. The managerial and analytical problems from causal ignorance about the effects of inspecting eating establishments are not unusual; they are par for the course.

Let us assume for a moment that our hypothetical city develops through analysis and "hard-headed business management" an inspection system that seems ideal by the standards of most city administrations. Each of the 2,200 eating establishments is inspected at least twice a year. Inspectors are low-paid and energetic. They run through their day and yet carefully check each of the 102 categories of possible violation on each inspection job. Inspectors are incorruptible because of bonding and supervisory checks.

Can we feel secure that such a service is effective and both managerially and economically efficient? Unfortunately, no. The effectiveness question is still indeterminate because of ignorance about the relationship between inspections and illnesses averted. Managerial efficiency is in doubt because there are other inspection-system configurations that might be devised to enforce the standards (as reflected in the 102 categories of possible violation) upon eating establishments. For example, we might (1) cut back to two inspectors; (2) get legislation passed that requires eateries to post surety bonds and imposes heavy fines for any violations found upon inspection; (3) communicate the standards that would be enforced and what the fines would be for violations to owners; (4) conduct unannounced, thorough inspections on a random-sampling basis; (5) publicize all violations and fines to all owners; and (6) guard against sloppy or corrupt inspections by having the supervisor select a few inspection reports randomly each week and reinspect those establishments. With this alternative design, we would pay few inspectors and give owners a strong financial incentive to maintain standards on the chance that they will be inspected. Fines could be used to support the inspection system. Such an alternative system might well be more efficient and more effective than conventional systems.

A slightly more radical alternative system would be to (1) employ one or two investigators and no inspectors, (2) conduct no inspections, and (3) pass legislation that requires owners to post large surety bonds and holds them legally responsible for avoiding all of the food-borne illnesses that initially motivated the inspection system. If an eating establishment is linked by investigation to a health incident, the penalty would range from a modest fine or partial forfeiture of the bond to full forfeiture and permanent closure. Once again, owners would have the desired incentives and the responsibility for avoiding what comprehensive inspection systems seek to avoid. Such a system, with low direct costs to government, might also be superior to current practice.

Considerations of general economic efficiency might take us even further. The most radical alternative would be for government to simply get out of the inspection business altogether; let the market operate within the larger legal system. Even now customers probably consider the cleanliness and safety of eating establishments in making their decisions about where to eat. If they are poisoned or infected by eating in some establishments, they will stop eating there, tell their friends to avoid the establishments, and they or their survivors can sue the owners for damages. There is no obvious failure in the food-serving market that makes it necessary for government to intervene. If the market could function properly without inspection systems, this would, at least in theory, be the most economically efficient way to organize the service. Government, with the exception of the legal system, would avoid all costs and responsibilities. Market mechanisms would determine optimal levels of cleanliness and food-borne illness. Prices in eating establishments might fall because owners would be free to find the most efficient, effective ways of delivering food service rather than having to meet onerous, nitpicking government standards that may have nothing to do with levels of food-borne illness. This move might be nearly Pareto optimal, with unemployed inspectors the only obvious losers. And they might, with their wealth of experience, open clean, safe restaurants and make more money than they did as inspectors.

The big worries about relying on natural markets in this instance are that food service is a complex product and the stakes associated with incorrect consumer choices are potentially high. All the data that customers need in order to evaluate the health characteristics of alternative food services are not available from an inexpensive, superficial look at the facility. It is easy to determine whether the floor and walls are reasonably clean, if not disinfected, but much harder to know when grease traps were last cleaned or whether food-handling employees always remember to wash their hands after using the toilet. Owners may cut costs by attending to those things that consumers can see and ignoring those health precautions that are not visible. The stakes that consumers face in markets for various goods and services range from minor cost and inconvenience to major costs and death. If you buy a dishwashing detergent that spots your crystal and silverware, your penalty is hand washing or living with the spots until you switch brands. If your Peking duck is served with salmonellae, you will be very sick and may even die. Your right and that of your heirs to spend a year or two at great personal expense trying to sue an owner who may declare bankruptcy in the face of a large judgment is very little consolation for the experience of salmonellosis.

With a specific example like restaurant inspection, it is easy to see the potential difficulties in devising and using a system for measuring and managing that would have a salutary effect on the efficiency and effectiveness of the service. The pressures to measure lead to the only practical responses, measures of quantities far down the means-ends chain. The measured quantities and the pressures to use them in managing the service lead to great emphasis on activities that have, at best, a tenuous relationship to the ultimate goals of the service. Goals are displaced; putting in the required time and going through the measured motions becomes much more important than accomplishing anything of value. If a health hazard is not on the inspector's list of 102 items, he probably won't see it. The problem becomes to check the 102 items, not to prevent food-borne illness.

If you were the manager of the inspection service, how would you go about improving its efficiency and effectiveness? Is there a system in your plans? Do the business methods discussed in the addendum to Chapter 2 suggest any reforms?

We could, at this point, move on to a discussion of the many stumbling blocks to the application of the concepts of efficiency, effectiveness, and productivity that exist in other functional areas: national defense, local police protection, postal delivery, cancer research, etc. However, the contextual richness of each area would soon begin to subvert our intentions. Because each area presents its own set of unique substantive details, the result would quickly assume the character of the fabled classification of animals in the ancient Chinese encyclopedia.

> (a) belonging to the emperor, (b) embalmed, (c) tame, (d) sucking pigs, (e) sirens, (f) fabulous, (g) stray dogs, (h) included in the present classification, (i) frenzied, (j) innumerable, (k) drawn with a very fine camel hair brush, (l) et cetera, (m) having just broken the water pitcher, (n) that from a long way off look like flies. (Borges, 1970, p. 15.)

Most of the problems described in the restaurant inspection example (e.g., the importance of controlling for the quality of the output and estimating what would have happened had the service not been provided) are generic enough to be relevant to any functional area. Our purpose is not to suggest that any attempt to measure the efficiency and effectiveness of government agencies is doomed to failure, only that it is almost invariably a very complex task that can, at best, be accomplished only imperfectly. If reforms whose objective is to improve government performance are to succeed, both of these facts must be recognized at the outset. Reforms that make sense in abstract principle may well not make any sense in practical circumstances.

WHY MEASURING AND MANAGING SYSTEMS FAIL

> The inevitable result of improved and enlarged communication be-
> tween different levels in a hierarchy is a vastly increased area of mis-
> understanding.
>
> MARTIN'S LAW OF COMMUNICATIONS

The several examples discussed in this chapter contain a number of lessons about when and how productivity measurement can fail as a guide to policymaking. One important problem is goal complexity. When there are a large number of organizational outputs of interest, the ability to evaluate agency performance depends on an ability to develop priorities. If the importance ascribed to 15 different measures of police department performance is unclear, it will be very difficult to decide whether the department is doing better or worse than during the previous year. What makes this problem particularly troublesome is that analysts can often do very little to make the task of choosing priorities simpler. In the best of all rational worlds, they would be able to help by doing a benefit-cost analysis for each output indicator. This would say something about the "value" of each output relative to all others. But in real life and certainly in the police example, it doesn't work this way. Analysis cannot reveal the value of a percentage-point decrease in murder rates as compared to a similar decrease in robberies or assaults. The relative weightings must inevitably be a function of values, and in an area such as law enforcement, values of different groups and individuals can be expected to clash more than they do in areas such as waste removal or restaurant inspection. Productivity measurement cannot resolve problems that are basically political. The measures may, ironically, only serve to sharpen disagreements and make it increasingly difficult for agencies to perform functions efficiently and effectively.

Another lesson involves the extent to which the utility of productivity measures depends on an understanding of service-delivery technology and the interrelationship of different outputs. A major reason why the police chief's explanation confuses council members is that they have no way of knowing whether concentrating on violent crimes or completing arson and robbery reports actually reduce the police's ability to make burglary arrests. Nor do they have any idea whether an increased budget of $400,000 is a reasonable request likely to achieve the desired results or whether it is something akin to bureaucratic extortion. The city council's understanding of the technology involved, of the interrelationship of different outputs, and of the relationship between funding levels, programs, and performance is far too primitive to permit a truly informed opinion. Fortunately, the same is not true in the case of waste removal. Here, the knowledge of the processes involved is almost thorough enough to justify "engineering" in planning and operating the function.

We understand, at least within tolerable limits, cause-and-effect relationships and the tradeoffs that exist between key performance measures (e.g., frequency of service and cost) in the area of waste removal. That understanding is not so secure that cities can implement new routing plans or make major equipment purchases without experimentation. There is still uncertainty about precisely what effect a given innovation will have, just as there is in steel manufacturing. But the technology of waste removal is sufficiently well understood that the results of a test can be interpreted and the appropriate adjustments made. The absence of a refined technology of law enforcement usually means that interpretation and appropriate adjustment are not possible. It is like trying to learn how to play the game of baseball solely by studying box scores. It is a good way to determine team standings and batting averages but a poor way to learn to pitch and hit.

The problems posed by an undeveloped and poorly understood technology are compounded by the uncertain impact of uncontrollable and frequently unknown external factors. When there is a high probability that output change is not purely a product of agency behavior, performance measures become a much less useful tool for decision making. This is the traditional difficulty with using crime rates as the basis for evaluating police performance. If one could confidently attribute changes in the burglary rates to changes in police patrolling patterns and crime-prevention programs, all would be well. But one cannot. Other factors, ranging from the weather to economic conditions, may also have had an impact. Various statistical techniques can help to specify what portion of the change is due to these other factors; however, the accuracy of the conclusions is still uncertain because it is unknown what all of these factors are and how they, in turn, are related to each other. Not surprisingly, the more factors there are and the more complicated the mechanisms through which they work, the harder it becomes to assign responsibility to any one of them. It is going to be a long time before city councils (or police chiefs) will be able to study a set of performance measures and arrive at confident conclusions about how well the police are doing and what budgetary changes should be made.

Of course, the problem of connecting output changes to program characteristics is not confined to the public sector. The same confusion exists in corporations. Corporate boards of directors are frequently confused as to the source of declining productivity or market share. Is management to blame, or has the company been the victim of forces beyond its control? The difference between the public and private sector is that in the case of corporations it is often possible to sidestep temporarily the ultimate issue of precisely why profits (or productivity) have fallen and instead analyze performance on related measures—such as turnover, quality control, or marketing costs—that are less susceptible to outside influence. This strategy can be implemented with some confidence because experience and economic theory have convinced decision makers that there is a strong, if slightly ambiguous, relationship between a dimension like quality control and profit. However, this understanding of the underlying technology of the organization and its relationship to outputs (especially effectiveness) is precisely what is lacking for many public-sector agencies. The relationships between arrest rates, patrol patterns, manpower levels, and crime rates are much more obscure than comparable dimensions within the corporation.

Another explanation for the failure to employ productivity measures in law enforcement also concerns technology. Here, however, the reference is not to the internal technology of the agency but to the innovations that are waiting to be evaluated. One of the major roles of any performance measurement system lies in the evaluation of new programs and techniques. The value of such a system for the organization is directly dependent on the quality and variety of the innovations that await evaluation. If there are many such innovations and the benefits they offer vary substantially (i.e., some are valuable and some are worthless), then a productivity measurement system will probably make a substantial contribution by enabling decision makers to choose among them. If, on the other hand, there are relatively few innovations to be evaluated or the quality of these new techniques and programs is uniformly low, performance measurement cannot be expected to make much of a contribution.

While a relatively large number of innovations are being evaluated in both waste removal and law enforcement, the value of those in law enforcement is probably much lower. The effect that truck configuration and crew-size changes have had on "tons of waste removed" or "cost per ton" has been much greater than the effect of police patrol patterns on crime rates or budgetary requirements. This means, in turn, that the payoff of performance measurement for sanitation departments has probably been greater than for police departments. This should be expected. The quality of proposals about how to improve a system's performance is inevitably a function of how well that system is understood, and relationships between police behavior and crime aren't very well understood at all. The net result is that until the set of innovations proposed for law enforcement begins to include some that are of very high quality (i.e., will increase productivity substantially), performance measurement won't seem very worthwhile to policymakers.

There is a final reason why measuring and managing systems often fail—a reason that has nothing to do with differences between law enforcement and waste and which is likely to cause problems in either area. It has to do with assumptions about how human beings will respond to the use of measurement systems. Here is the way V. F. Ridgeway summarized the problem 30 years ago.

> Quantitative measures of performance are tools, and are undoubtedly useful. But research indicates that indiscriminate use and undue confidence and reliance in them result from insufficient knowledge of full effects and consequences. Judicious use of a tool requires awareness of possible side effects and reactions. Otherwise, indiscriminate use may result in side effects and reactions outweighing the benefits, as was the case when penicillin was first hailed as a wonder drug. The cure is sometimes worse than the disease. . . .
>
> Quantitative performance measurements—whether single, multiple, or composite—are seen to have undesirable consequences for overall organizational performance. The complexity of large organizations requires better knowledge of organizational behavior for managers to make best use of the personnel available to them. Even where performance measures are instituted purely for purposes of information, they are probably interpreted as definitions of that job or activity and, hence, have important implications for the motivation of behavior. (Ridgeway, 1956, pp. 240 and 247.)

Ridgeway reflects the tension between the strong intuitive belief in the virtue of measures and the often contradictory experience with them in practice, a tension that has not lessened in the intervening years. Public (and private) organizations are most in need of performance measurement in situations that are fairly complex, but it is in precisely those situations that individuals and units accused of poor performance are most likely to reject their "scores" and/or attribute them to a variety of factors beyond their control. The debate that ensues can be enormously expensive, because it takes time away from directly furthering the objectives behind the outputs at issue and because it lowers morale and complicates future communications and coordination. The insensitive use of complex measures by management can thus make the cure worse than the disease. We shall further discuss behavioral responses to measures when we consider personnel systems (see Chapter 6).

CONCLUSION

> It is difficult to get a man to understand something when his salary
> depends upon his not understanding it.
>
> UPTON SINCLAIR

Productivity and performance measurement have a potentially important role to play in increasing government efficiency and effectiveness. Without them we can't fully understand how well agencies are serving us, we can't begin to acquire a more sophisticated understanding of service technologies, and we can't make intelligent decisions about the implementation of proposed innovations. Without good performance measurement, public-sector productivity will inevitably lag behind its potential.

Unfortunately, it is easy to forget that the step from measuring productivity to improving it is a long one, for the following reasons:

1. Goal complexity makes it difficult to summarize productivity with a single measure.
2. An incomplete understanding of the relationship between agency actions and effectiveness leads to problems in translating productivity findings into specific program and policy changes.
3. The uncertain impact of external factors on performance makes it difficult to determine the effect of individual and agency actions on decisions and, therefore, the extent to which individuals and agencies are responsible for outcomes.
4. The absence of high-quality innovations in some policy areas detracts from the potential contribution of productivity measurement through evaluation. Historically, productivity measurement has rarely led to the discovery of useful innovations; its role is limited to evaluating the potential of those already generated from another source.
5. The behavioral responses to systems for measuring and managing are at best complicated and at worst perverse.

These more or less technical problems are compounded by the politics of productivity measurement and can lead those involved to cease to support the efforts personally and financially. Productivity data can easily be turned against the bureaucrats and elected officials who gather them. If productivity drops—regardless of the reason—these people can be made to look bad. Officials are all too aware of this Pandora's box character of performance measurement and fear it, especially when they have reason to believe that performance changes may not even be under their control.

Unless the cost implications are impressive and easy to understand (neither of which is usually the case) top policymakers become bored with productivity measurement. The reason is easy to grasp: most of the information that is produced is only useful to someone who possesses a detailed understanding of the technology concerned. Allen Schick summarizes the problem nicely in his description of the indifference that greeted BOB's issuance of productivity measurement studies in 1964:

> All these applications were at a level of detail useful for managers with operating or supervisory responsibilities, but of scant usefulness for top-level officials who have to determine organizational objectives and goals. Does it really help top officials if they know that it cost $0.07 to wash a pound of laundry or that the average postal employee processes 289 items of mail per hour? These are the main fruits of performance measurements, and they have an important place in the management of an organization. They are of great value to the operating official who has the limited function of getting a job done, but they would put a crushing burden on the policy maker whose function is to map the future of action. (Schick, 1970, p. 41.)

Little wonder that productivity measurement programs have periodically arisen and then disappeared over the past 50 years.

If productivity measurement is to reach its full potential, a strategy of implementation must be devised that recognizes the technical and political problems it poses. In some cases this means moving very slowly. Where goal complexity problems are severe or the number of creative new innovations on the horizon is small, the costs of devising an elaborate productivity measurement system may outweigh the benefits. City planning, mental health services, and general administration are all examples of areas where productivity measurement is likely to be of little real value. Meaningful effectiveness measures in these realms are difficult to come by and the number of high-quality innovations waiting to be evaluated is small. Simple work-load measures are likely to be useful for planning and personnel control purposes, but major investments in productivity measures are probably unwarranted.

In areas where the measurement problems stem from an incomplete understanding of the technology of service delivery and the impact of exogenous variables, something more can be done. Here the enemy is an ignorance of critical organizational processes and environmental effects—rather than value conflicts, as in the case of goal complexity, or the absence of a fertile technological imagination, as in the case of scarce innovation. This sort of ignorance should prove easier to combat, although the battle will not be won overnight.

One of the first things that needs to be done is to institutionalize productivity measurement in such a way that it is less vulnerable to the recurring cycles of political interest and disinterest that have plagued the field since its inception. Basic productivity data must be collected by an agency that is permanently funded and exists beyond the reach of the political spoils system. The agency's head should be appointed for a term that is longer than that of the chief executive of the political unit in question (i.e., city, state, or federal government) and it should be charged with producing an annual report using a format that is relatively constant over time. Establishing such a permanent agency (or small office in the case of most cities) will make productivity measurement less subject to political caprice and help ensure that the data have more integrity than might otherwise be the case. As the importance of productivity information in the political process increases, so will the temptation to tamper with the figures in a way that makes the incumbent administration look good. An independent agency should help to discipline this temptation.

The role of this agency should be carefully limited to collecting data on a small number of key measures. No interests would be served if it had to maintain 32 output measures for a police department. This would be pointless as well as expensive, since no useful inferences could be made from most of the data. Inevitably the agency would be unsuited for performing the complex tasks of clarifying the relationship of internal technology to productivity or determining the impact of different exogenous variables. These tasks are best seen as a basic part of management and R&D, not oversight. Detailed productivity research must take place within the service agencies themselves, and they must have the opportunity to explore intricate and ambiguous questions without running the constant risk of creating political scandal. The difficulty lies in ensuring that service agencies have the funds to carry out the necessary research and the incentive to do so.

NOTES

1. A recent reviewer concluded that while the conceptual issues in productivity accounting were well worked out in the mid-1950s, it "has not been considered part of the information that will assist managers in their decision-making and control activities." See Kaplan (1982).
2. Work-load measures are simply measures of the total volume of work that is handled by a given agency. If the unit in question was the transportation agency or motor pool of a small city, work-load measures might consist of the number of vehicles that were serviced, the number of repair orders that were processed, and some measure (e.g., mileage) of how heavily the vehicles were used (Finz, 1980, p. 147). Unit cost or efficiency measures include most of the measures normally associated with productivity. In the motor-pool example, efficiency could be measured by the number of repair orders processed by each mechanic, the operation cost per vehicle-mile, and so forth.

   Effectiveness measures refer to the extent to which the agency accomplishes its goals. For agencies that provide direct services to the public, this means the extent to which the public is satisfied with the service that is being delivered. The percent of vehicles receiving preventive maintenance inspection, percent of repair failures, and number of driver complaints are typical effectiveness measures for a motor pool. Goals and objectives refer to nothing more than the existence of a set of documented intentions that may or may not be quantified. In the case of the motor pool, a goal could be satisfying the city government's need for vehicles or achieving a specific level of performance (e.g., "Cut maintenance per vehicle time by 8 percent").

3. Self-reporting also probably leads to inflated figures. Doubtless respondents occasionally give themselves credit for measuring performance because they think they should be doing so, not because they are.
4. Measures of efficiency based on effectiveness outputs might include "number of citizen complaints per dollar" or "number of environmental hazard-free days per dollar."
5. This example is hypothetical but based on an amalgam of the inspection function in several cities. The data are fictitious.
6. This is an actual checklist used in one large city.
7. It is worth noting these data are much more complete and detailed than the data easily available in any real situation. Such data, if they exist at all, exist on detailed records like data worksheets that are not compiled and analyzed.
8. Of course, to work with such standards we would want to keep the data on inspections by establishment as well as by inspector, by year, and by inspection type.

REFERENCES

Borges, Jorge Luis, quoted in Foucault, Michael. *The Order of Things*. New York: Pantheon, 1970, p. 15.

Bureau of the Budget. *Measuring Productivity*, Washington, D.C.: U.S. Government Printing Office, 1964.

Crane, Edgar. "Productivity in State Government." In *Productivity Improvement Handbook*, edited by George J. Washin. New York: Wiley, 1980.

Finz, Samuel A. "Productivity Measurement Systems and Their Implementation." In *Productivity Improvement Handbook*, edited by George J. Washin, New York: Wiley, 1980.

Kaplan, Robert. "Manufacturing Performance: A New Challenge for Accounting and Management Research." Graduate School of Industrial Administration, Carnegie-Mellon University, working paper #25-82-83, November 1982, pp. 9–10.

Kull, Donald C. "Productivity Programs in the Federal Government." *Public Administration Review* 38 (January 1978): 6.

Morris, Thomas D., et al. "Productivity Measures in the Federal Government." *Public Administration Review* 53 (1972)6:753–763.

Peterson, Peter G. "Productivity in Government and the American Economy." *Public Administration Review* 53 (1972)6:740–746.

Ridgeway, V. F. "Dysfunctional Consequence of Performance Measurement." *Administrative Sciences Quarterly*, September 1956, pp. 240–247.

Savas, E. S., et al. "Solid Waste Collection." In *Productivity Improvement Handbook*, edited by George J. Washin. New York: Wiley, 1980.

Schick, Allen. "The Road to PPB." In *Planning, Programming, Budgeting*, edited by Fremont J. Lyden and Ernest G. Miller. Chicago: Markham, 1970, pp. 25–52.

Washin, George J. ed. *Productivity Improvement Handbook*, New York: Wiley, 1980.

CHAPTER 4

Better Performance Through Better Analysis: Nothing But the Facts

> Far better an approximate answer to the right question, which is often vague, than an exact answer to the wrong question, which can always be made precise.
>
> JOHN TUKEY

One of the principal approaches advocated and attempted for improving government performance over the past 40 years is the use of analytic techniques in evaluating and designing policy options objectively and quantitatively. The rationale behind this approach is that many of government's performance problems stem from ignorance of decision consequences and from the failure to use techniques for systematic, informed, rational decision making. Potholes appear not so much because the contract for street resurfacing was awarded to the mayor's nephew but because the public works department did a poor job of estimating truck traffic, drainage conditions, and the relative durability of the various grades of asphalt or concrete. Mass transit systems go wildly over budget and take too long to complete because of an even larger set of similar problems. From the standpoint of the economists and operations researchers who employ the analytic methods discussed in this chapter, governments often perform poorly for the simple reason that they don't know what they are doing.

Although the most frequently mentioned goal of analytic methods is to inform particular decisions in the policymaking process, many proponents clearly believe that rational decision-making methods would also act to bring order and discipline to sometimes chaotic and arbitrary political processes. The attitude expressed by David Novick, an early proponent of analysis, is characteristic.

> Some authorities feel that political choices can best be made if politicians listen merely to voices in the air, observe straws in the political wind, or regard their occupation as an amusing bargaining game. Our position is that political choices can be improved if politicians are aided by information and analysis concerning the probable consequences of their acts. . . . Ultimately, decisions are made by individuals, groups or legislative bodies exercising their informed judgment. One can hope that such decisions will be improved if they are made in light of all available evidence and the evidence is marshaled in an orderly way. Furthermore, such procedure may help to avoid the political bargaining and logrolling that mars rather than makes the political process. (Novick, 1951, p. 51.)

Advocates of analytic methods such as Novick often see the methods acting as a surrogate for the competition that insures the efficient operation of firms in a free market. Good policy analysis and the wide dissemination of the results will force both elected officials and government bureaucrats to adopt efficient policy alternatives, because their failure to do so will soon become conspicuous in the same sense that an inefficient firm's high prices and/or inferior products are conspicuous. The advocates hold that regardless of how manipulative government officials might be, they cannot long survive by consistently choosing policy alternatives "proven" to be wasteful and inefficient.

Elaborate analytic approaches for making decisions "rationally" have been developed over the past 50 years. The most prominent of these approaches, economic analysis and operations research,[1] have their modern roots in the analysis of U.S. federal water resource projects in the 1930s and in U.S. and British analyses of military operations during World War II, respectively. Economic analysis, which in application to particular decisions consists largely of marginal analysis and cost–benefit analysis, has acquired an elaborate rationale in economic theory and some reasonably complicated techniques since it was first applied by the Bureau of Reclamation and the Corps of Engineers to water resource projects. Operations research is a set of loosely related mathematical and statistical techniques (e.g., inventory theory, queueing theory, stochastic processes, linear programming, dynamic programming, and decision analysis) for making decisions. Both approaches were motivated, at least initially, by dissatisfaction with intuitive, political approaches to decision making and the desire for better decisions. The approaches are quantitative and ostensibly explicit and objective.

Because analysis has been a major strategy for improving government efficiency and effectiveness, particularly since the 1950s, there is, at this point, considerable experience with some of the analytic techniques. This chapter considers a few specific analytic techniques applied to particular decision problems: what they are, what the hope was for using them to increase government efficiency and effectiveness, what the experience has been with applying the techniques, and what the prospects are for using analysis to improve government. The next chapter considers analytic systems, particularly resource allocation systems like PPBS, that depend in part on the widespread, systematic use of the analytic techniques discussed here.

The concepts associated with the analytic techniques are relatively simple; the technical details that one must master to apply the techniques sensibly are reasonably complex. Because of this technical complexity, we emphasize concepts and introduce only those technical details that are important conceptually. Simplified examples of applications of each technique discussed are given because one cannot properly appreciate the strengths and limitations of the techniques without the level of specific understanding that examples provide. The analytic techniques described in this chapter are cost–benefit analysis, cost–effectiveness analysis, and decision analysis. These are *normative* techniques for making decisions; they prescribe how decisions ought to be made. They are only a small part of the methods employed by operations researchers and economic analysts, but they are the techniques that have been applied most often to government.

The examples of the techniques given below are intentionally mundane. They deal with things like sidewalk design, local flood control, and traffic safety measures. There are two reasons for using the mundane. First, most of life within government consists of mundane activities about which decisions must be made. If analysis is ever going to contribute significantly to improving government performance, it will have to contribute through improving mundane decisions. Decisions like whether the United States should support Great Britain or Argentina in the Falklands/Malvinas dispute, whether the United States should sell AWACS to Saudi Arabia, whether a school district should adopt a controversial forced integration plan, whether the secretary of the interior should be permitted to sell oil drilling leases on the last nesting grounds of whooping cranes, or whether an MX missile system of some configuration should be deployed are dramatic, very important, and intrinsically interesting to most people, includng analysts, the media, and citizens. But such issues constitute a small part of what governments do, and the resources involved make up a small part of what governnments spend. Attending to mundane problems implies more weight to bureaucrats than to politicians.

> . . . bureaucrats at the bureau level normally have more impact than anyone else on the final allocation of program benefits. To some readers, this premise will seem odd and perhaps even preposterous. Most Americans still think of electoral activities as portrayed on television as the most crucial political events. Or they relate to Watergate-like deliberations matching President against Congress for extremely high stakes. On the other hand, the typical citizen hears the word [sic] "bureaucrat" and, if he knows what it means, immediately thinks of the license bureau clerk or a social worker. Bureaucracy conjures up images of red tape, burdensome regulations, and personal frustration from dealing with "those people." All of these visions present a biased and essentially incomplete view of how political decisions are made. Yet, as beliefs, they are understandable. Bureaucrats seldom get attention. They do not make their decisions in public, they are seldom followed by the press, and they need never be in the public eye to retain their jobs. Almost all their work goes on behind the scenes. (Browne, 1980, p. 6)

Second, analysis usually has more to contribute on mundane issues than on the more dramatic issues. Dramatic issues are often not amenable to rigorous analysis; the political value issues swamp other considerations. They are unique and nonrecurrent and usually come with enormous time pressures and intense interest on the part of top policymakers, conditions inimical to careful analysis.

DECISION ANALYSIS

> I think there is in the heroic courage with which man confronts the irrationality of the world a beauty greater than the beauty of art.
>
> SOMERSET MAUGHAM

Decision analysis is a prescriptive approach to decision making; it prescribes how you should make a decision if you aspire to rationality.[2] Decision analysis is both the oldest and the newest of the approaches examined in this chapter. It is the oldest in that critical parts of the approach, notably probability theory and utility theory, have been around for a very long time. It is the newest in that the synthesis of the various elements like probability theory into a coherent decision-theoretic approach and the application of the approach to a variety of decision problems have occurred in the last 20 years.

Decision analysis is more "conceptual framework" than "technique." It is a very general approach to decision making that might, in particular applications, subsume a benefit–cost analysis, an application of linear programming, or modeling of any complex phenomena by substantive experts.

Figure 4.1 shows a payoff matrix that is a "normal form" for representing decision problems. Figure 4.2 shows the same generalized decision problem as a decision tree. The A_i's are the various actions you might take. The S_j's, the possible states of nature, are factors beyond your control but that materially affect the outcomes, θ_{ij}. The $V(\theta_{ij})$ are dollar or utile valuations of the outcomes, θ_{ij}. The problem in both formats is to choose the "best" action, A_i, which usually means the action with the greatest expected (monetary or utile) value.[3] The general formula for calculating expected value is shown at the bottom of Figure 4.1.

The decision-analysis format is most useful for problems in which you can control only some of a sequence of actions and you are uncertain about what the "state of nature" will be. The format is extremely general because there is almost always only partial control in decision situations. Uncertainty is ubiquitous. The list of variables that can be neither predicted nor controlled but that can dramatically affect the efficiency and effectiveness of government programs could fill vol-

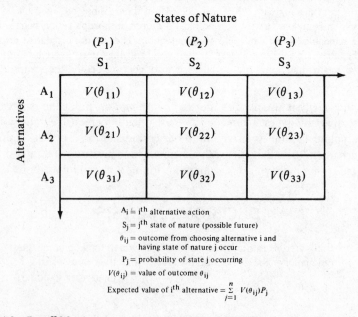

Figure 4.1   Payoff Matrix

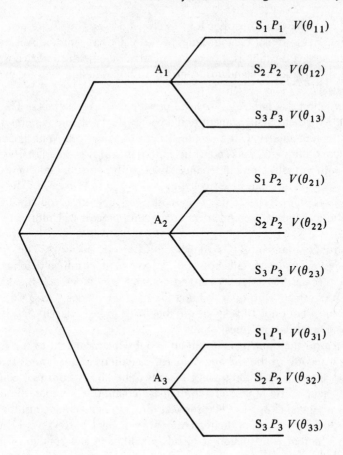

Figure 4.2   Decision Tree

umes: weather, stock market behavior, the actions of foreign governments, technological changes, business investment, etc.

DECISION-ANALYSIS EXAMPLE

> Hungry Joe collected lists of fatal diseases and arranged them in alphabetical order so that he could put his finger without delay on any one he wanted to worry about.
>
> JOSEPH HELLER, *CATCH-22*

Imagine that you are an analyst with the city manager's office in Gotham. The director of the Department of Building and Safety has come to you with a problem. Eighty percent of the sidewalks were built under the Work Projects Administration (WPA) in the 1930s and are now crumbling and becoming increasingly unsafe. The city recently lost a $10,000 damage suit filed by a lady who stumbled on a bad sidewalk and broke her leg. Twelve more such suits are pending. The director is convinced that the four miles of WPA sidewalk must be replaced; patching will no longer do. She is, however, uncertain about which of two widely recommended construction standards to specify when requesting bids for the replacement sidewalks.

Construction standard A (CS-A) will provide Cadillac sidewalks. The standard requires the highest-quality cement reinforced by steel rods and requires a sidewalk thickness of four inches with a section length of three feet. With good soil and drainage conditions, sidewalks constructed to standard A should last 100 years, on average, with virtually no maintenance. Even with poor soil and drainage conditions, CS-A sidewalks can be expected to last 50 years on average. The disadvantage of CS-A sidewalks is cost. They cost $400 per lineal foot on average; of course, the low bid in a competitive contracting process will ultimately indicate the price.

Construction standard B (CS-B) provides Chevrolet sidewalks. The standard requires only low-grade cement, no steel reinforcement, two-inch depth and a five-foot section length. With good soil and drainage conditions, CS-B sidewalks last 50 years on average; with poor soil and drainage conditions, CS-B sidewalks can be expected to last only 10 years before they have to be replaced. CS-B sidewalks cost only about $200 per lineal foot.

One reason the director is uncertain about which standard to use is that the city has no records of the soil and drainage conditions at the various sidewalk replacement sites scattered throughout the city. She knows from past construction that 60 percent of the time, soil and drainage conditions are poor; the rest of the time they are good. For $100,000 she can hire an engineering consulting firm to conduct soil surveys at all of the replacement sites. Such surveys would enable her to specify different construction standards for different soil conditions in the request for bids.

The city capital and operating budgets are very tight this year and probably will be for the next few years as well. It is important that the director find the most efficient replacement scheme. One way she could approach this would be to use decision analysis to minimize the cost per mile of sidewalks. Figure 4.3 is a schematic decision tree for the problem.[4] There are four alternatives. Alternative A_1 is to buy the soil and drainage data and then, on the basis of the data, build to CS-A on good soil and drainage conditions and to CS-B on poor conditions. The second alternative, A_2, is to buy the data and to build to CS-A for poor conditions and to CS-B for good conditions. Alternative three, A_3, is to go ahead without soil condition data and build all CS-A sidewalk. Alternative four, A_4, is to build without soil condition data all CS-B sidewalk. Let's consider the alternatives one by one.

Evaluation of A_1

The data cost $100,000. P_g is the probability (or proportion) of good soil and drainage conditions. $P_p = (1 - P_g)$ is the probability of poor conditions. Sidewalk built to CS-A costs $400 per foot, so that the expected cost for sidewalk on good

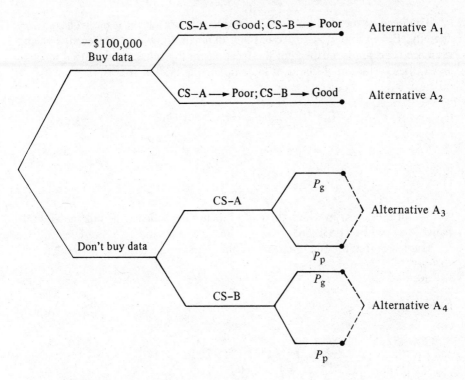

Figure 4.3 Sidewalk Example Decision Tree

conditions, $E(C_{g_1})$, is $P_g \times 21,120 \times \$400.$[5] The expected cost for CS-B sidewalk on poor conditions, $E(C_{p_1})$, is $P_p \times 21,120 \times \$200$. Expected total cost, $E(TC_1)$, is $E(C_{g_1}) + 100,000$. The mile-years for A_1, MY_1, are $P_g \times 4 \times 100 + P_p \times 4 \times 10^6$.

The criterion to minimize is TC_1/MY_1, the cost per mile-year. The calculations are as follows:

$$E(C_{g_1}) = P_g \times 21120 \times 400$$
$$= 8,448,000\ P_g$$

$$E(C_{p_1}) = P_p \times 21120 \times 200$$
$$= 4,224,000\ P_p$$

$$E(TC_1) = 8,448,000\ P_g + 4,224,000\ P_p$$
$$+ 100,000$$

$$MY_1 = 400\ P_g + 40\ P_p$$

$$TC_1/MY_1 = (8,448,000\ P_g + 4,224,000\ P_p$$
$$+ 100,000)/(400\ P_g + 40\ P_p)$$

The head of the Building and Safety Department says that on average across the city, $P_g = .4$ and $P_p = .6$. Absent any other information about what soil and drainage conditions to expect for the locations of the sidewalks that need replacement, these values might be used to complete the evaluation.

$$TC_1 = 3,379,200 + 2,534,400 + 100,000$$
$$= 6,013,600$$

$$MY_1 = 160 + 24$$
$$= 184$$

$$TC_1/MY_1 = 32,683$$

So, for every year in which there is a functioning mile of sidewalk under alternative A_1, it will cost $32,683.

The reasoning in evaluating each of the remaining alternatives is similar.

Evaluation of A_2

$$E(C_{g_2}) = .4 \times 21,120 \times 200$$
$$= 1,689,600$$

$$E(C_{p_2}) = .6 \times 8,448,000$$
$$= 5,068,800$$

$$E(TC_2) = E(C_{g_2}) + E(C_{p_2}) + 100,000$$
$$= 1,689,600 + 5,068,800 + 100,000$$
$$= 6,858,400$$

$$MY_2 = (.4 \times 4 \times 50) + (.6 \times 4 \times 50)$$
$$= 80 + 120$$
$$= 200$$

$$TC_2/MY_2 = 6,858,400/200$$
$$= \$34,292$$

Evaluation of A_3

$$E(C_{g_3}) = .4 \times 21,120 \times 400$$
$$= 3.379,200$$

$$E(C_{p_3}) = .6 \times 21,120 \times 400$$
$$= 5,068,800$$

$$E(TC_3) = 3.379,200 + 5,068,800$$
$$= 8,448,000$$

$$MY_3 = (.4 \times 4 \times 100) + (.6 \times 4 \times 50)$$
$$= 160 + 120$$
$$= 280$$

$$TC_3/MY_3 = 8,448,000/280$$
$$= \$30,171$$

Evaluation of A_4

$$E(C_{g_4}) = .4 \times 21,120 \times 200$$
$$= 1,689,600$$

$$E(C_{p_4}) = .6 \times 21,200 \times 200$$
$$= 2,534,400$$

$$E(TC_4) = 2,534,500 + 1,689,600$$
$$= 4,224,000$$

$$MY_4 = (.4 \times 4 \times 50) + (.6 \times 4 \times 10)$$
$$= 80 + 24$$
$$= 104$$

$$TC_4/MY_4 = 4,224,000/104$$

$$TC_4/MY_4 = \$40,615$$

The choice step in this problem is easy. The expected total costs, $E(TC_1)$ per mile-year of sidewalk were:

ALTERNATIVE	COST PER MILE-YEAR
A_1	$32,683
A_2	34,292
A_3	30,171
A_4	40,615

The alternative that minimizes the cost per mile-year of sidewalk is A_3, building all CS-A Cadillac sidewalks without buying information on soil conditions.

More realistic versions of the foregoing problem analysis would be much more complicated. The analysis might, for example, consider the null alternative[6] of not replacing sidewalks. This would require evaluating expected losses from injuries and suits such as the one brought by the lady who broke her leg.

It would almost certainly be desirable to do *sensitivity analysis* because the parameters and probabilities are uncertain. Sensitivity analysis simply asks "what if" questions about the analytic results. For example, what if $P_g = .75$ and $P_p = .25$ rather than the values that were used based on averages across the whole city? With these new P values, the alternatives' values become:

ALTERNATIVE	COST PER MILE-YEAR
A_1	$24,168
A_2	26,900
A_3	24,137*
A_4	26,400

The third alternative is still best by the criterion of minimum cost per mile-year.

If $P_g = 1$, meaning that there are no poor soil and drainage conditions, the values become:

ALTERNATIVE	COST PER MILE-YEAR
A_1	$21,370
A_2	21,620
A_3	21,210*
A_4	21,210*

It is usually wise to vary every uncertain parameter to see how sensitive the conclusions are to those estimates. In this case, the analysis should consider how the conclusions would change if the estimates of cost per foot or useful lives are wrong in one direction or the other. One of the most useful forms of sensitivity analysis is *break-even analysis*, which asks, "For what value of a particular parameter (e.g., P_g or cost per foot of CS-A sidewalk) will two alternatives be equal?" In the example, for what value of P_g is it true that

$$TC_3/MY_3 = TC_4/MY_4 \ ?$$

From above, one answer is $P_g = 1$. There may be other values of P_g that make the statement true.

Another complication to the analysis would be to consider the time value of money. The alternatives of (1) building one sidewalk at CS-A, with good soil and drainage conditions, that lasts for 100 years or (2) building and replacing a CS-B sidewalk at 50 years at the same nominal (current-dollar) cost evaluate quite differently if the value of taking half of the total nominal cost and investing it at going rates of interest is considered. Any normal consideration of the time value of money would make A_3 (building CS-A sidewalks) a questionable investment if full payment was required at the time of construction or if borrowing costs were high.

The analysis did not value the benefits, or mile-years of sidewalk. Thus it glossed over an important complication. From the analysis, it is not clear that any

---

*The preferred alternative by the criterion of minimizing cost-per-mile-year of sidewalk.

of the alternatives are worth undertaking. Is a mile-year of sidewalk worth $21,120? This is a cost–benefit analysis question. Sidewalks do not self-destruct overnight at 10, 50, or 100 years of age, as assumed in the problem formulation; sidewalks usually deteriorate slowly, and the value of the sidewalk is a function of its condition. Slightly deteriorated sidewalks may lead children to ride their bicycles on the street, increasing the probability that they will be struck by automobiles. What is the value of a child's life? What are the expected losses from injuries? If sidewalks are excellent, what are the expected losses from injuries to pedestrians struck by children riding bicycles on the sidewalks? These questions and many others would have to be answered to determine the benefits of so many miles of sidewalks of a given condition for a period of time.

What if the mayor's brother is the president of the only engineering consulting firm in town that can do a soil and drainage survey? Political factors that can alter the analysis often loom.

Alas, the life of the analyst is hard. Consider what a small part of a city's operating and capital budget building sidewalks is. Other possible topics for analysis include roads, stairs, bridges, buildings, vehicle maintenance, garage inventories, police patrols, fire station location, and thousands of others. Where does the analyst start and stop?

The flexibility of decision analysis is both its greatest strength and its greatest weakness. Some form of decision analysis can be used for any decision problem. But deciding what form the analysis should take is an often complicated and highly judgmental (read "arbitrary") task. As a recipe for decision making, decision analysis calls for pinches, or "add to taste," rather than definite measures of ingredients; it leaves the cook with a choice of flavorings and suggests that the dish bake for one or two hours in a medium oven or until it appears done. There is enough structure in the recipe to ensure a pastry rather than a casserole, but the quality of the dish depends critically on how the cook exercises discretion. Great cooks produce great dishes from ambiguous recipes. Great decision analysts produce useful decision analyses of the most complicated decision problems. Unfortunately, it is not always clear to mortal cooks and analysts how they should proceed to achieve comparable success.

One key ambiguity in decision analysis is the question: What aspects of complex, real problems can safely be ignored?

> . . . the farther we look ahead and the more refined our analysis becomes, the more complex the tree becomes, and if we carry matters to an extreme the tree begins to resemble a gigantic bush. Remember the analysis requires us to assign probabilities to all chance branches and utilities to all consequences at the tips of the tree. What a brutal task! In most realistic problems, in point of fact, one cannot possibly begin to chart out all the possible occurrences and choices far out into the foreseeable future. Compromises must be made; a touch of art must be combined with science. (Raiffa, 1968, p. 242.)

In the sidewalk construction example, there are clearly continuums for the types of soil conditions one might encounter and for the types and grades of sidewalk that might be built. Does the gross simplification of two types of sidewalk design and two soil conditions capture the essentials of the problem, or should the analyst consider five alternative designs and soil conditions? Or should they be treated as continuous variables? There is no easy answer. The decision analyst in this case should consult a civil engineer and perhaps a geologist about the design and soil condition variables. She might also need to consult a hydrologist about drainage, a financial analyst about probable costs and modes of financing, and a traffic engineer about projected levels of road usage and construction scheduling.

Decision analysis entails a lot of judgment on the part of the analyst, and the appropriate form of the analysis varies substantially with the problem. When the analyst finishes with sidewalk construction and moves to new problems like the purchase of refuse collection equipment or determining the optimal number of lawyers to have on city's legal staff, only the basic concepts (alternatives, states of nature, probabilities, outcomes, and expected value) will carry over from the sidewalk construction problem. A large part of each analysis must be sculpted anew. A large proportion of "art" in decision analysis is a problem because it calls on flexible analytic skills and sound substantive intuitions, both of which are in short supply. Decision analysis in the hands of a mediocre analyst is like a Bernaise sauce in the hands of mediocre cook; you may get a palatable product, but there is a significantly probability that you won't.

A further complication for decision analysis is that the analysis cannot be designed and executed with reference only to first principles from the logics of probability theory and utility theory; the analysis must take account of what the decision maker believes and what she or he can comprehend. Analysis is as much an exercise in persuasion as in logic. This poses a particular problem for decision analysis because of the great extent to which the analysis depends on information from decision makers. Probability and utility, central to decision analysis, are subjective quantities and must be elicited from the decision makers. They cannot be calculated independently by the analyst. Elaborate procedures have been developed for eliciting probabilities and utilities (see Keeney and Raiffa, 1978).

Elicitation is a problem in three ways.[7] First, elicitation takes the time and attention of decision makers, and these are their scarcest resources. It is hard to imagine a governor or large city mayor, much less the U.S. president or any legislative body, devoting the hours required to the formal procedures for eliciting probabilities and utilities. Eliciting the probabilities and utilities from lower levels (e.g., middle management) may be no help at all, since these individuals may not control the decisions and may not adequately represent those who do. Second, most decision makers, particularly chief executives and government officials, are not in the habit of being explicit about uncertainty and their values; such people would be uncomfortable with the explicitness of decision analysis. Although some very clever elicitation procedures have been devised, decision makers may resist being explicit and/or not have much confidence in results emerging from such an exercise. And third, public-sector decisions tend to belong to groups, not individuals. Elicitation procedures for groups and procedures for combining individual elicitations are not well developed.[8]

Most decision analyses are mathematical—nontrivially so for real, complicated problems. As a result, they are often resisted and distrusted by decision makers afflicted with the widespread "math phobia." Many with important decision-making responsibilities simply refuse, for reasons of capability or inclination, to understand mathematical analyses. Instead, they tend to ignore or mock results, particularly those that yield conclusions not consistent with their intuition or qualitative analysis. This is unfortunate, because the primary benefits of decision analysis are in problem structuring, not in the mathematical details. Getting the problem right in the amorphous world of government is a very important step, almost always more important than cranking out precise calculations.

The great strength of decision analysis for most problems is probably that it forces decision makers to think about what their problem is, what options are open to them, what values they care about, and what their primary sources of uncertainty are. This is a heuristic value, a value in discovery. The detailed calculations on a decision tree are often relatively unimportant; one may do them for the sake of completeness, but their contribution at the margin will probably be slight for most problems. Once a decision problem is formulated, the key ingredients have been specified, and rough calculations have been done, the alternative that should be chosen is often obvious. If the alternative is not obvious (e.g., there are several that are close), the detailed calculations are not apt to help much, because the errors in various estimates will be much larger than the differences in the expected payoffs.

As an approach to making government more efficient, decision analysis shares many other problems with other approaches to rationalizing discrete decisions. These general problems will be discussed in the last section of this chapter.

BENEFIT–COST ANALYSIS

Dear Sir:

In the affair of so much importance to you, wherein you ask my advice, I cannot, for want of sufficient premises, advise you what to determine, but if you please I will tell you how. When those difficult cases occur, they are difficult, chiefly because while we have them under consideration, all the reasons pro and con are not present to the mind at the same time; but sometimes one set present themselves, and at other time another, the first being out of sight. Hence the various purposes or inclinations that alternatively prevail, and the uncertainty that perplexes us. To get over this, my way is to divide half a sheet of paper by a line into two columns; writing over the one Pro, and over the other Con. Then, during three or four days consideration, I put down under the different heads short hints of the different motives, that at different times occur to me, for or against the measure. When I have thus got them all together in one view, I endeavor to estimate their respective weights; and where I find two, one on each side, that seem equal, I strike them both out. If I find a reason pro equal to some two reasons con, I strike out the three. If I judge some two reasons con, equal to some three reasons

Pro, I strike out the five; and thus proceeding I find at length where
the balance lies; and if, after a day or two of further consideration,
nothing new that is of importance occurs on either side, I come to
a determination accordingly. And, though the weight of reasons
cannot be taken with the precision of algebraic quantities, yet when
each is thus considered, separately and comparatively, and the
whole lies before me, I think I can judge better, and am less liable
to make a rash step, and in fact I have found great advantage from
this kind of equation, in what may be called moral and prudential
algebra.

Wishing sincerely that you may determine for the best, I am ever,
my dear friend, your most affectionately.

B. FRANKLIN,[9] LONDON, SEPTEMBER 19, 1772

Although benefit–cost analysis has become the centerpiece of applied economics,
the central notion in benefit–cost analysis, weighing and comparing the negative
and positive consequences of a contemplated action, is not an invention of modern economic theory.

Decision making can be viewed simply as a process of weighing, or analyzing,
the consequences associated with proposed courses of action. Costs are negative,
undesirable consequences flowing from actions (e.g., cash outlays, disruption of
natural settings, etc.). Benefits are positive, desirable consequences (e.g., averted
property damages and loss of life, etc.). A decision to proceed with a course of
action implies a belief that the project's benefits outweigh its costs. On the other
hand, a decision not to proceed with a course of action indicates a conclusion that
costs outweigh benefits. Where the decision maker faces a choice among courses
of action competing for the same limited resources, the action that appears to offer
the greatest expected benefits relative to the expected costs should be selected.

This sort of analysis is potentially important to government because resources
for projects are limited; it is simply not possible to undertake all of the projects
that are desired at any one time; and it is not possible to design all projects to the
highest standards. Some procedure for choosing among projects that are designed
to satisfy different objectives but that compete for the same scarce dollar resources
must be found. Also needed is a means of choosing among alternative ways of
accomplishing the same objective. Political processes provide one source of answers. Benefit–cost analysis seeks to provide information that will improve, if not
replace, political processes.

Benefits and costs can only be estimated in relation to an objective. The broad
objective for projects of this type is generally "to maximize the economic welfare
of the affected population." Benefits contribute to economic welfare and costs detract from it. Benefit–cost analysis always works with a "time stream" of costs and
benefits, a year-by-year forecast of costs and benefits from the outset of the project
to the end of its useful life. For example, the benefit–cost stream for a local flood
control project with a five-year life might appear as follows:

	T_0	T_1	T_2	T_3	T_4	T_5
Benefits	0	$10,000	$10,000	$10,000	$10,000	$10,000
Costs	$50,000	0	0	0	0	0

where T_0 is a construction year, T_1 is the first year when the project is in place, and so on.

A very large part of the effort in benefit–cost analysis must be devoted to generating the benefit–cost stream. In particular, estimating project benefits is often the most difficult and important task in benefit–cost analysis. Although information on project costs and construction scheduling is often routinely provided, information on project benefits is often missing entirely or incomplete and vague. The two primary reasons why adequate benefit information is not routinely provided are that (1) decision makers are not trained to perceive the need for explicit consideration of benefits and have no sense of what is possible and (2) estimating benefits is often a complicated task.

BENEFIT–COST ANALYSIS EXAMPLE

A simplified local flood-control project will be used to illustrate benefit–cost analysis. Background for the example is as follows:

1. The problem is that a small, somewhat isolated residential area has experienced sporadic flooding during severe storms and snow melts. The area is fully developed, with approximately $2 million of property value. Upstream and downstream effects can be ignored.[10]

2. Averted flood damage to property is the only important potential benefit from corrective actions. Loss of life, health hazards, aesthetics, dislocations, etc., are not important in this case and can be ignored.[11]

3. With no corrective action, serious flood damage is expected to occur only once every ten years.[12] The probability that a storm capable of causing such damage will occur in any given year is .1.[13] If damage occurs at all, it will cause the loss of 60 percent of the value in the area. The extent of the damage does not vary with the severity of the storm and flooding.[14]

4. Three projects have been proposed:

   a. To improve the existing surface drain at a cost of $200,000. With this project (Project A), flood damage would occur only in the event of a "25-year storm." The probability of a storm of an intensity equal to or greater than this in any one year is .04.

   b. To create an upstream impoundment and improve the existing drain at a cost of $500,000. With this project (Project B), flood damage would occur only in the event of a "50-year storm." The probability of a storm of an intensity equal to or greater than this in any one year is .02.

c. To create an upstream impoundment and a closed drain at a cost of $1.2 million. With this project (Project C), flood damage would occur only in the event of a "100-year storm." The probability of a storm of an intensity equal to or greater than this in any one year is .01.

5. All project costs are incurred at the outset.

6. There is no salvage return at the end of a project's useful life. The estimated useful life for all projects is 50 years.[15]

7. There is some nonzero probability that more than one storm of any given intensity may occur in any one year. It may be assumed, however, that if flooding occurs in any one year, no further damage is possible in that year.[16]

Knowledge of these characteristics/assumptions is necessary to generate a time stream of costs and benefits for each alternative. Table 4.1 summarizes some essential data for calculating costs and benefits. The calculations are shown in Table 4.2.

The analyst is interested in the marginal effects of projects. How will the world change as a result of particular actions? In calculating benefits for the hypothetical example, the importance of this "marginal view" is obvious (see Table 4.5 and associated discussion below). The benefits are calculated for each project as the difference between expected losses with the project and expected losses without the project; this calculation measures "averted flood damages." Costs in this hypothetical example require no calculation but are taken as given.

With benefit–cost streams, alternatives can be compared. In order to choose among alternatives, we need a definitive criterion or "test of preferredness." The three most commonly used criteria are (a) benefit–cost ratio, (b) internal rate of return, and (c) maximum gains minus costs (or maximum net present value). Before we discuss each of these criteria in the context of the hypothetical choice, some further assumptions are required.

The first additional assumption required concerns the interrelationships among the projects. For this example, assume that the projects are "mutually exclusive"; that is, it is not possible or sensible to undertake more than one of them.[17] A more complex choice might be to select a *set* of projects within a budget constraint where projects are independent (e.g., all projects can be done, physically if not

Table 4.1 **Basic Data: Storm Drain Example**

ACTION	CAPITAL COST	LEVEL OF PROTECTION*	PROBABILITY OF OCCURRENCE†
Status Quo	—	10-year storm	.1
Project A	$ 200,000	25-year storm	.04
Project B	500,000	50-year storm	.02
Project C	1,200,000	100-year storm	.01

*For any storm of an intensity equal to or greater than that indicated, flood damage occurs.

†This is the probability of a storm of an intensity equal to or greater than that indicated occurring in any one year.

Table 4.2 **Cost–Benefit Analysis for Flood-Control Project**

STATUS QUO

Expected annual loss $= (.1) (.6) (\$2,000,000)$
$= \$120,000$

PROJECT A

Expected annual loss $= (.04) (.6) (\$2,000,000)$
$= \$48,000$

Net annual benefit $= \$120,000 - \$48,000$
(averted flood damages) $= \$72,000$

PROJECT B

Expected annual loss $= (.02) (.06) (\$2,000,000)$
$= \$24,000$

Net annual benefit $= \$120,000 - \$24,000$
(averted flood damages) $= \$96,000$

PROJECT C

Expected annual loss $= (.01) (.6) (\$2,000,000)$
$= \$12,000$

Net annual benefit $= \$120,000 - \$12,000$
(averted flood damages) $= \$108,000$

financially) or interdependent (e.g., all costs and benefits of projects depend on which other projects are undertaken simultaneously). The analysis will also assume that each of the project alternatives can be financed if selected, an assumption that greatly simplifies the calculations.

Perhaps the most widely used criterion, and the one legally required in the analysis of federal water resource projects, is the benefit–cost ratio. The general formula for calculating this ratio is:

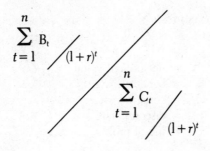

$$\dfrac{\displaystyle\sum_{t=1}^{n} \dfrac{B_t}{(1+r)^t}}{\displaystyle\sum_{t=1}^{n} \dfrac{C_t}{(1+r)^t}}$$

where B_t = benefits in year t
C_t = cost in year t
r = discount rate
n = expected life of
project (years)

In the example, assuming r to be equal to zero,[18] the formula is simply the sum of all benefits divided by the sum of all costs:

$$\sum_{t=1}^{n} B_t \bigg/ \sum_{t=1}^{n} C_t$$

The popularity of this criterion stems from its seemingly easy interpretation. The result is expressed as a single number, conveying a sense of precision and certainty. The general rules of interpretation are that projects with benefit–cost ratios less than 1 are not worth undertaking and that projects with larger ratios are preferred. On Table 4.3, Project A has a benefit–cost ratio of 18, almost twice that of Project B (9.6) and four times that of Project C (4.5). Using maximum benefit–cost ratio as the criterion, Project A is clearly preferred.

There are, however, a number of problems with the ratio criterion.[19] Its primary defect is an insensitivity to the scale of the projects. If the alternatives included a project that had one teenager working for an hour pulling large limbs from the ditch with costs of $5 and benefits of $100, a benefit–cost ratio of 20, this project would be preferred to all other projects by the ratio criterion. Project A is preferred to Project B by the ratio criterion (see Table 4.3), even though Project B's net benefits (total benefits minus total costs) are $900,000 more than Project A's net benefits. Project B does, however, cost $300,000 more than Project A. Although the ultimate choice between A and B would turn on the budget constraint and rate-of-return considerations, it is unlikely that it would be sensible to treat the teenager's hour as a full substitute for the other projects. Criteria, including the benefit–cost ratio, cannot be applied mechanically.

Before looking at two other possible criteria, the notion of "present value" of benefit–cost streams must be introduced. The formula for calculating net present value (with discrete compounding) is:

$$NPV = \sum_{i=0}^{n} \frac{B_i - C_i}{(1+r)^n}$$

where PV = net present value
B_i = benefits in year i
C_i = costs in year i
r = discount rate
n = life of project in years

In the example with r equal to zero, this reduces to:

$$NPV = \sum_{i=0}^{n} B_i - C_i$$

or simply the sum of the difference between benefits and costs for the life of the project. Determining the "present value" of a project's benefit–cost stream is necessary because *when* we receive a benefit or pay a cost affects the value that we place on it. A benefit of $1 million that will arrive in ten years is worth less than one of equivalent amount that will arrive in two years, because the latter could be invested and its value increased by eight years of interest before the first even arrived. To choose the first over the second would involve the sacrifice of potential interest—an "opportunity cost." Since alternative public projects will rarely if ever have all their benefits and costs restricted to a single year, it is necessary to translate them into present value before any sensible comparison can be made. The discount rate is simply a numeric representation of the rate at which the opportunity cost is accrued each year. It tells us how much we need to reduce per year (compounded) the value of benefits (or costs) that will arrive in the future.[20] Although we will discuss discount rates only briefly, the importance of the rate should be obvious. With the assumption of a zero discount rate in the example, the net benefits for Project C in year 50 are $108,000. If a discount rate of 10 percent were assumed, these benefits would be $920. Applying a 10 percent discount rate across all years might well result in a negative present value for Project C, indicating—like a benefit–cost ratio less than 1—that the project is not worth undertaking. Obviously, higher discount rates penalize (in terms of present value) projects requiring large cash outlays at the outset with benefits extending far into the future.

The second criterion, "internal rate of return," is that discount rate that makes a project's present value equal to zero. This criterion is not widely used, although it does have some virtue for choice situations with a large number of independent alternatives and no capital rationing.[21] The general choice rule is that projects with an internal rate of return below the prevailing market rate of interest are not worth undertaking and that higher internal rates of return are preferred. One problem with this criterion is that there may be no unique internal rate of return; there may be two discount rates that make a project's net present value zero.

A third and final criterion is "maximize benefits minus costs" or "maximize net present value." The last column of Table 4.3 gives the present value (with a

Table 4.3   **Summary Comparisons: Storm-Drain Example**

Project	Payback Period*	Total Benefits†	Total Costs	Benefit– Cost Ratio‡	Total Benefits Minus Total Costs
A	2.78	$3,600,000	$ 200,000	18	$3,400,000
B	5.21	4,800,000	500,000	9.6	4,300,000
C	11.11	5,400,000	1,200,000	4.5	4,200,000

*This is the number of years required for undiscounted expected benefits to equal total project costs.
†Sum of undiscounted, expected project benefits over the life of each project.
‡Total benefits divided by total costs.

zero discount rate) for each of the example projects. By this criterion at that discount rate, Project B with a present value of $4,300,000 is preferred to Project C with a present value of $4,200,000 and to Project A with a present value of $3,400,000. It is important to note that Project A, which was preferred with the ratio criterion, is the least desirable of the three projects by the criterion of maximum net present value. If benefits and costs can be expressed in dollar terms and projects are selected within a budget constraint, the criterion of maximum net present value is generally the most reliable, conceptually problem-free criterion that one can use.

Obviously, the choices of criterion and discount rate can determine the results of a cost–benefit analysis. Many of the assumptions employed in generating the benefit–cost stream can also strongly influence the results. Since it is inevitable that some of the choices made by the analyst will be debatable, any conclusion expressed as a single number or single set of numbers for comparison is symptomatic of poor analysis. This is as true for a hydrological analysis of any moderately complex system as it is for cost–benefit analysis.[22]

Some of the myriad technical and conceptual problems with benefit–cost analysis are apparent even in this simple example. The example chosen was relatively favorable to applications of benefit–cost analysis. Many of the standard difficulties—such as externalities,[23] valuing benefits, and selecting a discount rate—were assumed away. Selecting an example to make the analytic technique look truly ridiculous would be easy; almost any regulatory or social program would do, if only because of their sometimes amorphous, always difficult-to-measure outputs.

Most of the applications experience with benefit–cost analysis has been at the federal level on public works projects, particularly water resource projects. Indeed, benefit–cost analysis is the only analysis required by law. Federal agencies, in submitting any plan for a water resource project to Congress, must supply benefit–cost calculations. There are a set of published guidelines for federal agencies doing benefit–cost calculations (*Federal Register*, vol. 38, no. 174, September 1973). These guidelines are periodically updated. The fundamental requirement is that only those projects with a benefit–cost ratio greater than 1 (calculated in conformance with the guidelines) will be considered for authorization. There has not, to our knowledge, been a careful study of Congress's use of benefit–cost analysis, but Bradford and Feiveson's account (see also Ferejohn, 1974) is consistent with what most observers believe.

> The ratio of benefits and costs (the *B/C* ratio) is intended to play a twofold role. It should first form a loose guide both to the federal agencies and to Congress as to the priorities of projects, and second, play the role of a filter. Projects with a *B/C* ratio less than one will not be considered for authorization. The guidelines imposed by Congress, therefore, may be seen as a way of limiting the number of projects with which Congress must contend, but not so much that Congress loses discretion over which projects to fund. In this sense the guidelines represent a compromise: there should be a filter but one not too fine. In this screening process, seldom if ever does Congress inquire into the basis of a benefit–cost evaluation, faulty though it might be. Rather it has used benefit–cost analysis as a tool for controlling the bureaucracy, for imposing at least some modest amount of discipline on a set of agencies it otherwise has great difficulty controlling. The filter role for the *B/C* ratio is far more significant than its use in

setting priorities. By all accounts, so long as the *B/C* ratio is above one, and "comfortably" so, Congress pays relatively little attention to it. (Bradford and Feiveson, 1976, pp. 126–127.)

There have been fewer applications of benefit–cost analysis by state and local governments (David, 1979). One reason for this may be that the investments at these levels are smaller and do not warrant the same level of analytic effort. At some point the marginal benefits to be gained from elaborate analysis approach zero. It may also be that there are fewer analytic resources at the state and local levels. Good benefit–cost analysis requires considerable technical sophistication. Another reason is that the theory behind benefit–cost analysis incorporates a global, societal perspective not often appropriate for local problems. Localities have localized interests. On the kinds of large projects for which benefit–cost analysis would be appropriate (e.g., construction of a sewage treatment facility), there are myriad state and federal regulations that do not permit the locality to consider only its own interests and to treat effects on other localities as externalities. From a purely local perspective, Cincinnati's optimal sewage disposal is probably to dump raw sewage into the Ohio River at the extreme, downstream edge of the city limits. For Cincinnati residents, the procedure would be very cheap and effective. The economic virtue of this disposal method from a local perspective could be demonstrated analytically in benefit–cost analysis. But the downstream neighbors would not be happy with the costs imposed on them by such a method. State and federal agencies would not allow it. So Cincinnati's analysis would have to use a modified local perspective, internalizing the externalities. But these modifications in perspective required by state and federal regulations are so extensive that a pure benefit–cost analysis makes no sense for Cincinnati officials. Rather, the officials take the benefits implicit in the state and federal standards and look at the cost of alternatives for meeting the standards.

Like decision analysis, benefit–cost analysis is something less than a fully described algorithm for decision making. There is considerable art, if not arbitrariness, in the way a benefit–cost analysis should be performed. The high proportion of this "art" leads to contradictory results between two analyses of the same public program and provides enormous opportunities for manipulating the results to serve some ulterior political or personal motives.

Perhaps the best example of an essentially arbitrary quantity in benefit–cost analysis is the discount rate. The discount rate is often critical to benefit–cost analysis; varying the rate by few points usually alters radically the set of public projects that are economic ($B/C > 1$ or $NPV > 0$) and the preference orderings on projects (Project A>Project B>Project C). The appropriate discount rate for public projects has been the object of considerable academic debate, but the arcane details are irrelevant here; it is sufficient to know that it exists. There are those who argue that the rate should reflect the opportunity cost of capital with reference to private-sector costs of capital (e.g., the prime rate) because public uses of money should compete with private uses of money. Those on this side of the argument tend to have conservative political orientations. If these higher rates had been used over the past 30 years and the benefit–cost ratio rule (>1) had been enforced, few, if any, large-scale publicly financed capital projects would have been authorized. On the other side, there are those, usually liberal in their political orientation, who argue for very low discount rates for public projects. Three of the arguments for low rates are that (1) the discount rate should reflect a social rate of time preference that weighs the preferences of future generations; (2) private-sector rates are generated by firms that produce negative externalties, which are costly to correct; and (3) private-sector rates reflect a "risk premium" not applicable to public investments.

Regardless of one's preferences, it is always advisable to conduct sensitivity analysis on the discount rate rather than selecting a single rate. If a project is justifiable with a rate of 20 percent or unjustifiable at all rates greater than 1 percent, that is useful information. Projects whose economic justifiability turns on whether the discount rate used in evaluation is 7.5 percent or 9 percent probably will be authorized or denied on grounds other than the formal conclusion of the benefit–cost analysis.

Benefit–cost analysis does not handle uncertainty as explicitly or as naturally as decision analysis does. Sensitivity analysis can be extremely helpful, but the analytic output can become overcomplicated very quickly. For example, if you examine how the results change for ten values of each of three variables (say the discount rate, benefit estimates, and cost estimates) to reflect uncertainty in those quantities, you have a thousand ($10 \times 10 \times 10$) outcomes. There are ways, however, of summarizing such compendious results. You might, for example, represent the relationship between the discount rate and the benefit–cost ratio as shown on Figure 4.4. This figure gives the useful information that for the point estimate (best-guess) levels of benefit and costs, the project has a benefit–cost ratio greater than 1.0 for discount rates below 6 percent and less than 1.0 for greater discount rates. It is slightly more complicated and more cumbersome to explore the uncertainty in the estimates of costs and benefits. One way to proceed is to fix a discount rate. Figure 4.5 shows one way in which the relationship between the benefit–cost ratio and percentage error in the estimates of net benefits ($B - C$) might be represented. Each line represents the relationship at a different discount rate ($R = ?$).

Given the uncertainty inherent in benefit–cost analyses, this sort of information about the effects of uncertainty should always be provided, however complicated the presentation becomes. But it is not. Rather, government agencies provide summary ratios and recapitulations of benefit and cost calculations. This conveys less uncertainty than actually exists.

> One cannot help but be distressed by the illusion of precision the summary numbers in typical benefit–cost analyses present. At worst, these summary data are the resultant of a large number of possibly large errors; at best they will be merely clues about the consequences of a particular action. Instead of the crisp column of figures displayed in most benefit–cost analyses, perhaps what is needed is a sort of Rube Goldberg machine, with numbers popping out at odd times and places, to remind us all of the loose connections. (Bradford and Feiveson, 1976, pp. 157–158.)

A little honest sensitivity analysis would improve the quality of benefit–cost information and perhaps take a step toward the Rube Goldberg machine described above.

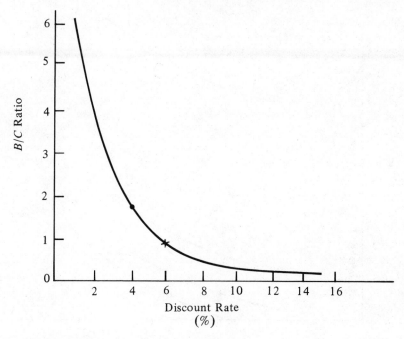

Figure 4.4 *B/C* Ratio as a Function of Discount Rate

A related problem with cost–benefit analysis in practice is that many analysts view the techniques as a sufficient procedure for making decisions rather than as a technique for producing information to premise decisions. There is a serious disjunction between what decision makers want and what analysts are most anxious to provide. Decision makers (sometimes) want information about the consequences of alternatives. They may get it from dispassionate analysts (an endangered species), from analysts representing the points of view of interested parties, or from the interested parties directly. The decision makers expect to integrate information from various sources and to exercise some discretion in the choice. More zealous benefit–cost analysts view their analysis as a sufficient decision procedure. They have worked very hard to insure that their analysis includes "everything that is important and legitimate to consider." When the analysis points to a definite conclusion, they cannot understand how a decision maker can possibly choose an alternative other than the one recommended by the analysis. For the more zealous analysts, decision makers who behave in this contrary way are either stupid or venal. Such zealots were common in the 1960s; they are rare in the 1980s. Perhaps there is natural selection in political processes.

The emphasis on analysis as a "decision rule," a sufficient decision procedure culminating in a definite recommendation, has been very destructive. It has led to the gross misallocation of analytic resources to the valuation and choice aspects of decision problems rather than to the problem formulation, alternative generation, and prediction aspects, which is where the help is most needed. Because of

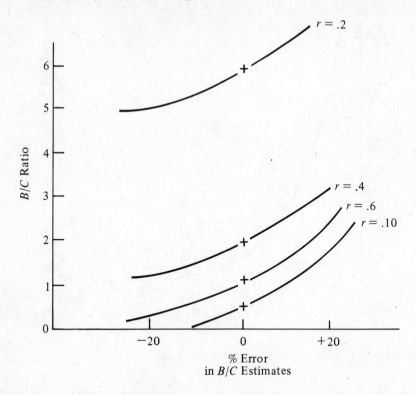

Figure 4.5   *B/C* Ratio as Function of Error in Estimates and Discount Rate

the many simplifying assumptions that must be made, the emphasis on valuation and choice leads to the premature suppression of uncertainty about what the problem (including goals) is and about what the consequences of various actions will be; it compels analysts to contrive measures that no one will believe.

If benefit–cost analysis is ever to become more useful, it will have to be viewed as an exercise in discovering values and alternatives and not as a sufficient decision procedure. Few benefit–cost analyses appear to have had much impact on decisions, but many of those that have had an impact have apparently considered real alternative programs and not just one real program and "straw-men programs" (Merewitz and Sosnick, 1971). Given the enormous uncertainties in the estimates of benefits and costs, the fact that the analysis almost always omits values important to decision makers, the essentially arbitrary choices that must underlie the analysis, and the care with which decision makers guard their decision prerogatives, it is ludicrous for analysts to provide decision makers with summary measures like benefit–cost ratios. It is also ludicrous that the law should require such measures. Government would be much better served by analysis that is directed at really learning something, analysis that explores alternatives and explicitly acknowledges uncertainty. Such analysis might even change minds once in a while and improve the efficiency and effectiveness of government.

Another "artful" aspect of benefit–cost analysis is determining the alternatives that will be analyzed. The usual resolution, a highly arbitrary one, is that a single program will be examined against the null alternative of doing nothing. While benefit–cost analysis has been advertised, in theory and in getting it accepted as a requirement for water resources projects, as an analytic tool for allocating scarce resources among competing projects, there is little competition in practice. There has rarely been simultaneous consideration of different public projects to accomplish the same objective or different projects to accomplish different objectives. There has never been, to our knowledge, comparisons of public projects with private projects except implicitly through complaints about the use of "artificially low" discount rates.[24]

Where the single public project that is analyzed comes from is never clear. Why that project and not others? Most public projects probably begin as a gleam in the eye of a citizen or politician who sees potential benefits or in the eye of an engineer in the Army Corps of Engineers who sees a potentially interesting solution to a flooding, irrigation, or water supply problem. There is no persuasive theory of "the optimality of gleams." Ignored alternatives are a major problem for benefit–cost analysis as a resource allocation tool. Pretensions to optimality are just that. The practice of benefit–cost analysis would benefit from procedures that force comparison of mutually exclusive alternatives for accomplishing the same objectives. Two new highways or a railroad subsidy might do as much for the economic development of the area benefited by the Tenn-Tom project as the waterway, and at a much lower cost.

Multiple, incommensurable values also pose substantial problems for benefit–cost analysis that focuses on allocative efficiency and quantitative evaluation of alternatives. There are always many more values associated with the forecasted effects of a project than are included in the "main analysis," the analysis that leads to a summary measure like the *B/C* ratio. Two classes of exclusion are most important. First, certain effects are dubbed "intangible" and not included in the main analysis. The best analyses list intangibles explicitly, even though they are not part of the main calculations. Indeed, listing intangibles is now a requirement for water resource projects. "Intangible" is often a synonym for "nonquantifiable." Any effect that is difficult to conceptualize, measure, or price is likely to be relegated to the intangibles category. The usual examples of intangibles include psychological variables (e.g., the "pain and suffering" associated with accidents) and certain kinds of "environmental spillovers" (e.g., the aesthetic impacts of a water resource project, damage to species' habitats, or the loss of archaeological treasures).

The exclusion of intangibles is important because for many public projects there is a strong suspicion that the intangible effects are more important than tangible effects.

> . . . the outcome of all too many cost–benefit studies follows that of the classic recipe for making horse and rabbit stew on a strictly fifty-fifty basis, one horse to one rabbit. No matter how carefully the scientific rabbit is chosen, the flavor of the resulting stew is sure to be swamped by the horseflesh. The horse, needless to say, represents

those other considerations among which environmental spillover effects loom large. For all that, mention of environmental spillover has until recently seldom taken up more space than a sentence or two in a footnote, or in the preamble to the expert's study which is, of course, the scientific rabbit, one having all the earmarks of professional competence.

In our growth-fevered atmosphere there is always a strong temptation for the economist, as for other specialists, to come up with firm quantitative results. In order to be able to do so, however, he finds that he must ignore the less easily measured spillovers. In so far as the ignored spillover effects are adverse, this common response to the temptation imparts a bias toward favoring commercially viable projects, irrespective of their ability to withstand more searching criteria. As a matter of professional pride, and of obligation to the community he elects to serve, the economist should resist this temptation. (Mishan, 1982, p. 149.)

While the foregoing comment was made over 20 years ago, the situation has not changed at all and is not apt to change in the next 20 (or 100) years.

The second important class of excluded effects comprises redistributive effects. Every public project redistributes income; it leaves some people better off and others worse off. From the perspective of allocative efficiency, the perspective of benefit–cost analysis, all that matters is that the benefits to the gainers exceed the losses to the losers.[25] Not surprisingly, however, politicians care a lot about who gains and who loses across constituency classes, and the exclusion of the redistributive effects has been one of the most important obstacles to giving benefit–cost analysis more impact on political decisions. While economists have experimented with different methods of including redistributive effects directly in benefit–cost analysis (e.g., by valuing benefits differently depending on what group receives them), the procedures are all very arbitrary and rarely used.[26]

Still another problem with benefit–cost analysis is that the results can vary enormously depending on who is doing the study. For example, three different groups have analyzed the costs of motor vehicle accidents. The results are shown on Table 4.4. Note the vast differences in estimated future earnings and medical costs. These costs are used by the groups to calculate benefits (as averted costs), which are then used along with program cost data to evaluate various interventions. The benefit–cost ratios for two such intervention programs are shown in Table 4.5. Not surprisingly, given the differences in estimated benefits, the variation is enormous. Under one set of calculated costs (by the Safety Administration), an intervention to improve bus passenger seating and crash protection is justified ($B/C > 1.0$): under the other two sets of calculated costs, the intervention is not justified.

What is a decision maker supposed to do with such contradictory results? One strategy is to try to understand the source of the differences in the analyses and choose the most "reasonable." In this case, the differences are clearly due to the treatment of "future earnings lost" and to the nine categories of cost included by the Safety Administration and excluded by NSC (National Safety Council) and the RECAT Committee (Regulatory Effects on the Cost of Automobile Transportation). But which estimates are correct? Even if you believe that the Safety Committee's estimates are more correct in that they are more complete, can you really

Table 4.4 **Estimated Costs of Motor Vehicle Accidents**

	Safety Administration	NSC	RECAT Committee
	(000,000 omitted)		
Costs estimated by all:			
Future earnings lost	$18,100	$ 3,700	$ 7,700
Medical costs	1,950	1,100	6,100
Property damage	7,100	5,000	4,900
Total:	27,150	9,800	18,700
Costs not estimated by RECAT Committee:			
Insurance administration	6,600	6,600	—
Costs estimated only by Safety Administration			
Home and family duties	4,500	—	—
Pain and suffering	3,800	—	—
Legal and court costs	1,050	—	—
Service to community	900	—	—
Time and money losses to others	800	—	—
Miscellaneous losses	800	—	—
Asset losses	300	—	—
Employer losses	50	—	—
Funeral costs	50	—	—
Total:	12,250	—	—
Total costs:	$46,000	$16,400	$18,700

Source: "*Need to Improve Benefit–Cost Analysis in Setting Motor Vehicle Safety Standards.*" Report to the Committee on Commerce, U.S. Senate, by the Comptroller General of the United States. Washington, D.C.: Mimeograph, 1974, p. 3.

Table 4.5 **Benefit–Cost Ratio**

Standard	Safety Administration	NSC	RECAT Committee
Windshield zone intrusion	16 to 1	6 to 1	7 to 1
Bus passenger seating and crash protection	222 to 1	.88 to 1	.96 to 1

Source: Need to Improve Benefit–Cost Analysis in Setting Motor Vehicle Safety Standards. Report to the Committee on Commerce, U.S. Senate, by the Comptroller General of the United States. Washington, D.C.: Mimeograph, 1974, p. 3.

believe the magnitudes? How many decision makers would be willing to think hard about the intricacies of estimating losses due to "home and family duties" foregone or contracted?" How many decision makers (or analysts) really believe that anyone can project and value losses in child care, household cleaning, washing and ironing, and so forth? And the "home and family duties" category is probably much easier to predict and value than the "pain and suffering" category.

The modeling requirements in the ideal benefit–cost analysis are enormous.

> . . . what is needed for any cost-benefits study is a model capable of performing two services: (1) predicting the future behavior of all the intervening economic variables, whether or not they are directly affected by the project; and (2) checking the optimality (in terms of allocative efficiency) of the present structure of economic activities in the study area, as well as its future structure at completion of the project. (Contini, 1969, p. 68.)

While it is possible to envision how government in the ideal world of theory should allocate resources, the relevance of this vision to a world in which no one can predict economic variables with anything like reasonable accuracy—and in which there is no meaningful social welfare function capable of defining "optimality"—is questionable.

Many of the complications in benefit–cost analysis arise in deciding what to count (and not to count) and in deciding how to value what is counted. The two most important rules about what to count are (1) count only changes in allocative efficiency and (2) count only marginal effects[27] and the estimation of "consumer surplus" (e.g., the maximum amount of money that a price discriminating monopolist could charge each user of a given service). (For a helpful discussion of both matters, see Gramlich, 1977.) We have already touched on the first rule in discussing the fact that benefit–cost analysis is insensitive to the issue of redistribution, but actually the matter is more complicated than simply ignoring the question of who benefits. Take the classic example of estimating the benefits associated with the building of a new highway. How should we deal with the increased business that is now enjoyed by firms located near the road and the increased value of the land that borders it? While it might seem that these should be counted as benefits, an economist would argue that these are not "real" but are "pecuniary" benefits in the sense that they are reflective of mere price changes. True, the businesses that border the highway are doing better than they were before, but this improvement is being offset by losses to businesses in other locales. Similarly, the increased value of land along the road has been offset by falling prices for the land along what are now less traveled routes. In neither case is there an increase in allocative efficiency in the sense that there is a net benefit in community welfare.

Marginal analysis is a central notion in microeconomic theory. The principle is best seen in an example. Table 4.6 summarizes the police and burglary situation for a small town adjacent to a large city. Each patrolman costs $25,000 (columns 1 and 2). Column 3 indicates the number of expected burglaries for each patrol level; the more patrolmen, the fewer the burglaries. Column 4 indicates the total social costs of burglaries ($2,000 each), and column 5 shows the marginal costs. The marginal value of each additional patrolman (the value of burglaries forestalled) is shown in column 6. Adding the fifth patrolman forestalls $40,000 in burglaries, which is greater than the $25,000 costs. Adding the sixth patrolman forestalls only $20,000 in burglaries, which does not cover the $25,000 cost. Analyzing the costs and benefits of a proposal to expand the patrol from five to ten men,[28] there are benefits of $38,000 ($500,000 − $482,000 from column 4 or $20,000 + $10,000 + $4,000 + $2,000 + $2,000 from column 6) and costs of $125,000 (the costs of five patrolmen); the proposal should be rejected.

In real instances an analyst almost never has available nor can the analyst create the sort of information given on Table 4.6, because causal relationships such as the relationships between the number of patrolmen and the number of burglaries are not understood. Also, even with a good idea of what an extra patrolman would cost, it would be hard to even conceptualize the social cost of a burglary or of the threat of burglary. Because of the psychological dimensions and other factors such as crimes that occur when burglaries are discovered in progress (e.g., assault and homicide), the social cost is much more than the original cost or replacement value of goods stolen. Even with narrower definitions of cost, there are problems: What is the value of a stolen family heirloom (e.g., your great grandmother's wedding ring) that contains $40 of silver and a semiprecious stone but is "irreplaceable"?

In the real world, there are several factors that make learning about causal relationships very difficult and that, in turn, make forecasts inaccurate. Causal relations are usually complex. The burglary rate is almost certainly a function of many factors, including economic conditions (e.g., some burglaries are committed by the unemployed trying to feed their families and others by drug users to support their habits), social arrangements (e.g., adequate welfare and unemployment compensation programs will make it unnecessary for some unemployed to commit burglary or effective drug rehabilitation programs will reduce users), judicial behavior (e.g., given apprehension, the higher the probability of conviction and the greater the expected severity of the sentence, the higher the expected costs of burglary and—by rational deterrence models—the fewer burglaries), homeowner behavior (e.g., trends in the use of home alarm systems and neighborhood watch systems), and the way in which patrols are used (e.g. one patrolman on the street in a high-burglary area is probably worth several patrolmen in a low-burglary area or an infinite number in the station house drinking coffee). The analytic methods available for unraveling such causal complexities as the effect of an additional patrolman at the margin on the burglary rate, given all of the other relevant factors, are, at best, feeble.

Quite often the world has not performed the experiments that might help to unravel causal relationships. In the police example above, the town may have had experience only with four patrolmen for 20 years and five patrolmen for 3 years. There is no historical basis for estimating what the burglary rate would be with no patrolmen or with ten and probably very little sympathy on the part of city council (or police unions) for the conduct of any formal experiments. The proposal to experiment with no patrolmen so that you can improve your analysis will probably encounter some political difficulties in even the most liberal communities.

Historical relationships are not necessarily stable and perfect understanding of causality in the historical period (something that never exists) might be a very poor

Table 4.6 Marginal Analysis of Patrol Size and Burglaries

(1)	(2)	(3)	(4)	(5)	(6)
Patrolmen	Cost	Burglaries	Social Cost	Marginal Cost	Marginal Value
0	—	500	$1,000,000	—	
1	$ 25,000	400	800,000	$25,000	$200,000
2	50,000	350	700,000	25,000	100,000
3	75,000	310	620,000	25,000	80,000
4	100,000	280	560,000	25,000	60,000
5	125,000	260	520,000	25,000	40,000
6	150,000	250	500,000	25,000	20,000
7	175,000	245	490,000	25,000	10,000
8	200,000	243	486,000	25,000	4,000
9	225,000	242	484,000	25,000	2,000
10	250,000	241	482,000	25,000	2,000

basis for forecasting future causal relationships. In the example, the construction of a freeway between the town and a nearby large city might improve access and make "getaways" easier, leading to many more burglaries.

Predicting the marginal effects of public programs is enormously difficult. Although it can and has been used retrospectively, benefit–cost analysis is primarily a prospective technique. The usefulness of the analysis depends directly on the accuracy of the forecasts of consequences. The accuracy of these forecasts, in turn, depends directly on our causal understanding of phenomena. And as one noted commentator on science puts it,

> We do not really understand nature, at all. Not to downgrade us; we have come a long way indeed, just to have learned enough to become conscious of our ignorance. It is not so bad a thing to be totally ignorant; the hard thing is to be part way toward real knowledge, far enough to be aware of being ignorant . . . It is a new experience for all of us, on unfamiliar ground. Just think, two centuries ago we could explain everything, out of pure reason, and now most of that elaborate and harmonious structure has come apart before our eyes. We are *dumb*. (Lewis Thomas, quoted in Bernstein 1978, p. 201.)

Prediction is *the* critical problem for benefit–cost analysis, but it is an aspect of the analysis that receives relatively little attention, particularly from economists. Perhaps this is because the forecasts require substantive expertise that economists usually do not have. The economists doing an analysis often take casual causal estimates from substantive experts—estimates with enormous error—and devote most of their attention and effort to the intricacies of selecting the "correct" discount rate or "shadow prices"[29] for the forecasted benefits. It is not unusual to find an economist exercising great genius (and spending a lot of time and money) in pricing "recreation user-days" or "pain and suffering" when the forecast quantities are only accurate within 200 percent.

Asserting that predictive accuracy is a major problem for analysis is not splitting hairs over 5 or 10 percent. There are gross inaccuracies that, in retrospect, make the decisions to go ahead with public projects very questionable. The Bay

Area Rapid Transit (BART) System is a good example. One retrospective analysis of BART concludes that

> The most notable fact about BART is that it is extraordinarily costly. It has turned out to be far more expensive than anyone expected, and far more costly than is usually understood. High capital costs (about 150 percent of forecast) plus high operating costs (about 475 percent of forecast) are being compounded by low patronage (50 percent of forecast) to make for average costs per ride that are twice as high as the bus and 50 percent greater than a standard American car. (Webber, 1981, p. 435.)

Tables 4.7 and 4.8 compare the forecasts and actuals for ridership and finances respectively.

Ridership and finances were the "easy variables" to forecast. Much harder to forecast, as the retrospective errors show, were such effects as the impact on suburban development and the impact on highway congestion. How can the analysis preceding the decision to build BART have gone so wrong? A project as large as BART would certainly seem to justify careful analysis before a decision is made to proceed. The error in this case probably stems from two primary sources. First, the analysis was biased to favor proceeding with the project. Those preparing the analysis probably had personal and professional stakes in seeing that the project went ahead. The standard pattern of partisan analysis, overstated benefits and understated costs, is obvious in the tables. Second, the technology and theories required to forecast such factors as inflation, which increase costs, and behavioral responses, such as the switching from automobiles and buses to the trains, are inadequate. BART's scope was well beyond historical experience, the most comfortable basis for most forecasts.

Benefit–cost analyses are subject to manipulation, usually to make a project look better than it is. One of the best examples of such manipulation is the analysis done over a 30-year period by the Army Corps of Engineers to promote the "Tenn-Tom" project.

> Thousands of confidential memorandums and other internal documents of the Army Corps of Engineers indicate a continuing practice of accounting manipulation, guesswork and misleading statements to Congress to justify construction of the $2 billion Tennessee-Tombigbee Waterway through Mississippi and Alabama. The government documents . . . show underestimates of costs and overestimates of benefits calculated to win approval for the most extensive project in the history of the Corps of Engineers . . . The economic justification for the waterway, the ratio of benefit to cost, was based on data derived from barge traffic projections that ranged from unlikely

Table 4.7 **Forecast as Against Actual BART Patronage, June 1976**

Route Segment	1961 Forecast for 1975	1976 Actual	Actual as Percent of Forecast
Transbay	77,850	53,880	69
East Bay	129,493	39,725	31
West Bay	51,153	37,765	74
Total:	258,496	131,370	51

Source: Webber, 1981, p. 418

to physically impossible. The cost–benefit ratio was also based on a channel width nearly twice as large as Congress authorized and included locks not in the approved design. Benefit figures used at various times to legally justify the project were based on the inclusion of hundreds of millions of dollars of improvements to 217 miles of the Tombigbee River that were not included in the project and have never been authorized by Congress. . . . In 1946, when Congress first authorized its construction, the corps cost estimate was $120 million. That estimate has already reached $1.8 billion, and before the waterway can be completed, probably in 1986, it seems certain to deplete public coffers by more than $2 billion. (Wayne King, *New York Times*, 1978, pp. 1, 32.)

This lengthy quote merely touches on the problems with the Tenn-Tom analysis, citing only the most blatant instances of manipulation. A more careful review of the analysis reveals consistent bias in favor of the project throughout. For example, the benefit–cost ratios reported, even today, are based on the extraordinarily unrealistic discount rate of 3.5 percent. Only members of Congress from Mississippi and Alabama or executives from the construction firms likely to win contracts are apt to believe that this rate reasonably reflects the opportunity cost of capital.

The many technical and conceptual ambiguities of benefit–cost analysis make manipulation almost inevitable. There are so many *judgment calls* in performing an analysis that it is hard to avoid some bias, particularly when the analysts are imbedded in an organization with an interest in seeing some projects go forward and others killed. While the impact of these judgment calls can be made explicit by the extensive use of sensitivity analysis, this is done far less often than one would hope. There are at least three reasons for this. First, it easily becomes too complex for almost anyone to understand, particularly top decision makers. Second, such analytic outputs are often viewed as wishy-washy because they make no definite recommendation. And third, such an analysis does work for opponents. The debate can immediately center on appropriate assumptions while a biased analysis promoting a project leaves opponents the task of discovering the biases and either attempting to discredit the analysis or attempting to provide a counteranalysis biased in the other direction.

The practice of manipulating analytic results is not exclusive to the Corps or the Tenn-Tom project.

Table 4.8 **BART Operating Revenues and Expenses (Fiscal Year 1975–1976)**

	millions of current dollars	
	1960 Composite Report	*Actual (Preliminary)*
Gross fare and concession revenue	$24.5	$23.7
Operating expenses	13.5	64.0
Net	$11.0 surplus	$40.3 deficit

Source: Webber, 1981, p. 424

Reluctantly, one is forced to conclude that the literature is unanimous in alleging that agency practices have the effect of inflating benefits or deflating costs, or both. Moreover, the differences between agency claims and the findings of independent reviewers are not small . . . economic evaluation, of course, is regularly used as a means of killing the more helplessly uneconomic projects . . . But having admitted this, one is still forced to conclude that one of the principal uses of benefit–cost analysis is to clothe politically desirable projects with the figleaf of economic respectability. (H. Marshall, in Kneese and Smith, 1966, p. 294.)

It is hard to devise procedures for doing analysis that eliminate the bias problem completely. As long as there are ambiguities (occasions for judgment) in the analytic technique, the analyses seek to inform political choices, and those performing or paying for the analyses have preferences on programs, some manipulation is inevitable. The danger in trying to locate responsibility for analysis in an independent agency that will not be involved in the construction or operation of a project—for example, the General Accounting Office instead of the Army Corps of Engineers—is that the analysts in the independent agency may not know enough about the substantive area to do sensible analysis. In consulting with the agencies that are substantively expert, analysts may still receive biased information. If they fail to consult, the analysis is apt to be inept and irrelevant. If they do enough independent research to become experts in their own right, the analytic enterprise will cost a fortune.

The last problem with benefit–cost analysis that we will mention here is incommensurable measures of consequences. Consequences are usually predicted in natural units. These units may be quite diverse—such as bushels of corn, kilowatt-hours of electricity, and recreation user-days for a hypothetical dam project. For comparison, it is often desirable to translate these diverse consequences into a common measure, usually dollars. Economists have developed an elaborate technology in cost–benefit analysis for pricing consequences. This technology is based primarily on how perfectly functioning markets would value the consequences; there is much use of "surrogate prices," analogies from private markets. This element is often a very major part of a cost–benefit analysis.

The difficulty in comparison and choice depends directly on what state the consequences are in from valuation. If the consequences are all in commensurate terms (e.g., all dollars) and consequences are treated deterministically, the criterion problem, finding a choice rule, can be fairly straightforward. If consequences are left in incommensurate terms (e.g., kilowatt-hours, bushels of corn, and dollars or the number of burglaries, the number of rapes, and the number of murders) and/or consequences are treated stochastically, the criterion problem can be much more complicated. There may be no explicit criterion that points to the best alternative. But finding a definite criterion is not a very serious practical problem for making benefit–cost analysis more useful. The analysis is not apt ever to become a sufficient decision procedure, and as long as the problems with single alternatives, predictive accuracy, and excluded values persist, worrying about the precise niceties of criteria is like "optimizing the arrangement of deck chairs on the Titanic rather than watching for icebergs."

One way of coping with the extreme difficulty of putting all consequences in commensurate terms is to do a cost–effectiveness analysis rather than a cost–benefit analysis.

COST–EFFECTIVENESS ANALYSIS

> There are never less than three conflicting criteria of merit. At best, operational research is nearly right.
>
> BLOGGINS' WORKING RULE #16

Cost–effectiveness analysis is very similar to benefit–cost analysis. The essential difference is that in cost–effectiveness analysis, the benefits are not put in units that are commensurable with the cost units. In benefit–cost, all costs and benefits are translated into dollars or utiles. In cost–effectiveness, benefits are expressed in natural units (e.g., bushels of wheat, lives saved, etc.) while costs are usually expressed in money terms.

Given the difficulty of valuing benefits for many public projects, cost–effectiveness is an important simplification of benefit–cost analysis. It enables the analyst to avoid valuing quantities such as deaths averted (lives saved) or the increase in the probability that a missile will survive a Soviet first strike, where any valuations are apt to be controversial with decision makers and other analysts.

Table 4.9 summarizes the results of cost–effectiveness analysis of alternative highway-safety control actions, with deaths averted as the chief benefit. Doubtless there are considerable uncertainties associated with the forecasts of both the "number of fatalities forestalled" and "cost," but given the extreme range in the cost–effectiveness measure ($500 per life saved from mandatory seat belt usage to $7,680,000 per life saved for roadway alignment and gradient), the figures can be off by a few hundred percent and still convey useful information for decision making.

Table 4.9 **Highway-Safety Control Actions Ranked in Order of Cost–Effectiveness***

Control Action	Number of Fatalities Forestalled	Cost (millions of dollars)	Cost per Fatality Forestalled (thousands of dollars)
Mandatory safety belt usage	89,000	45	0.5
Highway construction and maintenance practices	459	9	20
Upgrade bicycle and pedestrian safety curriculum offerings	649	13	20
Nationwide 55 mph speed limit	31,900	676	21
Driver improvement schools	2,470	53	21
Regulatory and warning signs	3,670	125	34
Guardrails	3,160	108	34

Table 4.9 (continued)

Control Action	Number of Fatalities Forestalled	Cost (millions of dollars)	Cost per Fatality Forestalled (thousands of dollars)
Pedestrian safety information and education	490	18	36
Skid resistance	3,740	158	42
Bridge rails and parapets	1,520	69	48
Wrong-way entry avoidance techniques	779	38	49
Driver improvement schools for young offenders	692	32	52
Motorcycle rider safety helmets	1,150	61	53
Motorcycle lights-on practice	65	5	80
Impact absorbing roadside safety devices	6,780	735	108
Breakaway sign and lighting supports	3,250	379	116
Selective traffic enforcement	7,560	1,010	133
Combined alcohol safety action countermeasures	13,000	2,130	164
Citizen assistance of crash victims	3,750	784	209
Median barriers	529	121	228
Pedestrian and bicycle visibility enhancement	1,440	332	230
Tire and braking system safety critical inspection—selective	4,591	1,150	251
Warning letters to problem drivers	182	50	283
Clear roadside recovery area	533	151	284
Upgrade education and training for beginning drivers	3,050	1,170	385
Intersection sight distance	468	196	420
Combined emergency medical countermeasures	8,000	4,300	538
Upgrade traffic signals and systems	3,400	2,080	610
Roadway lighting	759	710	936
Traffic channelization	645	1,080	1,680
Periodic motor vehicle inspection– current practice	1,840	3,890	2,120
Pavement markings and delineators	237	639	2,700
Selective access control for safety	1,300	3,790	2,910
Bridge widening	1,330	4,600	3,460
Railroad–highway grade crossing protection (automatic gates excluded)	276	974	3,530
Paved or stabilized shoulders	928	5,380	5,800
Roadway alignment and gradient	590	4,530	7,680

Source: The National Safety Needs Report, Department of Transportation, GPO, 1976.

*The above control actions include only those authorized by the Highway Safety Act. They do not include vehicle performance standards that are authorized under the Motor Safety Act.

The simplification of cost–benefit analysis in cost–effectiveness analysis is achieved at some expense. The analysis above, for example, does not tell us how much government should be willing to pay to avert a fatality. In the 1960s and 1970s, most valuations of human life employed a figure of about \$300,000 (Bick et al., 1979). With this value, a zero discount rate, and the (benefit/cost > 1) criterion, the control action of clearing roadside recovery areas (see Table 4.9) and the control actions above it, those with lower "cost per fatality forestalled" would be justified. Upgrading education and training for beginning drivers and all actions with higher costs per fatality forestalled would not be justified. With a more realistic discount rate, many fewer control actions would be justifiable.

Another conceptual problem with cost–effectiveness analysis is its inevitable tendency to focus on one or a very few benefits to the exclusion of all others. In the highway-safety example, one might also want to know what these control actions do to avert property damage and nonfatal injuries from accidents. Considering these other categories of benefit and calculating net benefits (or costs) might lead to a very different ranking than the one found on Table 4.9. For example, mandatory safety belt usage would probably reduce the severity of nonfatal injuries but do little or nothing to reduce property damage from accidents. On the other hand, the least cost–effective actions—such as bridge widening down to roadway alignment and gradient—would avert accidents altogether, thus reducing property damage, injuries, and loss of life. The least cost–effective actions also involve new construction, and if the programs were implemented to maximize the use of otherwise idle resources (personnel and materials), they might have significant secondary benefits in employing those resources. For example, the last few actions on Table 4.9 involve physical changes to roadways and are labor- and equipment-intensive. If unemployment is high among road workers and in the road-equipment manufacturing industry, and these workers would not be otherwise employed, it may be economically (and politically) justifiable to undertake some of these cost–effective projects. In a full cost–benefit framework, the rankings might be much closer or changed.

Cost–effectiveness analysis, then, is a simplification of cost–benefit analysis that is most useful when (1) benefits are much more easily specified than valued and (2) one category of benefit is the predominant effect of the alternatives being compared. The simplifications are accomplished at some cost.

EXPERIENCE WITH ANALYTICAL APPROACHES

> Experience is a dear teacher, but fools will learn at no other.
> POOR RICHARD'S ALMANAC

Analytical approaches to improving government and effectiveness are compelling. It is hard to object to a careful, calculating approach to important decisions on policies and programs. After all, how could such an approach possibly lead to worse decisions? Indeed, without analysis it is not even obvious how one would gauge the efficiency and effectiveness of governments' policies and programs. For government, there is no equivalent to the competitive pressure on business from "the market" that would induce efficiency and effectiveness or at least induce faith that existence (survival) is indicative of fitness. Analysis makes sense; better decisions should follow.

Yet, experience over the last 20 years with analytical approaches to improving government performance has been mixed at best. Certainly, the hope that many advocates of analysis held out in the early 1960s, that techniques like cost–benefit analysis would revolutionize government decision making, has not been realized. The enthusiasm that accompanied the introduction and initial development and applications of these techniques has largely evaporated. While there have surely been instances in which analysis led government to behave more efficiently and effectively than it would have without analysis, well-documented, well-analyzed success stories are distressingly hard to find.[30]

Most of the applications experience in government has been with cost–benefit analysis. Decision analysis has been applied, but much less frequently; and a significant proportion of the applications have been in defense areas, where the results are not widely publicized. Many of the applications of decision analysis in nondefense areas (e.g., airport siting and risk analysis of health and environmental decisions) are relatively recent. In addition, decision analysis has most often been applied to large, unique decision problems where evaluating the impact of the technique, which requires a model of how the decision would have been made without the technique, is very difficult.

There are two classes of problems that have hampered the effectiveness of analytical approaches. First, there are problems that arise from the feebleness of the analytical techniques vis-à-vis the problems. Second, there are problems that arise from the mismatch between analytical approaches to decision making and political and bureaucratic approaches.

FEEBLE METHODS AND FORMIDABLE PROBLEMS

> There is no virtue in not knowing what can be known.
>
> ALDOUS HUXLEY

The analytic techniques include no specific guidance to analysts on how to formulate decision problems or how to generate alternatives. Problem formulation is a very important element in decision making on matters about which very little is known either descriptively or prescriptively. The way in which a problem is represented—how you specify where you are now and where you want to be—often has profound implications for other elements in the decision process. Formulation determines to a large extent the alternatives considered. Obviously, the alternatives considered determine to some extent the quality of the alternative that will be chosen; it is not possible to choose a better alternative than the best in the set considered.

Consider a simple example of the importance of problem formulation. You are the manager of a city with serious automobile congestion on a two-lane bridge that connects the central business district with a major residential section. One way to formulate this problem is: "What is the most cost-effective means of moving x automobiles at y rate (an acceptable level of congestion) at peak commuting hours between the residential area and the central business district?" This formulation suggests alternatives such as widening an existing bridge or building another bridge or a tunnel. Other formulations—such as "How can we move commuters between origins and destinations at average rate z with standard deviation s most cost–effectively?"—suggest a much larger set of alternatives that include mass transportation or dispersing, through controls and incentives (e.g., zoning and relocation grants), the business locations currently in the central business district that are generating the demand for trips and contributing the congestion. In the 1980s, restricting the formulation to "moving automobiles" may seem stupid and the example unrealistic. But there are many examples of such narrow formulations from the 1940s and 1950s that led to solutions and that still contribute to congestion problems today. The decision techniques described in this chapter have almost nothing to say about how problems should be formulated, but their use can force explicit consideration of formulation.

An alternative is a course of action within control. The critical link between problem formulation and alternative generation was noted above; it is not possible to choose a better alternative than the best in the set that is considered. It is generally good advice to generate as many alternatives as possible, but it also helps to have an efficient, rational way of describing them or choosing among them without incurring enormous costs in predicting and valuing their consequences. Alternative generation is often the initial step in human problem solving and decision making. Someone makes a proposal that evokes counterproposals. Along the way, the group may even discover what problem it is that they are working on (and, incidentally, what their goals are). Generating alternatives is often a creative art.

The most common problem with alternatives in decision making is that there are too many of them and they are too costly to evaluate. Even seemingly simple problems become unmanageable. For example, assume you are a manager responsible for monitoring contracts in the Defense Department. You have 30 employees and 30 contracts. The employes have different strengths (efficiencies) in handling various kinds of contracts. How should you assign employees to contracts? Your first problem is that there are 30! ($30 \times 29 \times 28 \times 27 \ldots 2 \times 1$) ways of assigning employees. It would take you more than two years at one second per entry to merely write down the alternatives; much more to evaluate them. Finding good alternatives and discarding inferior ones cheaply is a central problem for prescriptive analytic approaches to decision making. The difficulty arises from the most common solution to the problem of too many alternatives. That solution is to pick, by the seat of your pants, one and only one alternative that will be developed and analyzed further. The only remaining competitor is the null alternative. There is little assurance that there are not better alternatives in the discarded set.

Analysis carries its own resource allocation problems with it. What problems and alternatives should be analyzed? With what techniques and with what intensity? The problems that stem from comparing a single alternative and the null alternative of doing nothing can be corrected simply by adding alternatives. Many of the problems of predictive inaccuracy can be solved by much more detailed planning of the alternative whose consequences are to be forecast; after careful engineering, the cost and benefit estimates for a dam project can be much more accurate than before. The snag is cost.

Analysis, particularly when it gets to the level of detailed architectural and engineering plans, is very time-consuming and expensive. In most instances, decision makers are reluctant, if not adamantly opposed, to incurring the costs of detailed planning for projects that may never be approved and built. If you analyze three alternatives for accomplishing the same objective, the costs of analyzing the two alternatives not selected are, for some, wasted. And usually as the planning becomes more and more detailed, the probability that the project will proceed increases; planning creates project constituencies. But without the data from detailed plans, decision makers have a poor basis for deciding which projects should be funded and which should be discarded. The ignorance problem is more serious when the knowledge missing requires basic scientific research. When the consequences depend on human behavior and there are no useful (accurate) models of behavior, it is not clear how to proceed. Do sensitivity analysis? Wait for the results of research costing many billions of dollars over the next 50 years?

Another important problem for the techniques discussed here is that they presume causal knowledge that often does not exist. The major contribution of the techniques with respect to causal knowledge is that they can sharpen conceptions of what information is relevant and what information is irrelevant. But finding out what you need to know is quite another and more difficult matter. The substantive theoretical knowledge required to make predictions to support decisions on government programs spans all of the physical, engineering, biological, and social sciences. The problems of predictive inaccuracy are perhaps most acute where human behavior is involved; the BART example given above is a case in point. The foibles of economists in predicting have become a sort of societal joke. Sadly, the other social and behavioral sciences rarely do better.

The purveyors of analysis have not grappled very well with the problem of predictive inaccuracy. As noted, economists devote enormous energies to valuing wildly inaccurate predictions of decision consequences. If the forecast of the increased bushels of corn that will result at the margin from a new dam is plus or minus 200 percent, there would seem to be little sense in employing exotic, complicated, expensive techniques to forecast the prices of bushels of corn; this is false precision of the worst kind. The only possible remedy for predictive inaccuracy is "basic research," research that improves our knowledge of how the world works. Of course, basic research comes with no guarantees: no one knows how to predict how much it will yield or what the ultimate limits are on our predictive capabilities.

One approach to improving analysis is to acknowledge the uncertainties explicitly and to design programs and projects so that they can be adapted as experience removes some of the uncertainty. Richard R. Nelson (1974, p. 386) has observed that "the strictures of the policy analysis tradition have been marked by a shifting of emphasis from before the fact analysis, to evaluation of programs *ex post*, to deliberate experimental developmental of policy." Each shift has been taken in response to experiential feedback, often negative, and reflects (1) a heightened appreciation of the formidable complexity of "real" policy problems vis-à-vis existing tools for policy analysis, (2) a reduction in the level of policy analysts' aspirations for impact on policy formulation processes where timing and magnitude of impact are key attributes of the aspiration level, and (3) a new focus of analytic attention (or "analytic strategy") in a continuing quest by policy analysts for a substantive role in policy formulation. These shifts in "scripture" have taken us from the euphoric pursuit of planning, programming, and budget systems (PPBS) in the 1960s to the carefully qualified program "experiments" of the 1970s. Each shift in emphasis has resulted in an analytic strategy that relies less than its predecessor on the existence of "usable" theories of behavioral processes—theories on how individuals and organizations do behave that can be systematically used to forecast responses to alternative program designs.

The extreme difficulty of providing accurate forecasts, particularly when the variables of interest are the outputs of behavioral systems, is a persuasive explanation for the shift from "before-the-fact analysis" to "evaluation of programs ex post." Program evaluation is not a single technique but a host of techniques that can be used in ex post (after the fact) appraisals of programs. The hope here is that by appraising the efficiency and effectiveness of programs after they have been in place for a while, the analysis will show ways to improve. The techniques discussed in this chapter can and have been used to evaluate programs, but statistics as a discipline is understandably more important to evaluation than all of the techniques belonging primarily to economics and operations research. Statistical techniques are much more general and flexible and come without questionable descriptive theoretical baggage. Of course, analysis is not necessarily easier in an ex post mode than in an ex ante (before-the-fact) mode. In place of predictions, ex post analyses must produce and use "counterfactuals" (i.e., projections of what the world would have been like without the program or with another program). Counterfactuals require analysts to do virtually everything they do in prediction; indeed, the same models (and theories) can be used for both tasks. The big difference between a forecast and a counterfactual is that an ornery politician or analyst can later check the forecast against some reality, while they can only argue about the assumptions and logic behind the counterfactual; counterfactuals are safer than forecasts for analysts.

The techniques discussed in this chapter assume forecasts but give analysts no real help in producing accurate forecasts. At best, the techniques sharpen notions about what forecasts are needed. Indeed, the analysts, usually operations researchers and economists, often lack the substantive background necessary to do the forecasting. Who the correct people are to do the forecasting depends on the alternatives being analyzed, but they are almost always substantive experts. For a dam project you may want an electrical engineer to forecast the hydroelectric power that will be produced; a hydrologist to project impacts on water supply; an agronomist to forecast the impact of increased water supply on crop yields; a commodities trader or an agricultural economist to forecast the value of changes in crop yields; and a recreation expert familiar with the area to forecast, in consultation with an ichthyologist and a psychiatrist, the recreational usages of the reservoir; and so on. Given prevailing human ignorance about such causal matters, it may be best to employ sets of such experts and use composite forecasts.

When the analysis requires, as it often does, forecasts of human behavior, the lack of causal knowledge (i.e., good theories of how the world works for forecasting) poses extreme problems. There are no good theories for predicting what increases in water supply or supply stability will occur from a large-scale dam project and what these will do to crop yields; the theories for predicting how human beings will price those yields or how they will react to a 55 m.p.h. speed limit are much worse.

All the techniques discussed here share another important common problem: where to get the numbers required to proceed with the analysis. Many variables such as those in the discussion of the benefits of sidewalks, above, are hard to conceptualize and much harder to measure and use. Implausible measures destroy the credibility of analytic work.

Values, objectives, and goals pose a number of serious problems for analysis. Part of the problem is that there are too many of them for analysis to handle comfortably. A related problem with goals is that analysis assumes that decision makers have them in a developed, useful form, when they usually don't. Analysis that assists decision makers in discovering goals is almost always more useful than analysis that assumes goals exist and presents conclusions based on the assumption. Governments and their constituent parts have interests that diverge to some extent from any particular visions of the "general welfare," like the one that underlies most cost–benefit analysis.

One popular fantasy is the belief that making applied analyses more "scientific" (and therefore objective) would lead to better decisions. While science may strive for objectivity, most scientists and knowledgeable commentators agree that the struggle is not won and not even winnable. If it is hard to sustain objectivity in the laboratory, it is impossible in political arenas.

THE MISMATCH BETWEEN ANALYSIS AND POLITICS

> When you have no basis for an argument, abuse the plaintiff.
> MARCUS TULLIUS CICERO

There are fundamental incompatibilities between analytical approaches to decision making and political decision making: (1) there are incentives to bias analyses, (2) analysis is orderly where politics is messy, and (3) there are weak incentives to do analysis and to follow the dictates of analysis when it is done.

Analytical approaches confront a dilemma. If the analyses are done by individuals or agencies with no regular standing in the decision processes, the analyses are apt to be "objective" but ignored or discredited by affected agencies who, for whatever reasons, disagree with the analytic conclusions. If, on the other hand, the analyses are done by agencies with regular standing in the decision processes, there are great pressures to manipulate the analyses so that they support predetermined positions.

> The water development agencies cannot survive without projects; and to have projects they must have favorable benefit–cost ratios for the simple reason that neither Congress nor the public would tolerate projects that were openly admitted to be economically inefficient. In producing favorable ratios for the politically desired projects, the employee knows that he is loyally serving not only his agency but the Congress and perhaps the President as well. (Marshall, 1966, p. 302.)

The number and complexity of the assumptions required to proceed on even a trivial cost–benefit problem, like the local flood control example given earlier, are truly impressive. It is easy to manipulate the assumptions. The bias problems have been most pronounced with cost–benefit analyses, but perhaps this is just because this is the technique with which there is the most experience.

One major difficulty with analytic approaches to improving government efficiency and effectiveness is that they greatly overestimate the orderliness possible in government decision making.[31] The analytic approaches to decision making seriously underestimate the difficulty in adopting a rational, contemplative style in the chaotic, often frenzied world of government. George Kennan's farm metaphor for planning in the State Department is descriptive of the lives of many government (and business) officials:

> I have a largish farm in Pennsylvania . . . . The farm includes two hundred thirty-five acres, and a number of buildings. On every one of those acres, I have discovered, things are constantly happening. Weeds are growing. Gullies are forming. Fences are falling down. Paint is fading. Wood is rotting. Insects are burrowing. Nothing seems to be standing still. The days . . . pass in a . . . succession of alarms and excursions. Here a bridge is collapsing. No sooner do you start to repair it than a neighbor comes to complain about a hedgerow which you haven't kept up—a half-mile away on the other side of the farm. At that very moment your daughter arrives to tell you that someone left the gate to the hog pasture open and the hogs are out. On the way to the hog pasture you discover that the beagle hound is happily liquidating one of the children's pet kittens. In burying the kitten you look up and notice that a whole section of the barn roof has been blown off, and needs instant repair. Someone shouts pitifully from the bathroom window that the pump must have busted—there's no water in the house. At that moment a truck arrives with five tons of stone for the lane. And as you stand helplessly there, wondering which of these crises to attend to first, you notice the farmer's little boy standing silently before you with that maddening smile that is halfway to a leer, and when you ask him what's up, he says triumphantly, "the bull's busted out and he's eating the strawberry bed." (Quoted in Hammond, 1978, pp. 22–23.)

The press of events is overwhelming. Decision occasions are ambiguous, beyond control, or both. Problems do not stay "solved" and decisions do not stay "made" in environments like governments, where control is distributed widely and the information premises for decisions are changing constantly. Analysis requires time (attention) and money not otherwise obligated; these are scarce resources.

There is a vicious cycle in an environment where "nothing seems to be standing still." Because of the press of problems, you resort with increasing frequency to stopgap solutions. These solutions ensure that the problems will recur with increasing frequency and increasing severity. The recurring problems increase the necessity of stopgap solutions. And so on. This is an administrative entropy that analytic approaches, at least as commonly applied, seem unable to stem.[32]

Governments shift their focus of attention constantly. This week in the U.S. federal government the most important topic for congressmen and executive officials is "the new federalism" and the size of the projected deficit. Next week the topic may be arms for El Salvador, the invasion of Grenada, aid for higher education, affirmative-action politics, or sanctions against the Soviet Union for its latest transgressions. Governments can focus on only a few issues/decisions at a time, which is why some of the most important decisions in government are about which issues to focus on at any particular time. When an issue is on the floor, government and the attending public have an enormous thirst for information about the issue, including formal analysis (as long as it is boiled down to one of two sentences that they can understand). The day after a decision has been made or attention has shifted for other reasons, even the best, path-breaking analysis will be ignored by everyone. Timing is almost everything. Decision makers are reluctant to reopen issues because there are so many other issues active and in the queue.

Many of the issues that capture governments' attention are not amenable to analysis. Issues that capture attention because of their moral, ethical, or prurient content are examples. The issues that are most amenable to analysis, particularly aspects of operations (e.g., the inventory policies of supply agencies), hold no political interest at all unless there is a scandal. Inefficiency in mundane government operations is hardly scandalous; it is expected. But money and incentives to change are tied to political attention. There is an enormous mismatch between political attention and where the opportunities for efficiency improvements are; the flamboyant issues have the attention and the mundane issues have the potential for large dollar savings in efficiency improvements.

Much more money is at stake during one week in the inventory decisions of the General Services Administration or in the Government Printing Office decisions about what they should print and what could be contracted at lower cost than is at stake in an entire year in all of the newsworthy "inefficiencies," such as a congressman hiring a female secretary for something other than typing or unnecessary congressional junkets on military airplanes or cabinet officers using chauffeured limousines. But inventory and printing costs are usually not newsworthy. The public interest, at least as reflected in the media's selective attention to issues, imposes a curious and very imperfect discipline on governments. There are few strong incentives to be efficient (or disincentives to be inefficient). But there are very strong disincentives to corrupt and immoral behavior. The congressman who is sniffing cocaine at a private party, even at home, is in much more political jeopardy than one who has a hand in wasting billions of dollars in a sincere, stupid way.

The upshot is that there are, at best, weak incentives to do analysis on the problems where analysis can potentially be most useful; and when analysis is done, there are often few incentives to do what the results indicate would maximize efficiency. We will have much more to say in the concluding chapter about how to deal with the weak incentives to be efficient in government.

There are fundamental incompatibilities between producers and consumers of analysis. Three sources of incompatibility are time (and timing), money, and language. Political decision processes need analyses before decisions are made, but there is enormous uncertainty about when decisions will be made. Until decision makers are attending to a particular issue and see a decision coming, they feel no need for analysis and consequently are unwilling to initiate and fund research. The situation is slightly better in federal agencies with analytic staffs and research budgets. But these staffs are, of necessity, highly responsive to the White House and Congress; on a moment's notice, they will turn all of their analytic resources to preparing congressional testimony or other forms of "quick and dirty analysis" to satisfy short-term pressures. In state and local governments the pressures are the same, but there are often fewer analytic resources.

Good research requires time, money, and periodic attention from decision makers during its preparation. A complex decision analysis or cost-benefit analysis may take a team of analysts several months to several years to complete. There are few examples of such sustained research efforts in nondefense areas. The usual mode is quick and dirty research in a few weeks or, at most, a few months. The real problem with this mode of analysis is that the knowledge base is so meager in the social and management sciences that quick and dirty research is just that. The research is apt to be superficial, adding nothing to the knowledge base and of questionable utility to decision makers.

A distressingly common use of research is to delay decisions. Although decision makers are more interested in timing than anything substantive the research might yield, this policy might result in slow, clean research relevant to some agendas. Unfortunately when the "further-study ploy" is used, the charge is usually given to a blue-ribbon panel, an interagency task force, or some other group without the resources to do the analysis intelligently and usefully.

The languages of analysis, mathematics, and jargons peculiar to techniques are not the languages of political and bureaucratic decision processes. Politicians and high-level bureaucrats who have the greatest voice in policy and program decisions are not selected for their analytic skills or familiarity with the languages of analysis. Given limits on their time and background, decision makers will not understand moderately complex materials. They will, in most cases, read the executive summary, perhaps ask their staffs to provide slightly more detailed critical summaries, set up hearings for analysts who disagree on the issue, and the like. Because they cannot work through the arguments behind the executive summary, they are apt to learn very little from the research, particularly if the summary is more recommendation than rationale. The probability that analysis will prompt them to think more deeply about an issue or change their mind is very low. Hence, most analysis will not lead easily and directly to improved efficiency and effectiveness.

Even if an analysis for a particular government decision is technically perfect, predictively accurate, and government officials heed the analysis and act accordingly, the outcome may not be improved performance. There is an important distinction between "decisions" and "outcomes." In a stochastic world, one can make a good decision and experience a bad outcome or make a bad decision and experience a good outcome. A trivial example can illustrate this important and simple but often overlooked point. Consider a coin-flip game in which you win $1 if the coin turns heads and you lose 50 cents if it turns tails. You must pay 20 cents to play and you can play only once. The coin is fair (i.e., there is equal probability of heads or tails). Should you play? If you can stand to lose 50 cents, the expected monetary value (EMV) is 25 cents.[33] If you played many times, you would expect to win 25 cents on average. The right decision is probably to play. You then throw a tail and lose 70 cents. You have made a good decision and experienced a bad outcome. In another game where you lose $1 for a head and win 50 cents for a tail and the promoter pays you 20 cents to play, the EMV is −5 cents. If you were to play, throw a tail, and win 70 cents, you would have made a bad decision and experienced a good outcome.

While we know of no systematic empirical evidence, casual observation strongly suggests that the distinction between the quality of decisions and the quality of outcomes has enormous significance in real organizations. There is a much lower ability in government and business to discriminate good from bad decisions than to discriminate between good and bad outcomes. Indeed, there is little ability to discriminate between decisions and outcomes; it happens that fools are promoted and competent individuals penalized and everyone in large organizations is more risk-averse than optimal.

A decision is a plan, a cognitive commitment to a course of action. But outcomes depend both on the plan and the implementation of the plan—the set of activities, cognitive and physical, that execute the plan. In the simple coin-flip example, the plan was to play, the implementation was the coin flip, and the outcome was the resulting face of the coin and associated payoff. In the example, because you could not control the result of the flip, the decision (plan) was much more important than the implementation to the outcome. In less trivial circumstances like a government water project, implementation is often much more important to the outcome than the initial decision (plan). Unless implementation is viewed as a sequence of increasingly specific decisions, the analytic techniques have nothing to contribute to implementation.

The bottom line is that decision makers in the public sector have almost no incentive to make decisions in accordance with the canons of rationality behind the various analytic techniques; indeed, the case is better for strong disincentives. First, as with benefit–cost analysis, the probable distributional effects dominate the probable allocative efficiency effects for politicians. It is hard to think of program decisions that do not have differential effects either geographically or by income grouping. Analysis that shows that a proposed change will result in large collective efficiency benefits at the expense of a particular political constituency will not be very persuasive to the politicians tied to that constituency. Second, there are a variety of constraints—such as guarantees of due process and publicness—on public sector decisionmaking that are often at odds with the canons of rationality. For example, it is hard to do the collectively efficient thing when you have to send notices to the adversely affected groups and hold public hearings inviting organized special-interest opposition to a disorganized, diffused collective interest.

The next chapter, "Rationalizing Decision Systems: Marching by the Letters," looks at several serious attempts to institutionalize analysis and to rationalize entire decision processes, particularly budget decisions. Given the problems in analyzing even one decision well, it is easy to anticipate the results of attempts to make thousands of decisions analytically year in and year out.

But before turning to these ambitious analytic systems, let us end on a more sanguine note about the prospects for improving efficiency and effectiveness through analysis. Governments are rife with problems that are amenable to analysis. For improving performance, some of the most solvable problems with the greatest potential for efficiency savings are often the least controversial and newsworthy. They are the problems of inventory, routing, purchasing systems, scheduling, and personnel allocation. They are recurring issues of low political salience. They are issues for which a variety of useful analytic techniques exist, primarily in operations research and statistics. These issues should be analyzed and reanalyzed on a periodic basis. Analysis is not likely to work efficiency miracles, but it is a necessary step toward improvements.

Since the analyses will require skills that are not widely available in government and because of the ever present dangers of self-serving biases, it will probably take special organizational arrangements to do the analytic work well. Existing employees, for reasons of ability or of organizational position, are not adequate to do the analyses. Because of the specialized skills required, the intermittent demand that any particular functional agency has for such skills, and the threat of bias, it does not make any sense to employ significant numbers of such analysts in each functional agency. An independent agency that serves as a consultant to the rest of government makes more sense. The Congressional Budget Office (CBO) and the General Accounting Office (GAO) have most of the required independence and have demonstrated the capacity for doing excellent analyses. These agencies are not, however, adequately staffed and funded to function as effective in-house analytic consultants and as clearinghouses for hiring and supervising external consultants. It would make a lot of sense to (1) maintain analytic groups in GAO, CBO and other similar organizations with responsibility for classes of procedures and decisions across the government and (2) provide the management of these groups with stable funding to be used to contract with private-sector analysts for some of the work. The approach is not entirely novel. The Bureau of the Budget until the 1960s had effective subgroups performing much of the internal consulting role that we are recommending here.[34]

NOTES

1. One could write a long, very boring, largely useless book that would attempt to bring semantic clarity to the labels of fields and techniques in the general area of analysis.

We will not waste time here trying to decide which techniques belong to economic analysis, statistics, operations research, and systems analysis. In practice, the labeling does not much matter; the best analysts from all of these interrelated fields use whichever techniques are appropriate to the problem at hand; the worst analysts apply their technique, often inappropriately, to any problem that arises.

2. One very good elementary reference on decision analysis is Raiffa (1968). A very good intermediate-to-advanced reference is Keeney and Raiffa (1976).

3. Usually because there are some circumstances when it may be more important to ensure that some minimum payoff is obtained rather than assuming more risk in quest of greater payoffs. The expected value of A_i is equal to $[V(\theta_{11})P1 + V(\theta_{12})P2 + V(\theta_{13})P3$

4. This tree is not labeled with the usual conventions. Usually the terminal nodes (extreme right) would have the value of each branch. That information and the calculations are provided in the text.

5. Four miles $= 21,120$ feet.

6. The null or do-nothing alternative is always available and should usually be evaluated in real problems because it is often best.

7. The reader should note that these problems are not peculiar to the public sector but are relevant to applications of decision analysis in the private sector as well.

8. "Elicitation" implies that the analyst is drawing out entities, probabilities, and preferences that the decision makers have in coherent form. There is an important line of psychological research indicating that people do not have coherent probabilities and preferences and that decision analysts are creating as much as eliciting. See Kahneman et al., 1982.

9. We are indebted to Kenneth R. MacCrimmon for this letter.

10. Property value in an area can change in a number of ways and, for real problems, it is often necessary to forecast changes due to further developments, appreciation of property, etc. Also, it is unusual to find a real problem in which upstream and downstream effects can be completely ignored even if these other areas are the responsibility of other drain commissions. New upstream development may increase runoff and hence flow in the problem area. This can change the nature of the problem.

11. It is always necessary to omit costs and benefits in the primary analysis because all benefits and costs cannot be measured and given a dollar value sensibly. However, competent benefit–cost analysis includes explicit consideration of such "intangibles" in side calculations (i.e., data are provided but not used in computing a benefit–cost ratio or net present value), leaving the task of imputing value to them to the decision maker.

12. Flooding is always a function of a more complex set of factors than the intensity of a storm or snow melt. This is, however, a simplification often employed by hydrologists in planning projects.

13. The information required here is a "probability density function" for the occurrence of flood conditions of varying levels of severity. For the simple example:

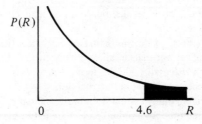

where R is inches of rainfall in a 24-hour period and $P(R)$ is the probability of occurrence. The area under the curve is 1. The hatched area in the diagram is the probability of occurrence in any one year (.02 in this example) of a storm as intense or more intense than one of an intensity expected only once in 50 years.

14. In real problems, the extent of flood damage does vary with the severity of flood conditions. The relationship might be:

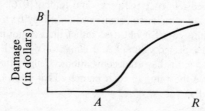

where R is the severity of flood conditions, A is the "level of full protection," and B is the upper limit on the amount of damage that might occur (always something less than total value).

15. Projects will usually have different useful lives and benefits and costs may vary with the age of a project. For example, many surface drains require periodic cleaning; their flow capacity is greatest immediately after cleaning and least right before cleaning.

16. This is an obvious simplification, but perhaps not an important one. The probabilities are small and recovery from flooding is not immediate.

17. The alternative of "doing nothing" is always available, as is the alternative of "generating more alternatives for consideration." In the event that all project alternatives (A, B, and C) detract from economic welfare, the "do nothing" and "plan further" alternatives should be considered.

18. There is an extensive literature on discount rates for public projects. One good reference is William J. Baumol, "On the Discount Rate for Public Projects" in *Public Expenditures and Policy Analysis*, edited by R. H. Haveman and Julius Margolis (Chicago, Markham, 1971), pp. 273–290. To simplify calculations $r = 0$ is assumed here; this assumption is discussed below.

19. Ratio criteria are, however, sometimes useful when benefits and costs are not expressed in the same terms. In such cases, ratios can be used to express the cost per unit of benefit or benefit per unit of cost. This is cost–effectiveness analysis, which will be discussed below.

20. Inflation complicates this somewhat. (See Gramlich, 1981, p. 94).

21. Projects are independent when they are directed at different objectives and the cost and benefits of projects are not interdependent. Capital rationing is simply "the existence of constraints (operative) on what one can finance . . . . the existence of a limited 'budget.' "

22. For example, the hydrologist might have to choose between different storm frequency curves (e.g., the Corps of Engineers and Brater and Sherrill). This choice may or may not be important to the analytic results, but to use a single curve as "right" is misleading in that it implies certainty.

23. Externalities are the effects of decisions that do not affect (i.e., no costs or benefits result) the decision maker but that do affect others. In the example, increased downstream pollution is an externality for the local agency. From a regional or national perspective, these effects would not be externalities.

24. It is hard even to imagine direct comparisons at the margin of public and private projects. If the resources required for a public project are left in the private sector as uncol-

lected taxes or a deficit increment not experienced, the resources are diffused throughout the private sector of households and firms and not associated with particular, comparable private projects.

25. This is, of course, the Kaldor-Hicks criterion of allocative efficiency, discussed in Chapter 1.

26. See Weisbrod, Burton A. "Income Redistribution Effects and Benefit-Cost Analysis," in S. B. Chase Jr., Editor, *Problems in Public Expenditure Analysis* (Washington, D.C.: The Brookings Institution, 1968).

27. Two other important but more complicated rules about what to count involve the correction of market prices to reflect social values (e.g., valuing the cost of using unemployed labor at less than its market or budget cost).

28. Ignoring other costs (e.g., a new facility to handle the doubled force) and other benefits (e.g., impact of increased patrol on other crimes and on the sense of community security).

29. The latter involves trying to put a price on goods (like travel time and human life) that are not priced in the market. Or it may involve adjusting a market price like that of steel produced by a monopoly supplier or by subsidized producers, where the price is believed to represent the goods' "true value" inaccurately.

30. There are at least two possible reasons for the scarcity of such success stories. First, there are few successes. Second, demonstrating success analytically is hard to do, and the best analysts are preoccupied with doing the original analysis, not in evaluating analyses.

31. Indeed, the problems with analytic approaches are common to most large organizations, public or private.

32. The chaotic issue environment is not strictly the province of government. Business executives, when forced to explain large differences between the list of their current problems in terms of importance with data on how they spend their time, have remarked, "I don't have time to work on my most important problems." (Pounds, *The Process of Problem Finding.*)

33. $EMV = .5(1.00) - .5(.50) - .20 = .25.$

34. See Schick, 1970, for an excellent discussion of the rise and fall of such groups.

REFERENCES

Baumol, William J. "On the Discount Rate for Public Projects." In *Public Expenditures and Policy Analysis*, edited by R. H. Haveman and Julius Margolis. Chicago: Markham, 1971, pp. 273–290.

Bradford, David F., and Feiveson, Herbert A. "Benefits and Costs, Winners and Losers," Chapter 4 in H. A. Feiveson, S. W. Linden, and R. H. Socolow (eds.), *Boundaries of Analysis: An Inquiry into the Tocks Island Dam Controversy.* Cambridge, Mass.: Ballinger Publishing Co., 1976, pp. 125–158.

Browne, William P. *Politics, Programs and Bureaucrats.* Port Washington, N.Y.: National University Publications, Kennikat Press, 1980.

Contini, Bruno, "A Critical Survey of Use of Cost-Benefit Analysis in Public Finance," Chapter 4 in *Quantitative Analysis in Public Finance.* New York: Praeger, 1969.

Federal Register 38 (September 1973) No. 174.

Gramlich, Edward M. *Benefit-Cost Analysis of Government Programs.* Englewood Cliffs, N.J.: Prentice-Hall, 1981.

Hammond, Kenneth R. *Judgment and Decision in Public Policy Formation.* Colorado: Westview Press, 1978.

Kahneman, Daniel, Slovic, Paul, and Tversky, Amos. *Judgment Under Uncertainty: Heuristics and Biases.* Cambridge, England: Cambridge University Press, 1982.

Keeney, Ralph, and Raiffa, Howard. *Decisions with Multiple Objectives: Preferences and Value Tradeoffs.* New York: Wiley, 1976.

King, Wayne. "Documents Indicate Corps Misled Congress on Major Southern Canal." *New York Times,* November 26, 1978, pp. 1 and 32.

Marshall, Hubert. "Politics and Efficiency in Water Development." In *Water Research,* edited by A. V. Kneese and S. C. Smith. Baltimore: The Johns Hopkins University Press, 1966, pp. 294 and 302.

Merewitz, Leonard, and Sosnick, Stephen H. "A Critique of Planning-Programming-Budgeting and Benefit-Cost Analysis." In *The Budget's New Clothes,* edited by Julius Margolis and Aaron Wildavsky. Chicago: Markham, 1971.

Mishan, E. J., *Cost-Benefit Analysis: An Informal Introduction,* Third Edition. London: George Allen and Unwin, 1982.

The National Safety Needs Report, Department of Transportation, GPO, 1976.

Nelson, Richard R. "Intellectualizing about the Moon-Ghetto Metaphor: A Study of the Current Malaise of Rational Analysis of Social Problems." *Policy Sciences* 5 (1974): 376–414.

Novick, David, *Program Budgeting: Program Analysis and the Federal Budget.* Cambridge, Mass.: Harvard University Press 1951, p. 51.

Pounds, William. "The Process of Problem Finding." *Industrial Management Review* 11(1969): 1–9.

Raiffa, Howard. *Decision Analysis: Introductory Lectures on Choices Under Uncertainty.* Reading, Mass.: Addison-Wesley, 1968.

Schick, Allen. "The Budget Bureau That Was: Thoughts on the Rise, Decline, and Future of a Presidential Agency." *Law and Contemporary Problems,* Summer 1970, pp. 519–539.

Webber, Melvin M. "The Bart Experience—What Have We Learned?" *The Public Interest,* Vol. 45, Fall 1976, pp. 79–108.

CHAPTER 5

Rationalizing Decision Systems: Marching by the Letters

The working of great institutions is mainly the result of a vast mass of routine, petty malice, self-interest, carelessness, and sheer mistake. Only a residual fraction is thought.

GEORGE SANTAYANA

One way to speed the widespread adoption of analysis in government decision making is simply to require that agencies employ a technique like benefit–cost analysis as part of the justification for major new programs and capital projects. This was the strategy adopted by the Army Corps of Engineers, and some judged it to have been fairly successful. However, for the most enthusiastic proponents of the rational approach to decision making, this strategy had two drawbacks. First, because past decisions were not reviewed, it implicitly supported the status quo. Inefficient programs and practices already in place could continue virtually forever regardless of whether funds could better be spent elsewhere. Second, the focus of this approach was within agencies. While it might lead an individual agency to spend its money optimally, it didn't guarantee that resources would be optimally allocated across agencies. To ensure this, benefit–cost analysis would have to be applied simultaneously to the spending programs of different agencies, with the results determining how much money should be devoted, for example, to health versus transportation versus crime control.

At the federal level, sophisticated advocates of the new decision-making techniques decided that the best way to both hasten adoption and dramatically broaden the realm of application was to work for the formal incorporation of analysis into the budgetary process. If agencies were made to realize that the size of their budgets would be a function of the quality of the analysis used to justify proposed expenditures, they would quickly adopt the new analytic methods. Self-interest would demand it. All that was required was to redesign the budgetary process so that the role of scientific analysis would be greatly increased at the expense of more parochial political concerns. Now, almost twenty years after the first efforts to accomplish such a reform began, we can confidently say that it is more easily said than done.

THE EVOLUTION OF BUDGETARY REFORMS

Adde parvum parvo magnus acervus erit. (Add little to little and
there will be a big pile.)

OVID

Budgeting as we know it is a twentieth-century phenomenon. Until about 1910,
the president, governors, and mayors did not prepare formal budget documents.
As Leonard D. White, one of the most prominent public administration scholars
of the first half of the twentieth century, noted, "A consistent balanced financial
program was unknown, the proper relation of expenditures to revenue was relegated to the background, and deficits were as common as mosquitoes in New Jersey" (White, 1948, pp. 259–260).

What distinguished the earliest budgeting from what we know today was a lack
of planning. The most primitive budgeting procedure, largely pre-Civil War, was
the "tax levy" in which "the apportioning of money to various departments was
done by city council in granting periodic contracts and permitting bills from
month to month" (Schiesl, p. 89). This was truly a pay-as-you-go system with no
pretensions to plans and forecasts. The legislatures approved expenditures and levied taxes throughout the year. There was no "budget."

A slight improvement was the "tax levy preceded by detailed estimates." Under
this procedure, the expenditure estimates were prepared to estimate the total tax
level required. Councils and departments were not bound by the expenditure estimates. This procedure, largely voluntary, introduced some planning but virtually
no control into the allocation process.

The next stage in the evolution toward the modern executive budget was the
"tax levy with detailed appropriations" (Schiesl, p. 89). Departments prepared detailed requests for spending and submitted these to the legislature. In spite of its
many defects, this procedure was a major improvement over the straight tax levy
system. Most tax was levied once a year and there were, for the first time, records
of how money was spent. The detailed appropriation estimates forced detailed
planning. Ironically, the detail was the problem. With binding appropriations at
the level of individual positions and specific quantities of materials and supplies,
the legislature (council or commission) was thrust into the day-to-day management
of city business in approving appropriation changes. Since many councils were
dominated by the "machines" of political parties, appropriations were subject to
the same abuses (e.g., padding of payrolls, partisan contracts, etc.) that originally
precipitated the reforms. Also, there was no forced coordination; appropriations
were piecemeal and changed constantly.

The solution was an organizational one: the executive budget.

> The essence of the great change which has been introduced in fiscal methods since
> 1910 (in the national government since 1921) is the grant to the chief executive of
> authority to control both the budget estimates and to some extent the use of the funds
> subsequently appropriated by the legislative body. Coordination, supervision, and con-

trol of finance are gradually replacing the unregulated and chaotic freedom of the various administrative agencies to deal directly with appropriations committees.

The immediate result has been a marked improvement in the care with which estimates are prepared for legislative consideration. A secondary consequence has been to amplify the administrative authority of the chief executive. Inevitably he who controls finance is in command so far as expediency and policy may dictate. The fiscal aspects of administrative reorganization form one of the principal bases on which the new leadership in administration rests (White, 1948, p. 259).

Of course, the reforms were not as simple as granting budget authority to presidents, governors, mayors, and city managers. More than a move to chief executives, the reforms were a move away from legislators. There were many variations of the reforms, including the creation of elected and appointed comptrollers and the formation of boards of estimate, many of which exist to this day as inefficient anachronisms.

So the early budget reforms were primarily directed at gaining an elementary level of control over government finances. Once the basic reforms were in place, reformers turned to more sophisticated strategies of improving efficiency and effectiveness. In 1907, The New York Bureau of Municipal Research recommended that the conventional "line-item" budget format that was based on objects of expenditures (personnel, equipment, etc.) be expanded to include classifications of expenditures by function and by work program.

> Classification by function—such as health, education, and law enforcement— would assist in setting the nature and level of programs and would provide data for the evaluation of results. Functional classification emphasizes "what" is to be done. Classification by work programs—furnishing data by organizational unit and type of activity in order to assist managerial control—would give detailed schedules of activities upon which work measurement programs and productivity improvements could be based. Work program classification emphasizes "how" activities are to be carried out. (Schultze, 1968, p. 9.)

In 1912, the Commission on Economy and Efficiency appointed by President Howard Taft recommended that the federal government adopt a budget reporting format designed along the lines of that recommended by the New York City agency. It argued that the present line-item format not only obscured important relationships between spending categories but, by insisting that funds be spent only on those items for which they were appropriated, eliminated important flexibility needed by executives to deal with unanticipated contingencies. Responding to these suggestions, Taft submitted an executive budget request in which expenditures were classified by function, agency, and type of activity, with extensive cross-references. Unfortunately Taft's successors were less convinced by the Commission's argument; after he left office the budget was once again submitted using the old line-item format.

The Budget and Accounting Act of 1921 created a Bureau of the Budget (BOB) in the Treasury Department, but did nothing to shift the emphasis away from the accounting and control perspective embodied in the traditional line-item budget. Throughout the 1920s, statements made by the directors of this fledgling agency reflected a preoccupation with what Charles Schultze has aptly dubbed "paper-clip efficiency."

> I want to say here again that the Budget Bureau keeps humble, and if it ever becomes obsessed with the idea that it has any work except to save money and improve efficiency in routine business it will cease to be useful in the hands of the President. Again I say, we have nothing to do with policy.
>
> Investigation by a representative of the department of which the bureau was a part disclosed loss or theft of towels by the hundred, while more than 500 soiled towels were discovered tucked away in desks, file cases, and closets. The simple and obvious requirement that an employee turn in a soiled towel in order to secure a clean one was immediately put into effect. In this same bureau there was great consumption of soap. Five barrels of Government soap were located in the home of one of the bureau employees and three barrels in the home of another. These industrious soap collectors are no longer in the Federal service . . . . In this bureau was discovered the enterprising employee with the elastic conscience who made from Government rubber bands a 10-pound ball as a plaything for his dog. He has now ample time for playing with the ball himself.
>
> The General Supply Committee here in Washington fell heir to seven barrels of spoiled, soused seal shoulders shipped from Alaska. They were unfit for consumption. The obvious course, and the course that would have been followed a few years ago, would be to throw them away. We have today, however, in the Federal service frugal minded people who have a heart for the taxpayer. One of these conservators found a market for the shoulders. They were sold for crab bait, yielding the Government $20. (Schultze, 1968, pp. 10–11.)

With the arrival of the Depression and Roosevelt's decision to commit the resources of the federal government to the task of softening its effects, BOB gradually shifted from the control orientation toward what Schultze describes as a more managerial approach. As government expenditures tripled from $2.6 billion in 1929 to $8.9 billion in 1939 and the number of new government agencies and programs grew proportionately, there was no way that a single central agency could keep up with all of the soiled towels, rubber bands, soused seal shoulders, and bits of string. Day-to-day auditing and fiscal control tasks had to be decentralized. At the same time, the vastly expanded bureaucracy required to administer the federal government's economic and relief programs threatened to run out of control. If the president were to manage this growing number of agencies and programs in the same sense that a corporation president manages a firm, it was clear he would need help.

In 1937, the President's Committee on Administrative Management, also known as the Brownlow Commission, issued a report criticizing BOB's excessive attention to routine accounting details. It urged the agency to aggressively assume a major role in coordinating agency activities under presidential leadership. Partly as a result, BOB was moved out of the Treasury Department in 1939 and shifted to the recently formed Executive Office of the President. From the beginning, it was clear that new responsibilities had come with the new location. Executive Order 8248 directed BOB to

> . . . keep the President informed of the progress of activities by agencies of the Government with respect to work proposed, work actually initiated, and work completed,

together with the relative time of work between the several agencies of the Government; all to the end that the work programs of the several agencies of the executive branch of the Government may be coordinated and that the monies appropriated by the Congress may be expended in the most economical manner possible to prevent overlapping and duplication of effort. (Schick, 1970, p. 37.)

All of the pressures created by the federal government's active role in coping with the Depression were dramatically intensified by the outbreak of World War II. The threefold increase in expenditures that had taken place between 1929 and 1939 was nothing compared to the almost tenfold increase that would take place in the next five years. Coordinating the war effort became the number-one priority at the White House, and BOB found itself ideally located to assume a major role. Paper-clip efficiency was pushed still further into the background; the managerial orientation had arrived to stay.

In the years immediately following World War II, the attention of reformers was directed toward making the budgetary process more efficient from a managerial standpoint. Now that the commitment had been made to use BOB and the budgetary process as instruments of managerial control, it remained to ensure that they operated as efficiently as possible. One obvious target for reformers was the formal structure of the budget. Despite the fact that the control orientation had been superseded both in spirit and in the mandate given BOB by the president, the budget was still structured as if the objects of expenditure were the principal concern. To bring the structure of the budget more into consonance with the new management orientation, the first Hoover Commission issued a report in 1949 calling for the adoption of what it called performance budgeting.

> We recommend that the whole budgetary concept of the Federal government should be refashioned by the adoption of a budget based upon functions, activities, and projects, this we designate a performance budget. Such an approach would focus attention upon the general character and relative importance of the work to be done, or upon the service to be rendered, rather than upon the things to be acquired, such as personal services, supplies, equipment, and so on. These latter objects are, after all, only the means to an end. The all important thing in budgeting is the work or the service to be accomplished, and what that work or service will cost. (Commission of the Organization of the Executive Board, 1949, p. 8.)

The performance budget was structured around the activities performed by government, rather than inputs, and was designed to help administrators evaluate the work efficiency of operating units. Budget categories were cast in functional terms and work-cost measurements were included so that policymakers could judge how efficiently tasks were being performed. If the Postal Service were to shift from a line-item budget to a performance budget, the major categories might change from personnel, equipment, capital projects, etc., to mail pickup, mail processing, mail delivery, and similar activities. Within each of these activity categories, efficiency data would be presented: number of letters sorted per employee-hour or cost of delivery per package.

Two underlying assumptions of performance budgeting were that efficiency would quickly become a major focus of policymakers' attention and that variation in agency efficiency was a simple function of agency effort. Yet, there were problems with both asumptions. For most agencies the political and technical difficulties connected with formulating a single index of productivity or efficiency were overwhelming. As a result, legislators in the House and the Senate who were interested in efficiency and productivity in the abstract found themselves having to cope with a seemingly endless number of pages filled with detailed performance figures. From a policymaking standpoint, what were they to make of the fact that the cost per residential mail delivery rose 8 cents during the past year or that the average number of pieces of mail sorted by an employee rose from 247 to 253 per hour? These figures might be useful for supervisors and executives within the Postal Service, but they meant little to the average congressman who had neither the time nor the inclination to become an expert in such matters.

Agency bureaucrats also had reason to dislike performance measures. From their point of view, the measures threatened to make the agency vulnerable to criticism for poor productivity regardless of whether or not the agency was actually at fault. How could a legislature be made to realize that the cost per delivery had risen because of increased maintenance costs, bad weather, and the continued growth of suburbs (where the cost per household delivery is higher than in the more densely populated urban areas), not because of poor management? In the minds of many agency professionals, the chances that the political decision process (or the press, for that matter) would use performance information in an intelligent, constructive fashion were almost zero.

There were additional problems. Putting together a performance budget could be a tedious and time-consuming process, especially in agencies that did not routinely gather the necessary data or regularly employ economists and statisticians. Some agencies found it difficult to quantify their goals in such a way that work-load statistics and productivity figures were meaningful. There was also the issue of bias. It was one thing to develop a few simple work-load statistics; it was often quite another to choose a set of performance measures that accurately reflected the agency's priorities and the full scope of its mission. The prospect that the performance of a multimission agency such as the Forest Service might be gauged by the examination of only two or three measures—because they were the only ones for which data were available—was a constant source of concern. Finally, there were the powerful forces of inertia and habit. Even if there had been no technical and political problems, performance budgets still represented a sharp departure from past practices. Asking a congressman who had been in office for ten or twenty years to stop thinking in terms of the old budget categories and embrace a new system was asking a lot.

For all these reasons, the management orientation that had come to dominate the budgetary process never dramatically altered the structure of the budget itself. While some progress was made in reducing the total number of appropriations necessary to implement the budget from 2,000 in 1940 to 375 in 1955, the basic object of expenditure format remained intact (Schultze, 1968, p. 13).

Somewhat ironically, even as the movement to performance budgeting had begun to fizzle, the intellectual foundations for a far more ambitious reorientation of the budgetary process were being laid within the RAND Corporation and the Department of Defense. The RAND Corporation had evolved out of "Project

RAND," originally created in 1946 to bring together former wartime operations analysts to advise the Air Force about research, development, and planning. If the task of planning expensive new weapons systems within the constraints of a peace-time economy was to be taken seriously, it was felt that analysts would have to adopt a systematic perspective in which the strategies and tactics of the individual military services were carefully integrated and in which the benefits of defense expenditures vis-à-vis those for civilian programs were thoroughly analyzed. The achievement of either objective would constitute a major reform of current policy-making methods and necessitate a fundamental reorientation of the budgetary process away from control and management and toward planning.

As currently structured, the budgetary process not only failed to foster an integrated defense policy among the services but actively discouraged it. Although legislation in the late 1940s and early 1950s made major advances toward centralizing control of the military under the secretary of defense, the budgetary process provided incentives for each service to go its separate way. BOB acting for the president would establish an overall budget ceiling for the Defense Department and the individual services would proceed to scramble to get the largest possible share. According to Charles Hitch, former chief economist at RAND, the results were precisely what anyone could have predicted:

1. Each service tended to exercise its own priorities: a. favoring its own unique mission to the detriment of joint missions; b. striving to lay the groundwork for an increased phase of the budget in future years by concentrating on alluring new weapon systems; and c. protecting the overall size of its own forces even at the cost of readiness. . . .
2. Because attention was focused on only the next fiscal year, the service had every incentive to propose large numbers of "new starts," the full cost dimensions of which would only become apparent in subsequent years . . . . (Lazarus, 1970, p. 361.)

The budgetary process provided the services not only with an incentive to pursue separate strategies, but also with ample opportunity. Despite the organizational reforms that had taken place, the secretaries of defense had neither the staff nor, it seemed at times, the inclination to integrate military planning with their budget requests. The Joint Chiefs of Staff (JCS) were (and are) a committee prone to logrolling solutions to budgeting. Although JCS has a chairman, the position has no particular staff or power. As a result, the budgets sent to Congress and the president were little more than a loose aggregation of three separate service budgets organized by line item. This structure made overlapping expenditures, conflicting priorities, inefficiency, and just plain "padding" inevitable and all but impossible to detect.

Furthermore, the responsibility for ensuring that long-term objectives such as continental defense and the creation of a survivable offensive capability would be met—even the responsibility for defining those objectives—was being laid entirely in the hands of three uncoordinated services. Alain C. Enthoven, another strong proponent of budget planning, offered this assessment of the situation:

[The pre-1961 system] had several important defects, perhaps the most important of which was the almost complete separation between planning and decision-making on weapon systems and forces, on the one hand, and budgeting on the other . . . In

other words, the long-range plans for weapon systems, forces, and all of their supporting elements were made by the Services on the basis of their estimates of the forces
required to assure our national security. Generally speaking, costs were not introduced
systematically, either to test the feasibility of the whole program or for the purposes of
evaluating the efficiency of the allocation.

Budgeting, on the other hand, had as its point of departure the guideline dollar
totals laid down by the Administration and based on estimates of the burden the economy could or should bear. The result was a gap. The "required forces" always cost
much more than the Administration and the Congress were willing to pay. The process
by which the conflicting interests were resolved was unsystematic and wasteful because
it led to unbalanced programs.

Moreover, cost data were presented and financial management was conducted at
the Defense Department level on a year-at-a-time basis. The full time-phased costs of
the proposed forces were not presented to the Secretary of Defense. Because the costs
of most programs are small in their first years, this led to the starting of many programs
that could not be completed at anything like existing levels. Although a certain amount
of this is a desirable hedge against uncertainty, it is clear that there were a great many
wasteful stretch-outs and cancellations of programs that would not have been started if
the costs of all of the approved programs had been anticipated. (Novick, 1965, p. 85.)

The solution that the RAND analysts recommended was the institution of what
they called program budgeting. As early as 1954, RAND had suggested that the
Air Force begin employing a function-oriented budget that classified expenditures
within the four major mission areas: strategic, tactical, defense, and transportation.
In each of these areas, major weapon systems and system support packages were
to be designated so that the relationship between a given input and its mission or
objective would be clear. A major feature of the program budget was to be an
elaborate analysis of different alternatives and the tradeoffs that existed between
them.

The RAND analysts believed that programmed budgeting could also bring a
measure of order to the tasks of planning and formulating appropriation requests
in the Defense Department as a whole. Instead of simply lumping the requests of
the various services together or treating each service separately, a programmed
budget would reveal the interrelationship of different service projects designed to
achieve a common mission. Under strategic weapons, for example, we would find
appropriation requests for the Navy's Polaris submarine and the Air Force's Titan
missile together with extended analyses of their capabilities and costs. If there was
overlap between the two systems such that increasing the size of one made increasing the size of the other unnecessary, or if one system was significantly more efficient than the other, this would emerge from a close examination of the budget.

RAND's persuasive arguments excited the interest of Kennedy's Secretary of
Defense Robert McNamara, who ordered that a program budgeting system be implemented under the supervision of former RAND analyst and then Assistant Secretary of Defense Charles Hitch. Hitch assumed office in 1961 and initially envisioned that the introduction of the new system would take place over a period of
several years. However, the managerial and technically oriented McNamara was
eager to begin. He wanted the system installed quickly enough for it to have a
visible impact on the FY1963 defense budget. This left Hitch with slightly more

than a year to set up a planning-programming-budgeting system (PPBS) that would contain five major elements:

1. A program structure in terms of missions, forces, and weapon and support systems. 2. The analytical comparisons of alternatives. 3. A continually up-dated five-year force structure and financial program. 4. Related year-round decision-making on new programs and changes. 5. Progress reporting to test the validity and administration of the plan. (Novick, 1965, p. 89.)

According to Alain Enthoven and Wayne Smith, two analysts who held positions in both RAND and the Defense Department during the years when the PPBS was being developed and refined, there were six basic ideas that motivated the experiment. First, and most important, there was the desire to develop explicit criteria that could be used to assess national defense needs and evaluate the adequacy of existing programs. It was recognized that this task would not be easy and that the criteria initially developed would be crude. Nonetheless, it was felt that only through the existence of such criteria could debate about national defense policy assume a rational character. It was impossible to reach an intelligent decision about the development of a new missile if U.S. objectives with respect to nuclear parity, deterrence, and retaliatory capability remained ambiguous and uncertain. If critics were unsatisfied with the criteria that were developed, it would be up to them to suggest better ones.

A second basic idea revolved around the explicit consideration of alternatives at the top decision level. "Given the nature of the issues involved, the huge costs, the judgments that must be made, and the uncertainties inherent in any defense program decision, it is not enough for the Secretary of Defense to consider only a single staff solution, no matter how well-reasoned it may be" (Enthoven and Smith, 1970, p. 486). If strategic weapons systems were being evaluated, the secretary of defense, the president, and other political leaders should be presented with a range of alternatives that included land- versus sea-based launching, different size missiles and payloads, and so forth. In retrospect, this innovation might seem to be no more than common sense. But if Enthoven and Smith are to be believed, the presentation of realistic alternatives to the secretary by the services had been the exception rather than the rule.

A third idea consisted of evaluating needs and costs together. In a world with unlimited resources, every military mission and weapons system that is deemed valuable can be implemented. In a world in which agency budgets are finite and there are competing claims for scarce funds, cost becomes an important determinant of the value of a project or goal. Thus a technically effective, antiballistic missile system, in spite of its praiseworthy objective, may not be worth developing at the present time simply because it would be too expensive. Prior to the implementation of PPBS, there had been a tendency to suspend discussion of cost considerations on the grounds that the life-and-death character of defense issues placed them above such narrow considerations. From an analytic point of view, this attitude was an exercise in self-delusion. Dollars that are spent on one life-and-death mission cannot be spent on another. If each dollar is not spent as effectively as possible, the result will be a less effective total program.

A fourth major idea of PPBS was the commitment to financial planning. We have seen that a drawback of present practices was that the long-term cost implications of key policy decisions were often obscure, sometimes made intentionally so by the services that wanted to conceal the size of the commitment that they were requesting. It was felt that the best way to remedy this situation was to insist that the cost implications of proposed projects and policies be spelled out in detail for a period of at least five years. This would force the comparison of needs and costs into a larger context. "If a decision-maker insists on seeing costs over a period of years, proponents of new programs find it harder to conceal the future cost implication of decisions made today, and thereby drive the 'thin edge of the budget wedge' into the program" (Enthoven and Smith, 1970, p. 489). It was also hoped that financial planning would help prevent some of the embarrassing coordination problems that periodically arose under the existing system.

> At that time there was an almost complete gap between force planning, which was long range, expressed in terms of combat units and performed mainly by military planners in the Joint Staff and the services; and financial planning, which was short range, expressed in terms of objects of expenditure, and performed mainly by civilians in the Comptroller organization. Given this situation, it is not surprising that there were serious imbalances in the defense posture—divisions without equipment and ammunition or the airlift to move them, aircraft without spare parts, and so on. (Enthoven and Smith, 1970, p. 489.)

A fifth idea basic to PPBS was that analysis and analytic staff must play a major role in directing budgetary choices. No one expected political considerations to become irrelevant or that the secretary of defense would begin delegating critical policy decisions to junior-level systems engineers, but there was a commitment to seeing that analysis was meaningfully integrated into the decision-making process. Virtually all of those involved in designing PPBS had been closely connected with the development of techniques such as benefit–cost analysis and cost–effectiveness analysis, and they were all too aware of the fact that these analyses were often filed away, unread, to gather dust in a cabinet. PPBS was designed to put an end to this by integrating analysis into every step of fiscal decision making and into the budget documents themselves. Top policymakers would be automatically exposed to serious analysis every time they picked up a budget request. Within the Department of Defense itself, a key policymaking role for the analytic perspective would be assured by creating a Systems Analysis Office reporting directly to the secretary.

The final idea embodied in PPBS was that analysis should be open and explicit:

> That is, each analysis should be made available to all interested parties so that they can see what assumptions were used and so they can retrace the steps leading to the conclusions. Open and explicit analysis is our best protection against persistence in error and against reaching conclusions on the basis of hidden or rigged assumptions. It also helps to build confidence in the results of an analysis. All calculations, assumptions, empirical data, and judgments should be described in an analysis in such a way that they can be checked, tested, debated, discussed, and possibly refuted. Adversary proceedings are the best stimulant to analytical progress. More importantly, analyses

should be tested, checked, and debated by all interested parties. Analyses should not be believed simply because they are analyses. It is the method—not the authority—of analysis that is important. (Enthoven and Smith, 1970, p. 450.)

Thus PPBS would set the ground rules for policy debates. Every voice would be heard if it were willing and able to abandon the language of emotional rhetoric and debate the issues in terms of realistic alternative, needs and costs, and a time horizon that went beyond the present year.

PPBS GOES PUBLIC: GREAT EXPECTATIONS

> One may solve one's problems not only by getting what one wants
> but also by wanting what one gets.
>
> RALPH BARTON PERRY

On August 25, 1965, President Johnson directed that all major civilian agencies begin using PPBS. It would, he believed, assist the government to:

1. Identify our national goals with precision and on a continuing basis.
2. Choose among those goals the ones that are most urgent.
3. Search for alternative means of reaching those goals most effectively at the least cost.
4. Inform ourselves not merely on next year's costs but on the second, and third, and subsequent years' cost of programs.
5. Measure the performance of our programs to ensure a dollar's worth of service for each dollar spent.

Clearly a grand experiment was about to begin. It is difficult in retrospect to appreciate fully the expectations that were held for PPBS, but Johnson's faith was typical. There were those who expected PPBS to revolutionize budgeting to the same extent that the transistor had revolutionized electronics or that computers were expected to revolutionize industry. Consider the scope of the following questions that Senator William Proxmire believed could be dealt with by the incorporation of more policy analysis into the budgetary process:

> What, for example, are the real national security costs of removing Southeast Asia from the primary defense perimeter and what are the budgetary savings from its removal? On the basis of very little evidence and information, I am inclined to say that the costs of removing Southeast Asia may well exceed the value of the budgetary savings that we would experience. However, I cannot make a rational decision on this matter, nor can my colleagues in the Congress, unless we have the best analysis available on the costs and gains of such a policy alternative.
>
> What are the total costs of eliminating a nuclear carrier force with all of its required support from our existing 15-carrier complex? What would be the loss in national security? How much elementary and secondary education could we purchase for the dollar cost of the new carrier? (Proxmire, 1970, p. 417.)

Part of the reason why the expectations for PPBS were so high was that the need for something like it was so great. All of the problems that PPBS was designed to help solve in the Defense Department were present in civilian agencies and the combined tasks of trying to manage, plan, and coordinate their activities constantly threatened to overwhelm both the executive branch and Congress. If there was ambiguity and uncertainty with respect to appropriate priorities within the Defense Department, it was nothing compared to that which existed between different civilian programs such as Head Start, antitrust, health care for elderly, and educational loans, or between civilian programs and defense programs. What was the relative value of the manned space program and oil depletion allowances? Should the federal government increase its support of mass transit systems or devote the money to new job training programs? What emphasis should be placed on direct military aid versus general foreign assistance? The questions were endless and the answers that were produced in the normal course of events by the unstable collaboration of the president and Congress often seemed excessively arbitrary and politically motivated.

Basic information about the goals and objectives of current programs and the amount of funds being spent in their pursuit was as difficult to obtain on the domestic side as it was for defense. It was a problem for BOB staff and elected officials to extract from each service's appropriation request the amount of funds being devoted to strategic weapons systems, but an equal amount of effort was needed to discover how many programs and how much money was being spent on the poor or on children's services. Ten or fifteen different federal agencies and literally hundreds of separate appropriations might be involved. Politicians and voters alike were becoming hopelessly confused about what they were getting as well as about what they wanted.

The same lack of knowledge about the long-term implications of present decisions that caused problems in the Defense Department also plagued the domestic side. A large water or power project could tie up funds for as long as a new weapons system and be just as burdened with unanticipated cost overruns. Even more dramatic were the long-term implications of decisions to establish new entitlement programs, such as veteran's pensions and national health insurance. These could tie up funds for decades to come and dramatically reduce future options in other areas. Many believed that such programs had already placed most of the funds in agencies like the Department of Health, Education, and Welfare outside the control of the secretary and President. It began to appear that it made no difference which political party controlled Congress and the White House—all of the important appropriations decisions had already been made.

Integrating evaluation into the domestic policymaking process was no less critical than it was in defense. Benefit–cost studies were just as likely to be ignored in civilian agencies, and there was a considerably lower probability that they would be commissioned in the first place. Dozens of ineffective programs were re-funded every year, while more promising alternatives languished in congressional committees for want of convincing evidence that corroborated what their advocates claimed. Inertia had become the hallmark of the budgetary process and PPBS promised change.

The basic components of the federalwide system were similar to what they had been in defense. Each agency had to develop a *program structure* composed of a series of objective-oriented categories that would encompass the total activity of the agency. It was anticipated—indeed, it was deemed desirable—that the program structure would not reflect an agency's organizational structure. Program categories were to cut across departmental boundaries in order to promote greater coordination and facilitate the discovery of service gaps or overlap. Thus it was suggested that the Forest Service, for example, could structure its budget according to timber production, outdoor recreation, water, and similar output-oriented categories—which had little to do with the internal organization of the service but summarized the actual mission of that agency. The general categories were then to be further broken down according to the same principles into program subcategories and program elements to permit even more detailed analysis.

The *program and financial plan* (PFP) was another key element. Its purpose, in BOB's language, was to translate "concretely specified agency objectives into combinations of agency activities and operations designed to reach such objectives in each of the stated time periods." In less formal terms, it was a plan that laid out what an agency intended to accomplish, how much each objective was going to cost, and when it would be attained. For most agencies, it was thought that the appropriate time horizon should be five years. It was felt that five years was a realistic compromise between the limited ability of agencies to forecast the future accurately and the length of time required by top policymakers to gain the perspective necessary for planning. A particularly critical feature of the PFP was its focus on quantitative descriptions of agency objectives, since these data would permit policymakers to see precisely what the agency expected to accomplish with the dollars requested. BOB's instructions to the agencies suggest what it expected:

> Express objectives and planned accomplishments, wherever possible, in quantitative non-financial terms. For example, physical description of program elements might include the additional capacity (in terms of numbers to be accommodated) of recreational facilities to be built in national forests, the number of youths to be trained in the Job Corps camps along with measures of the kinds of and intensity of training, the number of hours of Spanish language broadcasts on the Voice of America, the number of children to receive pre-school training, and the number of patients in federally-supported mental hospitals. In some programs, it may not be possible to obtain or develop adequate measures in quantitative physical terms such as these but it is important to do so wherever feasible. In any case, objectives and performance should be described in as specific and concrete terms as possible. (Bureau of the Budget, 1970, p. 411.)

Related to both the program structure and the PFPs was another element called the *program memorandum* (PM). This was to be a document that summarized the agency's policies within each program category and justified them. Agency objectives and their relationship to the needs of the American people in this area were to be described and various strategies—including those not adopted—designed to achieve those objectives were to be discussed in terms of their benefits and costs. It was hoped that this would provide a policymaker outside the agency with a thorough understanding of why the agency had chosen to pursue any given objective, what strategy it had selected to achieve it, and why alternative objectives and strategies had been rejected.

Two additional documents that played a significant role in the PPB system were *issue letters and special analytical studies*. Issue letters were simply directives from the head of BOB to agencies that defined major policy areas in which the administration was particularly interested. The agencies' task was then to develop program categories in a way that was responsive to these executive office priorities. Special analytical studies were just what the name implies: in-depth analyses of a particular project or problem. These were to serve as the basis for the program memoranda (PMs) and would ideally be commissioned months in advance of when the PMs were due.

Did this complicated apparatus transform the nature of budgetary decision making at the federal level? Did narrow self-interest and political rhetoric yield to rational calculation? The answer is no. In terms of the grandeur of its aspirations and the expectations it created, PPBS was something of a bust. It did not come close to recasting federal budgeting from "a repetitive process for financing permanent bureaucracies into an instrument for deciding the purposes and programs of government" (Schick, 1977, p. 556).

Interviews with several hundred officials in more than 30 agencies indicated that PPB's contribution to altering the basic character of the budgetary process was negligible (Wildavsky, 1979, p. 194). For the most part, agencies continued to plan, evaluate programs, and request funds in the same way that they had before PPBS came along. Even in the Defense Department, it appears that PPBS had only a limited impact. It brought no significant change in allocation patterns between the services and did not reduce the dominant role that the size of last year's appropriation played in determining the size of this year's budget. Expenditures were as incremental and bound to the past under the Johnson administration and PPBS as they had been under the Eisenhower and Truman administrations. The final admission that the grand experiment had failed came in June 1971, when the term "PPBS" was omitted from OMB requests for agency budget submission.

Perhaps the best way to appreciate the true character of PPBS's decline and fall is to consider the fate of the five components of the system, described above, as they were actually implemented. Up to this point we described them only in the abstract, as designers of PPBS hoped they would look. All too often, however, things do not work out as planned in the effort to reform government. Program structure is a good example. In the abstract, it appears to be an excellent organizing device that could enable agency bureaucrats and elected officials to coordinate programs, highlight objectives, reveal potential tradeoffs, and relate objectives to appropriations. The fact that agency officials might not be able to fit their programs into a single meaningful structure, that the selection of any particular structure might be disturbingly arbitrary, or that officials might not want to permit BOB and Congress the opportunity to alter its basic spending patterns tended to go unnoticed until the system was implemented. Agencies often solved the first and third problems simultaneously by creating program categories that were so ambiguous and vague that any activity could fit comfortably under any heading. Officials in the Department of Agriculture were the acknowledged masters of this strategy and worked with such flexible (if uninformative) categories as "Communities of Tomorrow," "Science in the Service of Man," and "Expanding Dimensions for Living" (Wildavsky, 1979, p. 203). Using such categories, they could place activities wherever they pleased and direct the attention of reviewing authorities away from sensitive issues involving overlap and controversial priorities that might catch their attention if a different program structure were used.

Actually, creating a program structure proved difficult even for officials who were more committed to the concept of program budgeting. In large part this was due to multiple and overlapping agency goals:

> Two of [the family planning program's] most significant outputs are a reduction in poverty and a reduction in infant mortality. Family planning reduces poverty by decreasing family size, thus decreasing the amount of income required to maintain a family at some specified minimum level of well-being. It reduces infant mortality by decreasing the number of children born to older women or to women with a large number of children. (The infant mortality rate for both these classes of women is several times higher than average.) Given these two outputs—and they are both substantial—one would have to ask where to put the family planning program if the program objectives were specified purely in terms of these ultimate outputs of reducing infant mortality and reducing poverty. (Seidman 1978, p. 346.)

> A first glance suggests that space projects are ideally suited for program budgeting because they are physical systems designed to accomplish different missions. Actually, there is a remarkable degree of interdependence between different missions and objectives—pride, scientific research, space exploration, military exploration and uses, etc.—so that it is difficult to apportion costs properly. Consider the problem of a rocket developed for one mission and useful for others. To apportion costs to each new mission is purely arbitrary; to allocate the cost to the first mission and regard the rocket as free for all subsequent missions is ludicrous. Making a separate program out of the rocket itself does violence to the concept of programs as end products. (Wildavsky, 1979, p. 188.)

Because planning was such a critical part of PPBS, the experience with the PFPs was particularly disappointing. When agencies were asked for figures about how much they would be spending and how much they planned to accomplish in the upcoming five-year period, they tended to submit wildly exaggerated estimates of both. Clearly they were responding with a description of the resources they would like to have in hopes that they could convince BOB to divert a great proportion of future funds in their direction. This practice tended, as one former BOB official noted, to make the entire exercise almost useless. BOB tried to get around this problem by restricting the content of the PFP to only those appropriations to which the government was committed by virtue of past or present decisions, but this change accomplished little. Each agency interpreted the term "commitment" differently, and BOB was left with the impossible task of reconciling the results.

PMs were of uneven quality. Most contained bits of useful information, but few came up to the standards that proponents of PPBS had imagined. Almost invariably some critical component of the PM was omitted or sloppily executed: realistic alternatives to the policies suggested by the agency were not discussed, policies were not analyzed in terms of specific objectives, future commitments were glossed over. Furthermore, agencies evidenced an understandable but frustrating tendency to argue their case with qualitative rhetoric rather than with facts and figures.

> Many of the PM's tend to be descriptive, verbose, non-analytic accounts of existing and proposed programs, together with impassioned pleas for funding at the full request. This is not very helpful in making resource allocation decisions, since it is difficult to know if an "urgent necessity" is more important than a "dire national need," a "must expenditure," or a "vital responsibility." (Carlson, 1970, p. 377.)

The special analytical studies are generally considered to have been the most successful part of PPBS, at least in the sense that they increased the amount of quantitative analysis conducted by federal agencies. While the conduct of these analyses did not usually result in any major shifts in agency priorities or program strategies, they did occasionally perform an important educational function. Inevitably, however, the benefits of the studies were restricted by the limitations of the analytic techniques described in the last chapter and by the absence of agency personnel trained to employ the analytic methods intelligently.

Issue letters, the mechanism by which the interests of BOB were to be introduced into the analytic programs of the agencies, also had their problems. One was timing. It often took BOB so long to get its priorities straight that issue letters were not sent to the agencies until well into the budget cycle. This left the agencies with insufficient time to develop competent responses before their budget requests were due and often meant that the issues raised could not be addressed in requests. In addition, agencies resented the implicit movement toward centralization that the issue letters represented. Career bureaucrats were protective of their privilege to define key problems and issues, and they valued the freedom to experiment with different policies outside the constant scrutiny of BOB and elected officials. Finally, limited numbers of trained personnel were again a problem. Many agencies simply did not have the manpower to respond to a series of issue letters that required fresh analysis.

PPBS: A POSTMORTEM

> Is it progress if a cannibal uses a knife and fork?
>   STANISLAW J. LEE

This brief account of the problems that plagued the formal components of PPBS is sufficient to provide an understanding of how the system failed. The more interesting question of *why* it failed remains.

Aaron Wildavsky, an early, eloquent critic of PPBS and other "rational" budgeting schemes, has conducted an elaborate autopsy of PPBS that has come to be accepted as correct by most political scientists. To begin with, Wildavsky argues that the preconditions that made the move to PPBS in the Defense Department at least appear to be reasonable were absent in much of the rest of the federal government. DOD possessed a large cadre of talented personnel who had spent years applying advanced analytic techniques to defense problems. As we have seen from the experiences connected with issue letters and special analytical studies, other agencies were not so fortunate. While it was possible for an agency like the State Department or HEW to hire away some of the Defense or RAND analysts, they could never hire enough to meet all their demands, and those they did hire possessed little knowledge of the substantive problems and peculiarities of the context in which they now had to work. Although sensitive to the subtle bureaucratic and political issues that existed in the defense field, it was difficult for them to become anything other than narrow technical consultants when relocated.

Wildavsky points out that top officials in the Defense Department understood the technical aspects of PPBS and were committed to its success. Neither was the case in many civilian agencies. For defense officials, PPBS had slowly emerged as a custom-made response to a real and well-established demand; for most civilian officials it burst upon the scene as an unexpected imposition. Civilian agency executives were predictably resistant, even disoriented by the new system. Allen Schick, a perceptive scholar of the budgetary process who shares many of Wildavsky's views, explains the failure of PPBS to achieve the same prestige in civilian agencies as it had in the Defense Department this way:

> The main problem was that unlike McNamara, whose initiative enabled him to forge his own PPB system, civilian department heads were ordered to graft an alien, standardized system onto their regular budget processes. In formulating a government-wide PPB system, the Bureau of the Budget gave little consideration to the preferences or problems of individual departments. It adopted the Defense system, including most of its procedures and terminology, and directed the civilian departments to fall in line. From the vantage point of departments, PPB was something manufactured by and for the use of the Budget Bureau. The departments did not have an opportunity to design their own systems or procedures, nor were they able to relate PPB to established budgetary practices. In fact, several departments were compelled to abandon or revamp analytic efforts and budget improvements launched prior to the introduction of PPB. (Schick, 1977, p. 559.)

Because they were unfamiliar with the language of the new system and skeptical about the relevance of the techniques it represented, civilian agencies tended to isolate the reporting and analytical apparatus of PPBS from key decision-making tasks. Decisions about appropriations requests and internal allocations were first made in the traditional manner and then "translated" into PPBS terms by lower-level bureaucrats. The fact that BOB continued to require that agencies submit a conventional line-item budget only served to reinforce the tendency of civilian agency executives to treat PPBS as a bureaucratic obstacle course rather than as an integral part of the budgetary process.

What might be described as the "analytic environment" was also different in the Defense Department and civilian agencies. Often, the goals of civilian programs were simultaneously more amorphous and more numerous than those of defense programs. This made it difficult to define program objectives so that achievement could be estimated quantitatively and made it expensive to carry out benefit–cost analyses. In fact, because the cost of civilian programs was usually much less than those in defense, there were those who questioned whether the prospective benefits of analysis were worth the cost. Spending $200,000 to analyze alternative strategies for a program that costs only $1.5 million might well be a waste of money. Another difference involved the quality of the alternatives that were being evaluated. For a given mission of the Defense Department, there were usually a variety of alternative technologies or weapons systems that were worthy of serious consideration. Analysis was frequently necessary to discriminate among them. In civilian agencies, realistic alternatives to current polices had often not been developed. While there was an active technological research establishment generating alternative weapons systems and battlefield procedures, there was no such research establishment generating ingenious new ways of eliminating unemployment, reducing crime, or slowing the rise in health care costs.

Wildavsky also argues that it was easier to implement the results of analysis in the Defense Department. There, the object of analysis was usually a new program or weapon system, whereas analysis in civilian agencies was more likely to be directed at proposed increases to a program already in place. New programs are somewhat less likely to have developed a large, entrenched constituency of interest groups ready to contest the results of any analysis threatening their domains. Wildavsky believes that implementation was made easier in the Defense Department by a tradition of centralized control that was often lacking in civilian agencies. While it was true that the Defense Department often had problems convincing the individual services to accept its leadership, there was at least an accepted hierarchy of control within those services. In civilian agencies, the lines of authority were often more blurred; it was not unusual for the character of programs to be determined as much by consensus as by mandate. This was particularly true when different levels of government were involved in the management of a program—a situation that never arose in the Defense Department but was commonplace in agencies like HEW, where state and local governments were often involved in service delivery.

If all of PPBS's problems arose from an insensitivity to these differences between the Defense Department and other agencies, much of it could probably have been salvaged. Analysts could be trained, executives sympathetic to its basic premises could be placed in positions of power, and implementation could be delayed in less technically oriented agencies. Yet Wildavsky passionately believes that PPBS is fundamentally flawed by a defect so serious that it could never work even in the most benign environment. PPBS is, he contends, politically irrational. This irrationality exists at two distinct levels. First, PPBS naively (and perniciously from Wildavsky's point of view) seeks to alter the basic relationships between Congress, the president, interest groups, and voters by assuming (1) that agency objectives are determined outside the political process and (2) that economic rationality is the only relevant criterion for evaluating the worth of a particular project. Yet a traditional aspect of our political system is that means as well as ends are influenced by what policies various political actors can agree upon and that political benefits and costs play as essential a role in determining the basis for that consensus as do economic benefits and costs (Wildavsky, 1979, p. 193).

> . . . there is no simple division of labor in which the "politicians" achieve consensus on . . . objectives while the "analysts" design and evaluate—from efficiency and effectiveness criteria—alternative means of achieving those objectives . . . choice of means, particularly among domestic programs, is almost equally as freighted with political values as is the choice of ends. (Charles Schultze, 1968, pp. 2–3.)

To displace the role of politics by an exclusive reliance on the criterion of economic efficiency threatens to undermine the role of political institutions, something that Congress in particular was not anxious to have happen. Little wonder then that congressional hostility proved to be a critical stumbling block for PPBS. Anxious to preserve the policymaking authority of committees and subcommittees, Congress continued to insist that the budget be presented in the conventional format that embodied that committee structure. This is why BOB was forced to order that agencies prepare two different budgets, a request that encouraged agency executives who were not boosters of PPBS to view it and the conventional budget as two different things.

PPBS was politically irrational at the organizational level as well. Because perfect information and foolproof technologies are not available to "real world" government agencies (or businesses), they must be willing and able to correct their mistakes. Line-item budgets make such corrections easy to execute. Because the categories do not directly relate to programs, programs can be altered without sacrificing resources and possibly threatening the very existence of the agency. Program budgets, on the other hand, link objectives, programs, and budgets so strongly that the rejection of an objective or program inevitably implies a budget reduction. What agency could be expected to cheerfully supply information that might result in the loss of jobs, resources, and prestige? Unless the agency had a replacement program that it knew to be acceptable to reviewing authorities, PPBS created an incentive to doctor information so that all programs appeared to be a smashing success, even in those cases when the agency itself knew the program was not working and would like to change or replace it.

Allen Schick extends this argument still further by pointing out that a basic element of the traditional budgetary process that is responsible for its efficient operation is its abhorrence of protracted and intensive conflict.

> Budgetary warfare brings challenges to those interests which are advantaged in the budget; it invites political and administrative disruption; and it may mean payless paydays, program cuts, reduction-in-force, and even agency terminations. It is no small accomplishment that 250 billion potential conflicts are negotiated with minimal strife each year. While the problem is not free of conflict—it couldn't be with so much at stake—it has available many devices and strategies for regulating and containing discord. (Schick, 1977, p. 563.)

Each of the mechanisms that Schick goes on to describe conflicts with the philosophy embodied in PPBS: continuing resolutions, informal understandings between congressional committees, and a widening gap between appropriations and authorizations. All these represent a compromise between political and economic rationality, and under PPBS they must be discarded. But can the system survive this reform? Without such mechanisms, conflict that had previously been successfully managed or that had remained latent might well up and paralyze the decision-making process. In a modern industrial state in which government plays a critical regulatory and redistributive role, such paralysis would be intolerable. Schick understates the case considerably when he observes: "The prospects for bolstering governmental tolerance of prolonged budgetary impasses are not bright. An essential mission of all budgeting is to keep agencies and their activities in business" (Schick, 1977, p. 565).

There was a kind of cognitive irrationality associated with PPBS as well. One of the reasons that is always given for PPBS's failure and one that we have already discussed is that there weren't enough trained analysts who could conduct expert benefit–cost studies and assist in putting program structures together. While there is no question that there were fewer such analysts in civilian agencies than there were in the Defense Department and that it would have helped if there had been more, there is reason to doubt that there could ever be enough analysts to meet the knowledge requirements of PPBS. The problem isn't simply that objectives are often difficult to quantify or that many programs have multiple goals. Of equal or greater concern is the sheer magnitude of the task and the limited amount of time in which it must be completed. If PPBS was to work in the manner initially envisioned, the analysis of agency programs and alternatives was not something that would be confined to new projects. Virtually every program would have to receive a thorough reanalysis each year in light of changing objectives and conditions. The manpower demands of this requirement are such that it is administratively and financially impractical *regardless* of whether there are large numbers of trained analysts or not. No government can afford to devote 30 to 40 percent of its budget to analysis; indeed, it would be inefficient and ineffective to do so.

Another aspect of this cognitive irrationality was its naive faith in the powers of prospective analytic techniques, such as benefit–cost analysis, that attempt to evaluate the merits of a program or alternative before it is implemented. Too often, for all of the reasons discussed in the previous chapter, this technology was totally incapable of doing the job. In areas where data were lacking or where the programs being evaluated represented sharp departures from what had been done previously, the estimation of benefits and costs became an almost mystical process in which analysts relied more on intuition than on facts. The analysts weren't being irresponsible in the sense that they were ignoring data; they were doing the best they could. It was just that the technology they were using made assumptions that could not be met.

In conclusion, we have seen that there are many explanations for PPBS's demise. There were not enough trained analysts; top officials did not understand it and felt threatened; the goals of civilian agency programs were numerous and difficult to measure; realistic alternatives that were worth analyzing were not always present; interest groups and decentralized control made the results of analysis difficult to implement; the system was politically irrational in its attempt to alter the basic relationships among political institutions and was therefore distrusted by

Congress, which insisted that the old budgeting format continue to be used; it ignored agency incentives to preserve resources; it encouraged political conflict; it insisted that an unreasonably great amount of analysis be conducted in an unreasonably short time span; and it rested on a mode of analysis that was not capable of carrying the load thrust upon it. PPBS had, in fact, so many problems and they are so interconnected that it is impossible to isolate confidently one or two that can be said to be primarily responsible for its failure.

No matter. The value of PPBS as the premier case study of an attempt to reform the budgetary process stems precisely from the fact that it was so ambitious in its demands and expectations that it uncovered a number of factors that would have to be considered in any subsequent reform. We will now learn more about the relative importance of these factors as we consider two other reforms, management by objectives and zero-based budgeting, which were attempted while the memory of PPBS was still fresh.

MANAGEMENT BY OBJECTIVES

The search for the best is the enemy of the good.
VOLTAIRE

Although the principles upon which it is based owe much to performance budgeting and similar public sector innovations extending back to the turn of the century, the term "management by objectives" (MBO) comes to us from the Austrian-born management consultant Peter Drucker. In a series of books and articles beginning with the *Practice of Management* (1954), Drucker focused on the tendency of managers in the private sector to become diverted from their firm's true goals and slip into unproductive behavior. A major source of this misdirection was the almost inevitable narrowing of vision that takes place when a manager is given responsibility for some functional area such as personnel or market research. Because it is only natural for an aggressive manager to want to succeed, he or she strives to develop the most efficient personnel system in the industry or the highest-quality scientific market research. This is fine as far as it goes, but it often directs the manager's attention away from the more fundamental goals of the enterprise.

> The functional work becomes an end in itself. In far too many instances the functional manager no longer measures his performance by its contribution to the enterprise, but only by his own professional criteria of workmanship. He tends to appraise his subordinates by their craftsmanship, to reward and promote them accordingly. He resents demands made on him for the sake of business performance as interfering with "good engineering," "smooth production," or "hard-hitting selling." (Drucker, 1954, p. 123.)

Differences in the location of managers within a firm's hierarchy also cause problems. Top management speaks in a language that often has little direct relevance to the job of a manager in production or accounting. This frustrates efforts at coordination, with the result that managers in different parts of the organization and at different levels can be inefficiently attending to partially conflicting goals without even knowing it.

Drucker believed that the basic solution to this general problem of misdirection is for every manager in the firm, from the chief executive to the assembly-line foreman, to operate on the basis of a set of carefully integrated, clearly spelled out objectives. These objectives would tell the manager what his or her group is expected to produce, how this contribution relates to the attainment of the company's goals, and what the manager can expect from other units that affects the unit's achievement. Critical to the success of this solution is that objectives be quantitatively defined, so that achievement can be unambiguously measured and each manager can develop objectives without undue interference from higher-level management. This last requirement is somewhat surprising given the centralizing role that MBO was supposed to play in the Nixon administration, but Drucker held that it was important. While higher-level management must, of course, reserve the right to approve or disapprove what the lower-level manager proposed, it should not dictate. Objectives and performance standards should be settled through negotiation, with the lower-level manager granted the bulk of the initiative. That manager must be allowed to control his or her performance: "Self-control means stronger motivation; a desire to do the best rather than just enough to get by. It means higher performance goals and broader vision. Even if management by objectives were not necessary to give the enterprise the unity of direction and effort of a management team, it would be necessary to make possible management by self-control" (Drucker, 1954, p. 131). So seriously did Drucker regard the principle of self-control that he insisted that the results of performance evaluations be reported to the immediate manager in charge, not to his or her superior.

Possibly because the principles of MBO laid down by Drucker are so general and abstract, the name has been applied to a wide variety of management systems. In fact, it often seems that any attempt to devise performance standards and measure achievement, something that has been taking place for as long as organizations have existed, is heralded as yet another example of MBO's spreading popularity. However, neither the range of systems that claim the name nor the all-encompassing nature of MBO's definition are at issue here. We need only concern ourselves with the basically straightforward brand of MBO that has usually been applied in the public sector. Most government MBO programs have been made up of three elements: (1) the definition of quantifiable objectives, (2) the creation of an annual operating plan that sets performance objectives and synchronizes their achievement, and (3) the evaluation of performance.

It should be obvious that this variation of MBO has much in common with performance budgeting. Both are heavily oriented toward program accounting and the measurement of goal achievement. The major difference between them is that while performance budgeting emphasizes efficiency and concentrates on minimizing the cost of service, MBO emphasizes effectiveness and concentrates on maximizing coordination. The differences between PPBS and MBO run deeper and are similar to those that distinguish the managerial and planning approaches to budgeting. MBO concedes that objectives are politically rather than analytically determined. In restricting itself to quantifying, prioritizing, and coordinating agency objectives, MBO's ambitions are far more modest than PPBS's goal of estimating the value objectives in dollars and cents. The role of analysis is less institutionalized in MBO as well. Unlike PPBS, MBO does not stress the importance of employing benefit–cost analysis to choose between alternative ways of pursuing the same objective. Nor does it exploit the use of experimental program evaluation to conduct retrospective analyses. True, MBO requires the periodic evaluation of agency performance, but the focus of the evaluation is usually on a governmental unit rather than a policy or program. The question asked by MBO is not whether food stamps or cash payments are a more efficient way of dealing with the food problems of the poor but rather how well the Department of Agriculture is fulfilling its objective to provide a given level of assistance. This variety of MBO is also much less ambitious with respect to planning. Whereas PPBS had worked with a five-year time horizon and attempted to uncover the long-term implications of present choices, planning in MBO was confined to the fiscal or calendar year.

On April 21, 1973, President Nixon ordered that MBO be implemented in 21 of the largest federal agencies. From his standpoint the system must have seemed particularly attractive. Nixon and most of his advisors venerated the private sector as the source of all management wisdom and MBO possessed impeccable private sector credentials. Not only was it the creation of one of the world's most famous management consultants, but it had become something of the rage at the Harvard Business School, which supplied Nixon with a number of his top staff. Although some members of that staff were willing to concede that there may be some important differences between the public and private sectors—remember we are now into Nixon's second term—they remained committed to the idea that the hard-headed, rational management practices used in business could make significant inroads toward eliminating waste and inefficiency in government. Perhaps equally important, MBO promised to help centralize control of a bureaucracy that Nixon viewed as inept and disloyal to his programs. Drucker and other designers of MBO systems may have stressed the importance of participation and decentralization, but the potential it offered as an instrument of control for monitoring agency achievement of administration objectives was well appreciated.

Nixon's Watergate problems and Ford's subsequent indifference to the program prevented MBO from really taking root as a governmentwide management system. In the first year of its operation, the Office of Management and Budget (OMB) maintained a calculated low profile in order to minimize the kind of agency resistance that had crippled PPBS. Agencies were permitted to determine their own objectives, and OMB made every effort to act only as a resource that was available for consulting purposes if asked. Although it was generally presumed that this policy of decentralization would end once the agencies were acclimated to the new system, before this transition could take place Nixon had resigned and Ford took office. When Ford did nothing more than endorse the second set of objectives formulated by the agencies, the system as a whole began losing momentum. By 1975, only two years after it had been introduced, governmentwide MBO was in a state of suspended animation, with agencies no longer required to identify their most important objectives and with OMB no longer meeting with the agencies to discuss the program. MBO continued in this state until officially terminated with the Carter administration's introduction of zero-base budgeting.

Given the tentative manner in which it was introduced and the confused conditions under which it had to function, it would have been surprising if MBO had a dramatic impact on the way the government functioned. It didn't. It brought about no major reallocation of funds between agencies. Presidential control of the bureaucracy did not increase. Programs in different agencies with related objectives were not coordinated with any new precision.

Boosters of MBO often argue that it did have an impact on the performance of individual agencies, but their evidence is far from overwhelming. One supposed success story that has been widely reprinted is described by Rodney H. Brady in an article aggressively entitled "MBO Goes to Work in the Public Sector," published in the *Harvard Business Review*; it relates the experiences that Brady, a former business executive and management consultant who had used MBO before coming to Washington, had in introducing MBO in HEW after he was appointed chief administrative and management officer. After describing how MBO worked and the problems that it encountered during its first three years, Brady proceeds to claim that the system yielded a number of substantial, measurable results:

1. During the fiscal year 1972, the Food and Drug Administration increased by 50 percent the number of import products inspected. This objective was met despite delay caused by a dock strike.
2. In fiscal year 1971, the Social and Rehabilitation Service (SRS) was able to train more than 40,000 welfare recipients, a figure that exceeded its objective by 5,000. (Brady, 1979, p. 125.)

Unfortunately, in neither case was any indication given of what either agency would have achieved without MBO or what the cost of the increased achievement is in terms of accomplishing other objectives. It seems highly improbable that it was MBO alone that was responsible for the gains described, and it is even more improbable that the gains were realized without cost. It is certainly not clear from this "evidence" that the existence of MBO was an essential prerequisite for either achievement. In some sense, the character of the evidence Brady suggests illustrates the difference in perspective between PPBS and MBO more clearly than any formal comparison of their attributes: these are the claims of a management consultant, not an analyst.

Of course, the fact that Brady's evidence is unimpressive doesn't prove that MBO wasn't useful. Clarifying objectives and trying to measure performance is sometimes a good idea, and it would be hard to believe that some benefits were not realized. Nonetheless, it appears possible to make a case as strong as Brady's for MBO having had virtually no impact at HEW. We know, for example, that there was no major change in the allocation pattern within the agency that is traceable to MBO. A study of MBO in SRS—the same agency from which Brady chose his evidence—showed that its chief effects "are an increase in paperwork and in discussion of objectives and a decrease in time spent on programmatic activity" (Wildavsky, 1979, p. 185).

Some of the reasons generally given for MBO's limited impact bear a close resemblance to those we have looked at in connection with PPBS: agency executives saw MBO as an attempt to centralize authority; agency objectives were hard to define and quantify; personnel familiar with the system were in short supply. MBO also ran afoul of politics, although in different ways than PPBS. The problem wasn't that MBO threatened to bring about a major shift in the balance of power between the major branches of government but rather that it concerned itself with objectives that held little political interest for the president and OMB. Richard Rose, a political scientist who has written extensively about the implementation of MBO at the federal level, estimates that 81 percent of the objectives forwarded to OMB by the agencies in 1973 were apolitical in the sense that they represented noncontroversial tasks such as completing reports by a given date. "The absence of controversy made such objectives safe for bureaucrats to present to political superiors. But it also meant that busy Executive office staff had no positive incentive to take an interest in them, and paid a high opportunity cost in time to monitor noncontroversial achievements of government, where there were many controversial issues to seek to influence" (Rose, 1977, p. 68). MBO seemed to suffer more from political irrelevance than political ambition.

But perhaps the most serious shortcoming of MBO was its excessive faith in the power of objective clarification and productivity measurement to increase government performance. In the article by Rodney Brady referred to earlier, he quotes the following dialogue between the secretary of HEW and an agency head that took place at an objective setting meeting.

Here is a typical dialogue between former HEW Secretary Elliot L. Richardson and an agency head as they formulated an objective.

Agency head: One of our agency's most important initiatives this year will be to focus our efforts in the area of alcoholism and to treat an additional 10,000 alcoholics. Given last year's funding of 41 alcoholism treatment centers and the direction of other resources at the state and local level, we feel that this is an achievable objective.

Secretary: Are these 41 centers operating independently or are they linked to other service organizations in their communities? In other words, are we treating the whole problem of alcoholism, including its employment, mental health and welfare aspects, or are we just treating the symptoms of alcoholism?

Agency head: A program requirement for getting funds is that the services involved must be linked in an integrated fashion with these other resources.

Secretary: I am not interested in just looking at the number of alcoholics that are treated. Our goal ought to be the actual rehabilitation of these patients. Do you have data to enable you to restate the objective in terms of that goal?

Agency head: As a matter of fact, Mr. Secretary, we have developed a management information and evaluation system in which each grantee will be providing quarterly data on the number of alcoholics treated, as well as on the number of alcoholics who are actually rehabilitated.

Secretary: How do you define "rehabilitated?"

Agency head: If they are gainfully employed one year after treatment, we regard them as being rehabilitated.

Secretary: Please revise this objective, then, to enable us to track progress on how effective these programs really are in treating the disease of alcoholism and in rehabilitating alcoholics. (Brady, 1979, p. 120.)

This conversation has been widely reprinted in public administration texts and seems to represent for their authors, as it obviously did for Brady, a fine example of MBO at work. The implication is that with tough-minded exchanges like these taking place, improvements in government performance are just around the corner. But are they? How much does the refinement of objectives really contribute to more efficient and effective government? If one views government as a potentially efficient machine crippled solely by indecision and confusion about goals, MBO makes a lot of sense. If, however, the problem lies in uncertainty not only about what should be done but how to do it, MBO is less helpful. A young doctor who decides that he would like to find a cure for cancer or a stockbroker who sets a yearly income goal of $450,000 still may have problems despite the fact that both objectives are commendable, specific, and concerned with outcomes, not merely inputs or activities. They are likely to have problems because the detail of precisely what actions they have to take to reach their goals remains.

So it often is with government. While confusion about what an agency should be trying to do often contributes to poor performance, not knowing the best way (or even a pretty good way) to reach a goal about which there is little disagreement can be a far greater problem. What keeps the inflation rate high, health costs rising, inner cities deteriorating, and reading scores of high school students dropping is not a lack of clarity about what objectives should be. It is knowing what to do. In the context of the dialogue between the secretary of HEW and his agency head, the mere act of setting an objective in terms of the number of alcoholics gainfully employed after one year may have very little connection with having that objective realized—unless the agency provides an effective technology of alcoholic rehabilitation.

Advocates of MBO inevitably assume that if an agency does not possess an effective technology prior to its introduction, feedback from its periodic evaluations will assure major strides in this direction. If all goes according to schedule, an agency will introduce a program, obtain feedback through productivity evaluations, and then make whatever policy adjustments are necessary to bring performance up to the desired level. Yet whether this cycle will actually result in an improved technology and performance is by no means a foregone conclusion. For one thing, the presumption is made that the agency will be able to locate the source of the problem. Often this is not that easy. Suppose our young stockbroker has a system whereby he carefully reviews his net worth every month. After six months he discovers that he is $440,000 short of his yearly goal of $450,000, with six months to go. How much has he learned? He knows that things are not working out the way he hoped and that his investment choices might have been better. But what next? Which of the thousands of alternative investment strategies remaining to him are most likely to pay off? The source of failure may be no more clear in the case of HEW's alcoholic rehabilitation program, especially because there are a variety of outside factors such as the job market that can affect its success (rehabilitation is obviously harder when it is more difficult to find jobs for those in the program). Even when the source of failure is known, there is no guarantee that we will be able to formulate better policy. The dilemma facing the physician who would like to find a cure for cancer is not that he can't get high quality feedback about the success of experimental drugs. He knows that many of them don't work, but that does not tell him what to do next.

Like PPBS, MBO has its good points. Virtually all of its ambitions are laudatory. In organizations with extremely unsophisticated managements, public or private, MBO activities to clarify objectives and measure productivity are apt to be useful. For the reasons given above, however, the effects will probably be modest. In more sophisticated environments where goal specification and evaluation are already basic management activities, MBO is less likely to have an effect—except to generate new paperwork. For these organizations MBO has nothing new to say and their problems require something more.

ZERO-BASE BUDGETING

Practice by no means makes perfect—for without development,
practice simply reinforces, intensifies and perpetuates early mistakes.
SYDNEY HARRIS

In 1977 when Jimmy Carter ordered that all federal agencies begin employing zero-base budgeting (ZBB), it may have appeared that he was doing nothing more than engaging in what by now had become an administrative ritual at the federal level. The introduction of a new management system provided inexpensive but tangible evidence of a commitment to government efficiency and seemed to have become obligatory for each new president. But Carter didn't approach the introduction of ZBB as mere ritual. Possibly because of his background as a naval officer and engineer, he had demonstrated an early commitment to rational budgeting methods and had introduced ZBB in the state of Georgia when he was governor. The implementation of ZBB at the federal level was a campaign promise with which he identified far more strongly than did Johnson with PPBS or Nixon with MBO.

Like MBO, ZBB was imported from the private sector. It had been developed in 1969 by Peter Phyrr for use by Texas Instruments[1] as a means of controlling the growth in overhead costs and was quickly adapted for more generalized applications in other corporations. The system gets its name from its aspiration to overcome the almost invariable tendency of traditional budgeting to focus attention only on those activities that are connected with changes, usually increases, in the proposed budget over that of the current year. The current year's expenditures (i.e., the "base") are commonly accepted as the starting point for negotiating next year's budget and the activities they represent are generally considered to be immune from review. ZBB, on the other hand, grants no such immunity. Its basic premise is that the entire range of an agency's activities should be scrutinized annually in order that only the most efficient and effective may be permitted to survive.

The preparation of the zero-base budget is a four step process:

1. "Decision units" are identified.
2. "Decision packages" are created for each decision unit.
3. Decision packages are evaluated and ranked.
4. Detailed operating budgets are prepared.

The decision unit represents the lowest-level entity for which a budget is prepared. Its definition is purposely left flexible so that the system can be easily adapted to the flow of responsibility in any particular agency. The only requirement is that there be a single manager responsible for each unit. From the standpoint of implementation, a major advantage of this flexible approach to defining decision units is that an agency could easily keep its present budgetary format intact within the ZBB structure. In fact, OMB encouraged this by advising that each decision unit should, "to the extent possible, reflect existing program and organizational structures that have accounting support" (Schick, 1979, p. 226).

The decision package contains an analytical presentation of the programs and activities of the decision unit. Its purpose, according to Phyrr, is to describe each decision unit in such a way that upper-level management can "(a) evaluate it and rank it against other decision units competing for funding and (b) decide whether to approve or disapprove it" (Phyrr, 1978, p. 323). The precise content of the decision package can be expected to vary, but it would normally include all of the information one might associate with either MBO or PPBS. The objectives of the decision unit would be defined, the benefits and costs of alternative politics would be evaluated, performance data about the current level of achievement would be supplied, and future intentions would be discussed.

The critical difference between the type of analysis associated with other management systems and that included in the zero-base budget was an added emphasis on examining the benefits and costs of different *levels* of agency effort and funding. Choosing between alternative methods of testing air quality is one thing, determining how many test sites to establish and how much money to spend on the task is another. ZBB represented a commitment to the ideal that decision makers should be made aware of the full range of implications associated with various levels of program support.

To accomplish its analytic goals, ZBB required decision units to submit not just one decision package but several. Each package represented a different level of service activity and, by implication, a different level of funding. By convention, three such packages were generally prepared. The first dealt with the services that the agency would perform under a minimum level of effort. The minimum was defined as "the critical level of effort, below which the operation would be discontinued because it loses its viability or effectiveness" (Phyrr, 1978, p. 324). The second package contained an analysis of the activities necessary to maintain the current level of service. The budget required to support this level of service was not necessarily identical to that of the current year. Productivity improvements might make it possible to deliver the same service for a lower cost, or, as was more commonly the case, inflation and other problems may have driven that cost substantially higher. The third package contained an analysis of the activities necessary to provide a higher level of service and inevitably involved greater expenditures.

Thus as a result of its dual concern with alternative means of performing a service and the consequences of different levels of effort, ZBB required what amounted to two separate analyses. Phyrr provides a compact example of what the two analyses might look like in connection with solid waste disposal in a small city in the southwest:

1. Different ways of performing the same function.

a) Recommended means: City provides the collection service, requiring the use of plastic sacks for all refuse. Plastic sacks are purchased by each resident. Refuse trains are used for heavily populated areas. Front loading refuse trucks are used to empty the refuse trains on the route to transport the refuse to the landfill. Other types of trucks are used for the less-populated areas and country runs. Cost—$790,300.

b) Alternatives not recommended:

—Collection without the use of plastic sacks: Additional man required on each crew if garbage cans are used in place of plastic sacks. Added cost of $96,000.

—Collection of all refuse by the trains. Use of other types of equipment (shu-packs and barrel trucks) are more efficient in less densely populated areas. Purchase of three additional refuse trains and two front loaders would be required, plus eight additional personnel, for an additional cost of $150,000.

—Contract city refuse collection to a private contract: Cost $1,108,800 for twice-a-week collection; $900,000 for once-a-week collection.

The recommended means was chosen because the alternatives did not offer any additional advantages and were more expensive.

The residential refuse collection manager completed his zero-base analysis by identifying different levels of effort for performing the function. In this case, the manager believed he could reduce the level of refuse collection from twice a week to once a week and still satisfy the minimum sanitary requirements. Therefore, he completed his analysis by identifying the minimum level and additional levels of effort for his recommended means of refuse collection as follows:

2. Different levels of effort for performing the function:

a) Residential Refuse Collection (1 of 3): cost—$607,000 minimum level; Collect residential refuse once per week; brush pick up on Thursday and Friday.

b) Residential Refuse Collection (2 of 3): cost—$142,800 (Levels 1 + 2 = $750,300). Add one additional collection per week, so that refuse is collected twice per week.

c) Residential Refuse Collection (3 of 3): cost—$40,500 (Levels $1 + 2 + 3 = \$790,300$). Collection of brush and white goods an additional two days per week, so that brush collected every collection day (Mon., Tues., Thurs., and Fri.). (Phyrr, 1978, p. 261.)

After the decision packages are developed, they are ranked by priority. If we are speaking in terms of only one decision unit performing a single activity, this ranking has already been done in conjunction with determining the three basic packages. By definition, the activity level represented by the first or minimum package has the highest priority. Often, however, a decision unit will generate several sets of decision packages, each of which relates to a separate activity. If the department responsible for waste removal is also responsible for waste disposal, it might generate six different packages; three for each activity. In this case, the ranking of each package is no longer obvious. The department might want to recommend, for example, that the service level in collection be reduced to the minimum and that more resources be devoted to disposal. If so, the decision package representing the current level of effort in removal would be ranked lower than the third disposal alternative. Obviously ranking becomes increasingly important as we move to successively higher levels of management, where each manager has the responsibility to review the decision packages generated by dozens of units and to determine the priorities among them.

Once the ranking process is complete, the detailed operating budget can be prepared for legislative review. ZBB does not magically generate the optimal budget total. That is basically a political question. What ZBB does try to do, by making the decision packages and rankings available to the legislature, is to make the service implications of any budget cuts (or additions) precisely understood.

Taking advantage of some of the lessons from the PPBS and MBO experiences, proponents of ZBB like President Carter and Phyrr cautioned against expecting miracles when it was first implemented. They acknowledged, for example, that it was politically unrealistic to expect any immediate and dramatic shift in basic allocation patterns. The Defense Department was not going to have its budget cut by 30 percent, nor was the Labor Department going to get a 40 percent increase. They also realized that ZBB, like its predecessors, would pose a threat to program managers anxious to maintain their level of funding. Nonetheless, they believed that the introduction of ZBB would bring about many (and in most cases measurable) benefits:

1. It would focus the management process on analysis and decision making rather than on the size of incremental funding increases.
2. It would eliminate or reduce low priority programs.
3. Managers would be forced to examine the cost-effectiveness of their programs.
4. It would permit quick, rational budget adjustments during the year, if revenue falls short of projections. Reference to the priority rankings would ensure that the money was taken from those programs that were least valuable.
5. It would show the growth rate of taxes by insuring that agencies used existing resources more efficiently.
6. It would broadly expand management participation in the budgetary process.

Those opposed to the introduction of ZBB were less enthusiastic. They saw it as another futile variation on the PPB theme and particularly resented the implication that every federal program would be completely reevaluated each year from a base of zero. They argued that entrenched political interest groups were not the only reason why yearly basic shifts in budgetary allocations were impossible. A substantial portion of the budget (at least 75 percent) is committed by virtue of major legislative entitlement programs (like Social Security, veteran pensions, payment of interest on the national debt, and governmental contracts). The idea that a group of analysts would be handing down an annual recommendation as to whether Social Security or payment on the national debt seemed of sufficient priority to warrant continued support seemed absurd. Such expenditures were inevitable. Critics viewed the resource requirements of ZBB with equal disbelief. Could any rational person believe that enough analysts existed on the face of the earth much less in the federal government to conduct a yearly analysis of every program? There weren't enough trees from which to produce the paper that would be needed for all the reports.

Those in favor of ZBB acknowledged that the name of the program and some of the rhetoric used to support it might occasionally produce exaggerated expectations, but they defended its underlying principle and argued that the manner in which ZBB would be implemented was sensitive to the budget commitment and paperwork problems. The fact that the first decision package was to focus on the minimum level of activity necessary to sustain the integrity of the agency was tacit recognition that certain expenditures and activities could not be realistically considered as candidates for elimination. As for the potential deluge of paperwork that might have to accompany the introduction of ZBB, OMB could regulate this by setting a limit on the length of decision packages. The limit was immediately set at two pages.

ZBB was also charged with being bureaucratically naive. Were program managers really going to submit program packages that suggested their agencies could absorb a substantial budget cut with only a minimal loss in service? Opponents doubted it. It seemed more likely that decision packages would be prepared so as to make it appear that the smallest cutback would have disastrous consequences and that an ever-increasing amount of funds was needed for the agency to continue offering its current level of service. James Q. Wilson, a Harvard political scientist whose antipathy for budgetary reform systems is only slightly less than that of Wildavsky, imagined how ZBB would work in the Park Service:

> "Here is what we will do," the Director continued. "Smith, you tell Senator Henry Jackson, the chairman of the Interior Committee, that we are considering what would happen if we closed all the national parks." "Even those in the state of Washington?" Smith asked incredulously. "Especially those in Washington," the Director replied. "But stress to the Senator that it is just a mental experiment, a planning exercise. We probably won't really close any of the parks in his state." Suddenly, a beatific expression of sudden enlightenment spread across Smith's face. "Gotcha, chief." "Gorstwinkle, I want you to get right to work on making up a list of national parks in the order of their importance, so we will know which ones to leave open if we can't reopen all of them," the Director said. Gorstwinkle started to giggle uncontrollably: "Right away. Of course,

I won't be able to keep the list secret, chief. You know, Freedom of Information and all that . . . . " He broke up in laughter. "I understand," the Director replied, allowing a thin smile to crease his stern features. "Nothin's ever secret any more. I suppose the Sierra Club is bound to find out that we are thinking of closing Yellowstone." "The Audubon Society will suspect that we might be cutting back on bird sanctuaries," someone remarked. "Wait until the Daughters of the American Revolution finds out that we are . . . . " the speaker gasped for breath, as he shook convulsively with laughter, "that we are analyzing whether it makes sense to leave Independence Hall open!" Howls range through the room. One man staggered to the drinking fountain, and another had to loosen his tie to avoid choking. Pettypoint bristled. "You are not looking at this constructively." "Oh, but we are, Mr. Pettypoint," the Director replied. "I firmly believe that, as a result of this ZBB exercise, the public will realize we need more money for more parks." (Wilson, 1978, p. 335.)

President Carter felt that such problems could be solved by establishing a dialogue between the executive office and the agencies that emphasized what ZBB could do *for them* rather than *to them*. "For unlike traditional approaches, zero-base budgeting offers them a genuine opportunity to increase their resources where they can demonstrate greater effectiveness or need" (Carter, 1978, p. 332). Phyrr trusted to the integrity of the system itself: "If the decision packages are formatted adequately to display the alternative considered, workload and performance data, descriptions of action, and enough cost data so that discretionary items cannot be built into the cost estimate, it becomes very obvious when such gamesmanship is attempted" (Phyrr, 1978, p. 330). Critics, however, remained skeptical that either approach would work. Being told that ZBB promises the opportunity to get a large budget increase may make agencies eager to prove the merits of their programs, but it does not necessarily increase their enthusiasm for revealing program defects. Phyrr's trust in the information revealed by the decision packages might be appropriate if those packages were painstakingly constructed and detailed, but OMB was speaking in terms of packages that were two pages or less. What sort of integrity would be ensured by a scant two pages of analysis? To nonbelievers it appeared as though an avalanche of paperwork was being avoided at the high cost of institutionalizing the sort of superficial analysis that agencies could easily manipulate.

From an administrative perspective, the implementation of ZBB was a striking success, at least compared to PPBS or MBO. Complaints about excess paperwork and White House interference were few during the first year, as more than 9,500 agency managers prepared about 25,000 internal decision packages for subsequent review by higher-level officials. After consolidation and the elimination of low-ranking packages, about 10,000 decision packages were forwarded to OMB in September 1977—just five months after the program had been initiated.

Allen Schick attributes this painless process of implementation to the compromises that we have already mentioned rather than any great enthusiasm on the part of agencies for the zero-based concept. Agencies did as they were told not so much because ZBB offered them so much as because it cost them so little.

This rapid penetration of budgetary practice betrays ZBB's superficiality. ZBB could be speedily installed because it did not alter the two things that matter most in budgetary technique: the data used for making program and financial decisions and the form in which the data are classified . . . . There is not a single bit of budgetary data unique to ZBB. Nowhere do OMB guidelines command agencies to gather information (other than ranking scores) not already used in budgeting. Nor do the guidelines require agencies to abandon their existing decisional structures. (Schick, 1979, p. 224.)

Given the limited demands that ZBB placed on the agencies and the limited amount of new information that it generated for decision makers, ZBB's impact seemed destined to be no greater than that of PPBS or MBO. It was not.

The fiscal 1979 budget (unveiled on January 23, 1978) hardly terminates or curtails anything of significance, continues most spending at inflation-adjusted levels, and offers few program initiatives. It projects an expenditure growth of $40 billion, all but $8 billion of which—2% of the budget total—is due to mandatory inflation and workload increases. Even this 2% overstates the amount of discretion exercised by the nation's number one budgetmaker. MR current service estimates assume no inflation adjustment for entitlement programs (such as veterans' benefits) which are not linked by formula to the cost of living, or for grant-in-aid programs which do not have spending increases already scheduled in law. When inflation is added for these two categories, there appears to have been almost no exercise of presidential power. Virtually every function, subfunction, and major program is funded at or slightly above its current service level. The small number of program reductions sprinkled throughout the budget certainly are not due to zero-base technology. There are fewer such reductions than in any previous 1970s budget, though this was the first one graced by the new waste-purging methods. The fiscal 1979 budget comes out just about where disembodied incrementalism would tend to. (Schick, 1979, p. 223.)

In short, there do not seem to be *any* significant changes in spending that have occurred as the result of ZBB. Certainly there is no concrete evidence to substantiate Carter's expectation that management's attention would be focused on anaylsis rather than incremental funding increases or that ZBB would act to eliminate or reduce low-priority funding programs. Nor, for that matter, has anyone produced data attesting to any visible increase in program effectiveness or the more efficient utilization of existing resources.

Defenders of ZBB might argue that it was unreasonable to expect results after only one year. Perhaps they would only begin to come several years down the road after agencies had become comfortable with the system and OMB felt freer to increase the system's analytic demands. This, of course, was the strategy behind the "incremental" introduction of MBO by the Nixon administration, and it may well have been the thinking behind the Carter administration's undemanding brand of ZBB. If so, however, it appears that the proper adjustments were never made. At least up until the time of this writing, no new evidence has been introduced that would lead us to change the flavor of Schick's assessment of ZBB's impact.

The record of ZBB's achievements at the state and local level seems equally modest even in those cases where the system has been in place for three or four years. While bold claims of success have occasionally been made, the evidence presented in support of them has invariably been weak and inconclusive. Interestingly, applications of ZBB at the state and local level tend to reveal the same sort of compromises with the pure ZBB concept that were felt necessary at the federal level. The base for the minimum package is usually no less than 85 percent of current spending and the amount of analysis that agencies are ordered to present in support of their arguments is usually limited. When ZBB was implemented in

Missouri, Idaho, and California, for example, there wasn't even a requirement that expenditures included in the minimum package be justified with any analysis (Wildavsky, 1979, p. 209).

Undoubtedly the most exhaustive examination of ZBB's impact on the state or local level has taken place in Georgia, where Carter first introduced it when he was governor. A dozen or so studies have been conducted and their findings are consistent with the portrait of ZBB's performance at the federal level drawn by Schick. While it was true that 278 agencies were "eliminated" during the first year of ZBB, it is easily demonstrated that this was the consequence of a massive reorganization that was unrelated to any recommendation generated by ZBB. Despite the initial rhetoric that ZBB had "put an end to incremental decision making," there was no sign of any great change in the basic allocation of resources among state agencies. Indeed, one study concluded that during the period from 1973 to 1975, no function received less funds than it had in the previous year (Wildavsky, 1979, p. 212). Although there is some suggestion that ZBB may have had some microorganizational impact within programs, no data and analyses have been presented to substantiate this claim.

Just as significantly, comments solicited during interviews with program managers and legislative staff in Georgia revealed a notable lack of enthusiasm for some of ZBB's most cherished elements. Here is how they viewed the task of determining the minimum level of funding:

> The minimum is a waste of time . . . no one looks at that. We determine where we want to be and work back to 85%.
> The minimum level is a pain in the ass. It is inconceivable that you would only fund 85% of the current level.
> See that machine over there? [A deck calculator] I prepare my current level to which to my way of thinking is not the same dollars as this year, but what it will take to provide the same level of services . . . then I hit those keys and multiply by .85 of the current to get the minimum. (Lauth, 1979, p. 188.)

The reasons given for ZBB's failure to transform the character of fiscal decision making in Georgia are all too familiar. A substantial portion of expenditures were locked in by statutory and constitutional requirement and thus virtually uncontrollable. Many programs were supported by powerful interest groups whose views were not swayed by rational argument. Agencies were protective of their budgets and refused to cooperate with executive office analysts. The Legislative Budget Office refused to use ZBB. And so on. Thomas Lauth summed up the situation nicely:

> In short, incremental budgeting continues amid the procedures of zero-based budgeting because it serves participants well as a useful decision premise when operating within a political environment. The pervasive characteristic of that environment is pluralism. According to this interpretation of American politics, conflicts among competing interests over the distribution of socio-economic benefits and burdens are frequently resolved by negotiated and partial accommodations with which the participants can live, at least temporarily. Many of those accommodations are recorded annually with the adoption of the budget. By assuming that existing programs will normally be continued, political accommodations arrived at on earlier occasions by previous actors are reaffirmed and the range of political conflict is restricted. By asking "How can we adjust

what we are doing?" rather than abrogating prior agreements and asking anew each year "What should we be doing?" conflict over basic values and public purposes is minimized. Zero-base budgeting has had a difficult time penetrating existing budgeting practices precisely because those traditional practices have served the political interests of most of the participants in the budgetary process. In one sense ZBB did successfully penetrate the routines of building and justifying a budget in Georgia. The format and procedures of ZBB were installed throughout the government during the first year with only minor difficulties. In a more important sense, however, ZBB has failed to fundamentally change the decision rules used by those who prepare budgets in the State of Georgia. (Lauth, 1978, p. 200.)

CONCLUSION

There's always an easy solution to every human problem—neat, plausible and wrong.

H. L. MENCKEN

Born of analytical idealism, political naiveté, and (except in the case of PPBS) private-sector evangelism, the various decision systems examined in this chapter each promised to improve public sector performance dramatically. As we have seen, however, when measured by an objective, empirical standard, their individual and collective performance fell far short of this goal. Government productivity did not boom, red tape did not disappear, heavily bureaucratized agencies were not suddenly transformed into paragons of efficiency and effectiveness.

Yet to say that PPBS, MBO and ZBB failed to achieve their goals is not to claim that they had no impact. The unprecedented demand for policy analysis that they created brought large numbers of talented economists, operations researchers, and accountants into the public sector at all levels. While the efforts of these individuals may not have been sufficient to transform the allocation processes of government fundamentally, they did act markedly to improve the level of discourse that surrounds policy debates, especially at the state and local levels where the tradition of policy analysis was often less well developed and certainly less well funded than it was at the federal level. The implications of a given piece of zoning legislation or a county drainage project may still be only imperfectly understood by decision makers and public alike, but there has been some improvement over the kind of information that was generally available in the early 1950s. While opponents of the decision systems might argue that such improvements could and probably would have taken place without the complicated apparatus and broken promises that accompanied the implementation of the decision systems, the fact remains that these systems have contributed to what might be called the institutionalization of policy analysis in government decision making. Just as the mass employment of lawyers by government has created an internal interest group that is extraordinarily sensitive to issues of due process, so has the mass employment of economists and other analysts created a bureaucratic constituency that is sensitive to efficiency concerns.

Perhaps the most profound long-term contribution of PPBS and the other decision systems is the deepened understanding of the policy process that these natural experiments have produced. As commentators like Wildavsky and Schick have persuasively argued, there are important lessons to be learned here that have implications for the design and probable success of future administrative and budgetary reforms.

One lesson is that the budgetary process is permeated with politics: party politics, interest-group politics, institutional politics, and bureaucratic politics. This means, as Wildavsky constantly reminds us, that any budget reform is also a political reform, and its success will depend on its political as well as administrative rationality. To assume that Congress will permit major policy decisions to be made solely on the basis of benefit–cost analysis or that agencies will disinterestedly contribute information that is likely to result in the elimination of one of their principal programs is pure folly. Politics may be a frustrating aspect of the budgetary process, but there is every indication that it is a permanent aspect.

A second lession is that the budgetary process can provide an uncongenial environment for the development of high-quality policy analysis. As we have seen, both the time pressures and the incentives that surround the budgetary process act to subvert the integrity of data gathering, analysis, and the search for realistic alternatives to present policies. Policy analysis obviously has an important role to play in budgetary decision making, but when the character of that analysis is excessively determined by the pressures and constraints of budgeting, its integrity and ultimately its usefulness are lost. The requirement of ZBB that agencies annually produce dozens of decision package analyses that must be summarized in two pages is a good example of a situation in which a well-intentioned decision system ensured that neither good analysis nor good budgeting could take place. The competent evaluation of complex programs requires patience and objectivity, neither of which is widespread in budgetary processes.

NOTE

1. Given the somewhat disastrous performance history of TI over the last 15 years, it would be interesting to have a case study of ZBB at TI. To what extent and for how long was it adopted? If adopted, what role did the system play in the many decisions that led to TI's problems?

REFERENCES

Brady, Rodney H. "MBO Goes to Work in the Public Sector." In *Contemporary Approaches to Public Budgeting*, edited by Fred Kraemer. Cambridge, Mass.: Winthrop, 1979, pp. 12–129.

Bureau of the Budget. "Planning, Programming, Budgeting." Bulletin No. 66–3. In *Planning, Programming, Budgeting*, edited by Fremont J. Lyden and Ernest G. Miller. Chicago: Markham, 1970, pp. 405–421.

Carlson, Jack W. "The Status and Next Steps for Planning, Programming, and Budgeting." In *Public Expenditures and Policy Analyses*, edited by Robert H. Haveman and Julius Margolis. Chicago: Markham, 1970, pp. 367–412.

Carter, Jimmy. "Jimmy Carter Tells Why He Will Use Zero-Base Budgeting." In *Current Issues in Public Administration*, edited by Frederick S. Lane. New York: St. Martins, 1978, pp. 334–335.

Commission on the Organization of the Executive Branch. *Concluding Report*. Washington, D.C.: U.S. Government Printing Office, 1949.

Drucker, Peter F. *The Practice of Management*. New York: Harper & Row, 1954.

Enthoven, Alain C., and Smith, K. Wayne. "The Planning, Programming, and Budgeting System in the Development of Defense." In *Public Expenditures and Policy Analysis*, edited by Robert H. Haveman and Julius Margolis. Chicago: Markham, 1970, pp. 485–501.

Lauth, Thomas P. "Zero-Base Budgeting in Georgia State Government: Myth and Reality." In *Contemporary Approaches to Public Budgeting*, edited by Fred A. Kraemer. Cambridge, Mass.: Winthrop, 1979, pp. 182–206.

Lazarus, Steven. "Planning-Programming-Budgeting Systems and Project PRIME." In *Planning, Programming, Budgeting*, edited by Fremont J. Lyden and Ernest G. Miller. Chicago: Markham, 1970.

Novick, David. "The Department of Defense." In *Program Budgeting*, edited by David Novick. Cambridge, Mass.: Harvard University Press, 1965, pp. 81–119.

Proxmire, William. "PPB, The Agencies, and the Congress." In *Public Expenditures and Policy Analyses*, edited by Robert Haveman and Julius Margolis. Chicago: Markham, 1970, pp. 413–423.

Phyrr, Peter. "The Zero-Base Approach to Government Budgeting." In *Current Issues in Public Administration*, edited by Frederick S. Lane. New York: St. Martins, 1978, pp 302–319.

Rose, Richard, "Implementation and Evaporation: The Record of MBO." *Public Administration Review*, 37 (1977) 1:64–77.

Schiesl, Martin J. "The Politics of Efficiency." *Municipal Administration and Reform in America, 1880–1920*. Berkeley, Calif.: University of California Press, 1977.

Schick, Allen. "The Road to PPB." In *Planning, Programming, Budgeting*, edited by Fremont J. Lyden and Ernest G. Miller. Chicago: Markham, 1970, pp. 26–52.

Schick, Allen. "A Death in the Bureaucracy: The Demise of Federal PPB." In *Public Expenditures and Policy Analyses*, ed 2, edited by Robert Haveman and Julius Margolis. Chicago: Markham, 1977, pp. 556–576.

Schultze, Charles L. *The Politics and Economics of Public Spending*. Washington, D.C.: Brookings, 1968.

Seidman, David R. "PPB in HEW: Some Management Issues." In *Public Budgeting*, ed 3, edited by Fremont J. Lyden and Ernest G. Miller. Chicago: Rand McNally, 1978, pp. 341–359.

White, Leonard D. *The Federalists*. New York: Macmillan, 1948.

Wildavsky, Aaron. *The Politics of the Budgetary Process*. Boston: Little, Brown, 1979.

Wilson, James Q. "Zero-Based Budgeting Comes to Washington." In *Current Issues in Public Administration*, edited by Frederick S. Lane. New York: St. Martin's Press, 1978.

CHAPTER 6

From Hubris to Helplessness

> The belief that enhanced understanding will necessarily stir a nation
> or an organization to action is one of mankind's oldest illusions.
>
> HACKER'S LAW

One of the well-known dangers of promising too much is the cynicism that it eventually inspires. If a long succession of highly publicized reforms assume a willingness to follow the dictates of analysis that isn't there or require resources far in excess of what is available, they will fail. Over time, this experience can come to play a major role in determining the public's view of government performance. Ineptness in reform is at least as conspicuous as ineptness in day-to-day administration. In the end, the broken promises and dashed hopes can even help shape a government's image of itself.

This chapter begins by examining reorganization and personnel reform, two strategies for improving government performance that have engendered a great deal of publicity and a great deal of cynicism. Unlike zero-base budgeting (ZBB) or the planning-programming-budgeting system (PPBS), they are not defined by any specific agenda of reform or identified with any specific administration but have meant many different things in many different contexts. What they share in common with PPBS and ZBB is that they have consistently failed to live up to the expectations created by their press releases.

In the second half of the chapter, we examine a tangible consequence of the growing cynicism toward government's efforts to reform itself: the tax- and expenditure-limitation movement. This reform strategy is representative of what can be termed the "helpless" approach to managing government. The philosophy reflected is that government is not an instrument that, if only it were better designed and better managed, could be used actively to solve society's problems. Rather, an inevitably inefficient and ineffective government is part of virtually every problem. From this perspective, the most essential reforms are not those that attempt to improve the ability of government to manage but those that curtail government's activities.

In the late 1970s and early 1980s, politics have increasingly reflected the helpless approach to government. Successful candidates of both major parties are more apt to ridicule government and to call for gross reduction and simplification of its activities than to offer ambitious programs. Nothing represents this new spirit (or absence of spirit) better than the attempt to control government growth and increase efficiency by restricting revenue and/or expenditure growth. These extremely popular reforms are premised on the unassailable logic that a government cannot waste resources it does not have. Whether or not the reforms actually lead to a more efficient use of the available resources is a much trickier question; there are good reasons to believe that they will not.

REORGANIZATION

> We *trained hard* . . . But it seemed that every time we were beginning to form up into teams we would be reorganized . . . . I was to learn later in life that we tend to meet any new situation by reorganizing; and a wonderful method it can be for creating the illusion of progress while producing confusion, inefficiency, and demoralization.
>
> PETRONIUS ARBITER, 210 B.C.

Any conscious alteration in the structure of government, the process by which it operates, or its responsibilities can be termed a reorganization. Obviously this covers a lot of ground: regulation, deregulation, the New Federalism, increased federal assumption of welfare funding and state assumption of primary and secondary education funding, the creation of single-purpose districts at the local level, the consolidation of school districts, the creation of the Departments of Defense and Health and Human Services, the adoption of the city manager plan to operate cities, and so on. If we include minor internal reforms that might involve having a city planning director report or not report to the city manager, or having a state department of economic development report or not report to the governor, the universe of reorganizations contains tens of thousands of reforms.

Increasing government efficiency has always been a major goal of reorganizations. At the local level, reorganizations like the commission plan, the city manager plan, school consolidations and, more recently, home rule initiatives have all been seen as solutions for specific efficiency problems such as corruption, the spoils system, and the lack of professional management. Efficiency is also used as a justification for federal reorganizations. For example, the Defense Reorganization Act of 1949 was motivated in part by the desire to reduce costly competition and duplication among the armed services.[1]

To even begin to describe all these reforms much less evaluate them is well beyond the scope of this book. Our interest is restricted to the much narrower question of why, despite the fact that almost every president, governor, and mayor recommends a reorganization before or immediately after taking office, it is increasingly hard to find anyone who seriously believes that reorganization is an effective strategy for increasing efficiency.

One possibility is that our image of reorganization, like that of the public sector in general, has fallen prey to the combined effect of poor evaluation methodology and selective perception. Perhaps reorganizations are accomplishing things that go undetected and too much emphasis is placed on isolated instances of failure. Certainly it is no easy matter to demonstrate rigorously the efficiency effects of a major reorganization. A comparison must be made of the costs and benefits stemming from the new form of organization and those that would have resulted had the old form existed in the present context. This is relatively easy if agency personnel and the context in which it operates stay the same, but they almost never do. The clients that an agency serves may increase or change in character, costs may rise for critical supplies and resources, unscheduled maintenance problems may develop, or the mix of services that the agency offers may change. Try to envision all of the changes in defense operations that have taken place between 1948 and today and then imagine the task of isolating the long-term efficiency consequences of the reorganization that took place in 1949. As Miles (1981, p. 126) claims, such calculations are close to meaningless. To make matters worse, the very definition of what is a cost and what is a benefit can change following reorganization because program goals are often affected. As Simon notes: "When we change the organization, we change the picture that the people in it have of the concrete tasks to be done and the concrete goals to be achieved—their concept of the program. When we change the concept of the program, we change the relative emphasis that the various parts of the complex whole will receive, we alter allocations of resources and relative priorities among goals" (Simon, 1976, p. 334).

Selective perception is another possible source of bias in trying to obtain an accurate picture of the benefits of reorganization. Because there have been so many reorganizations, it is inevitable that there would have been some failures. The tendency to focus on the worst cases could be partly responsible for the present cynicism with which reorganization is viewed. Certainly all reorganizations have not failed. One kind that has met with some success is the creation of single-purpose "special districts" in which independent local governments agree to cede their functional responsibilities for a single issue (e.g., water, sewage) and some revenue-raising capability to a special government body. Although there have been some spectacular failures both functionally and financially, these consolidations have probably been, on balance, a success story. Redundant staff positions have been eliminated, better technical assistance has become available, and service has often improved. A related success story has come in the area of intergovernmental cooperation. In cases where formal consolidation is impractical, a large number of local governments have agreed to cooperate functionally. They do this through joint purchasing, equipment sharing, and personnel sharing. Such initiatives have helped overcome the economy-of-scale problems faced by modest-size local governments; one small city may not be able to fully employ or afford a Ph.D. horticulturalist, but three or four such cities may be able to hire one.

Does this mean that the cynical stance that most observers take toward reorganization is largely without justification? We don't think so. While there have been few rigorous evaluations of reorganizations, there have been a large number of informal studies and their message is consistently negative. Whether we are speaking in terms of reorganizations at the state and local level in the United States or reorganizations at the national level in this and other countries, the judgment of March and Olsen is typical: "In terms of their effects on administrative costs, size of staff, productivity or spending, most major reorganization efforts have been described by outsiders, and frequently by participants, as substantial failures. Few efficiencies are achieved; little gain in responsiveness is recorded; control seems as elusive after the efforts as before . . . " (March and Olsen, 1982, p. 288).

Another explanation for the cynical attitude toward reorganizations that also accounts for why they continue to occur is that efficiency is less a goal of reorganization than a justification for it. According to this view, politicians and bureaucrats don't believe that reorganization will make government operate more efficiently, but they do believe that the best way to realize their real goals is to cloak their strategies under the mantle of efficiency. The structure of an organization or government reflects political interests. As the balance of power among those interests changes, it is not surprising that pressure builds to change that structure in response. It is convenient for politicians to dub these responses "reorganizations" and justify them at least partly on the grounds of increased efficiency. Thus we have the cases in which entire agencies are created by liberals who desire a new service to be offered or a part of the private sector to be regulated and other instances where agencies are eliminated by conservatives who want to eliminate the service or deregulate the industry. At the same end of the spectrum are the governmental reorganizations—such as the adoption of the city manager plan by a local government or changes in a legislature's seniority rules—that result in a fundamental change in the capacity of various groups and officials to influence key decisions. Of somewhat less consequence for the operation of the organization concerned, but of considerable political importance, are changes that increase the public visibility of a favored official (e.g., by taking the Department of Corrections out of the Department of Social Services) or that increase the proportion of appointed versus civil service executives in a particular agency.

It also seems clear that some reorganizations are carried out with no other political goal in mind than to appear to be concerned about efficiency. This was, of course, Petronius Arbiter's point in the quotation that begins this section and is the inspiration for the well-known maxim "When in doubt, reorganize." As Branch observes, reorganization is one of the principal tools that bureaucracies use in dealing with criticism. "If the heat is on, a department should go through six months of shuffling the organizational charts and then hope the crisis has passed, as is usually the case" (Branch, 1977, p. 163).

Yet while Branch is correct in observing that reorganization is a useful tool in coping with the demands of a crisis, its greatest symbolic value seems to be in creating the sense that a newly elected or appointed executive is different from his or her predecessor. This is to be expected. The most common reason for installing a new executive is the desire to do something innovative; quite often, the precise character of this innovation is not clear to anyone, least of all the new executive. Under these circumstances, what makes more sense—from the point of view of the president, governor, mayor, (or chief executive officer)—than to boldly announce the necessity of carrying out a major reorganization in order to increase efficiency and effectiveness? The temptation is nearly irresistible, particularly when there is virtually no chance that the consequences of the reorganization will ever be systematically evaluated; one can proclaim success with impunity. This goes a long way in explaining why most reorganizations take place near the beginning of a new administration. It also accounts for why civil servants who "pay" for each major reorganization by having to cope with new telephone directories, new budget formats, office changes, and the like often greet the prospect of a change in administrations with reactions ranging from irritation to horror.

While the political motivations for reorganization are very important and have become increasingly so during the past 15 years, the evidence suggests that administrators have learned to be cynical about the efficiency implications of reorganization; they did not (at least as a group) undertake reorganizations with the belief that enormous efficiencies will result. The purely manipulative bonding of efficiency and reorganization is the product of a long history of disappointment and frustration on the part of elected officials, administrators in both the public and private sectors, and scholars interested in organizations. It is impossible to read the debate and commentary surrounding the Brownlow Committee, the first and second Hoover Commissions, the Price and Heineman Task Forces, the Ash Council, or that associated with any proposal to reorganize the federal executive branch and come away with the belief that the individuals involved felt that reorganization had nothing to do with government efficiency. On the contrary, it is obvious that they believed strongly that the performance and structure of government were intimately connected. Many had been educated, by academics who believed these ideas, in a tradition that emphasized the key role of variables like centralization, span of control, and specialization in determining organizational performance in the public and private sectors. Max Weber, one of the founders of modern sociology, preoccupied himself with structural variables that are the focus of reorganizations because he believed them to be important determinants of organizational performance. The tradition he began runs through scholars such as Luther Gulick and Henri Fayol to the structuralists today.

The structural tradition is alive and well in the practical arena of government reform. The Grace Commission (PPSS) report released in January 1984 is filled with proposals for structural reforms ranging from the creation of a new office of financial management that would centralize many of the administrative functions of the executive branch in federal government to changing the spans of control in specific functions. Given the history of reorganizations, the faith that this group of business executives places in structural reforms for achieving billions of dollars of efficiency gains in federal government is nothing short of astounding. As we shall see in more detail in the next chapter, the Grace Commission report sets a new standard for insensitivity to the politics and complexities of government organization.

The most important explanation for why reorganizations have not lived up to expectations in terms of improved efficiency begins with the work of Herbert A. Simon. Simon pointed out that most of the guidelines built on concepts like span of control and specialization were of little use to anyone trying to structure an organization so as to maximize efficiency (Simon, 1976, pp. 20–45) because the concepts are indeterminate. Managers are told that efficiency is enhanced by limiting the number of subordinates that report to any one individual. Seemingly sensible advice. On the other hand, they are also told that efficiency is promoted by minimizing the number of levels through which an issue must pass before it is acted upon, another piece of seemingly sensible advice and something to be remembered when planning a reorganization. The problem is that limiting the number of people reporting to a given superior tends to increase the number of organizational levels, and decreasing the number of levels tends to increase the number reporting to any given official. Like the proverbs "Absence makes the heart grow fonder" and "out of sight, out of mind," we have two pieces of advice that contain some wisdom but little real guidance. At precisely what point do the marginal benefits of decreasing the number of levels become less than those of decreasing the span of control? Is this point always the same across all organizations and in every context?[2] The mere existence of a contradiction between two principles of organizational design is not in itself a cause for great concern. Other realms are filled with the same contradictions. Automotive engineers, for example, manage to cope with the contradictory goals of designing cars that are simultaneously powerful and fuel-efficient. Those in the auto industry realize that a compromise has to be made and that the challenge lies in making cars that best reflect the values of the buying public. With two factors such as fuel-efficiency and power this requires some experimentation to explore where the tradeoffs are and (at the simplest level) a good marketing research unit that can tell the engineers how many buyers are more interested in using their car for hauling trailers than going to the supermarket and conversely. Cars are then made with differing characteristics and in differing quantities for different market segments. One important difference between the auto problem and organization design problem is in the clarity of the design tradeoffs; it is much easier to engineer cars than organizations. The efficiency implications of the tradeoff between span of control and levels of hierarchy are affected by dozens of organizational and contextual variables, all of which interact with each other. Sometimes decreasing the span of control at the expense of increasing the level of hierarchy will increase efficiency, sometimes it will decrease efficiency, and sometimes (perhaps most often) it will have no effect at all. In short, span of control has no single effect on efficiency; it has many effects and they can be markedly different.

The notion that there is one maximally efficient span of control throughout the hierarchy of a large, complex organization (i.e., that would hold for those reporting to a CEO, to a regional sales manager, to the secretary of defense, and to a supervisor of keypunch operators in the Air Force Logistics Command) and across many such organizations (i.e., that would hold for ITT, Hospital Corporation of America, Kinney Shoes, the Department of Defense, and the Securities and Exchange Commission) is truly foolish. There are no useful rules of thumb; 1:1 is probably too few and 50:1 is probably too many (unless the employees work on chores that are easily monitored).

Those academics interested in creating a science of organizational design have barely begun to explore the contingent effects associated with even the most prominent variables that are manipulated in the course of a reorganization. They are able to tell us next to nothing about the efficiency implications of "secondary" variables like span of control and level of hierarchy under various conditions. This wouldn't matter so much if we could be assured that altering a particular factor had a positive but indeterminate impact on efficiency. While we couldn't predict exactly how much efficiency would increase when this factor was increased, at least we would know that we were making some contribution to our goal. But we didn't even know this. Our ignorance is so great that our efforts could actually lead to a decrease in efficiency.

In this context, reorganization can be thought of as a process by which a dozen factors thought to be connected with efficiency are simultaneously manipulated without any real knowledge of how any one factor effects efficiency. To predict confidently that such a reform will improve the performance of government is foolhardy. Part of the hubris associated with reorganizations stems from the pretense of knowledge where it does not exist, another part lies in underestimating the difficulty of implementing the reorganization. It is one thing for proponents of a reorganization to get a clear mental picture of what they want it to accomplish and quite another to translate this image into reality. Perhaps the classic reason for being unable to do this is an insufficient appreciation of the extent to which the present organizational structure reflects networks of power and interests. A reorganization that attempts to alter these relationships will be resisted by those who will lose power; a reorganization that naively disregards these interests runs the risk of being ignored. In the first instance the reorganization is likely never to be implemented; in the second, it will be meaningless.

Opposition by interest groups (including Congress) has led to the collapse of numerous reorganization plans at the federal level alone. In their excellent review of government reorganization during the twentieth century, March and Olson point out that opposition forced the abandonment of reorganization proposals during the Wilson, Johnson, Truman, Nixon, and Carter administrations and note that 100 Democratic congressmen deserted Roosevelt to defeat the 1938 Executive Reorganization bill (March and Olson, 1983, p. 285). Often the opposition to reorganization on the part of interest groups is evidenced less by an overwhelming defeat on some key vote than by the length of time that passes before the reorganization is even voted on. Stalling tactics are often used to avoid a confrontation on reorganization, its opponents resting securely in the knowledge that if they delay long enough, the executive's attention will wander off to other, more pressing matters. As the authors observe, "Although it is hard to predict what specific crisis, scandal or war will divert presidents from the reorganization arena, it is easy to predict that something will" (March and Olson, 1983, p. 286).

Reorganizations that succeed on paper but are ignored in practice are just as common. March and Olson discuss a case where control of federal employment security policy continued to rest with a coalition of state agencies and employer groups even after a reorganization had assigned the Department of Labor responsibility for this activity (March and Olson, 1983, p. 284). Basically the same thing occurred after the Defense Reorganization Act of 1949, which attempted to achieve a wide variety of efficiency gains by creating the Defense Department to oversee the four armed services. Although its aspirations were high, it was not able to redistribute power sufficiently away from the services toward the new department to ensure that these aspirations were carried out. In the first few years at least—ex-secretaries of defense would argue that the period runs until the present—the Defense Department was not so much in control of the services as tolerated by them.

State and local governments are witness to the same process. During the 1960s, for example, many states attempted to reduce friction and promote cooperation among welfare, health, and correctional agencies by consolidating them within "umbrella" or "super" agencies such as a department of human services. Proponents of such schemes soon discovered that the political price for getting various interests to agree to the reform was that the individual agencies retain substantial amounts of their autonomy. As a result parochial agency interests and hostilities almost always survived the reorganization.

Given how little is known about the consequences of manipulating the dimensions of reorganization and the difficulty in implementing them, it should not surprise us that people are skeptical about the claims made on their behalf. Given the potential symbolic and manipulative aspects of reorganization, it is not surprising that they retain a great deal of their popularity—if popularity can be measured by the percentage of governments and government agencies that undertake reorganizations every year.

PERSONNEL REFORM

> If the public accepts the common stereotype of the lazy, venal "bureaucrat," it will not expect efficient, responsible government, and it will not get it. To the extent that the public recognizes that the problems of efficiency in government are as serious as, but no more serious than, these problems in other large-scale organizations, we can expect substantial progress toward these goals.
>
> HERBERT A. SIMON

Personnel system reforms have much in common with reorganization as a means of increasing government efficiency. They are extremely popular. They can be used symbolically to pursue political ends in the name of efficiency or to attest to an administration's commitment to efficiency. There is a great deal of skepticism about their usefulness. And proponents consistently overestimate their ability to design reforms that can overcome informational and political problems.

Throughout history, government has been a labor-intensive activity. Once we exclude contractual work and the major transfer programs such as Social Security, the vast majority of government expenditures go toward personnel. Given the limited opportunities to improve the productivity of agencies through capital substitution and the creation of new work procedures and organizational forms, improving the motivation and skill of the government work force would seem to be a promising area for productivity gains. This is especially true if one believes, as most Americans do, that the lassitude of government workers is a chief source of inefficiency.

The central problem in designing government personnel systems has always been that of creating a bureaucracy that responds to the legitimate management initiatives of elected officials but in which professional competence rather than political or personal loyalty is the primary criterion of selection, promotion, and advancement. Because the balance between responsiveness and professional autonomy is so delicate, the history of personnel system reform in the United States and elsewhere oscillates between the twin perils of "spoils systems," in which politics is everything, and highly insulated civil service bureaucracies, in which incompetence is protected by law.

Under a spoils system, political or personal allegiance play a dominant role in all personnel decisions. Workers are hired not because they are the best qualified but because they have political connections or were active in securing the election of the present government. The excesses wrought by the most notorious spoils systems were countless. Budgetary surpluses were regularly distributed as bonuses to favored employees at the end of the year. Ward officers who could barely read or write were placed in supervisory positions as accountants and civil engineers. Because many of the jobs required little or no work, employees were often more than happy to return substantial portions of their salaries as campaign contributions or direct kickbacks. Subordinates with political connections openly defied their superiors.

Even under the "best" spoils system, where corruption was less conspicuous, highly competent people were regularly dismissed. The following letter, written in the 1880s for one of the victims of a spoils system, makes the criterion for retention absolutely clear.

To Whom It May Concern:

It affords me great pleasure to be able to certify to the fact that my intercourse with Mr. Lewis N. Rollins, former clerk of this office under Mr. John H. Sellman, formerly collector and my predecessor, was of the most pleasant and satisfactory character and such as to enable me to ascertain that he was a most conscientious and efficient officer, and a gentleman of the strictest integrity and honor.

He was requested to resign his position by me for no fault whatever, save that we differed politically, thus coming under the old rule that "to the victor belongs the spoils."

I can commend Mr. Rollins with confidence to anyone who may desire the services of a faithful and efficient employee.

J. K. Roberts, Collector
District of Maryland

Reforms beginning with the Pendleton Act of 1883 and touching all levels of government had the dual purpose of expunging political influences from public service and instilling the "merit principle" for personnel selection, remuneration, and promotion. The reforms instituted a variety of fairly rigid rules and strong employee protections that made great strides toward an apolitical bureaucracy. However, it was not very long before problems began to surface. Some argued that the reforms should be less negative and more positive. "Keeping the rascals out" was a praiseworthy goal, but it did not solve the problem of getting well-trained people into public service and providing sufficient incentives for them to remain and excel. As Charles Beard, a contemporary commentator put it, "the time has arrived for giving more attention to lifting up the strong and wise than holding down the wicked" (Beard, 1916, p. 219).

An even more basic problem involved the fundamental paradox of personnel system design: if you protect employees from political and personal caprice, you inevitably run the risk of providing them with the ability to ignore even legitimate directions. In the limiting case you end up with the stereotypical civil service system in which you can't make employees work, can't fire them if they refuse to work, and can't control promotions and pay differentials between the most competent and least competent employees. What is needed is a system that protects employees from the evils of a spoils system but also leads to the development of a responsive and efficient bureaucracy.

For many, the answer appeared to lie in a personnel system based on the objective measurement of worker productivity. If selection and advancement decisions were based solely on productivity, then we could rest assured that politics and personal loyalty were not involved and that bureaucratic inertia would not be allowed to run amok. Initial confidence that worker productivity could be measured accurately was characteristically high. Carl Schurz (the bearded gentleman on the 4-cent stamp) had introduced one of the first efficiency based personnel systems in the Office of the Interior Department in 1879. He confidently asserted:

> We can ascertain with almost mathematical certainty the proportion of work done by each clerk in the Pension Office in point of quantity as well as quality, the number of claims disposed of and the accuracy of the work. . . . When the efficiency record is before me, those who have done the most and the best work are promoted, and those who have fallen behind are reduced. The system has proved to be a powerful stimulus, and the result is that almost everyone in the Pension Office does his utmost. (White, 1958, p. 356.)

With the initial civil service reform, the Pendleton Act, in place and the experience in the Department of Interior, President Benjamin Harrison in 1891 directed all departments of the federal government to adopt an efficiency rating system as quickly as possible. Yet they soon ran into trouble from a source that President Harrison could not have anticipated from the Department of Interior experience. The problem was interoffice competition. Because the performance of a subordinate reflects the quality of his or her supervision, each supervisor of clerks in an office had a strong incentive to make his clerks compare favorably with the clerks of other supervisors in other offices. Everyone ended up rated near the top of the scale, separated by the smallest permissible intervals. The effort was a failure. (White, 1958, p. 358.)

What is often referred to as the first modern personnel performance appraisal system, the graphic rating scale, was installed in 1923. The instrument that formed the basis of this system is shown in Figure 6.1. This system was in part a reaction to the inadequacies of previous systems that had been based almost entirely on production (output) data. The graphic rating scale was an attempt to recognize explicitly and systematize the subjective element in personnel judgments. Production data were relegated to the fifteenth item on a 15-item scale and were only required where good output records existed.

Ironically, this system, designed to recognize and handle inherent imprecisions in personnel evaluations, foundered in large part because of pretensions to precision. A numerical rating that had to be calculated to 0.01 percent was taken from the crude instrument in Figure 6.1 and played a major role in pay, promotion, demotion, and layoff (now RIF, Reduction in Force) decisions. The legislation required a "normal" average of 82.5 and as many ratings below as above average. This average provision led to some "weird manipulations."

> If A secured a rating of 90 in 1930 to ensure his increment, he might be reduced to 80 in 1931 to make possible a rating of 90 to B without disturbing too seriously the sacred average of 82.5. Naturally A became disturbed at these gyrations, especially when in 1933 and 1934 many layoffs occurred which were based in part upon the efficiency rating. (White, 1958, p. 357.)

After 12 years, the system was reviewed and replaced by another that abandoned the artificial precision of the first and loosened the connection between ratings and personnel decisions. Perhaps predictably, it was soon discovered that the new system left too much discretion to individual supervisors and was drifting away from the goal of objectively measuring productivity. Several years later, the cycle continued when this system was replaced by still another that focused more on outputs.

Thus began a seemingly endless series of oscillations bewtween highly structured systems with great pretensions to precision and more subjective ones that amounted to having no system at all. The only constants were the failure to increase efficiency to any noticeable extent and the undiminished enthusiasm and self-confidence of proponents of each ensuing reform. These attitudes are, of course, reminiscent of those possessed by advocates of reorganization and were so pervasive that they played a central role in Leonard White's insightful review of the experience with personnel rating systems through 1948.

> American experts have pushed their experiments toward an "objective" and automatic system boldly and hopefully, but not always with adequate insight into the hazards of their venture.
>
> Inspired by an extraordinary faith in the validity of various schemes, they have been put to work in some jurisdictions with a thoroughness which cast caution to the winds. Men and women have been singled out to lose their jobs, to sacrifice a part of their income, and to abandon the prospect of promotion because a mathematical conversion of a series of check marks by supervisors totaled less than an arbitrary sum. The effort to control the judgment of supervisors to this degree and to govern the fate of individuals in this way is not sound personnel policy.
>
> The defense made for it is that unless a formal record is established and made conclusive, the bias, prejudice, or ill will of supervisory officials will produce even worse results. There are doubtless illustrations of personal malice or poor judgment among a small minority of officials; but no one should suppose that they will be more reliable in making out an efficiency record than in taking any other action. The only cure is more intelligent and trustworthy supervisors. In other words, a formal rating by a supervisor cannot be expected to achieve indirectly what the supervisor does not intend or is not able to do directly. (White, 1958, p. 358.)

Figure 6.1

GRAPHIC RATING SCALE

Efficiency Rating Form No. 3

NON-SUPERVISORY _____
SUPERVISORY _____

☐ (CHECK ONE)
☐

CLASSIFICATION SYMBOLS

SERVICE	GRADE	CLASS

Name _____

(Surname)   (Given Name)   (Initial)   Department _____

(Bureau)   (Division)   (Section)   (Subsection)

NOTE: MARK ONLY ON ELEMENTS CHECKED IN LEFT-HAND MARGIN

ELEMENT NUMBER	SERVICE ELEMENTS						Do not Use Space Below
☐ **1**	Consider accuracy; ability to produce work free from error; ability to detect errors.	Highest possible accuracy	Very careful	Careful. No more than reasonable time required for revision	Careless. Time required for revision greatly excessive	Practically worthless work	
☐ **2**	Consider reliability in the execution of assigned tasks; dependability in following instructions; accuracy of any parts of product appraisable in terms of accuracy.	Greatest possible reliability	Very reliable	Reliable	Doubtful reliability	Unreliable	
☐ **3**	Consider neatness and orderliness of work.	Greatest possible neatness and orderliness	Very neat and orderly	Neat and orderly	Disorderly	Slovenly	
☐ **4**	Consider the speed or rapidity with which work is accomplished; the quantity of work produced in a given time; the dispatch with which a task of known difficulty is completed.	Greatest possible rapidity	Very rapid	Good speed	Slow	Hopelessly slow	
☐ **5**	Consider industry; diligence; attentiveness; energy and application to duties; the degree to which the employee really concentrates on the work at hand.	Greatest possible diligence	Very diligent	Industrious	Inattentive to work	Lazy	
☐ **6**	Consider knowledge of work; present knowledge of job and of work related to it; specialized knowledge in his particular field.	Completely informed	Unusually well informed	Well informed	Poorly informed	Lacking	
☐ **7**	Consider judgment; ability to grasp a situation and draw correct conclusions; ability to profit by experience; sense of proportion or relative values; common sense.	Perfect judgment	Excellent judgment	Good judgment	Poor judgment	Neglects and misinterprets the facts	

#	Consideration					
8	Consider success in winning confidence and respect through his personality; courtesy and tact; control of emotions; poise.	Inspiring	Unusually pleasing	Pleasing	Weak	Repellent
9	Consider cooperativeness; ability to work for and with others; readiness to give new ideas and methods a fair trial; desire to observe and conform with the policies of the management.	Greatest possible co-operativeness	Very cooperative	Cooperative	Difficult to handle	Obstructive
10	Consider initiative; resourcefulness; success in doing things in new and better ways and in adapting improved methods to his own work; constructive thinking.	Greatest possible originality	Very resourceful	Progressive	Rarely suggests	Needs detailed instruction
11	Consider execution; ability to pursue to the end difficult investigations or assignments.	Completes assignments in shortest possible time	Completes assignments in unusually short time.	Completes assignments in a reasonable time	Slow in completing assignments; or does not complete assignments	Takes inordinately long and accomplishes little
12	Consider organizing ability; success in organizing the work of his section, division, or department, both by delegating authority wisely and by making certain that results are achieved; ability to plan so as to complete tasks on schedule.	Highest possible effectiveness	Effective under difficult circumstances	Effective under normal circumstances	Lacks planning ability	Inefficient
13	Consider leadership; success in winning the cooperation of his subordinates and in welding them into a loyal and effective working unit; decisiveness; energy; self control; tact; courage; fairness in dealing with others.	Most capable and forceful leader possible	Very capable and forceful leader	Capable leader	Fails to command confidence	Antagonizes subordinates
14	Consider success in improving and developing employees by imparting information, developing talent, and arousing ambition; ability to teach; ability to explain matters clearly and comprehensively.	Develops employees of highest possible caliber	Develops very efficient employees	Develops competent employees	Fails to develop employees	Discourages and misinforms employees
15	QUANTITY OF WORK (To be used only where accurate and comprehensive OUTPUT RECORDS are kept.)	Highest possible output	High output	Good output	Low output	Practically no output

On the whole, do you consider the department and attitude of this employee toward his work to be satisfactory? Answer "Yes," "No," or "Fairly so" _____

Rated by: _____ (Rating officer) (Date) _____ Reviewed by: _____ (Reviewing officer) (Date) _____

Total _____

Final rating _____

The subsequent history of personnel reforms would not have pleased White. For the most part, it has provided little more than the opportunity to rediscover old problems and identify others that should have been obvious from the outset. Take the current experience with the Civil Service Reform Act (CSRA) of 1978 that required a merit pay scheme based on "objective indicators" of relative performance for federal supervisory and managerial personnel in grades 13 to 15. In a recently published review of the federal experience with the system so far, Pearce and Perry (1983, pp. 315–325) concluded that "there is no indication that the merit pay experiment at grades 13–15 has been sufficiently successful to proceed with plans to include employees in grades 1–12." They attribute difficulties with the programs to three factors.

First, "the new performance appraisal system does not effectively measure performance and therefore does not serve the purpose of the merit pay program to link pay to performance." As we have seen, this is a problem with precedents.

Second, Pearce and Perry attribute some of merit pay's problems to an "inherent contradiction in the guidance that calls for accurate appraisals based on consultation with the ratee along with "managed" ratings to ensure against payout-inequities." After the initial "objective" ratings are made, "pay-pool managers" and personnel specialists assume that ratings are naturally distorted and that there are equivalent distributions of performance in all employee pools. They therefore revise the "objective" ratings to achieve equity across pools. This is, of course, a version of the interoffice competition problem that Schurz's system encountered 100 years ago. The modern solution penalizes the more honest ratings.

Third, they argue that merit pay encountered some problems peculiar to the public sector. These include an environment in which it is more difficult to measure performance, tight budgetary constraints, the necessity of freedom of information regarding individual salaries, unclear authority relationships, and changing organizational goals. (Pearce and Perry, 1983, p. 324.) They probably exaggerate the extent to which most of these problems are peculiar to the public sector. With the exception of salary disclosure, these problems are present in the private sector and cause the same sorts of frustration and inequities; recall the tenuous link between the fabled bottom line and executive compensation. Nonetheless, their claim that these problems cause difficulties for personnel systems seems unassailable.

Pearce and Perry describe the "theory" behind the latest federal attempt at performance appraisal and merit-based pay as "Vroom's expectancy theory." They say that, in its simplified form, it

> . . . . posits that if individuals expect to receive a valued reward for high performance, they are more likely to strive for this level of performance, than if there were no "payoff." Federal merit pay is expected to increase effort and, therefore, performance by changing the probability that performance will lead to the outcome (salary increase) that is assumed to be positively valued by most managers. (Pearce and Perry, 1983, pp. 315–316.)

This is hardly deep theory but rather a slightly pompous restatement of a belief about motivation held by most parents, athletic coaches, managers, and anyone else responsible for influencing the behavior of others. It is the basis of all compensation schemes where pay is contingent on performance. In many cases, as with salespersons on straight commission or seamstresses on piecework rates, the contingency is direct and unambiguous: no performance, no pay—more performance, more pay. In the instance of the CSRA merit pay system, the link between pay and performance is much less direct. It is relative, not absolute, performance that counts, and there is a lot of ambiguity in how performance is defined and measured.

The problems with the CSRA merit pay scheme are fundamental. As we saw in the discussion of productivity measurement in Chapter 3, the obstacles to constructing meaningful measures of performance are formidable. There is evidence suggesting *that even if the federal government succeeded in constructing a meaningful performance appraisal system and in linking pay to performance, the desired motivational effects might not follow.*

Difficult as it may be for enthusiastic proponents to believe, performance appraisal is a treacherous business. In their review of empirical research on the topic, Ilgen et al. (1979, p. 367) concluded that "feedback is often either misperceived or not accepted by the recipient . . . " and that "negative feedback is very likely to be misperceived and not accepted." Kay et al. (1965), in a study of comprehensive year-end appraisal interviews in a real organizational setting, found that most of those whose performance was being reviewed did not respond constructively to praise or criticism; the performance of those praised did not improve and the performance of those criticized usually worsened. In this particular study, the authors attributed these results to the length of time between appraisals and the presence of the formal appraisal system, causing managers to "save up" appraisal comments rather than giving them as they occurred. But others (Ilgen et al., 1979, p. 367) note that "increasing feedback frequency may not only fail to improve performance but actually may be detrimental to it." Chapanis (1964) found experimentally that knowledge of performance had no incentive effects on the performance of repetitive, monotonous tasks (e.g., keypunching); subjects with knowledge of their performance did not outperform those without feedback on performance. Explicit, quantitative measures that are held by management to define functions adequately are a standing invitation to employees and organizations to interpret them literally and to do exactly what the measures call for and nothing else. One need only look at the experience with unions who chose to "work to rule" (e.g., railway unions in the 1950s and 1960s) rather than strike to understand how devastatingly dysfunctional such literal interpretations can be. Because of our inability to prespecify all essential aspects of such functions, even fairly simple operations grind to a complete halt when employees do only what is specified in their job descriptions. If you add behavioral force to such a measurement system by directly and mechanically tying compensation to performance on measures, you are inviting trouble, because most functions are not amenable to a "piecework" arrangement. As the Soviets discovered, shoe factories rewarded for the number of shoes may produce many left shoes, nail factories rewarded on the number of nails produce many, small nails, and so on.

Fortunately, it seems clear that portions of the private (and, we suspect, the public) sector have already learned some of these lessons.

While it is true that the good companies have superb analytic skills, we believe that their major decisions are shaped more by their values than by their dexterity with numbers. The top performers create a broad, uplifting, shared culture, a coherent framework within which charged-up people search for appropriate adaptations. Their contributions from very large numbers of people turn on the ability to create a sense of highly valued purpose. Such purpose invariably emanates from love of product, providing top-quality services, and honoring innovations and contribution from all. Such high purpose is inherently at odds with 30 quarterly MBO objectives, 25 measures of cost containment, 100 demeaning rules for production-line workers, or an ever-changing, analytically derived strategy that stresses cost this year, innovation next, and heaven knows what the year after. (Peters and Waterman, 1982, p. 51.)

A merit pay scheme like the CSRA reform that rewards the relative performance, ambiguously measured, of a fixed proportion of an employment population (e.g., 25 or 30 percent) is apt to have all sorts of undesirable motivational effects that may actually lower individual and organizational performance. Individual expectations are a serious problem. If you reward the top one-third in relative performance, employees who are not selected but nonetheless consider themselves among the top third in performance are apt to be angry and may take their anger out on the job. Their response may be to become less efficient rather than to strive to be included in the top one-third in the next review, particularly if they believe that they are already there and that it is only poor measurement, politics, discrimination, and the like that says otherwise. Mikalachki (1976) reviews research showing that 70 to 90 percent of managerial and technical employee groups consider themselves in a top 30 percent performance group. For example, "86% of the engineers working in research laboratories in a number of different companies rated themselves in the top 25% of excellence in performance. The other 14% saw themselves in the top 50% of performance excellence" (Mikalachki, 1976, p. 178). In an environment like this, the efficiency benefits in rewarding the 25 percent may be offset by the cost of having more than twice that number disaffected and bitter. This is not to say that it is never a good idea to raise some workers' salaries more than those of others—obviously, very efficient workers can react strongly to a lockstep arrangement in which incompetent colleagues receive the same rewards as they do, but it is to argue that very mechanical decision rules like "reward only the top 25 percent" applied in organizations where performance is difficult to assess with precision can cause as many problems as they are designed to solve.

Relative performance measures also introduce competition into hierarchical systems where cooperation is often essential to overall organizational performance. Consider Bill and Charlie who are research engineers in the same laboratory and members of the same pool of employees competing for merit pay on the basis of their individual productivity. They have equal resources (e.g., the same number of assistants, the same equipment, etc.) and their output for purposes of performance appraisal is defined in such a way that cooperative efforts do not count for either individual—a likely situation because of the conceptual problems in defining and measuring outputs. It is inevitable that there will be instances where the overall organizational performance will be best served by having Bill and Charlie pool their resources—say to perform an experiment that neither has the resources to perform alone—or by having Bill lend Charlie half his resources for a week to speed the completion of a critical line of work (and incidentally improve Charlie's case for merit pay and worsen Bill's case). In such instances, the existence of competition for merit pay may be to discourage cooperation and lower performance if employees are not unusually dedicated and self-sacrificing. Organizations are, by definition, entities whose performance depends on cooperative efforts; the impact of any individual on overall performance depends on the activities of other individuals. It is not clear that pitting these individuals against each other in competition for pay will increase overall performance. Individual productivity is related to group productivity in other nonsimple ways.

> Although a carefully organized production record is the best single index of efficiency, it is not always adequate standing by itself. An employee with a high production index may be blessed with a personality that irritates colleagues to the point where their own efficiency is adversely affected. And conversely an employee with an average production record may have that rare type of personality that makes for harmony, good will, and *esprit de corps* in his group; such an employee may be worth infinitely more than a mere production record would indicate. (White, 1958, p. 409.)

As long as an index of performance does not capture all of what we want from an employee on the job, including his or her interrelationships with other employees, measuring and managing systems will often fall short of generating the desired motivational effects and improved overall organizational performance.

The fact that personnel rating systems are imperfect need not bar experimentation with different systems. Obviously some are more imperfect than others, and it would be foolish to argue that a formal evaluation system, with all of its attendant problems, is necessarily inferior to every informal system. We are interested here in the potential and limitations of personnel rating systems and in personnel reform more generally as a vehicle for achieving the dramatic efficiency gains that have been promised by their more vocal proponents. At the turn of the century, when the spoils systems was dominant and a few broad reforms such as the institution of a merit-based civil service system could change the complexion of government overnight, limitations such as the complexity and ambiguity of public agency goals and the uncertain link between feedback and motivation were largely irrelevant. Now that these more dramatic reforms have been instituted, the potential of personnel reform is much less and the limitations loom large.

Unhappily from the point of view of personnel systems reformers, we seem to have reached the point where most of the reforms they propose are only useful at the margin or are unworkable. Thus while the Merit System Protection Board (MSPB) instituted as part of the 1978 reforms may play an important role in protecting the system from some of the abuses that took place under the Nixon administration, its contribution to increasing the efficiency of government as a whole is unlikely to come up to the level of earlier reforms. For example, ensuring that the Civil Service Commission stops operating a special referral unit to circumvent merit procedures for special political appointments—a task of the MSPB—is a reasonable but minor idea that will not increase government efficiency in any dramatic way because it will not affect most appointments. More ambitious proposals for schemes like merit bonuses and streamlined methods for dismissing employees can be expected to yield disappointing results, either because they ignore important technical problems surrounding performance assessment or because they ignore certain fundamental realities of government like the inevitable tension between politics and administration or the ultimately political source of much inefficiency. It will always be more difficult to fire workers in public agencies than private corporations because of the constant threat of the abuses of a spoils system in which party or personal loyalties are more important than competence. Similarly, no personnel system, regardless of how cunningly designed or rich in resources, could cope with the "inefficiencies" whose source is pork-barrel politics or redistribution.

The current balance between "spoils" and "merit" is not obviously unreasonable. Chief executives can appoint their own teams for their own reasons to top policy/managerial positions, while lower-level positions, where specific expertise and continuity are critical, are more insulated from politics, so that substantive merit is more important than political allegiances in all aspects of personnel management. There are still spoils. Edwin Meese was not confirmed as attorney general of the United States because of his personal rectitude, the depth of his jurisprudential knowledge, or his demonstrated ability to manage effectively large legal organizations, and Bert Lance did not become the Director of OMB because of his personal rectitude, the depth of his knowledge about the federal budget, or his demonstrated genius at managing complicated financial affairs. Joseph Califano and Martin Feldman were not made uncomfortable in Washington because they lacked substantive ability. But there is merit at work as well; physicists are not given political litmus tests prior to employment as physicists in national laboratories. The most promising lines for future improvement lie not in changes in the number of political appointments or in more elaborate performance measurement/pay systems but in electing and appointing better quality people, people who place a greater value on substantive competence than on personal allegiance and who are less likely to confuse the two.

TAKING THE MONEY AWAY

This opposition to higher taxes on the part of the property owner has . . . placed the public official in a difficult situation. On the one hand the citizens are demanding more service, while on the other, taxpayers demand lower taxes. Both sets of demands must be satisfied . . . if the official is to hold his position. But the only way in which both of these conflicting desires can be gratified is by greater efficiency on the part of the office holder . . . . The screws have been turned on the office holder by taxpayers and consumers of the public service.

HENRY GEORGE, 1916

By the mid 1970s the accumulated frustration of countless failed reforms had begun to take its toll. Highly touted managerial systems like ZBB and MBO were being discarded soon after adoption, and there was no agreement among experts on what to do next. Although reorganizations and personnel reforms were still implemented by new administrations as evidence of their commitment to efficiency, few people inside or outside of government took them seriously anymore. Everybody (particularly candidates for elected office) still "knew" that government was terribly inefficient, but no one seemed to have any new ideas about how to attack the problems.

The effect of doubts about government's ability to increase efficiency was compounded by a similar loss of confidence in its ability to solve the larger problems of society. The programs of the Great Society were under attack as expensive and ineffective and were being dismantled. A variety of monetary and fiscal policies appeared to be failing miserably in dealing with inflation, unemployment, and increasing federal deficits. New York City was on the verge of bankruptcy. Domestic and international markets were lost to foreign competitors, particularly the Japanese and Germans. The Organization of Petroleum Exporting Countries had been able, without effective retaliation, to expropriate a substantial chunk of our national wealth, and we all sat in line to give domestic oil companies a fair chunk of what was left. Drug use and violent crime increased at a rate that was exceeded only by the rate at which academic achievement in public schools declined. The list of problems that government wasn't able to solve seemed endless. The confidence of the early 1960s that government could do anything had degenerated into despair.

It was against this background that a new strategy for limiting the growth of government and for increasing government efficiency gained popularity. Its logic was simple: control government expenditures by restricting the amount of available revenue. The strategy was motivated by two interrelated beliefs about the nature of government spending behavior that seemed quite reasonable. First, governments cannot waste financial resources that they do not have at their disposal. If you believe that governments are wasting a substantial proportion, say 80 percent, of each dollar that they collect, one good way to reduce waste in government is to take the money away. For each dollar you take away, you save 80 cents. Second, from the perspective of the average citizen there is a declining marginal utility associated with government expenditures. As governments grow more affluent, they spend an ever-increasing proportion of tax dollars on services that many citizens view as marginal if not frivolous. Mobile libraries, county environmental coordinators, and psychological counseling services are often viewed as falling into this category. If government revenues are restricted or cut back, it is believed that only these basically irrelevant services will suffer and not the really essential services like police and fire protection at the local level and defense and social security at the federal level.

The strategy of controlling government growth and increasing efficiency by restricting revenue has been widely employed in recent years. Between 1970 and the passage of California's widely publicized Proposition 13, at least 15 states adopted some form of sweeping financial reform, including ceilings on expenditures and restrictions on revenue sources with the property tax as the favorite target. In 1979, reform limitations passed in 12 of 16 states that had them on the ballot. In 1980 and 1981, the passage of Proposition 2½ in Massachusetts and the Reagan administration's strong initiatives to cut federal taxes and domestic spending are evidence of the continuing vitality of the fiscal reform movement. All levels and types of government have been affected by the movement over the past decade.

The duration and ultimate consequences of this movement are still unclear. There is some systematic empirical work on the consequences of various tax and expenditure limits,[3] but it is much too early to know if the consequences identified thus far are transitory or structural. For example, it may be that the initial reductions in expenditures or slower growth in government budgets will be offset by surges in expenditures in future years. Short-term responses, such as the state "bailout" that followed passage of California's Proposition 13, have only recently begun to be displaced by less ad hoc and more institutionally durable arrangements. At any rate, it still will be several years before the most interesting counterfactuals can be rigorously addressed. (Are government budgets smaller than they *would have been* without the fiscal reform movement? How are service and employment patterns different from what they would have been?)

Reducing taxes and spending money are the two tried and true ways for politicians to win friends and influence votes through financial decisions. Unfortunately for aspiring philanthropists occupying nonfederal offices, budgets are legally required to balance. Estimated revenues must equal estimated expenditures in each budget year, and the governments cannot by law run recurring deficits. The central problem that a tax limitation measure such as Proposition 13 poses for politicians and bureaucrats is a projected budget imbalance. The specter of reduced tax receipts or receipts that grow at a slower rate than the costs of providing services leaves officials with three categories of alternatives: (1) develop additional sources of revenue; (2) reduce expenditures by cutting the level of services; and (3) reduce expenditures by increasing "efficiency" (i.e., delivering the same level of services at lower cost). Optimistic sponsors and voters believe that officials will choose the third option. That is, only unnecessary services will be cut and the rest of the loss absorbed by the implementation of more efficient management practices. Regrettably, there are good reasons for arguing that such changes have not been and will not be the modal response. As a result, increased efficiency will probably not be an important outcome of the various fiscal reform measures.

THE MOTIVATION FOR FISCAL REFORM

You can be sincere and still be stupid.

CHARLES F. KETTERING

The expansion of proponents' arguments for adopting revenue and expenditure restrictions has mirrored the growth of the movement itself. Proposition 13, for example, was initially offered as a method to reverse the dramatic growth in California's property taxes. As the campaign proceeded, the measure was promoted as a method to secure governmental tax relief, slow inflation and halt governmental expansion. Finally, as the election approached, it was described by sponsors as a method to promote governmental efficiency and eliminate waste (Break, 1979, p. 54). A defense of the beleaguered taxpayer had evolved into an aggressive offensive directed at supposedly inept and spendthrift politicians and bureaucrats.

There are a number of interesting discussions of voter motivations in approving tax and expenditure limitations.[4] Virtually all of these studies emphasize the centrality of the efficiency argument. For example, one of the few examinations of voter motivations across states concluded that

> . . . the experiences of 1979 and the data available for the past several years call into question some of the prevailing notions about the causes of the tax and expenditure limitation movement. Neither states with high tax burdens nor states that have experienced rapid growth in tax burden enacted limitation measures more often than states with low tax burdens. Similarly, the "excessive spending" argument is difficult to sustain because state and local spending has actually declined as a percent of the gross national product in recent years. Moreover, survey data indicate that most voters do not favor spending cuts for the majority of public programs. This study suggests that perceived inefficiency and waste in government rather than tax burden or excessive spending are more strongly related to the fiscal limitation movement. (National Governor's Association Center for Policy Research, 1979, p. 2.)

There is, of course, a difference between being motivated to institute a given reform to punish perceived inefficiency and realistically expecting the reform to result in greater efficiency. Simply cutting back the amount of money that government has to spend may punish bureaucrats, but it would not represent an authentic gain in efficiency unless the money that is still being spent produces greater output per dollar. While most surveys have been more concerned with motivations than with expectations, there is some evidence that voters really expect improved efficiency from the reforms. In a very limited empirical study, Balbien (1978) asked: "Do you agree or disagree Jarvis-Gann (Proposition 13) would force government to be more efficient?" His results are shown in Table 7.1 and suggest that a belief in the instrumental value of Proposition 13 to increase governmental efficiency played a central role in voter's decisions to support or oppose it. Why isn't this belief reasonable?

Table 7.1 **Results of Survey on Proposition 13**

Efficient Government	For (%)	Against (%)	Undecided (%)	
Agree	77.0	10.7	12.7	100
Disagree	15.1	73.6	11.3	100
Total sample	44.6	30.4	25.0	100

Source: Balbien, 1978, p. 5.

REVENUE RESPONSES

Why does a slight tax increase cost you two hundred dollars and a substantial tax cut save you thirty cents?

PEG BRACKEN

State and local governments receive money (revenue) from four basic sources: (1) revenues for general operating purposes, usually from taxes; (2) fees (and penalties) for the provision of various goods and services; (3) borrowed monies that are usually designated for specific uses (e.g., capital improvements); and (4) transfers from other levels of government, some for general purposes and others designated for special purposes.

When faced with an impending budget deficit, officials will usually try to find alternative sources of revenue rather than cut expenditures. In large part, revenue solutions are preferred because their burden can usually be diffused through a large population. It is frequently easier to make a large, faceless, and inattentive public a little mad than to make a smaller but always present and always attentive crowd—like public employees and program constituencies—very mad. To the extent that increases are gradual and avoid public attention and ire, revenue solutions minimize the amount of righteous (and politically costly) indignation that must be borne by politicians. There is also the matter of administrative ease and continuity. Revenue solutions are least disruptive of current service levels and personnel policies.

The tendency for government to seek revenue solutions has been appreciated by those drafting tax limitation initiatives. Most endeavor to make it very difficult for affected governments to increase old taxes or create new ones. However, those who expect a reform like Proposition 13 to reduce total revenues (and the total tax burden) in an amount corresponding to the loss of property tax receipts do not fully appreciate the flexibility on revenue sources that cities and counties possess.[5] The architects of fiscal reform measures would be well advised to study the history of attempts to reform the U.S. Income Tax Code to appreciate the frustrating "string pushing" character of their task. The lesson in that history of having two loopholes appear for every one you close is that however clever one is in devising controls, the human capacity for devising responses (many of them ingenious and wholly unpredictable) that subvert the original intent of the controls is nothing short of remarkable.

Most of the specific state reform measures are primarily attacks on one of the most visible, and hence objectionable, general-purpose taxes—the property tax. Tax visibility is largely a function of two attributes: (1) the ability to separate and identify the amount of tax paid as tax and not as a "legitimate" part of the price in a larger transaction, and (2) the degree to which the payment forces nonroutine, negative adjustments in financial behavior. The size, periodicity, and expectability of the required payment determine the "nonroutineness" of adjustments. "New" and separable taxes, like customs duties for first-time travelers or a newly imposed surcharge, are most apt to have the highest visibility and thus attract the most attention and ire. On "old" taxes, large, noticeable, unexpected increases in required payments (e.g., property reassessment after three years of inflation) are most apt to evoke anger.[6]

Taxpayers experience the greatest pain when required to write an unexpectedly large check for taxes (e.g., income-tax surcharges not withheld or property taxes paid annually without escrow after large assessment increases) that forces them to borrow, withdraw savings and/or curtail other "regular" expenditures. The pain is somewhat less when a tax is identifiable but paid on a regular, anticipated basis (e.g., income tax withholding, estimated income tax payments, or monthly property tax payments to escrow). There is little pain associated with small, regular tax payments that are closely tied to other transactions. The sales tax is a good example of such a payment. There is no pain, at least no pain directly attributable to government's tax actions, associated with taxes shifted through the price of goods and services (e.g., shifted corporate income tax). When it is possible for those directly paying taxes (e.g., corporations paying income tax or owners of rental property paying property tax) to shift the tax burden to others, there is often no substantial resistance to the tax.

When Ronald Reagan, as governor of California in the late 1960s, objected to the proposal to withhold state income taxes in favor of having citizens pay directly once a year, he did so in the belief that citizens would be more supportive of his fiscally conservative policies if they were fully aware of their tax burden ("taxes should hurt"). State and local officials have long known that different tax payment procedures have different psychological impacts and that avoiding shocks (i.e., avoiding large divergences between actual tax billings and citizen expectations with respect to tax levels) is central to harmonious government–taxpayer relations. Localities that reassess property periodically (e.g., every three years) often spread the increase over more than one year to minimize possible tax shocks. In other communities where politicians can raise tax rates without seeking permission from the electorate, an all-too-frequent ploy is to publicize the expectation of a large tax increase before implementing a smaller tax increase. Citizens are then grateful to the politicians for "holding the taxes down."

Excepting principled conservatives like Ronald Reagan, most politicians and bureaucrats will prefer less visible, more stable revenue sources. If citizens cannot calculate and know the level of taxes they are paying, accountability is problematic and there is almost no chance of a "revolt." With extreme pressure on visible tax sources, there should be increased use of less visible sources, sources that lead citizens to underestimate their tax burdens. State governments have access to a much broader set of revenue instruments, particularly unobtrusive sources, than local governments. A common two-stage response to the "tax revolt" is likely to be as follows: (1) states assume a greater financial (if not administrative) responsibility for services that have been provided traditionally by local governments and (2) states increasingly rely on unobtrusive sources of revenue.

This shift is an unintended and perhaps undesirable consequence of otherwise well-intentioned fiscal reform measures. The shift is especially undesirable for those who hope for more directly democratic and responsive institutional forms. Citizens will be increasingly less able to calculate and react to the costs of government. Needless to say, there is some irony in fiscal responses to citizen initiatives that lower the probability of future initiatives by reducing citizen knowledge.

Another increasingly familiar revenue available to local governments is the increased use of fees for service or user charges. Existing fees for service can be increased to cover at least the full costs of providing the service (including the overhead costs) and, in many cases, to cover full costs plus the costs of other government activities perhaps only tangentially related to the service. Cost accounting is still as much art as science. In calculating service costs, there are many essentially arbitrary choices about what is included and what is excluded. Conventions that formerly guided these choices are changed under fiscal pressure to reflect "full costing." Many service functions that were formerly supported from general tax revenues are put on a fee for service (or special tax), self-sustaining basis. Services (e.g., symphonies and refuse collection) with identifiable benefits and beneficiaries are obvious candidates for such changes (Comptroller General, 1979, p. 22). In many locales across the United States it has become much more expensive in time and dollars for citizens to park (legally or illegally), to acquire copies of official documents, to be late in paying fees for service, and to engage in a host of transactions with government. One-time fees, such as those for utility connections and planning applications, often become very expensive (see Gabriel et al., 1980). There is no way of directly determining the value of many of these services. Absent a competitive market, prices (fees) can soar.

Governments can also become much more vigorous in their administration of tax assessments and collections. They assess and collect the maximum allowable amounts and devise severe penalties to punish those who are late in paying tax bills. They become more insensitive and "bureaucratic" in dealings with individual citizens. To the average citizen, these characteristics might already seem endemic to all tax collecting agencies, but one way in which tax systems remain adaptive is through intentional ambiguity and discretion in administration. There are always specific cases where the application of general rules, however well devised, violates our sensibilities, and administrative discretion is a common means of coping with such cases. However, in the wake of fiscal reform, taxpayers can expect much more literal interpretation of the laws from officials than they experienced before if such interpretations increase revenues.

Increasing intergovernmental transfer revenues (e.g., state and federal grants) and making their provisions more flexible is another important revenue response. The use of California's state budget as a source of increased local aid evolved from an important temporary solution in 1978–79 (when a surplus existed) to something that now appears permanent. There are also some transfers of functional responsibilities from local governments to states where, as in the California case, the limitations were applied to local government and not state government. A complementary strategy is to convince state and federal agencies to relax the "strings" on existing grant programs so that more state and federal dollars can be used to continue existing services currently supported from locally collected revenues.

As financial creatures, local general-purpose governments consist of several "funds," including a "general fund" and a number of special funds. Each fund has associated revenues from one or more functional activities to which monies are budgeted and for which they are spent. The general fund is the largest (in dollar terms) and supports the most personnel and day-to-day operating expenditures. As a result, the general fund is where most of the financial activity is and where property tax revenue is directed. Understanding the difference in funds is important to predict government responses to reform measures, because some of the responses inevitably consist of moving money and service responsibilities from fund to fund. For example, the water fund may be assessed a new overhead charge payable to the general fund for all of the services general government provides to the Water Department.

The redefinition of operating expenses as either capital expenses (that are not paid out of the general fund) or legitimate expenses for designated funds are ways of reducing pressure from a tax limitation on a general fund. As the experience in recent years with New York City, Washington, D.C., Cleveland, the Bay Area Rapid Transit System, and numerous other governmental entities has shown, the distinction between capital and operating obligations is a definitional matter. Under certain conditions, very creative definitions are possible. The redefinition of operating expenditures sustains service input levels but shifts financial responsibility from the general fund to other funds and other revenue sources. A particular advantage in redefining operating expenditures as capital expenditures is that revenue from bond sales can then be used. A particular disadvantage is that necessary and legitimate capital projects may be postponed for too long and cost too much.

In sum, potential revenue solutions to the budget problem are many and varied. They have, however, one thing in common: they will do little or nothing to improve the efficiency or effectiveness of government operations.

EXPENDITURE RESPONSES

Nothing is easier than spending public money. It does not appear to belong to anybody. The temptation is overwhelming to bestow it on somebody.

CALVIN COOLIDGE

Despite the motivation and opportunities for devising revenue solutions to the budget problem posed by reforms to "take the money away," it is reasonable to assume (at least in the first few years) that local government resources will be somewhat lower than they would have been without such measures.[8] Many of the short-term revenue solutions are small compared to the cuts in revenues, and both the voters and media watch government more closely than usual following the adoption of a reform. Despite protestations to the contrary, government officials do behave differently in the glare of public attention. Some reductions in expenditures can be expected.

Faced with budget cuts in a short period of time, politicians will usually choose to do one or more of the following:

1. Freeze all hiring, promotions, and periodic cost-of-living pay increases (COLAs in the federal lexicon).
2. Mandate across-the-board percentage cuts, leaving the means (e.g., attrition, lay-offs, shortened work weeks, and nonpersonnel cuts such as postponing purchases of capital improvements and new equipment) to the discretion of functional managers. In some cases, "essential" services, like police and fire protection at the local level or national defense and Social Security at the federal level, will be exempt from cuts.
3. Eliminate whole departments or programs. The focus will be on those that are likely to be assumed by another level of government, that will not entail personnel cuts (i.e., subsidy and purchase of service arrangements), and/or that involve substantial intangible (unmeasurable) benefits (e.g., recreational and life-enrichment services).

The adoption of these broad-stroke tactics rather than the careful implementation of detailed efficiency improvements is a function of the bureaucratic and political realities in government. In an economically rational world, officials would appraise the value of agency programs at the margin and allocate resources to maximize value or, equivalently, to minimize value lost in the retrenchment. In a complex, moderately intentional, frequently incomprehensible, uncontrollable, and unpredictable world, crude, broad-stroke cuts predominate.

There are many reasons for the popularity of "meat axe" decision rules in cutting budgets. One important reason is that differential treatment in cuts is a statement of priorities different than the priorities implicit in what the government is doing at the time cuts become necessary. Budgetary decisions that violate historically grounded expectations often require extensive justification in public settings. Those advocating or deciding on particular cuts must be able to defend them. Yet everyone is all too well aware of the fact that we do not know how to calculate the precise consequences of cutting of $1,000 from recreation rather than police or $1 billion from Medicare rather than defense. Because such choices are frequently made does not imply that they are made informedly, much less rationally. Officials rarely have the time, information, staff, or analytic capacities to evaluate and compare agency performance. Such limitations are exacerbated by reforms that force very rapid budgetary responses.

Standards of efficiency are usually taken from one of these sources: (1) the historical performance of the same organizational subunit, (2) the performance of comparable subunits in other organizations during the same time period, or (3) an analytic model. Whatever the standard employed, the one certain response is that those affected adversely by the application of a particular standard will do everything possible to invalidate it; they will argue—often cogently—that "times have changed; agency X is not really like us; or the model is founded on unreasonable assumptions."

Even if there is some efficiency standard accepted by a dominant coalition, it is not clear that taking money away (e.g., cutting the budget) will result in increased efficiency. Managers may not know why their operation is relatively inefficient nor how to change the operation to make it more efficient. Budget cuts will often be translated into reductions in output (i.e., effectiveness cuts). It is much easier to find and implement effectiveness cuts (e.g., mowing park grass and cleaning public toilets less frequently or patching and repaving fewer miles of road) than it is to find efficiency improvements (e.g., mowing park grass and cleaning toilets with the same frequency at lower cost or patching and repaving the same number of miles of road at less cost).

Inevitably, a few specific services will be singled out for extensive reduction, if not wholesale elimination, but the characteristics that they will share are not inefficiency. It is more probable that they will be distinguished by their small and relatively unorganized constituencies inside and outside the bureaucracy. Services that are purchased by, rather than directly provided by, government and therefore do not involve "regular" (e.g., civil service) personnel will be prime targets (Comptroller General, 1979). "Life enrichment" and recreation programs frequently fall into this category, since they are often staffed by part-time personnel. The same is true of heavily subsidized performing arts (e.g., opera, symphony). When the loss of regular personnel is unavoidable, difficulties will be eased somewhat by concentrating on relatively new programs, where few workers have seniority and where external constituencies have not had enough time to become powerful interest groups. Alternatively, they may cut using a "neutral" strategy such as attrition, a strategy that can be defended to complaining constituents on equity grounds.

The importance of constituency pressure in determining the vulnerability of services to budget cuts raises the larger issue of service visibility. One reason that officials find it easier to save money by relaxing preventive maintenance schedules or the prosecution of health code violations as opposed to reducing the number of waste pickups is that the former are almost invisible. While the visibility of a particular service may occasionally correspond to an economist's estimate of its marginal social benefit, this is clearly not always the case.

Even when invisible services cannot be entirely eliminated—generally the case—they can often be postponed with few immediate consequences. Expenditures can be reduced in the current period by deferring the maintenance of vehicles, roads, and buildings or by maintaining rather than replacing these items. Because the effects of such actions may not be apparent for 30 or 40 years (i.e., the time it takes for a capital facility that should last 100 years to deteriorate because of substandard construction or improper maintenance), they are attractive to officials (and some citizens as well) with short time horizons. Unfortunately, when viewed over several decades, the postponement of problems tends to inflate the cost of maintaining a given level of service, thereby reducing efficiency.

Current officials both are captive of such actions by past officials and contribute to the efficiency problems of future officials. With intense pressure in the form of tax and expenditure limitations, current officials are apt to make enormous contributions to future problems while being applauded for a commitment to responsive public service and efficiency.[9]

Visibility can be important in an opposite way. It is a common ploy for officials to single out highly visible and valued services as targets for major cuts in order to emphasize the need to have funds restored. This tactic is known to budgeters as the Washington Monument ploy in honor of the National Park Service, which many years ago talked about closing the Washington landmark in response to budget cuts. When Governor Brown requested that the University of California develop contingency plans to implement a large budget cut, no one suggested that such a cut would have grave implications for their maintenance budget. Indeed, members of the university administration alluded to the possible need to reduce the number of campuses or shut down one of the medical schools, obviously among the most visible and unpopular cuts that could be made. While it might be argued that in this case there was little probability that either action would ever be taken (thus reducing the effectiveness of the tactic), this is not always true. Officials and bureaucrats are often quite willing to reduce the services that will be the most sorely missed if they believe such action will result in the restoration of funds.

The probability that the eliminated service will be reinstituted by another level of government is another program characteristic that will determine vulnerability to cuts. In the 1960s and 1970s, local governments were aware of their ability to coerce state and federal agencies into providing, or at least funding, important services in areas such as water quality control, education, and social services simply by reducing or eliminating local effort. Consequently, such services could be cut with a reasonable probability that higher levels of government would assume responsibility. Times have changed with Reaganomics and the massive federal deficits. It is now the federal government that is in the business of shifting functional responsibilities to state and local governments. The Grace Commission proposes a number of such shifts and proceeds to calculate the "efficiency savings" to the federal government.

A particularly dramatic example of just how explicit this "blackmail" can become was related to one of the authors by the principal staff member of a regional water quality control board located in California. The board had been frustrated by the slow response of a small city to its orders to improve water quality by carrying out some expensive renovations to that city's reservoir. After innumerable requests to remedy the situation, the board took the matter to court, hoping to obtain an order fining the town for noncompliance. Twenty-four hours later, the head of the water board received a deed to the reservoir in the mail, compliments of the city manager. The suit was dropped.

If all else fails, the government can declare bankruptcy, as the San Jose Unified School District did a few years ago. This extreme strategy shifts the problem to court-appointed receivers who are apt to find more cooperative teachers' unions, taxpayers, and bondholders. Some efficiencies that were infeasible politically may become feasible.

Many of the citizen-initiated and citizen-approved local government reforms have sought to eliminate "spendthrift" transfer programs (e.g., welfare services), and proponents are consistently amazed that such programs survive budget crises. Yet it is often the case that there are many more federal or state dollars in such programs than locally collected tax dollars. Hence their real "cost" to local officials may be slight and the financial incentives for local governments to even lobby against such programs, however wasteful they may believe the programs to be, are negligible. They can usually do nothing more than lobby because the programs are controlled at higher levels. Voters who support reforms of local governments (e.g., Proposition 13) with the expectation that social services and welfare will be immediately reduced are likely to be disappointed. They are striking out against government units that have virtually no control over and almost no money in the irksome programs. These units may well have to cut back on programs the reformers like in order to cope with revenue shortfalls.

A third common response to tax and expenditure restrictions—freezing new hiring and salaries of current public employees—may actually result in improved efficiency in the short run. This is because it is difficult for agency heads to translate a wage freeze into effectiveness or service cuts. Assuming no behavioral backlash (e.g., employees cutting their productivity because they are disgruntled at reductions in real wages), services will be provided at lower cost than they would have been with wage increases. Given that local services are highly labor intensive (70 to 85 percent of expenditures for most services are for personnel), the savings can be substantial. Wage freezes do not, however, accomplish expenditure reductions; they simply fix the costs of some service inputs, cutting the rate of growth in expenditures. Cuts require a reduction in input levels. For personnel, this can be accomplished through attrition (with a hiring freeze), layoffs, or firings. Attrition, the most popular method with officials (and employees) for cutting because of its voluntary and nonjudgmental character, is an unreliable approach to improving efficiency. Vacancies rarely occur in the right office at the right time, and it is usually the best employees who leave. Too often, cuts by attrition worsen efficiency rather than improve it.

Another significant disadvantage of salary freezes is political. Public-sector unionism is not noticeably decreasing and, to date, the militancy of these unions has proved difficult to handle, particularly where uniformed services (fire, police) are involved. Once the "reform crisis" has passed, the pressure to catch up can be expected to become extremely strong. One unintended effect of limitation measures may be to increase the levels of existing unions' militancy and of new unionization. Should this occur, governments will become still harder to manage, and management is essential to maintain or improve efficiency.

EFFICIENCY RESPONSES

> I had an immense advantage over many others dealing with the problem inasmuch as I had no fixed ideas derived from long-established practice to control and bias my mind, and did not suffer from the general belief that whatever is, is right.
>
> HENRY BESSEMER

While all of the evidence is not yet in, it is not very likely that governments subject to tax and expenditure limits will choose efficiency solutions as an important part of what becomes essentially an internal budgetary problem. This is neither a condemnation nor an apology for officials charged with the efficient operation of governments. *Feasible* efficiency measures, alternative ways of accomplishing a given set of objectives at less cost, are simply hard (and often expensive) to devise; not as hard to devise as many officials would have us believe at times, but hard nonetheless. Three important and interrelated constraints on the ability to design and/or implement efficiency measures are ignorance, institutional structures, and politics.

As we have argued throughout this book, we are ignorant (as managers and as social and management scientists) about causal relationships in the provision of public services, knowledge that is essential to plan service delivery systems systematically. Even where we have some of the requisite knowledge (i.e., in areas with physical outputs and engineering theories), there are bureaucratic and political obstacles to utilizing it.

> Local government is a low-change system by design. A maze of procedural requirements on budgeting, on hiring and firing, on purchasing, and on contracting make any change from the modus operandi very difficult. New ideas must undergo the scrutiny of a city council and sometimes an independently elected comptroller as well as the overhead agencies such as budget and personnel. The civil service system and, frequently, employee unions add to the difficulties.
>
> The result is, that in local government, the cards are stacked against new ideas. There will rarely be strongly supportive forces in the community. The inertial drag of the system will make internal progress slow and difficult. The political risks are substantial. (Hayes, 1979, p. 27.)

There are comparable obstacles at the federal and state levels.

Taking the money away does little to increase either the resources or the incentives to overcome these obstacles. The resources of time, manpower, and dollars required to develop and implement better methods of accomplishing specific tasks—a classic source of increased efficiency in the private sector—are viewed by reformers and many voters to be irrelevant to the task of increasing efficiency in the public sector.

The dominant image of government appears to consist of two overpaid clerks doing the work of one and, given the image, the reform of cutting the work force in half is compelling. Complicate the image by adding concerns about police and fire department manning, water quality, and declining reading scores in elementary schools, and the relevance of resources to devising more efficient operational methods becomes somewhat clearer. Unfortunately, this more complicated world is not conducive to the success of heroically simple proposals for achieving across-the-board improvements in efficiency.

The relationship between fiscal reforms and the incentive for public officials to become efficient is also widely misunderstood. The dominant operational goal in budgeting for any particular year is not to maximize community welfare or improve efficiency but to balance estimated receipts and estimated expenditures. Other goals are pursued secondarily. By leading to a condition where prospective revenues are no longer enough to cover projected expenditures, fiscal reforms greatly exacerbate the difficulties that must be overcome by officials to solve this budget-balancing problem. While it is true that obtaining greater efficiency may offer officials cost savings, these savings are apt to be small relative to yields from revenue raising and broad-stroke expenditure cutting responses. Efficiency gains solve less of the larger, primal budget problem and there are fewer resources to devote to finding efficiencies.

The prospects of increased efficiency and effectiveness in government as an important result of the reforms to take money away are not good. Increased revenues from new and less obtrusive sources and reductions in service levels will be more important in restoring balance to budgets than efficiency moves will be. The reforms will have some salutary impacts on efficiency because they create a political climate conducive to adopting actions previously identified but politically infeasible. Nonetheless, this climate is as fleeting as public attention, and most efficiency measures require some persistence and initiative by government officials.

Taking the money away is an act of helplessness. As a reform, it communicates general dissatisfaction, not specific problems and constructive solutions. Improved government performance will not be an important consequence of taking the money away.

CONCLUSION

> Government is the most precious of human possessions; and no care
> can be too great to be spent on enabling it to do its work in the best
> way. A chief condition to that end is that it should not be set to work
> for which it is not specially qualified, under the conditions of time
> and place.
>
> ALFRED MARSHALL

Until recently the greatest temptation for someone interested in improving government performance was to adopt what we have termed the "hubris" approach to reform. This involves ignoring both the disappointing performance of past reform attempts and the realities of public-sector management in favor of an idealistic vision of how decisions should be made and the effect that a particular proposal should have. It is this approach that brought us PPBS, ZBB, and countless government reorganizations.

Times have changed. While a charismatic reformer at the state or local level may still be able to convince a small group of followers that a new budgeting system is the answer to every problem, it is getting harder to convince most politicians, editorial writers, and informed citizens. Past failures have induced enormous cynicism about the motives and potential of politicians and governments. Now the greatest temptation is to replace hubris with the ideology of helplessness. The weak version of this tells us that because the problems with which we expect government to deal (e.g., poverty or crime) are basically intractable or because their solution could only be achieved at the expense of valuable features of the existing political system, little should be attempted. The stronger version of the ideology of helplessness tells us that government is incapable of performing any task with the efficiency regularly found in any private firm and persistently interferes with the efficient operation of the general economy. The ideology asserts that government is not a cure for problems, it is a problem—perhaps the biggest problem.

NOTES

1. The recent initiative to reorganize the Joint Chiefs of Staff so that the chairman has more power than the other chiefs is the latest in a long line of attempts to solve the still unsolved problem of competition and duplication.
2. The Grace Commission confidently asserts that "a goal of 7:1 (for span of control) is standard in the private sector" (PPSS, III-274). Like most of the "private sector standards" invoked in the Grace Commission report, this one is invoked with no indication of where the number comes from and no defense of its use.
3. Balbein (1978), Chaiken and Walker (1979), Comptroller General (1979), Eribes and Hall (1981), Pascal and Menchik (1980), Oakland (1979), Pascal (1980), and Rafuse (1979).
4. Citrin (1979), Kuttner and Kelston (1979), Levy and Zamolo (1979), National Governor's Association Center for Policy Research (1979), Oakland (1979), Pascal et al. (1979), and Shapiro et al. (1979).
5. Special-purpose units of government, like schools and special districts, operate under much more restrictive rules and have much less room to maneuver in response to restrictions.
6. For futher discussion of "fiscal illusion (i.e., the form of tax determining the taxpayer's perception of burdens), see Buchanan (1967), Goetz (1977), and Wagner (1976).
7. The first stage took place in California immediately following the passage of Proposition 13. The state's share of education financing, for example, increased from 40 to 70 percent (Danziger, 1979, p. 62).
8. Some reductions have already appeared, and in California reductions have accelerated as the cushion of the state surplus disappeared. See Balbien (1978), Comptroller General (1979), Chaiken and Walker (1979), Eribes and Hall (1981), Oakland (1979), and Rafuse (1979).
9. Postponing problems can take other forms. If all else fails (i.e., there are insufficient revenue and expenditures solutions), local officials will prepare "optimistic" budgets. Budgets are, after all, plans; like all plans, they rest on forecasts. By being optimistic (high) in forecasting revenues and optimistic (low) in forecasting expenditures, the budget can be "balanced." When revenue comes in lower and expenditures higher than forecasts, the government can engage in short-term borrowing to manage its cash flow. This is not a "solution" to the budget imbalance problem in the same sense as the other solutions discussed here. It contributes to a solution of the current year's problem by postponing it. As New York, Cleveland, and other northeastern cities have shown us, it is possible to postpone the problem for years, if not decades, before it becomes wholly unmanageable and obvious to the public.

REFERENCES

Balbien, J. A. "A Note on the 1978 Jarvis-Gann Election." Social Science Working Paper 329. Pasadena, Calif.: Institute of Technology, 1978.

Beard, Charles A. "Training for Efficient Public Service World." *Annals of the American Academy of Political and Social Science* 64 (March 1916):219.

Branch, Taylor. "We're All Working for the Penn Central." *Inside the System*, ed. 3, edited by Charles Peters and James Fallows. New York, Praeger, 1977, p. 163.

Break, G. F. "After Proposition 13—the Deluge?" *Challenge* 10 (1979)1:54–56.

Buchanan, James M. "Public Goods in Theory and Practice: A Note on the Minasian-Samuelson Discussion." *Journal of Law and Economics*, 1967, pp. 193–197.

Chaiken, Jan M., and Walker, Warren W. *Growth in Municipal Expenditures: A Case Study of Los Angeles*. Santa Monica: The Rand Corporation, N–1200–RC, June 1979.

Chapanis, Alphonse. "Knowledge of Performance As An Incentive in Repetitive, Monotonous Tasks." *Journal of Applied Psychology* 48 (1964)4:263–267.

Citrin, J. "Do People Want Something for Nothing: Public Opinion on Taxes and Government Spending." *National Tax Journal* 32 (June 1979)2:

Comptroller General of the United States, National Highway Traffic Safety Administration, Department of Transportation. *Need To Improve Benefit–Cost Analyses in Setting Motor Vehicle Safety Standards*. Report to the Committee of Commerce, United States Senate. Washington, D.C.: U.S. Government Printing Office, 1979.

Danziger, J. N. "Rebellion on Fiscal Policy: Assessing the Effects of California's Proposition 13. *The Urban Interest* 1 (1979)1:62.

Eribes, R. A., and Hall, J. S. "Revolt of the Affluent: Fiscal Controls in Three States." In *The Impact of Resource Scarcity on Urban Public Finance*, edited by J. McCaffery. Special issue of *Public Administration Review* 41 (January 1981):107–121.

Gabriel, S., Katz, L., and Wolch, J. "Local Land-Use Regulation and Proposition 13." *Taxing and Spending*, Spring 1980, pp. 73–81.

Goetz, C. J. "Fiscal Illusion in State and Local Finance." In *Budgets and Bureaucrats: The Sources of Government Growth*, edited by T. E. Borcherding. Durham, N.C.: Duke University Press, 1979.

Hayes, Frederick O'R. *Productivity in Local Government*. Lexington, Mass.: Lexington Books, 1977.

Ilgen, Daniel R., Cynthia D. Fischer, and M. Susan Taylor. "Consequences of Individual Feedback on Behavior in Organizations." *Journal of Applied Psychology* 64 (1979)4:349–371.

Kay, Emanuel, Meyer, Herbert H., Frank, Jr., John R. P. "Effects of Threat in a Performance Appraisal Interview." *Journal of Applied Psychology* 49 (October 1965) 5:311–317.

Kuttner, R., and Kelston, D. *The Shifting Property Tax Burden: The Untold Cause of the Tax Revolt*. Public Policy Report, Conference on Alternative State and Local Policies, mimeograph, 1979.

Levy, F., and Zamolo, P. *The Preconditions of Proposition 13*. Working Paper 1105-01. Washington, D.C.: The Urban Institute, 1979.

Mikalachki, A. "There is No Merit in Merit Pay." *Business Quarterly*, Spring, 1976.

March, James G., and Olson, Johan P. "What Administrative Reorganization Tells Us About Governing." *The American Political Science Review* 77 (June 1983): 284–286.

Miles, Rufus E., Jr. "Considerations For a President Bent on Reorganization." *In Approaches to Organzing*, edited by Robert T. Golembiewski. Washington, D.C.: American Society For Public Administration, 1981, p. 126.

National Governors' Association Center for Policy Research. Research Notes 5, Washington, D.C., 1979.

Oakland, William H. "Proposition 13—Genesis and Consequences." *National Tax Journal* 32 (June 1979) 2:387–407.

Pascal, Anthony H. *User Charges, Contracting Out, and Privatization in an Era of Fiscal Retrenchment*, P–2417. Santa Monica, Calif.: The Rand Corporation, April 1980.

Pascal, Anthony H., and Menchik, Mark David. *Fiscal Containment: Who Gains? Who Loses?* R–2494/1–F–RC. Santa Monica, Calif.: The Rand Corporation, September 1979.

Pearce, Jone L. and Perry, James L. "Federal Merit Pay: A Longitudinal Analysis," *Public Administration Review*, (July/August 1983) 2:315–325.

Peters, Thomas J., and Waterman, Robert H. *In Serach of Excellence: Lessons from America's Best-Run Companies*. McKinsey & Co., 1982, p. 51.

Rafuse, R. W. Jr. "Proposition 13: Initial Impacts on the Finances of Four County Governments." In *Proceeding of a Conference on Tax and Expenditure Limitations*, edited by D. Puryear et al. *National Tax Journal, Supplement*, 32 (1979) 2:229–241.

Shapiro, Perry, Puryear, David, and Ross, John. "Tax and Expenditure Limitation in Retrospect and in Prospect." In *Proceedings of a Conference on Tax and Expenditure Limitations*, edited by David Puryear et al. *National Tax Journal, Supplement*, 32 (1979) 2:1–22.

Simon, Herbert. *Administrative Behavior*, Third Edition. New York: Free Press, 1976, pp. 20–45.

Simon, Herbert. "The Business School: A Problem in Organizational Design." In *Administrative Behavior*, Third Edition. New York: Free Press, 1976, p. 335.

Wagner, Richard E. "Revenue Structure, Fiscal Illusion, and Budgetary Choice." *Public Choice* 25 (Spring 1976)4:45–62.

White, Leonard D. *The Republican Era: 1869–1901*. New York: Macmillan, 1958.

CHAPTER 7

What is to be Done?

Today the people no longer look to Washington as the Emerald City
with magic solutions to every problem.

PRESIDENT RONALD REAGAN

With the failure of past reforms still fresh in our collective memory and the election of a president deeply committed to reducing the size and influence of government, it is hardly surprising that the "helplessness" philosophy has dominated the reform agenda of the early 1980s. Problems like poverty, crime, pollution, and unemployment, which had preoccupied previous administrations, were viewed either as basically intractable or resistant to direct intervention by government. While there was continued interest in increasing the efficiency of government, the approach to improving efficiency had become, first and foremost, to divest government of as many of its activities as are "not necessary" or that can be "handled" by the private sector. Almost as an afterthought in this approach, the remaining activities should be run in a businesslike fashion. Hubris was out, helplessness was in.

Or so it seemed. For in January 1984 hubris returned with a vengeance in the form of the President's Private Sector Survey on Cost Control in the Federal Government (PPSS), popularly known as the Grace Commission after its vocal Chairman, J. Peter Grace (chairman and chief executive officer of W. R. Grace & Co.). This was not, however, the hubris of the 1960s, when officials believed that calculated government intervention could eliminate any social problem. Most of those connected with the Grace Commission were passionately dedicated to the principle of minimal government: the government should do as little as possible. Yet the portrait of government operations contained in the Commission's report and the reforms that it proposes reveal a level of arrogance and self-satisfaction equal to that of the most starry-eyed reformer of any previous decade.

AMAZING GRACE: A NEW HUBRIS?

Nobody talks more of free enterprise and competition and of the best
man winning than the man who inherited his father's store or farm.

C. WRIGHT MILLS

217

While aspects of the PPSS or Grace Commission have been discussed in passing throughout this book, the report deserves special and separate consideration for several reasons. First, the PPSS is one of the most extensive and ambitious efforts in U.S. history to bring the management experience of the private sector to bear on the management problems of government. The sheer magnitude of the effort and the prominence of the participants commands attention. In its entirety, the report stands 10 feet high, encompasses 47 unindexed volumes, and contains 2,478 "cost cutting" and "revenue enhancing" recommendations that "would save $424 billion in three years, rising to $1.9 trillion per year by the year 2000 (PPSS, p. 1). The project was overseen by a 161-member executive committee, primarily chief executive officers of large corporations, who directed the efforts of 2,000 individuals participating in the survey as task force members, survey management office personnel, or PPSS advisors. It was "self-financed" through a private, not-for-profit foundation that raised approximately $3.3 million in cash and in-kind contributions. Further, "a rough calculation of private sector contributions in terms of time and personnel resources dedicated to the PPSS effort totals over $75 million" (PPSS, sec. VI, p. 11).

Second, the PPSS report warrants special attention because it represents the most visible contemporary attempt to reform government in the name of efficiency. President Reagan has repeatedly referred to it as one important approach to reducing the record federal deficits. It has captured considerable media attention, ranging from news items and editorials to a string of advertisements by the Mobil Corporation. It has inspired a number of congressional hearings. And, perhaps most conspicuously, J. Peter Grace has apparently decided, in the twilight of a long career running the family business, to devote a substantial proportion of his personal time and not insignificant financial resources to publicizing the Commission's recommendations. He is "on the stump" speaking at chamber of commerce, Rotary, and trade association gatherings around the country. According to recent news accounts, he gave 107 speeches on government waste in 1984 and has already scheduled 47 more in 1985.[1] With Jack Anderson, the columnist, he has formed a group, called Citizens Against Waste (CAW), which has produced at least one television commerical (so far denied public service advertising time on the networks because it is too partisan and controversial) and through promotions in *Penthouse Magazine* is attempting to get 50 million signatures on a petition urging fiscal restraint upon the White House and Congress. He has published a summary of the report as a book provocatively entitled *Burning Money* and has become a familiar, indeed unavoidable, figure on television.

Yet a third reason for discussing the Grace Commission report here is that its rhetoric and recommendations nicely illustrate many of the more abstract points made throughout this book about the somewhat futile history of efficiency reform. In particular, the Commission provides a number of fresh, contemporary examples—both positive and negative—to illustrate what we call the "lessons of reform."

Before reviewing those lessons, however, it is important to understand why the PPSS effort represents the most recent example of reform hubris, albeit a different type of hubris. Basically, the hubris stems from three core assumptions in the

Commission's work: (1) that the private sector is far more efficient than the public sector and is the repository of all management wisdom, (2) that the public and private sectors are similar enough that the former can be dramatically transformed by techniques imported from the latter, and (3) that the reform efforts of the past have little to teach present-day reformers.

THE WISDOM OF EFFICIENCY

> Grace wants to sell the Hoover Dam, but who in the hell wants to buy it?
>
> REPUBLICAN CONGRESSIONAL STAFF MEMBER

Given the Grace Commission's composition, its presumption that the private sector is vastly more efficient than the public sector is hardly surprising. It is also not surprising that the Commission saw no need to defend that presumption seriously. Except in isolated instances using highly suspect data, little attempt is made to compare the performance of the two sectors directly. It is enough to find instances of gross inefficiency (the sampling problem) and appeal to the inevitable consequences of a lack of competition (argument by syllogism). The Commission was not, after all, mandated to conduct a balanced and intellectually defensible research project but to recommend ways to improve government performance.

By itself the presumption of greater relative private-sector efficiency is relatively harmless; indeed, it is a common presumption that panders to widespread beliefs in the population. The presumption enjoys a grain of truth. Private-sector organizations are probably more efficient on average than government organizations, although the systematic evidence for that proposition is not (as we saw in Chapter 2) very compelling and the innate differences are also probably much less than groups like the Grace Commission believe.

The companion assumptions permeating the Grace Commission report, that all management wisdom resides in the private sector and that differences in performance stem from government mismanagement, are far more damaging. They are harmful because they encourage the delusions that government bureaucrats know next to nothing about management and that a few simple-minded nostrums that might appear in a junior achievement pamphlet or chamber of commerce brochure can produce miraculous improvements in public sector efficiency. What is even worse—given the enormous resources that the Commisson had at its disposal, particularly in terms of managerial talent— is that the assumptions kept the Commission from really trying to understand why given problems exist. The best management consultant firms in the private sector are not those that begin from the premise that the firm that they are called in to help is operated by fools who are totally ignorant of good management practices and that the situation can be changed overnight by the application of a few principles of management.

The effects of these presumptions are strewn throughout the Commission's two-volume summary report. In discussing the information problems of the federal government (which are, in fact, quite severe), the authors tell government managers that they have to "assess their information requirements." The private sector, they proudly proclaim, has discovered the interesting, if not profound, fact "that often a limited amount of carefully selected information can serve to manage essential functions" (PPSS, Sec. III, p. 21). Does the Commission really believe that this is a discovery that has eluded all bureaucrats and that simply mentioning this obvious point will help solve the problem? Since questions such as, "Why aren't agencies gathering the right sort of information?" and "What needs to be done to enable agencies to more efficiently gather data?" are never raised, the answer is apparently yes. Similarly, the report frequently asserts that effective government management is being stifled by a lack of consensus about basic goals, poor planning, and the absence of high-quality performance measures.

Doubtless the Commission again believes that it makes a significant contribution by simply making this observation, because it offers few clues as to how these problems that have been recognized since the dawn of reform might be solved. It is as if the solution for the absence of clear, measurable goals is simply to go out and develop goals that are clear and measurable; in this spirit, the solution to poverty is to earn money and the solution to a low golf score is to hit the ball straight and long. Lest readers who have lacked the patience or stamina to wade through the voluminous Grace Commission summary report believe that this point is exaggerated, consider the following summary of what to do about strategic planning in government research and development:

> R&D management suffers from a lack of clearly defined goals. Existing planning efforts do not establish priorities for R&D programs, cannot eliminate marginal programs, and do not serve as a base for operational management. . . . [recommendations include] focusing efforts by top management on the development of clear, measurable standards of R&D goals; developing systems necessary to translate goal statements into complete plans; and committing to the use of effective strategic planning guide the operations of agency. (PPSS, Sec. VIII, p. 102.)

In short, the Commission appears to have embraced the implausible and incredibly arrogant notion that problems exist because no one in government has noticed them and that they will go away if the collective genius of the private sector points them out. Yet if this is so, what does it tell us about the contribution of the hundreds, probably thousands, of business executives who have been appointed to top posts by Eisenhower, Nixon, Ford, and Reagan, as well as their Democratic counterparts? Have "current Federal management activities . . . evolved over many years with little recognition of the need to provide central guidance and direction to achieve a well-coordinated overall process" (PPSS, Sec. III, p. 15) in spite of the efforts of outstanding managers like Robert McNamara, William Simon, Roy Ash, Michael Blumenthal, David Packard, Donald Regan, and a host of others who have arrived in Washington following extremely successful careers in business? It seem unlikely. More probable is a state of affairs that the Grace Commission rarely entertains: that the public sector's problems are very difficult and very different from those that private-sector management faces and that it will take more than hackneyed solutions and business maxims to solve them.

If the Grace Commission report shows little respect for the people who manage the federal government, including many of their own kind, and for the difficulty of the problems with which they must deal, its attitude toward the qualifications and expertise of its own authors borders on idolatry. They are described as "the top business and managerial talent in America" and the "best and the brightest" who worked like "tireless bloodhounds" in identifying waste and inefficiency (PPSS, Sec. VI, p. 5). Clearly the implication of such adjectives is that members of Congress and the public alike can trust the recommendations that emerge from such an august group.

While it is almost certainly true that the Commission engaged some very gifted managers, a government bureaucrat weary of being patronized and scorned by his or her private-sector colleagues might adopt some of the Commission's own tactics and point out that not all of the Commission members' managerial credentials are all that impressive. Thirty-seven of the affiliated companies finished dead last or next to last in their respective industries in terms of five-year return on equity— widely accepted as one of the most important dimensions of the infamous "bottom line" that inspires firms to be efficient. Over 60 of the affiliated firms were below median in performance and far below the best performers in their industry on the same criterion.[2]

What, the much maligned federal bureaucrat might wonder, did the "best and the brightest," "individuals who had proven ability to effectively and efficiently manage their own enterprises" and "the top business and managerial talent in America" do managerially to lead their firms to the bottom of their industry? What possible help, he or she might ask, could managers from Continental Illinois Corporation, recently the recipient of a $4.5 billion federal bailout to avert bankruptcy caused by "disastrous management practices," offer to the Department of Treasury? The bureaucrat might wonder, if life in business is really so much more demanding than life in government, what sorts of managerial talent were these companies actually willing to send away to study government for months on end? Why would the CEO of a company ranked dead last in its industry and fighting for survival in the hard, cruel, unforgiving, highly competitive world of the private sector send the company's "best and brightest" managers, managers who would be by definition central to turning the company's situation around, off to Washington on an extended philanthropic mission to help the federal government with its problems? Why would the board of directors, representing shareholders, allow such an allocation of personnel resources?

Obviously the fact that not every company that supported the Grace Commission's work was among the business elite in terms of their most recent five-year return on equity does not automatically invalidate the Commission's many recommendations. Neither, however, does it encourage us to view the recommendations as a distillation of infallible managerial wisdom accumulated down through the ages. The Grace Commission is not, however, comparably charitable to managers in federal government. Problems there are treated as indisputable evidence of managerial incompetence or worse.

THE BUSINESS OF GOVERNMENT

The society of money and exploitation has never been charged, so
far as I know, with assuring the triumph of freedom and justice.
ALBERT CAMUS

The second assumption, that private-sector management wisdom in the form of
standard business practices and principles is easily applicable to the public sector
and will result in substantial efficiency gains, is no less problematic. One difficulty, as discussed in the addendum to Chapter 2, is the lack of consensus among
business executives, consultants, and business school academics on exactly what
the principles and practices of successful business are. Even within industries for
companies of roughly the same size, many different principles and practices appear to work in the sense that managerially diverse companies survive and are
profitable. Survival and profitability are, of course, not conclusive evidence of absolute efficiency; even in "competitive" industries, only relative efficiency is required to prosper. Managers of moderately efficient firms in industries populated
with less efficient firms can be profit heroes without knowing very much about
good management practices that are relevant to other industries and government.

Another difficulty is that many of the principles and practices, whatever those
might be, that enable one to make a profit, the primary strategic problem of businesses, are not appropriate to the strategic problems of governments, such as medi-
ating interest-group values, redistributing resources, defending the political system
from external threats, sustaining efforts to solve important and seemingly insoluble
problems, and the like. The strategic problems are qualitatively different. It is not
surprising that when a group such as the Commission views the activities from the
perspective of making a profit (or at least breaking even), that a very large number
of the activities make no sense at all. But this is about as sensible as a pole vaulter
and a javelin thrower trying to understand the other's technique in light of their
own objectives. The pole vaulter notes that the javelin thrower can never gain any
height because she throws her pole at the end of the approach, while the javelin
thrower notes that the pole vaulter will never throw the spear for any distance as
long as he insists on sticking it into the ground at the end of his approach.

The Grace Commission makes much ado over the federal government's failure
to pursue its own narrow financial interests on issues such as price supports and
subsidies, user fees that cover much less than the full cost of providing services,
generous military and civilian pensions, the large number of post offices and veterans hospitals, the laws governing wage rates paid by government contractors, the
price of hydroelectric power in the western states, the level of fees for leased graz-
ing lands, the way in which school lunch benefits are treated for income tax
purposes, or the size of social security cost-of-living adjustments. These are, of
course, redistributive elements in programs. The elements do not exist and persist
because the federal government is incapable of doing break-even analysis in setting
prices or of calculating the net financial savings from changing an entitlement formula. The calculations are frequently done and there are many financially sub-

stantiated proposals in every administration and Congress for changes and some of these changes are enacted. The arguments about changes are primarily arguments about the distribution of benefits and costs in the society and, until recently, only secondarily arguments about impacts on the financial position of the federal government. The fact that some 73 percent of its recommendations require explicit congressional approval should have suggested to the Commission that a good deal of what it views as government waste stems not, as it so persistently implies, from bureaucratic mismanagement and wanton sloth but from conscious political decisions and the character of the resulting programs that bureaucrats are directed to administer.

The "business principle" that the Commission values more than all others is that of *working with a manageable set of clear operational goals;* it continually exhorts government to realize the virtues of doing so.

> In the private sector, corporate strategy is viewed as a means of reducing general corporate objectives to manageable proportions, thus enabling employees across the country to work in unison toward the achievement of clearly defined goals and objectives. This unifying direction is critical for the successful coordination of management initiatives that cross departmental and functional boundaries, and for integrating disparate departmental projects. The same principles apply to the public sector. (PPSS, Sec. IV, p. 19.)

Yet, as we have seen, agency officials—even those who grasp the advantages of a small number of measurable goals—often have far less discretion in the way that they organize and manage programs than their private-sector critics imagine, and sometimes no discretion at all in determining the objectives of those programs. Those who attempted to implement such reforms as PPBS and ZBB, and most students of American government, have discovered that nebulous and contradictory goals coupled with a desire to solve some very intractable problems are an inevitable outcome of our particular political system. To argue too stridently for a romantic vision in which a president (alias "national chief executive officer") organizes activity around a simple set of perfectly consistent goals raises the suspicion that the critic's problem lies as much with the basic nature of American democracy as with inefficiency. Considering the Commission's attitude toward congressional interference in administrative matters (PPSS, Sec. VIII, pp. 133ff) and the manner in which Peter Grace has dealt with Congress about its recommendations, this suspicion may not be far off the mark.

Government in the United States is intentionally adversarial. By design, government is the arena in which competing views of what the problems are and how they should be solved are pitted against one another. In the same way that antitrust legislation is designed to prevent any single firm from "winning" their competition to the extent that they have an unassailable monopoly, the design of government seeks to prevent any one set of interests from gaining complete ascendance over opposing interests. While a substantial majority may hold power and manage by "clear operational goals," the structure of government assures a loyal opposition with opposing goals and the right to promote those. Most of us, except in passing fits of frustration and megalomania, would not have it any other way.

Next to goal consensus, the principle of administration that the Commission most highly values is obviously *centralization*. According to the report, policies and procedures concerning data processing, accounting, regulation, management information, procurement, real property disposition, and bill collecting should all be standardized and coordinated by one specific agency or office. They recommend the creation of an Office of Federal Management (OFM) and a Federal Information Resource Manager (FIRM) that would centralize executive management and the acquisition of automatic data processing, respectively. The implication is that the federal government's problems can be solved by creating focused responsibility for vast functional areas; there will be one (well-paid?) person in charge with command of enormous information resources, with one view of what the problems are and how to solve them, who will be held accountable just as a CEO in a large corporation is purportedly held accountable for results. These new agencies will, of course, enjoy the new high degree of consensus on a clear, operational set of goals.

Although some of the specific centralization proposals have some merit and will be discussed below in more detail, they are unlikely to bring about the efficiency gains that the Commission envisions, primarily because of scale problems. While the Commission acknowledges the fantastic size and complexity of the federal government when it wants to emphasize the need to reduce it, it consistently fails to understand the problems these attributes pose for reformers. Even if it were scaled down substantially through privatization and service reductions, the federal government would still be orders of magnitude larger than any corporation. Just as the managerial techniques and reforms that work in a small factory or mom-and-pop grocery store may have questionable relevance for IBM, so the techniques and reforms that work for IBM may have questionable relevance for the federal government.

It is more than a little ironic that centralization is such a dominant theme in a report purporting to bring business experience to bear on government management problems. Our reading of the contemporary literature on managing large-scale enterprises, particularly conglomerates that provide the closest analogue to government, suggests the importance of decentralization, delegation, and deregulation. While it always seems as though centralization should produce greater efficiency, it does not always turn out to be true—even in the private sector.

It is naive to believe that whatever works in the private sector will also work in the public sector. It is just silly to assume that any differences between them signify that the public sector is doing something wrong. The Commission becomes indignant, for example, when it is unable to comply with President Reagan's request that it "look at the various departments and agencies as if they were candidates for a merger or takeover." It discovered that this was impossible because the "information necessary to make a buy or no-buy decision was not available" (PPSS, Sec. VIII, p. 131). Regrettable no doubt, but is this the sort of information that should be given the highest priority, and is it really necessary that this information be readily available in order for the agency to operate at a satisfactory level of efficiency? Should the government, as the Commission also recommends, take steps to bring the ratio of white collar and blue collar workers closer to the mean value found in private industry? If so, should stockholders in investment banking firms take steps to encourage their corporate officers to do the same thing, since their ratios are far greater than those in the mining or food-processing industries? Given that there are enormous differences in the spans of control, corporate structures, pay structures, and retirement systems in successful business firms, why presume that any departure from the private sector "average" by the public sector is so disastrous?

It may be, as Peter Grace asserts, that "if the federal government were a private company, it would probably be bankrupt." But is it equally true that "if most private companies were governments, they would not survive very long politically." The government is not and can never become a business on many important dimensions. If businessmen were ever to attempt to run the federal government in accordance with the broad "business principles" that are the basis for much of the advice in the Grace Commission report, they would learn a lot about the practical limitations of their principles in government and, to everyone's benefit, the voters would leave them with a lot more time on their hands to apply the principles to their businesses, perhaps increasing profitability and their companies' industry rankings on five-year return on equity.

DON'T LOOK BACK

The best substitute for experience is being sixteen.
RAYMOND DUNCAN

Armed with enormous faith in the power of business methods and with the strength of its convictions that the problems of the federal government exist and persist because of a failure to utilize those methods, the Grace Commission devoted little attention to studying the experiences with past reform attempts. Consequently, the Commission report repeats recommendations that have been made regularly for the past 50 years without ever touching on the questions of why the prescriptions were not embraced the first time they were proposed or why they were ineffective when previously implemented.

The Commission calls for objective-based management, goal clarification, better planning, and the development of performance measures without referring to the long history of reforms like PPBS, MBO, and ZBB, which were devised and implemented to accomplish many of the same managerial ends. Why should the Commission members or anyone else believe that these proposals will succeed now where better-developed versions have failed before? Perhaps the Commission believed that the past failures were due entirely to an absence of sufficient political will on the part of the president and an absence of sufficient pressure for reform from voters, and that both these requisite conditions for success are now present. But if this is its belief, it is a naive one. Political will is important, but so are a variety of other factors that we have seen play a role in the demise of these reforms.

The historical vacuum in which the Commission operates reduces the credibility of even perhaps reasonable proposals like the establishment of a far more powerful Office of Federal Management. This agency—which would subsume OMB, OPM, and GSA—is intended by the Commission to put more emphasis on reviewing regulations, developing and monitoring financial accounting systems, and planning management information systems than occurs with the current organizational structure. They want to put the "M" back in OMB. We agree with the Grace Commission that the executive office should pay more attention to such managerial matters as financial reporting and information systems. We have no particular objection to the proposed new agency except that the history indicates that it will not have the desired effect.

The history of reform demonstrates nothing so much as that there is often difficulty in translating praiseworthy objectives into political reality. The Commission should realize that many of its objectives were sought by earlier reform groups. Taft's Commission on Economy and Efficiency in 1912 changed financial reporting. The Budgeting and Accounting Act of 1921 created the Bureau of the Budget within the Treasury Department, with an accounting control perspective. Roosevel's Brownlow Commission in 1937 moved budgeting from the Treasury Department to the Executive Office of the President and gave it much broader management and agency-coordination responsibilities. Then there were PPBS, MBO, and the change from BOB to OMB, which was intended to be much more than a name change. There have also been a host of intraorganizational changes, such as growth in the White House staff and reorganizations of that staff directed at increasing the president's managerial control.

The Grace Commission should realize that the present OMB, with its preoccupation on the second of its two mandates, the "B," evolved out of an agency, the Bureau of the Budget, that possessed and lost something of the sort of financial control and management orientation that the Commission recommends the new agency have. It should think about why this evolution took place. If it occurred because of some foolish choices on the part of successive Democratic administrations that were insensitive to the need for good management practices, then maybe we do not have to worry about it. A wise (conservative) leader can simply order that the new goals be adopted, and everyone will live happily ever after. If, however, the management orientation has proved to be very difficult to create and maintain in OMB because of incentives and constraints that are still in place (e.g., the budget is far more politically salient than management issues or it is simply too large and complex for oversight to be handled by a single agency), then we face the prospect of having the same cycle take place all over again and the reform effort will ultimately fail.

The tendency of the Commission to repeat recommendations that have been made over and over again without ever bothering to speculate about why they have never been successfully implemented makes its report much less useful than it should have been. Much of the administrative genius possessed by members of the Commission doubtless lies less in dreaming up totally novel management strategies than in being able to implement, creatively, well-known techniques in environments that frustrate less talented individuals. Since government bureaucracy and the complex political environment in which it must operate presents about as challenging an environment as any members of the Grace Commission could imagine, the fit should have been perfect. The collective talent of hundreds of skilled administrative problem solvers from the private sector could have been applied to the knotty implementation problems that have thus far prevented some very obvious "solutions" from working. Unfortunately, this never happened. The Commission virtually ignored the critical issue of implementation and opted instead for the easier task of repeating recommendations now decades old.

It is hard to escape the conclusion that the Grace Commission report ignores implementation questions and the history of past reforms not only because it assumes that such brilliant recommendations have never been made before but also because the commissioners have no real interest in understanding how government works. They believe in a world of clear and well-articulated goals, of centralized authority, of complete information, of fair prices for products and services, and of docile boards of directors. To the extent that government is not like this, that is government's problem. It is the Commission's task only to point out the problems and tell how they would be solved *if government worked as it should work*. This explains the intolerance and insensitivity of the Commission and particularly its chief spokesman, Peter Grace, toward politics. It leads the Commission to argue that its recommendations do not "endanger the substance or legislated intent of Federal programs" (PPSS, Sec. II, p. 1) while proceeding to recommend numerous "reforms" that obviously will have precisely this effect (e.g., reducing funding for EPA grants, eliminating the Small Business Administration, and counting benefits from the school lunch and child nutrition programs as income in determining food stamp eligibility). But while the Grace Commission may not know the difference between efficiency changes and policy changes, Congress does. Indeed, there is already some evidence on how many of the proposed policy changes will be received. The Senate has voted by an almost three-quarters majority (with unanimity among senators from states west of Missouri) to extend the provision of federally subsidized power for another 30 years despite a survey recommendation to charge market rates for the power.

Nothing in the Grace Commission effort indicates its contempt for and indifference about the way government actually operates as clearly as the strategy that the chairman and his assistants have taken in attempting to have the recommendations adopted. The centerpiece of this strategy is apparently a frontal assault on Congress, blaming it for much of the inefficiency and waste in government and attempting to intimidate it into acting with the threat of a populist uprising by beleaguered taxpayers (who pay one of lowest tax rates in any industrialized country) and businessmen in the event Congress does not act. He is reported as uttering such gems of insight for implementation as "You've got to be tough with these people, they know only one way of acting," and "You can't be polite, not in politics," and "You've got to scare the hell out of these people, that's the only language they know."[3] Such tactics may be effective for the chairman and majority stockholder of a company in dealing with a hand-picked, usually servile, board of directors, but the tactics are an almost certain recipe for failure in dealing with 535 often fiercely independent agents in the business of protecting the interests of the constituents who elected them. As Senator Robert Dole, now majority leader, understated it, "Bashing Congress isn't going to help him get his proposals through." [Quoted by Laurie McGinley, "Touted Report Won't be Heeded," *The Wall Street Journal*, Friday, November 30, 1984.]

The assumptions that all management wisdom originates in the private sector, that private-sector techniques are equally effective in the public sector, and that the failures of similar past reform efforts have nothing to teach us all reinforce what is generally regarded as the report's most prominent feature: its tendency toward wild hyperbole.

WHAT'S A FEW BILLION AMONG FRIENDS?

In the opinion of people who are well informed, the savings estimates [of the Grace Commision] are enormously exaggerated. We've had things like this since the Hoover Commission that purport to save huge amounts that don't materialize.

HERBERT STEIN

Both the severity of the government's problems and the benefits of PPSS recommendations are routinely overstated by the Grace Commission. The "one-third" of the budget supposedly consumed by waste and inefficiency includes numerous redistributive programs as well as federal employee benefits that are generous in some regards but certainly not uniformly so (it is not clear that generous retirement benefits compensate middle- and upper-level federal executives for 20 or 30 years at a salary level well above their private-sector counterparts). These programs and policies may be wasteful if your politics say that they are unnecessary, but they are the product of conscious political decisions and not mismanagement or waste in the usual sense. The 100 percent of the tax revenues that "are gone before one nickel is spent on services that taxpayers expect from their Government" (PPSS, Sec. 1, p. 4) include transfer payments to Social Security, which most politicians, including President Reagan, now acknowledge as a program that taxpayers—and voters—strongly favor.

The Commission concedes that the three-year net savings and revenue enhancement figure of $424.351 billion that it so freely bandies about is based on figures that are of a *planning* rather than *budget* quality, but it neither explains this interesting distinction nor speculates about its implications for the estimated total. Another interesting but never fully explained distinction is that between Category I ("fully substantiated and defensible"), II ("substantially documented and supportable"), and III ("potentially justifiable and supportable") recommendations. Our guess is that it means the numbers in Category I and II are so shaky that if a public official used them in decision making, the Commission would level charges of managerial incompetence. The use of Category III numbers is out of the question, even for the Grace Commission. We also doubt that there are many underestimation errors.

There are assumptions behind the numbers that are never adequately explained to those eager to save $424 billion. For example, most casual readers and listeners are left with the impression that the estimates apply to the next three fiscal years. Alas, they do not.

> The work of PPSS focused on both short-term and long-term opportunities. In many instances, some of the PPSS recommendations can be easily and immediately implemented at the agency or department level. In other instances, implementation of PPSS recommendations will require Congressional legislation and, therefore, will take a much longer time period for implementation. For this reason, reference in the reports is made to "Year 1," "Year 2," and "Year 3," rather than to any specific fiscal year or time frame. PPSS considers its recommendations ageless. (PPSS, Sec. VI, p. 12.)

Thus, in the $424 billion savings figure is an estimate of the savings that would result in an arbitrary three years after all of the recommendations are implemented. Some of the savings would occur in FY 2000 and not in FY 1985 through FY 1987. The survey's estimated savings for the immediate three fiscal years is $298 billion. The Congressional Budget Office estimates that the savings for the same period and programs would be more like $98 billion if all of the proposals were adopted, including those that have nothing to do with efficiency. The Grace Commission's calculations and reporting are feckless, not ageless.

The survey makes much ado about "netting out" duplications across the savings estimates from the 47 task forces in arriving at its "net" $424 billion figure. Apparently, this ado is intended to increase the listener's confidence in the accuracy of the numbers; after all, they could have claimed much more. But there are other "net" calculations that the Commission apparently does not do. One of these is "net" to government as a whole and not just the federal government. A number of the Commission recommendations achieve savings at the expense of state and local governments by curtailing transfers. For example, EPA recommendation 1-1 suggests that the federal government "redirect construction grants program to the states" at a saving of $46.3 million.[4] For the taxpayers, these savings are "net" in a narrow financial sense only if the state and local governments decide to drop the service rather than to increase state and local taxes to fund it themselves. In the broader sense, these savings are "net" only if the activities funded by the grants have no value.

A second "netting" anomaly concerns the "savings" that are claimed for internal pricing changes, particularly schemes where one federal agency charges other federal agencies for goods and services provided. For example, recommendation number 22 for Agriculture says that the department should "require recipient departments to budget and pay for USDA commodities they use" with an estimated "revenue enhancement" of $1,205 million.[5] It is not at all clear how these revenue enhancements can be "net" to the federal government, since the payments are effectively transfers to USDA from other lines in the federal budget. It is also not clear that the Commission recognized this and adjusted for it.

Yet another "netting" anomaly can be found in those recommendations that save money by transferring functions from one federal agency to another. For example, recommendation number 53 for the Department of Agriculture is to "transfer selected human nutrition research programs to HHS" with an estimated savings of $99 million.[6] It may be that this and comparable "savings" are netted out of the $424 billion advertised, but we cannot determine that this was done from the compendious, unindexed documentation.

Many of the PPSS estimates, particularly those associated with particular cost-saving recommendations, are not easily criticized because they are so poorly documented. The erstwhile critic must first infer from sketchy descriptions what procedures were used to get the numbers and then evaluate those procedures. While the numbers are so fallacious and so poorly documented that they neither warrant nor support much detailed critical treatment, the casual consumer of the Commission's public pronouncements in the various media will not, and in many cases cannot, understand just how "fast and loose" the Commission has played in arriving at its estimates.

More important than what is "net" are the specific savings or revenue enhancements that will result from specific recommendations. The research and analysis supporting them is much worse than uneven. It is mostly absent. One area that reveals some of the problems is that of Automatic Data Processing/Office Automation (ADP/OA). This area was stressed throughout the report.

> PPSS found Federal automated data processing activities to be disorganized and inefficient, falling far short of the potential for productivity improvements and consequent savings that exist in state of the art computer systems. More than half of all Federal ADP systems are obsolete, with an average age about twice that in the private sector. Further, ADP systems are not acquired with coordinated planning and the Government's computer systems are, therefore, generally incompatible. PPSS recommendations center on the establishment of a Federal Information Resources Manager who would direct a coordinated government-wide effort to upgrade and replace existing systems. . . . (PPSS, sec. III, pp. 66–77.)

The sum necessary to reduce the average age of the government's computers to a point comparable to that of the private sector's—that is, from approximately 6.7 years to 3 years—would be astronomical. To begin with, there are equipment and equipment maintenance costs in billions and billions of dollars, whether the government is buying or leasing. Then there are the systems development, training, and conversion costs that will run into many more billions. There is also the potential for service disruption costs. New systems have a nasty habit of failing to perform reliably, sometimes for years, until all of the bugs are worked out.

One can just imagine the political response and potential for human suffering if the checks to veterans, Social Security recipients, private-sector accounts payable, or tax refunds are delayed for a few weeks or a few months while the government experts and highly paid private-sector consultants work out "a few bugs" in their "much more efficient" new system.[7] It may be that those who depend on the checks to pay rent and to eat would be mollified by abstract arguments about the importance of increasing governmental efficiency by bringing the government's computing equipment up to date with an arbitrary private-sector standard for average age, but we doubt it. The predictable strategy in implementing the new systems, aside from avoiding election years, would be to run, at considerable additional cost, the old and new systems in parallel until there is sufficient confidence in the reliability of the new systems.[8]

Moreover, simply because a computer is old does not mean that it is inefficient, wasteful, or inappropriate for the task to which it is being applied. The differences between the capabilities of 3-year-old and 6.7-year-old computing technology can be considerable. The newer hardware technology is on the whole more compact, higher-capacity, faster, and cheaper. The improvements in central processing units and peripherals over the past few years are nothing short of revolutionary. There have been dramatic improvements in software, particularly for minicomputers and microcomputers. What the Commission neglects to recognize, or at least acknowledge, is that most of these improvements are largely irrelevant to the bulk of government applications of computing. The bulk of the applications are mundane tasks such as data-base management, text processing, and check writing, for which one does not need bit-mapped graphics or the speed of a Cray supercomputer. Being able to search a data base and print a report in three minutes rather than eight minutes is apt to have a negligible impact on the efficiency of most administrative functions. And these are just the sorts of improvements that the newer technologies bring to mundane administrative applications. In such applications, most of the expense is in designing and installing the system in the first place, in creating and maintaining enormous data bases, and in training and retaining staff to operate the system. The equipment you use can be important, but there are few easy generalizations. What the most efficient ADP technology is must be determined on a case-by-case basis with a level of detailed research that the Grace Commission simply does not provide. Such analysis might even reveal that certain systems, now computerized, might be more efficiently implemented with pencils and paper.

The Grace Commission was also critical of many other aspects of the federal government's use of ADP/OA. They noted that the lack of a coordinated acquisition process has led to a situation in which many of the government's systems cannot "talk to each other," and therefore it becomes very difficult to share computing capabilities across agencies. While there is a great deal to be said for compatibility in standards and protocols, the Grace Commission's problem diagnosis in this area fails to recognize or acknowledge some deep technical and organizational problems that exist.

The technical problems are difficult because there are few well-established and widely adhered to industry standards on the machine and software characteristics that are the key to communicating among machines. For reasons of competition and convenience, manufacturers have intentionally gone their own way in terms of character sets, operating systems, communication protocols, and the like. Some characteristics are even closely guarded trade secrets. IBM, for one, has always, at least prior to the introduction of its personal computer, worked with "closed architecture" and differentiated its hardware and software from its competitors and potential competitors. This strategy has been the heart of one of the most effective marketing strategies in the history of world business. By ensuring a high degree of incompatibility with other computer suppliers and a high degree of upward compatibility within their own line of machines and software, IBM has been able to make the prospective costs of shifting to another supplier very high. The federal government cannot sole-source computing equipment. It may be able to go further than it has to date in announcing technical standards that further compatibility and then buying or leasing only equipment that adheres to the standards. But if the Department of Defense's experience in trying to set standards in software to solve what many have called its "Tower of Babel problem" with the ADA language is any guide, it will take a long time to set the standards, the resulting standards will be technically inefficient compromises, and enforcing the standards will be nearly impossible. Regardless of the standards set, the rapidly advancing technology will ensure that they are more trouble than they are worth by the time they are set.

Then there are the organizational issues. Compatibility is a serious problem in organizations of all kinds. With the advent of powerful minicomputer and microcomputer technology, there have been, for example, many reports of incompatibility problems in corporations. The existence of incompatible computing technologies is not, as the Grace Commission asserts, evidence of enormous organizational inefficiencies calling for radical organizational solutions. The imputation of problems seems to stem from some vision of enormous economies of scale in acquisition and use. With coordinated acquisition based on some centralized plan, the government will save a lot of money on the acquisition of computers in the same way it gets a cost break on bulk purchases of four-ply toilet paper. And in a phantasmagorical world of complete compatibility and coordination, the government will be able to smooth computer usage so that no agency ever runs short while other agencies have idle capacity; every last byte can be harnessed in the service of those clear objectives that the Commission urges the federal government to get.

One set of organizational problems for the Grace Commission recommendations in the ADP/OA area is found in the disputes over the control of computing in the midst of a revolution in computing technology. Traditionally, government and business organizations have had centralized data processing operations that controlled all aspects of computing for the organizations. This was a natural and frequently efficient way of organizing when computing technology consisted entirely of very expensive "mainframe" equipment that required a lot of space in a carefully controlled environment, a lot of expertise to operate the machines and to troubleshoot problems, and very specialized technical knowledge to program the machines to accomplish the various computing tasks.

The technological times have changed and continue to change with the accelerating proliferation of powerful, portable, easy-to-use minicomputing and microcomputing. The computational power of a moderately large mainframe computer of 1975 can now be put in desk-top machines, and the power of the larger mainframes of 1975 can be put in cases about the size of three-drawer file cabinets. The machines are much hardier, requiring a less controlled environment, less operator expertise, and less repair. The cost per unit of computational power has declined markedly over the last several years. There has been a companion revolution in software. With sophisticated data-base, statistical, and spreadsheet packages, managers with very modest technical training can do in hours what once took teams of excellent programmers weeks to do.

The upshot of these tandem revolutions in the cost and performance of hardware and software is that it is now feasible to distribute computing throughout organizations. Indeed, distributed computing with distributed control is becoming the most efficient form for most organizations. Naturally, a lot of vested interests were built up around the centralized mode of organizing. Career paths from the entry level of programmer or systems analyst to deputy assistant secretary (or senior vice president) for data processing were established. The most serious problem for exploiting state-of-the-art computing technology in government (and private industry) that the Commission identifies and seeks to remedy—a lack of centralized coordination on acquisition and use—is not the real problem. The problem is exactly the opposite: centralized computing and entrenched managers of centralized "data centers" who utilize mainframe technologies and resist the introduction of the new, distributed technologies. The Commission's advice, increased centralization, is exactly wrong.

Other organizational difficulties that argue for the further decentralization of computing in the federal government are the need for secure data bases and the managerial costs of time-sharing computing. Virtually every federal agency—not just Defense, the Central Intelligence Agency, and the Internal Revenue Service—has data that must be confidential. One of the main ways that they protect the data is by restricting access to the systems. It may be attractive conceptually to time-share computing capacity on the basis of need across agencies, but working out the rules of access and priority has always been and will always be a managerial nightmare, even within agencies. All users always believe that their computing requirements of the moment should take precedence over the requirements of other users. In the days of expensive, limited-capacity centralized computing resources, strife over access was unavoidable; priorities had to be set, sometimes at the highest levels of the organization. To an increasing extent, the strife is avoidable at least at the high levels. Decentralize!

The Grace Commission cannot really be serious in recommending that *all* federally owned computers "talk to one another." There is probably not now and never will be any good reason for the dedicated Wang word processors in the Department of Housing and Urban Development to communicate with the Cray supercomputers in Los Alamos. While this is an extreme case where it is obvious that one should not be willing to pay much for compatibility, there are a host of less extreme cases where it also does not make sense. The variety of tasks requiring computing in the federal government is enormous and will call for a corresponding variety in computers. Compatibility should be pursued on an agency-by-agency and office-by-office basis. The acquisition of smaller computers for the sake of bulk-purchase discounts should be handled in exactly the same way as the bulk purchase of other capital goods (e.g., air conditioners or typewriters) is handled and not by a czar of computing in the New Executive Office Building. The virtues of increased centralization as proposed by the Grace Commission are not obvious.

There are almost certainly substantial problems with the acquisition and use of computing in the federal government and substantial opportunities for improvements in both efficiency and effectiveness. The scale alone assures this. There may even be excellent ideas in the Grace Commission report as to how ADP/OA can be improved. But given the style and substance of the report, it is impossible to identify such meritorious ideas. Certainly, the estimates of "cost savings" that the Grace Commission offers in the areas of ADP/OA are grossly overstated. The substantive advice on organizing for computing is not even very good, costs aside.

While it would be very difficult to prove conclusively, we expect that the only savings estimates that are at all reliable are those associated with the recommendations that have the least to do with managerial efficiency and that will be the most difficult to implement politically. It is much easier to get reasonable estimates of the net financial effects from scrapping a program or office entirely or from cutting personnel benefits or changing an entitlement formula than it is to estimate the net effects from replacing a 1978 vintage computer with a 1983 vintage computer or from installing a new inventory system.[9] As was argued in earlier chapters, finding demonstrable efficiency improvements in governments that do not affect policies is never easy. The small number of such improvements in the 2,478 Grace Commission recommendations is excellent evidence for the point.

The Commission got into the spirit of bandying about incomprehensibly large numbers in communications as well as calculations. For example, in the press release announcing the "cost savings of more than $1.8 billion over a three-year period" in the Environmental Protection Agency (EPA), Small Business Administration (SBA), and the Federal Emergency Management Agency (FEMA), the survey rounded up the detailed estimates by $43 million before modifying $1.8 billion with the phrases "more than" and "at least." Of the 71 recommendations it describes for these agencies, only 10 have estimated savings greater than $43 million, the rounding amount. Behind the blaring headline "TASK FORCE REVIEWING PERSONNEL REVEALS NEARLY $40 BILLION WORTH OF SAVINGS POTENTIAL" (PPSSCC press release, April 5, 1983) are estimated "savings" of $38.178 billion. We do not know how many average taxpayers $1.822 billion, the rounding amounts, represents, but we suspect that it is a lot; and if the general taxpayers are not impressed with this amount, the farmers or students would love to have the amount added back to their programs in the FY 86 budget.

The final instance of the Commission's hyperbole to be mentioned here is represented by its statements of how little the PPSS effort cost the federal government. These are, we feel, particularly revealing. The report claims:

> Except for the one full-time Government employee assigned it, PPSS cost the Federal Government *nothing*. A private, not-for-profit Foundation was established for purposes of raising gifts in kind as well as financial contributions to support the work of the Survey Management Office (including space, equipment, and support staff) and the overall administration of the Task Forces. Approximately $3.3 million was raised by the Foundation.
>
> More specifically, members of the Executive Committee, the Survey Management Office and the Task Forces served without cost to the Federal Government. All their salaries and expenses, including travel, hotel, and other out of pocket costs, were paid

by their private sector employers who volunteered their services or by them personally. A rough calculation of private sector contributions in terms of time and personnel resources dedicated to the PPSS effort totals over $75 million. (PPSS sec. VI, pp. 10–11.)

This sounds very much like the proverbial "free lunch." While there are no easy ways of calculating the costs of the survey to federal government, there are at least three categories of costs in addition to the direct cost of the one assigned federal employee. First, there are the costs in the amounts of income taxes lost from contributors who claimed their contributions as business expenses or charitable contributions. While the precise tax loss depends on the amounts claimed and the marginal tax rates of the individual and corporate contributors, the amount almost certainly runs into the millions of dollars. Second, there are the costs in the time of federal employees who spent many hours with PPSS workers educating them about particular aspects of the federal government and the costs of providing them with the documentation. The value of the time spent by federal employees, time that might have been spent on performing their function or improving their function, if calculated as the sum of hours spent times the salary and fringe benefit costs of each employee plus the value of the services that were lost, would certainly run into many more millions of dollars. The documentation costs were perhaps a trivial amount if the Grace Commission paid prevailing rates for copies of the various documents they used. If not, one can only imagine the costs of the documentation that was eventually distilled into a 47 volume study costing about $715 to purchase from the National Technical Information Service (NTIS). We will resist the temptation to imitate the survey's procedure of feigning a precise dollar estimate in an amorphous circumstance and then translating it into the number of average income taxpayers that the amount represents.

The cost of the study, like so many other numerical claims in the Commission's report, is so distorted and stated with such arrogant, self-congratulatory certitude that it is hard to believe that purportedly competent businessmen were serious in the assertion. If they were serious, we can only hope that it was an atypical, careless mistake and neither a deliberate misrepresentation nor an example of how they usually work with cost estimates in their own businesses. If the Grace Commission's financial analysis fairly represents the premises that the "best and the brightest" managerial talent in the United States uses as premises for their investment and management decisions, our prospects in the international industrial competition with Japan, Germany, Korea, Taiwan, and other developed countries are somewhat frightening.

The Grace Commission would have a very hard time finding CPAs willing to attest to the dollar estimates in their report as "conforming to generally accepted accounting principles" and "fairly reflecting the financial condition of the government." The hyperbole in the financial claims is unfortunate. A lot of time and effort has been wasted by the Congress, the White House staff, the GAO, the CBO, the media, and others in arguing about what the savings from various Commission proposals would be and when they would occur. This is time and effort that would be better spent examining a few of the Commission's more interesting and novel proposals and proposals from other sources.

Given the magnitude of the financial, managerial, and political problems the federal government actually faces over the foreseeable future, it is not at all clear why the Commission felt compelled to engage in as much hyperbole as it did. The tactic does nothing but hurt the credibility of the report.

Having said all of this we do not want to give the impression that the Grace Commission report is totally without merit. Twenty-five hundred recommendations cannot be all bad. If one can get past the gratuitous vilification of the public sector and the childlike faith that the effortless application of standard business methods can quickly bring enormous efficiency gains, there are some helpful prescriptions to be found that are, as we shall soon see, very much in keeping with the lessons that emerge from our analysis of the experience with earlier efficiency reforms.[10] The time has arrived to reflect on just what those lessons are.

The Lessons of Reform

That which we call sin in others is experiment for us.
EMERSON'S INSIGHT

THE GRAND-STRATEGY PROBLEM

Our plans miscarry because they have no aim. When a man does
not know what harbor he is making for, no wind is the right wind.
SENECA

One problem with many past reforms is that they have taken a comprehensive, strategic approach. They have usually been directed at all agencies or all programs in the target government and have been aimed at the highest-level decisions. There has been a corresponding and notable disinterest in more modest tactical reforms directed at a single agency or program and at decisions that affect relatively small budget allocations.

There are a number of reasons why this bias toward strategic reforms exists. First, hype and oversell are the stuff of which democratic politics is made. How otherwise could aspiring reformers possibly divert scarce money and political attention away from more politically colorful issues like the Soviet threat, abortion, the Equal Rights Amendment, inflation, insurgency in Central America, trade deficits, budget deficits, and the arms race that occupy the federal political agenda at any point in time? Second, the widely held view of government bureaucracies as hopelessly inefficient invites sweeping strategic reforms. Anything less pales beside the perceived problems. If it is widely believed that billions are casually tossed away through bureaucratic waste, it is hard to capture much political attention and inspire political support by advocating modest programs that save a few hundred thousand or even a million dollars.

A third reason for the emphasis on strategic reforms is that the grander and more ambiguous the reform, the more easily it can trade on the most treasured symbolic values in society. Efficiency ranks with motherhood, apple pie, citizen participation, and balanced budgets as a fundamental American value. But all these values are best espoused as general principles with no specific programs attached. Motherhood is fine as long as you do not have to take a position on a mother's right to have an abortion and on who should pay the costs of day care. Apple pie is fine as long as you do not have to worry about the effects on human health of the insecticides used in orchards; about the relative subsidies in the production of apples, tobacco, and soybeans; or about the calories in the pie contributing to obesity, which, in turn, leads to health problems that increase Medicare and Medicaid costs. The same pattern holds for most reform goals. Balanced budgets are fine as long as someone else's favorite programs are cut to achieve the balance. Citizen participation is fine as long as you do not have to specify the groups, the forms of participation, and the precise impact of participation. Sim-

237

ilarly, efficiency is fine as long as you do not spell out details that enable politicians to project the specific impacts of the proposed reform on their constituencies and learn that they are among those who will lose influence or funds. It is always somewhat harder to sacrifice for principles when the level of sacrifice can be computed—particularly in election years.

Yet while the absence of specifics may be an important positive feature of reforms when one is seeking political approval and resources, it becomes an important negative feature when the time comes to do the actual reforming. The details, with all their associated distributional consequences, must still be worked out in highly politicized contexts in which efficiency must compete with other values. Until such details are mapped out, the reforms will have little or no impact on the day-to-day operations of governments, where the work load consists of accomplishing specifically prescribed tasks and not in embracing principles.

The problem with most strategic reforms is that they involve so many details with important consequences for "Who gets what, when, and how" that they can never be implemented without losing their basic character to the point that they are unrecognizable as well as ineffectual. Most of the time they do not get implemented at all but simply persist in the background as hollow monuments to great expectations and great naivete. These tragic flaws of the hubris approach to reform—in which the emphasis on strategic reforms plays a major role—were identified long ago by political scientists like Aaron Wildavsky, who argued that global reforms such as PPBS can best be viewed as major political reforms that seek to alter the distribution of influence and the character of the most basic government institutions in the name of efficiency. There is no way that a reform like PPBS could work as it was designed to do without changing the role and relative influence of Congress. Because members of Congress realized this, PPBS was persistently and thoroughly undermined.

Not only do strategic reforms fail but they simultaneously distract us from the gains that can be and, in fact, are achieved through more modest reforms and undermine our confidence that any improvements are possible. In the world of politics, where attention grabbing means so much, the promises of savings that will run into the billions have always tended to drown out the reality that—short of major policy changes—all that can usually be saved is a few hundred thousand dollars or a few million here and there. Perhaps even worse, a real savings of $1 million is often worth much more in advancing one's career than ten separate $100,000 savings. Unfortunately, promises do not reduce budget deficits. Even in the "world of many zeros" (the federal government), there are far more opportunities to save $100,000 than to save $1 million. To make matters even worse, the size of the savings is not the only or even the most important determinant of the "pressworthiness" of an efficiency act. Frequently the incentives are greater to harangue, in the name of efficiency, a governor for using the state police to shuttle his children to and from school or to introduce a bill, in the name of efficiency, barring the use of limousine services by top officials than to propose changes in more complicated, less politically salient areas where efficiency savings are orders of magnitude greater.

The failure of strategic reforms has also distorted our view of what efficiency gains are possible. Because strategic reforms are most often attempted and most often given press coverage, we begin to feel that government can do nothing to improve efficiency. Because strategic reforms require major changes in the structure of government institutions and the relationship of these institutions to each other, we conclude that any efficiency gain would require that we rewrite the constitution—a price too high. Fortunately, the managerial-consultant character of the Grace Commission report and the intensity of the effort ensured that some attention would be paid to tactical reforms. Many of the 2,478 proposals contained in the 35 individual reports and the 11 special studies focus on specific problems in individual agencies. The following proposals certainly fall into this category:

- That the Department of Defense consolidate some of its 30 wholesale depots in which only 68 percent of the space is presently being utilized (PPSS, sec. III, p. 8).
- That payroll processing in the Department of Energy be handled in one location instead of eight as is presently the case and that the agency's monthly books be closed on a single day (PPSS, sec. III, p. 37).
- That the Treasury Department pay bills only when they are due rather than on a first-in, first out basis (PPSS, sec. III, p. 39).
- That the Internal Revenue Service add 2,500 employees to its Examination Division staff. (PPSS, sec. III, p. 43).
- That federal employees utilize government-issued credit cards to pay for official travel (PPSS, sec. V, p. 4).
- That the Federal Employee Health Benefit Program conduct open enrollment only in alternate years and require that enrollees remain in a plan until the next enrollment period (PPSS, sec. III, p. 313).
- That premiums for the Department of Agriculture's Federal Crop Insurance Program be actuarially determined and that the federal government no longer administer crime or riot insurance (PPSS, sec. III, p. 235).
- That the Education Department require cosigners for all student loans (PPSS, sec. III, p. 211).

LOYALTY TO THE POLITICAL STATUS QUO

I obeyed every order with which I agreed.
ADMIRAL HYMAN RICKOVER
(reflecting on his long naval career)

While there is considerable truth in Wildavsky's observation that the fatal flaw of PPBS and similar systems was that they naïvely required fundamental transformations in basic political institutions, it is important to avoid the trap of arguing that any reform that affects the distribution of influence among governmental institutions threatens to undermine the American political system. The role of the president, Congress, and the courts has shifted countless times in the past (almost) 200 years as the result of a variety of internal and external forces. Is the appropriate influence of the office of the president that which it exerted in 1824? 1865? 1938? or 1983? Seen in this light, it makes little sense to judge a reform unthinkable simply because it has some effect on the policymaking initiative of Congress vis-à-vis the president or acts to strengthen political parties.

We say this because one important category of tactical reform involves altering what might be called secondary institutions. These are those complicated and boring procedures and organizational arrangements that are legitimately (either through law or tradition) part of government but that can be altered to improve efficiency without changing the government's "basic character." Although "basic character" is obviously ambiguous, our argument is that many of these secondary institutions are constantly in flux and that if they can be altered so as to increase the efficiency of government without violating its fundamental underpinnings and the basic relationships among institutions, so be it. For example, the elimination of the spoils system as it existed in the beginning of the twentieth century and the establishment of the civil service system was an important political reform in the sense that it altered the scope of executive authority and the benefits of elected office. Yet by almost any estimation except those of political bosses or dispossessed workers, this was an important and legitimate political reform that should not be denigrated simply because civil service is far from perfect or that subsequent personnel reforms were often disappointing.

Dozens of other reforms—ranging from the partial abandonment of the seniority system in Congress to the installation of the city manager form of urban government—might be argued to fall into the same category. They are political reforms justified in large part by their efficiency consequences and given intellectual support by efficiency reformers. Eventually, of course, we get to the point where the magnitude of what is proposed on the grounds of increasing efficiency is so great and the definition of efficiency so arbitrary that we are dealing with nothing less than fundamental political change, but there are a large number of effective reforms that can take place before that point is reached. For example, one avenue of reform explored later in this chapter is the establishment of agencies that function as independent sources of information about the efficiency and effectiveness of other parts of government, such as the Congressional Budget Office. This agency was established as part of the 1974 Congressional Reform Act to counter what many perceived to be a monopoly of information about the operations of government by the executive branch. In the years since its establishment, the information that it has produced on government spending, revenue and expenditure forecasts, and the behavior of specific agencies such as the Defense Department and the Environmental Protection Agency has almost certainly made a significant contribution to the cause of increased efficiency and effectiveness by raising issues and questions that were not previously raised. Yet it has also altered the relationship between Congress and the executive branch. Does this mean that it should never have been established? We do not think so.

Many of the Grace Commission proposals have been criticized as involving infeasible changes of a basically political character. To the extent that they are indeed infeasible (and many are), this criticism is helpful, but to simply argue that they are impractical because they are more political than managerial is unfair—at least it would be unfair if the authors of the report did not claim that the report was basically nonpolitical. There is no question that the suggested repeal or amendment of the Davis-Bacon or Walsh-Healy Acts (which set wage scales for government contracts) is squarely in the realm of politics, but this does not mean that their mere contemplation violates the basic structure of American government. The same is true of changes in price supports and subsidies or proposals that user fees at airports and national parks be increased. Individually these proposals may be wise or foolish, but they and others like them deserve a hearing with as much evidence as supporters can muster. There is simply no way that significant efficiency gains will be achieved without abandoning the notion that they can be obtained primarily through the institution of strictly apolitical, administrative reforms.

THE WRONG-PROBLEMS PROBLEM

The Puritans objected to bearbaiting not because it gave pain to the bear but because it gave pleasure to the spectators.

THOMAS MACAULEY

Despite their press releases, many reforms have been inspired by problems that are not really efficiency problems at all. Reorganizations, for example, are frequently promoted as efficiency reforms when in reality they are designed to achieve quite different ends, such as increasing the political advantage of a newly elected executive. It has been no less common to propose complicated procedural reforms or budget cutting to deal with bureaucratic inefficiency when the performance problem actually has its roots elsewhere. The roots of society's inability to reduce crime, make American energy-independent, eliminate inflation and unemployment, or provide sufficient low-income housing lie in an absence of technology, resources, and political will. They are not products of bureaucratic ineptness or lazy and indifferent government workers. The belief that government's incapacities are the product of such failings may make election rhetoric more colorful and protect us from the pain of dealing with difficult problems and hard choices, but it brings none of these goals any closer.

Reorganizations, PPBS-like reforms, and budget cuts are also proposed to fight the waste that people see when they mistakenly use a personal rather than a collective utility function to value government output. Liberals propose them to fight the rampant inefficiency that they invariably see in the Department of Defense, while conservatives invoke them to fight the problem in the Department of Health and Human Services. While either department could doubtless be made to operate somewhat more efficiently than it presently does, the magnitude of each problem is almost certainly less than either group perceives, and the particular sources of inefficiency that do exist are unlikely to be eliminated through such broad and heavy-handed changes. If, for example, the failure to require that bids be submitted for spare-parts contracts or overly generous cost overrun provisions are principally responsible for the real (as opposed to ideologically based) component of Defense Department inefficiency, they are capable of surviving any number of reorganizations or PPBS-type reforms.

The existence of multiple goals in almost every public agency leads to the same problem. If the due-process or redistributive goals that frequently play a central role in the mandate of a public organization consume resources that a private organization would spend on the primary mission alone, then the public agency is, by definition, vulnerable to a charge of inefficiency by private-sector standards. This sets the stage for still another round of reforms that have nothing to do with the "real" problem, which has roots that are political in the most fundamental sense. How is a reform designed to guarantee that a government agency efficiently pursues its objectives going to reduce a variety of "inefficiency" that is a direct consequence of those objectives? How will a reform that is designed to ensure that a government worker gives a full day's work for a full day's pay help? They will not because the problem—if there is one—lies in the goals of the agency, not in their manipulation.

The wrong-problem problem runs deeper than this. Not only are misperceptions about government performance a constant inspiration for political platforms and misdirected reforms, they operate to prevent the implementation of the sort of useful tactical reforms that we have described. By constantly keeping the bureaucracy in a state of chaotic upheaval and disparaging the current performance levels of government workers, these reforms create a negative and hostile environment for government that makes performance difficult. If there is one consistent message in the "secrets of good management" literature directed largely at the private sector, it is "get your employees enthused about the organization and its objectives and give them the freedom to pursue those objectives as avidly and creatively as they can." Yet misdirected reforms and the misperceptions that motivate them work in almost precisely the opposite direction.

It is not easy for government managers to get employees to take pride in working for organizations that most of society, apparently including most "captains of industry" (if the members of the Grace Commission are a representative sample), disdains. It is bad enough that the only time that most government agencies hear from their "consumers" is when something goes wrong; it is far worse that they and their employees are *assumed* to be inefficient when very little is going wrong. Agencies try to cope with this situation by motivating employees through internally generated incentives, but they are severely constrained in the methods they can use. Big bonuses and rapid promotions, like those prevalent in the private sector, are generally viewed by politicians and the public as unnecessary and wasteful, while nonmonetary honors like the 1.6 medals awarded for every soldier who participated in the invasion of Grenada can quickly become a debased currency. In any event, there is a limit to the extent that any organization can prevent its employees from being damaged by a hostile environment. No number of rapid promotions could have prevented the readiness of the U.S. military from sagging badly during the period of post-Vietnam recriminations.

The tendency of many reformers to treat all government employees as incompetents and laggards not only reduces their energy and enthusiasm but all too frequently disenfranchises them from the entire reform process. One of the main reasons that efficiency reforms often fail in both the public and private sectors is that they are designed by people who are too remote from the realities of day-to-day functions and operations. In business this group is best exemplified by executives thrust into top-management posts who are unfamiliar with a company's operations but who are nonetheless committed to "revitalizing" the firm. In government this group is usually composed of newly elected officials who have campaigned to eliminate waste. Neither group has been notably successful.

The private sector has recently made attempts to supplement the recommendations of top officials by devising ways of systematically incorporating the knowledge of lower-level employees. Quality circles and incentive award programs are examples of two such innovations. Unfortunately, despite the entreaties of numerous management consultants and public administration experts, very little of this participative philosophy appears to have found its way into the larger efforts to reform government. For the reforms that are directed at improving the decisions on defense expenditures versus domestic expenditures, the failure to consult a GS-7 clerk-typist in the Department of Health and Human Services is understandable. Less understandable is the failure to solicit the opinion of agency analysts and middle- and lower-level managers about the wisdom of proceeding with the newest reorganization or budgetary reform and the failure to encourage proposals for the sort of "tactical" reforms already discussed.

POOR BASE INFORMATION

Life is the art of drawing sufficient conclusions from insufficient premises.

SAMUEL BUTLER

In spite of the enormous volumes of data they generate each year, governments leave a very incomplete, distorted, and often unusable record of their past activities. The data required to get a start on learning what causes what or on forecasting the consequences of various actions often do not exist. Surprising as it may seem, the federal government has a very poor idea of how much money it has given out to which state and local governments over the past 20 years and only the vaguest idea of what these funds have been used for. States frequently do not have accurate records of which highways and bridges they are responsible for, let alone what condition they are in. Cities (especially old cities in the East and Midwest) are often even more in the dark about the location and condition of their sewer and water pipes. How can one mount a "rational" capital expenditure or maintenance program without these data? And this is just the tip of the iceberg: the state of base information that governments have available to formulate policy is appalling. Obviously without a rich, accurate, and easily retrievable information base, the fancier analytic techniques that have characterized many recent reforms are a complete waste of time and money.

One important reason for the poor information base is that little priority and inadequate resources are given to collecting and storing data in an easily accessible form when there is no immediate use in sight for the data. Data activities are often vulnerable in times of financial stringency or in the periodic moves to reduce paperwork. The Reagan administration, for example, is busily destroying data-collection systems in many areas, such as that of the Federal Trade Commission, on corporate finance and outputs. These data, the first of their kind, offered some hope of fruitful research on such topics as the impact of trade and antitrust policies on business. If the administration succeeds, as it appears to have done, the information necessary to improve our understanding of such issues so that government might behave more rationally will be lost for another generation and the money that was spent on collecting the five or six years of data will have largely been wasted.

Another important reason for the poor information base is that much of the information produced by government, particularly textual information, is subject to politically motivated strategic manipulation. The historical record is written for political purposes. Some information is suppressed while other information is highlighted. Even without sins of commision, the sins of selective omission and emphasis can dramatically change the record. The Congressional Record has a very tenuous relationship with the substance of what occurs on the floors of the Houses of Congress (e.g., the casual reader of the record or of a congressman's speech, extracted from the record and mailed to all cosntituents, might actually believe that there was an audience of more than five in the House at the time the speech was delivered). Gubernatorial and mayoral budget messages are often riddled with strategic distortions of the facts. Even special prosecutors and independent blue ribbon commissions are often negotiated representations of events.

Yet another contributing factor is the poor and rapidly changing specification of what data various governments are required to record, of the forms in which they are to retain it, and of how long they are to keep it. This factor is important even in areas such as finances and budgeting, where one would not expect it to be. For analysts, incomplete data and data that are definitionally inconsistent across time or across comparable governments is a severe problem. The analytic technologies are weak enough without the added complication of incomplete and error-prone base information.

There is no doubt that many decisions are made each year at every level of government that could be improved—made more congruent with the values of the electorate and decision makers—if information that is accessible but for some reason remains unrevealed was disseminated. This may appear to be the same basic prescription of benefit–cost and productivity advocates and to some extent it is. Although proponents of these approaches exaggerated their applicability and accuracy while underestimating their many problems, they understood the potential value of information and, at least in the case of proponents of benefit–cost analysis, they understood that a principal source of government inefficiency lies in making "bad" decisions rather than in bureaucratic red tape and sloth. Employed "tactically" rather than "strategically," both techniques have their uses. However, we are talking about something much broader here than a single variety of analytic information.

There are, for example, the institutions and processes ensuring that information that goes against the interests of an incumbent administration will see the light of day and thus have the opportunity to affect the political process. Every time a more reliable set of cost estimates emerges from the Congressional Budgeting Office or the General Accounting Office about the cost of a subsidy, regulation, missile system, welfare program, or Grace Commission, the cause of efficiency is served. To expect such information to emerge naturally from within a bureaucracy controlled by an administration committed to these projects is naive, as the experience with benefit–cost analysis has demonstrated.

We agree with the Grace Commission that arbitrary and ill-considered congressional reporting requirements frequently lead to a waste of agency resources and that this problem has to be addressed. But it is naive to believe, as the Commission seems to, that the executive branch can be counted on to behave as a disinterested provider of information about its own activities. It is, after all, the executive branch that is the home of much of the alleged inefficiency. There is a continued need for much more legislative attention at all levels of government to specifying the data that agencies must collect and report. Once this has been specified, much weight must be given to maintaining consistency in these formats, since after a series is broken, much of its value is lost. At present, many data and reporting conventions are far too discretionary and changeable. A secretary of commerce, a director of EPA, a governor, or a mayor who is hostile to analysis or wants to gut the capacity of government to monitor private-sector activities can have a large impact that will have implications far beyond his or her term of office. Only with stable statutory requirements is the base information apt to improve dramatically. This must also be a patient process. It may be ten or twenty years before enough information is amassed to be truly useful in analysis, but it is often worth the effort. There are excellent models for data collection, processing, and reporting such as those of the Bureau of Labor Statistics in the Department of Labor, where elaborate procedures exist to ensure consistent data and an absence of political tampering. As for the issue of excessive congressional reporting requirements, it might be useful for Congress to create an agency of its own to deal with what has obviously become a very real problem. Other "process" solutions—such as periodically requiring that reporting requirements be reviewed and justified—might be considered.

NO RESOURCES TO SAVE RESOURCES

The meek shall inherit the earth but not the mineral rights.
GETTY'S REMINDER

Ironically, one of the principal obstacles to improving government performance is a lack of money. Virtually all efficiency improvements require some new expenditures, an investment. Just as it take money to make money in business, it takes money to save money in government. Training, reorganization, analysis, new equipment, and all of the other elements that might be required for any particular efficiency improvement are costly. Few, if any, government agencies have an "efficiency line" in their budget or the slack in their work loads and budgets that would enable them to take advantage of opportunities to improve efficiency as they arise. As a result these agencies are like the individuals who are too busy to get organized, whose lack of organization decreases their efficiency in accomplishing their work, so that they are increasingly busy, and so on. There is a degenerative cycle here that at some point guarantees that the work load will become overwhelming. The same cycle operates in many government agencies that have all of their resources dedicated to performing their function and none available to improving the way in which they perform their function. Even in those agencies where there is slack in the work load or budget, the employees who might be temporarily assigned to improving efficiency are sometimes incapable of doing that work—or there are elaborate control systems designed to prevent the misuse of public monies that have the side effect of preventing their sensible, efficiency-increasing use for anything not foreseen by the legislature when it appropriated the money.

The Grace Commission report is filled with suggestions for reforms that require substantial initial expenditures before any downstream savings can be achieved. The recommendation to substantially increase federal executive salaries from 20 to 30 percent in order to attract and keep skilled executives who now choose to pursue the greater economic rewards offered by the private sector falls into this category (PPSS, sec. III, p. 252). So too do the sensible recommendations that decentralized appellate tax boards be established to deal with backlogged tax cases (PPSS, secs. III–VIII, p. iii) and that the government be more aggressive in seeking to collect loan payments due it. Yet the funds required to implement these minor improvements pale in comparison to the amount required to implement one of the Commission's favorite recommendations, that the government's computer and management information systems be upgraded to the same standards of age, compatibility, and capability as those *purportedly* found in the private sector. As we noted at the beginning of this chapter, correcting the "problem" that government computers average 6.7 years of age while those in business average 3.0 years of age entails an astronomical investment. The Grace Commission is not clear about where this money would come from (increased income taxes or larger deficits?), and in calculating the "cost savings," the Commission does not obviously take an investment perspective in its calculations that nets out the capital costs, including the opportunity cost, of such an investment.

There is no question that it would be helpful if the Department of Housing and Urban Development had a consolidated financial control system (PPSS, sec. III, p. 73), if the reliability of the Navy's supply monitoring equipment were improved to the point that they were no longer plagued with inaccurate inventory records (PPSS, sec. VIII, p. 87), and if the National Technical Information Service data base were expanded (PPSS, sec. III, p. 223). The problem is that all of them would require a significant investment before any savings would be realized, and this fact needs to sink into the consciousness of legislators and government reformers alike. To behave as the Grace Commission does and rarely, if ever, acknowledge that these up-front costs exist—and the savings may be years off—and instead focus exclusively on the enormous savings that are "just around the corner" creates false expectations about the process by which real savings are achieved.

As hard as it may be for some ardent critics of government to believe, agencies like the Internal Revenue Service and the Department of Defense do not continue to use obsolete computer equipment because they don't know that better equipment is available or are unable to use it effectively. They don't have the resources (or are not allowed to spend the resources they do have) to buy new equipment. Recommendations to create task forces, hire a federal information resource manager, and upgrade the computing operations are not of much value unless there is also a recommendation on where to find the money in a budget with record deficits.

Some provision must be made to set aside resources, money, and trained personnel for improving performance. These resources cannot be subject to the same vicissitudes from the ebb and flow of financial and political fortunes as the resources devoted to directly performing the functions. As things now stand, the analysts who are the "efficiency experts" are often among the first personnel to go when cutbacks are made for reasons of financial stringency because the financial problems are immediate and the experts' solutions are not. This is the degenerative cycle in action—it is "eating the managerial seed corn"; to disrupt this degenerative cycle, institutions of government must be mandated to represent efficiency interests—institutions that are not subject to the short-term pressures of politics and budgets.

SHORT-TERM POLITICAL TIME HORIZONS

> Patience is a most necessary qualification for business; many a man would rather you heard his story than granted his request.
>
> CHESTERFIELD

The longest period of time that a large number of elected officials can think about is the period from now until the next election. Not surprisingly, this perspective introduces enormous biases in what politicians attend to at any given moment and in their program preferences. Politicians' short time horizons have played a significant role in the failure of the reforms we have described. They also play a key role in reducing the performance of government generally. It is those short time horizons that motivate politicians to court strategic reforms and to disdain tactical reforms. It is those short time horizons that encourage city officials to cut "invisible" expenditures—such as those on maintenance and equipment—to give the impression of efficiency and frugality while ignoring the long-term effect of neglected highways and buses. It is those short time horizons that make it very difficult for governments to work successfully on the large, complex problems that are such an important part of what they are supposed to do.

Many of the decisions that public organizations make are temporally interdependent in the sense that most decisions made now have important implications for other decisions that will be made in the future. Sometimes this temporal interdependence is direct. Solutions to current problems can obviously affect the amount of resources that are available to solve future problems. If a university spends part of its endowment for current operating expenses or gives tenure to a large proportion of its faculty, its future budget and personnel problems are going to be different than they would be if these actions were not taken. If a government relies on optimistic revenue forecasts to balance its budget, borrows cash against future resources to pay today's bills, or agrees in labor negotiations to expensive but deferred fringe-benefit packages, that government has altered its future budget and personnel problems. If such behavior is sustained over many years, as in the case of New York City, the problems may eventually become insoluble and default may loom as the only alternative.

Sometimes the temporal interdependencies are less direct, with the effects of current decisions on future decisions mediated through a complex array of individuals and organizations. Automobile manufacturers that control costs and prices through such measures as reducing expenditures for rear shielding of gasoline tanks may face, in future periods, altered consumer perceptions of product quality, increased direct regulation, and new, more punitive product liability laws. Universities that balance budgets by raising tuition, increasing class sizes, and reducing student support services may face declining enrollments and reduced tuition revenues. City governments that raise visible (e.g., property) tax rates rapidly or fail to reduce rates to dampen the tax-payment effects of inflation on property valuations may be inviting citizen-initiated limitations on revenues and/or expenditures.

In addition to varying in their directness, temporal interdependencies also vary in the immediacy and perceptibility of consequences. While the operating budget implications of a new indoor recreation facility may be obvious when the time arrives to staff, heat, and light it, the operating budget implications of changing the design of drainage for a road base to save a few thousand dollars in construction costs per mile may not be obvious even when the potholes appear in 10 to 20 years with greater frequency and severity than they would have with the original design. Learning is more likely in the first case than in the second because of the differences in elapsed time and in the relative difficulty of understanding the outcomes causally. By the time the potholes appear, the officials who changed the road design will probably no longer be in office. The new officials will be more interested in solving the pothole problem, perhaps using money generated from lowering design standards on current road construction, than in learning from the history of the current pothole problem to improve current decision making.

Drinkers do not acquire cirrhosis of the liver through some holistic, prescient choice procedure, they acquire it a sip at a time over an extended period. The result reflects the cumulative effects of many prior decisions, each of which, taken by itself, may have appeared unconnected to the cirrhosis condition and relatively unimportant. The terminal condition is unintended and undesirable. From the vantage of hindsight in a hospital bed, the patient's normative view of the many prior decisions (how they should have been made) may differ considerably from the descriptive view (how they were made). Unfortunately, the physiological state of the liver has by then been altered in largely irreversible ways. It is too late for changed values or increased insight into the consequences of drinking to reflect in the decisions important to the patient. The learning process is faulty, in part because the data that would permit adaptation—change values or improve one's understanding of consequences for subsequent decisions—are disguised over much of the period in which the decisions (to sip or not) are made. Even (or especially) for the well informed, the consequences of cirrhosis are unpleasant to attend to at the time of decision. There is utility in terms of immediate sensations in not attending to undesirable, imperceptible consequences of our every act, particularly when the act–consequence connections are stochastic and studied in a scientific field, medicine in this example, that we neither follow nor understand. For the moderately well informed, sometimes calculating individual, there is always the hope that medical science will discover either a means of reversing the physiological processes, that a foolproof liver transplant procedure will be developed, or that you are a physiological type not prone to cirrhosis. Or the reasoning may be that "something else will get me before cirrhosis and I may as well take my pleasures while I can."

Current officials, who are busily capturing their successors, are to a large extent captives of decisions made by their predecessors. For example, if their counterparts 20 years earlier cut corners on road construction standards and sewer maintenance programs, acquired extensive park and recreation facilities (with their attendant operating costs), and chose not to fund the pension plan fully, it may be current officials who must either solve the problems (e.g., find the revenues to replace or maintain the facilities or abandon them) or devise a means of shifting the problems onto future officials. Like the drinker's liver, much of the context for government has a memory—its structure is gradually transformed both by actions officials take and by forces beyond their control.

There is another way in which short time horizons contribute directly to the perpetuation of governmental inefficiency. As we noted at the outset of this section, short time horizons make it very difficult for governments to work successfully on the large, complex problems that are such an important part of what they are supposed to do. Incomplete programs, outputs, and reforms are an important source of public-sector inefficiency. Many tasks are undertaken but never completed because of such factors as a change of administration, the advent of a short-term financial crisis, or a shift in political attention. Given the difficulty of changing the institutions to give their administrators the capacity for a longer attention span, perhaps we need to think about how to change the way in which the problems for the public sector are defined. Herbert Simon's parable of the two watchmakers clearly demonstrates the implications of defining problems and structuring your work on them in different ways:

> There once were two watchmakers, named Hora and Tempus, who manufactured very fine watches. Both of them were highly regarded, and the phones in their workshops rang frequently—new customers were constantly calling them. However, Hora prospered, while Tempus became poorer and poorer and finally lost his shop. What was the reason?
>
> The watches the men made consisted of about 1,000 parts each. Tempus had so constructed his that if he had one partly assembled and had to put it down—to answer the phone, say—it immediately fell to pieces and had to be reassembled from the elements. The better the customers liked his watches, the more they phoned him and the more difficult it became for him to find enough uninterrupted time to finish a watch.
>
> The watches that Hora made were no less complex than those of Tempus. But he had designed them so that he could put together subassemblies of about ten elements each. Ten of these subassemblies, again, could be put together into a larger subassembly; and a system of ten of the latter subassemblies constituted the whole watch. Hence, when Hora had to put down a partly assembled watch to answer the phone, he lost only a small part of his work, and he assembled his watches in only a fraction of the man-hours it took Tempus.
>
> It is rather easy to make a quantitative analysis of the relative difficulty of the tasks of Tempus and Hora: suppose the probability that an interruption will occur, while a part is being added to an incomplete assembly, is p. Then the probability that Tempus can complete a watch he has started without interruption is $(1-p)^{1000}$—a very small number unless p is 0.001 or less. Each interruption will cost on the average the time to assemble $1/p$ parts (the expected number assembled before interruption). On the other hand, Hora has to complete 111 subassemblies of ten parts each. The probability that he will be interrupted while completing any one of these is $(1-p)^{10}$, and each interruption will cost only about the time required to assemble five parts.
>
> Now if p is about 0.01—that is, there is one chance in a hundred that either watchmaker will be interrupted while adding any one part to an assembly—then a straightforward calculation shows that it will take Tempus on the average about four thousand times as long to assemble a watch as Hora. (Simon, 1969)

If political time horizons remain short relative to the time required to solve the large, complex problems common in government, there are good reasons—efficiency and effectiveness for starters—to rethink our penchant for defining grandiose problems and devising grandiose solutions. For example, rather than defining the problems in defense procurement that lead to overpriced parts as a flaw in the grand design that stifles competition, etc., and proposing grand solutions such as dual-source contracting and massive information systems based on new computers providing data for a highly centralized decision-making process *across the board* in defense procurement, perhaps we should set an agenda of solving a sequence of much smaller problems so that there is at least some progress while we are waiting for Godot.

The Grace Commission emphasized the problems with short time horizons as a "lack of continuity of management."

> Because of the rapid turnover of key executives, a condition endemic to the political process, Government functions lack continuity of management. Key appointed officials change every 18 to 24 months. It is not possible to implement and sustain meaningful management improvement in an environment characterized by persistent changes in management. (PPSS, sec. III, p. 14.)

The Commission proposes two primary solutions to the problem. First, it recommends the creation of an Office of Federal Management (OFM) under the president that would "include OMB, GSA and OPM and have Government-wide responsibility for establishing, modernizing, and monitoring management systems." Second, it recommends increases in top-level executive compensation (presumably with lower benefits) to stem defections to the private sector. These proposals are not very promising because they do not change the time horizons and, if anything, increase the scope of the problems that are to be solved within the time limits—the watch is to be larger and with many more parts. The OFM would still be politically controlled and subject to wholesale personnel changes with each turn of administration. No matter how much you pay a political appointee in OFM and no matter how much he or she wants to stay on that job, a new administration of either party is apt to change personnel in key positions so as to have "its own team." All the top jobs in OFM would be key positions.

Clearly, some new disciplines are required for public officials, particularly those elected officials who are preoccupied with the short-term symbolic consequences of their actions at the expense of a concern for their substantive consequences. One line of reform that has been proposed to deal with this long-recognized problem is to extend terms of office and restrict officials to a single term. Presumably the extended term would force officials to confront the implications of some of their actions, since they would still be in office when those implications became clear. The logic behind the single term is simply that it would free elected officials from the short-term bias that is caused by constantly having to prepare for the next election.

Such proposals have their virtues, but the problem of long-term accountability still remains. The period between acts and consequences in public programs sometimes is in excess of 20 years—far too long a period to impose accountability by manipulating the length of time officials spend in office. A more promising direction for reform is to build constraints into the decision-making processes that bias decisional outcomes for long-term consequences. These would have to be somewhat ad hoc by program area. For example, in the capital area, laws could be written requiring officials in municipal governments who are building roads, bridges, and other facilities to include in the initial allocation for construction "permanent allocations" to maintenance and replacement funds. Payments to these funds would be made automatically off the top of each budget over the estimated life of the facility. Because it is never a good idea to create total inflexibility, the laws might be written so that a three-quarters (or some other) majority of the legislature could decide to change the payments in any given year.

There are comparable steps in the area of federal budget deficits. Rather than imposing hard-and-fast limitations and balance requirements as many are proposing, we might require (with independent forecasts of revenues and expenditures) a 60 percent majority for projected deficits from 0 to 10 percent, a 70 percent majority for deficits from 11 to 20 percent, and so on.

MISALLOCATIONS OF POLITICAL ATTENTION

The only practical problem is what to do next.
ANONYMOUS

There are gross misallocations of political attention other than attention to the short term at the expense of the long term or a taste for strategic reforms as opposed to tactical reforms. The experience with budgetary reforms during the 1960s and 1970s also teaches us that there is a consistent preference for simple issues at the expense of more complicated issues and for colorful issues at the expense of boring issues. One need only recall the indifference with which most performance reports generated by MBO were greeted in Congress. These biases are understandable; most of us share them. The problem is that most of what government does—and most of the potential efficiency gains—lies in areas that are reasonably complicated and boring for elected officials and citizens. Yet while the design of a sewage treatment plant, road construction standards, and inventory systems for office supplies or military spare parts involve highly technical issues that inspire few passions when compared to school prayer or abortion laws, they involve a great deal of money.

The preoccupation with the colorful and technically simple creates and then helps to perpetuate a situation in which most of us have no knowedge of most of what government does and no basis for forming reasonable expectations about what government ought to do. If an automobile traveling along a divided highway below the speed limit hits an icy patch, goes through the guardrail, and crashes down a steep embankment, the responsible government is almost never viewed as responsible. Yet there is little or no excuse for such an accident; the technology exists to keep highways clear of ice and to construct guardrails that can deflect the largest, most overweight truck. In the winter of 1984 such an accident took the life of an individual with a Ph.D. in electrical and computer engineering, a field that is suffering from a critical shortage of trained personnel. The attention and other resources that might have gone to new guardrails and better road-clearing programs may well have gone into new programs to encourage students to major in computer engineering or for economic development subsidies to attract high-technology industry. If so, a good case could be made that it would have been more efficient to have paid more attention to road design and maintenance.[11]

There are numerous other examples of situations in which politicians are paying too little attention to issues that have important efficiency implications or are asking too little of governments. The experience with environmental pollution is a classic example of the price that eventually has to be paid for ignoring the technical, complex issues surrounding industrial development and land and water management. Virtually every EPA "superfund expenditure" to clean up toxic waste could have been avoided at a fraction of the cost if the political attention and the resources were made available at an earlier point. On a more mundane level, signal and traffic-flow technologies exist that would enable city governments to cut significantly the amount of time that we all spend sitting at red lights and waiting in long lines of congested traffic.

Like misperceptions of governmental performance, the misallocation of political attention is a difficult problem to solve because it entails changing what people know, believe about, and expect from government. It is obviously foolish simply to propose that politicians abandon strategizing about reelection in favor of learning more about highway design or the other technical skills that might provide helpful information about potential efficiency gains. This belongs to the same category as the prescription that politicians should stop promising things that cannot be delivered. It is a noble waste of breath. Nonetheless, things can and are already being done to increase the quality of information available to decision makers. At almost every level of government, staffs are larger and better educated than ever before and entire agencies are organized around the idea of providing better analysis. The trick, as we will be arguing again and again, is to ensure that those hired to inform have the freedom and incentive to do so. It is also possible to enlist in the cause of efficiency the intelligence and critical abilities of professional groups and associations outside government. If the associations of specialists (e.g., civil engineers) were strongly supported and encouraged, they might do more in certifying specific competencies for those eligible to bid on highway contracts and play a much more active role in making "feasible standards" of service more widely known. While it's always necessary to recognize and monitor the inefficiencies that are embedded in the self-interests of such professional associations, they can still make a difference—as indeed they already have in areas such as public health and waste management.

INADEQUATE REPRESENTATION OF THE EFFICIENCY VALUE IN POLITICS

> There are a lot of mediocre judges and people and lawyers, and they are entitled to a little representation.
> SENATOR ROMAN L. HRUSKA (arguing the virtues of one of Richard Nixon's nominations for a seat on the supreme court)

Perhaps the most important lesson that the history of reform teaches us is that the basically political character of most government inefficiency cannot be overcome through the installation of a program, organizational structure, or system that is controlled by the same people who have an incentive to protect values other than that of efficiency. The founding fathers did a remarkable job of designing a structure that avoids the "tyranny of the majority" and any drift toward autocracy. They did this by separating and distributing powers and by pitting interest against interest and ambition against ambition. They did an adequate job of ensuring the representation of the interests of the different geographic areas and the interests of the propertied class, the dominant concerns in securing approval of the Constitution. They did much less well in ensuring the representation of other interests such as those of women, minorities, and the poor; but many of these representational flaws have been partially remedied over the past 200 years and are active items on political agendas.

One remaining flaw, a very serious flaw for the concerns of this book, is the inadequate representation of efficiency interests in our political processes. It is easy to understand this oversight. Government in the time of the Founding Fathers did not do much beyond represent the nation abroad, fight occasional wars, deliver the mail, set broad policies and laws, and collect taxes. There was no basis to foresee the sort of activist government engaged in producing a wide range of goods and services that has evolved. Consequently, there was little reason for them to worry about ensuring efficiency in the government's production of goods and services. It is less clear why we have failed to remedy the insufficient representation of efficiency interests just as we done for other omitted interests over the past 200 years. One likely reason is that efficiency is a collective value with no natural constituency; it is everyone's general concern and, simultaneously, no one's primary concern.

As we noted in the discussion above, one source of these problems has been the tendency to treat efficiency as an absolute value that should not be traded off against other values and that should somehow be imposed on political processes that tend to inefficiency. Reforms based on these premises fail because other legitimate values such as equity, the self-interests of individuals and groups, and due process are effectively represented in legal and political processes while efficiency is not. To design effective reforms, we need to understand the nature of efficiency as a value and from that nature, what it will take to institutionalize its effective representation.

What needs to be done is to institutionalize the effective representation of efficiency concerns in the political system. This is not a wholly new perspective. For example, Charles L. Schultze, in advocating PPB, argued that

> Decision making is done by advocacy and bargaining. PPB introduces the "efficiency partisan" into the debate. At the bureau level, the program evaluation staff, to be effective, must operate within the constraints and basic values associated with that bureau. They are, however, more likely to be interested in questions of efficiency than the rest of the bureau. Given the current values and constraints of the bureau, the program evaluation staff can be expected to promote the selection of efficient means of achieving the bureau's values. The total level of resources going to the bureau may, indeed, be too large, viewed from some outside vantage point. And part of the program analyst's time may well be devoted to helping his bureau chief protect those excessive resources. Nevertheless, given a budget level however determined, the program evalua-

tion staff can be advocates for optimizing the use of that budget from the standpoint of effectiveness and efficiency. They can also be advocates for testing, at the margin, the elasticity of those constraints that reduce the efficiency with which the bureau's resources are used. (Schultze, 1968, p. 95.)

While Schultze's vision has been realized to some degree—analysis has probably improved government performance to some extent (see Chapters 4 and 5) because there are more analysts in government and those analysts are predisposed by training to understand and articulate efficiency concerns—he overstates the effect of this form of representation. To a greater extent than he anticipated, analysis has been turned to the service of other values in political and bureaucratic processes. It is not just "part of the analyst's time . . . devoted to helping his bureau chief protect . . . excessive resources," but assignment after assignment taking the form of: "I want to do X. Do an analysis that shows that X is efficient and effective." If the analyst refuses such assignments or obeys the canons of his or her profession and produces an unbiased anlaysis that shows that X is neither efficient nor effective, the usual result will be an analyst who, if still employed, is in no position in the internal political scheme to advocate anything effectively, including efficiency, in the future. The problem, of course, is that the PPBS form of representing efficiency interests, as interpreted by Schultze, leads inevitably to conflicts between efficiency interests and individual self-interests that are, just as inevitably, resolved in favor of the individual's interests most of the time.

Schultze's efficiency advocate is in an untenable position. In order to engage in "whistle blowing," the analyst, even a secure civil servant, must have an independent base of power. The analyst is dependent on the organization for salary and promotions. The analyst may, as Schultze believed, place much greater weight on efficiency than other bureaucrats do; but he or she is not evaluated on the basis of his or her success in representing those different values. Inevitably, the analyst depends on his or her success in representing the values most dear to the organization and its most influential individuals, values with which efficiency must inevitably compete. It is unrealistic to expect large numbers of such analysts to have the devotion to efficiency, the strength of character, and the bureaucratic acumen that would be required to withstand the pressures of other values, individual and collective, and to represent efficiency effectively.

The analyst as efficiency advocate must operate with other handicaps. There is the hindrance of a foreign language. The analyst speaks "technocratese" (algebra and worse) that is largely unintelligible to nonanalysts. The values that Schultze would have the analysts represent are bound up in theories and in technical explications that have little or no salience to nonanalysts. For politicians, political appointees, and ambitious bureaucrats whose careers depend, at least in part, on the judgments of politicians and political appointees, reducing "excess burden" or increasing the neutrality of the tax system is inherently less salient than delivering another half-billion dollars in program benefits to some critical constituency.

We are not arguing that the circumstance described above is good or bad but merely that this is the way things are, and that reforms to improve government performance must recognize and work around such realities. Individuals and groups may and sometimes do sacrifice their own interests for collective values, but the assumption that they will do so with regularity regardless of the pressures and temptations is a poor basis for designing effective reforms. As the Federalist papers and the Constitution attest, the founding fathers were not enamored of such assumptions. In arguing for the separation of powers, Madison (*The Federalist*, No. 51) argued that

> In order to lay a due foundation for that separate and distinct exercise of the different powers of government . . . it is evident that each department should have a will of its own; and consequently should be so constituted that the members of each should have as little agency as possible in the appointment of the members of the others. . . . It is equally evident that the members of each department should be as little dependent as possible on those of the others for the emoluments annexed to their offices. . . . Ambition must be made to counteract ambition. The interest of the man must be connected with the constitutional rights of the place. It may be a reflection on human nature that such devices should be necessary to control the abuses of government. But what is government itself but the greatest of all reflections on human nature? If men were angels, no government would be necessary. If angels were to govern men, neither external nor internal controls on government would be necessary.

In designing future reforms, it is important to view efficiency[12] as one among many competing values in political processes. The problem in reforming governments to improve their efficiency is that of ensuring effective representation of the value of efficiency in political processes. To do this effectively will require that those charged with representing efficiency be given a large measure of independence from those charged with representing other values in the political processes and that the individual and agency interests be aligned with the efficiency interest.

Before going into detail on the reforms that the representational view of the efficiency problem implies, it is useful to say more about the unusual characteristics of efficiency as a value in political processes and about why efficiency is currently underrepresented. Very often there are direct beneficiaries of inefficiency, just as there are direct beneficiaries of other program values. Money lost to inefficient activities is not burned; it goes to people directly or through organizations. When an activity is labeled inefficient, it means that someone somewhere is getting *something for nothing* according to the prevailing moral calculus. This may be as simple as an employee who is getting a fair day's pay for something less than a fair day's work or a contractor who is being paid more than a reasonable market price for his or her good or service. It may be as complicated as everyone involved working hard and being paid market prices for an activity with little or no value. The people and organizations involved in the inefficient activity are benefitting from it and have incentives to protect it. While they cannot argue directly in public on behalf of inefficiency and the benefits they enjoy from it as they can for meritorious program values, they can be very skillful at identifying (and inflating) positive values that preserve the inefficiency. They may well be the only ones who fully perceive the inefficiency and as beneficiaries, they have a disincentive to talk about it, much less eliminate it. The political rub is the difficulty of distinguishing between those who are simply the beneficiaries of inefficiency and those who are deserving beneficiaries of somewhat inefficient programs.

Inefficiency is not a value that stands by itself but one that is associated with the means of accomplishing other values. It is very difficult to find situations in which more efficient means can be effected without changing any of the other values. These other values have specific constituencies; efficiency, as a collective value, does not.

Several possible reforms are suggested by the perception of the problem as one of representing the value of efficiency as adequately as other values are represented. One distinct possibility is to create agencies within governments that are explicitly charged with representing efficiency by ferreting out corruption and inefficiency and are effectively buffered from political forces that would limit the scope of their inquiries. Madison's discussion of emoluments and dependency and of having "ambition counter ambition" is relevant.

Some key features of such an agency would include:

1. A budget and employees that are not under direct, short-term political control.
2. Employees who are legally barred from engaging in political activities and from leaving the agency and going to work for any part of the government that the agency evaluates or for any organization, public or private, funded by the government.
3. The right, by subpoena if necessary, to examine all records and to interview any officials, past or present, in the government.
4. Having the resources available to actually fund all or part of the investments required for efficiency improvements. If the agency were simply created to evaluate line agencies and identify possible efficiency improvements, not much would happen—for reasons that have been discussed.

The GAO in the federal government is something of a model, but we would go even further in the direction of independence. As it now operates, the GAO is an agency reporting to the Congress headed by a comptroller general who is appointed for 10 years and subject to removal only by impeachment. This is a good start, but a weakness in the current arrangements is the dependence of the GAO on Congress for its year-to-year appropriations. If the GAO were to issue a series of highly critical reports on programs favored by substantial majorities in Congress, there is the possibility that the appropriation would be drastically cut. A solution is to set aside, perhaps constitutionally, a percentage of the budget or of income tax collections as the appropriation. This need not be an entirely new net expense for governments. They could for example begin the agency by building on an existing agency, like GAO for the federal government, and by moving as many of the audit and control activities as possible from the various line agencies into this new agency.

The agency might have a paid board of directors with overlapping multiyear terms who are appointed by Congress with the consent of the president and whose salaries are set at the level of a congressman. The board, in turn, would be responsible for appointing a chief executive every six to ten years. The chief executive could be removed by a substantial majority of the board.

A persistent problem with regulatory agencies is the "capture" of the regulators by the regulated. After a period of time, the two come to share the same information and view of the world and the adversary relationship, somewhat necessary to effective regulation, is lost. The problem can become particularly critical if the regulators are permitted to go to work for the regulated agency. Federal agencies are, for example, populated at supergrade levels by many former OMB budget examiners and CBO analysts. The problem can be largely avoided by legally barring agency employees who leave the agency voluntarily from working for any other agency in the government or for any organization that derives more than 25 percent of its revenues from the government for 10 years. This provision should be a lot more stringent than the provisions that now apply to retired military officers working for defense contractors.

There are comparable organizations that would be sensible for state and larger local governments. For the smaller local governments, which are all creatures of states, the state might require and support a centralized agency to perform much the same functions. The sort of independent institution that we are advocating to represent efficiency will be something of a monster to many elected and appointed officials because it potentially represents an attentive, uncontrollable source of information about their activities. On the other hand, it is not the sort of proposal that is easy for a politician to be against because it seems reasonable that the more competent and well-meaning an official is, the more he or she should favor the creation of such an institution. Our expectations for the short-term impact of such a new agency are fairly modest. Many details would have to be worked out before a formal proposal could be prepared and during the processes of political consideration. The impacts would depend very much on the character of the top appointments, but the experience in the GAO over the last 20 years provides an encouraging example of just how much competent, well-meaning people can accomplish in the areas of control and efficiency.

There is also the problem of selective inattention and manipulation of information in areas that the president might want to ignore. Is it simply coincidental that the Grace Commission's report often mentions that the independent GAO has uncovered a particular management problem but rarely attributes any such discovery to OMB that works so closely with the president? We cannot help being suspicious that, regardless of its other merits, the Grace-proposed OFM may not always possess the incentive to develop control mechanisms that tie the hands of an ambitious president or that discover problems with a favorite presidential program. Oversight is needed, and this can only be provided by a more independent agency.

CONCLUSION

Business will be better or worse.

CALVIN COOLIDGE

A large part of this book has been concerned with popular and expert beliefs about governments and their performance. We believe, after examining a large body of evidence, that:

1. Governments in the United States are much more efficient and effective than most citizens believe. Their efficiency has improved dramatically over the past 100 years and compares favorably with that of their foreign counterparts. Moreover, the efficiency of government bureaucracies is much closer to that of private-sector bureaucracies than is generally acknowledged. Substantial problems with government performance remain, however, and these problems are much harder to solve than those of the past, which were connected with widespread graft and corruption and the absence of accounting systems. The chances are slim that there will be a technical or conceptual breakthrough in improving government efficiency that will have the impact that the discovery of broad-spectrum antibiotics had on medicine or that the discovery of the transistor or microchip had on electronics. The chances are nil that the solutions to governments' managerial problems already exist in the management technologies of the private sector.

2. The bulk of the improvements in government efficiency that have taken place in recent years have resulted not so much from overt, grandiose reform schemes as from a host of modest, tactical reforms. There appears to be an inverse relationship between the amount of fanfare associated with any given reform and its positive effects on government performance. Business methods are much less appropriate to improving the efficiency and effectiveness of government than is commonly believed. The "methods" are not the panaceas for inefficiency and ineffectiveness in government (or business) that some believe them to be. There are intrinsic differences between the functions of government and the functions of business, and these require different managerial methods.

3. There are real limits to the efficiency and effectiveness that any government can achieve. These limits arise from the nature of the problems that governments are obligated to address, from the constraints that governments must honor in attempting to solve the problems, from the large scale of many government organizations, and from the intentionally adversarial character of government processes.

4. Contemporary U.S. governments have not reached limits on their performance potential. There are real opportunities to improve government performance, but availing ourselves of these opportunities will require very different reform strategies than those that have been tried in the past. It is important that this country take a less negative, less destructive approach to government than it has in the past two decades. Governments have essential roles to play in this society, and one of those roles is that of "dumping ground" for the societal problems that are too important to be ignored and are unlikely to be addressed effectively by the private sector because the problems are hard or there is no obvious way to make a profit. A government that is paralyzed by gratuitous criticism and "reform" attempts cannot give those problems the attention they deserve. Hubris is not the answer. Helplessness is not the answer. There are alternative approaches, some of which we have suggested here.

NOTES

1. Sandra Salmans, "A Budget Cutter Who Won't Quit." *The New York Times*, February 24, 1985, p. F8.
2. The appendix to this chapter contains data and further discussion on selected companies affiliated with PPSS from *Forbes* magazine's "37th Annual Report on American Industry" (January 14, 1985).
3. Salmans, op. cit.
4. PPSSCC press release, April 5, 1983: PRIVATE SECTOR PANEL DETAILS COST REDUCTION PLAN FOR EPA/SBA/FEMA OF AT LEAST $1.8 BILLION.
5. PPSSCCF press release, April 5, 1983: PRIVATE SECTOR SURVEY TO RECOMMEND $11 BILLION IN AG SAVINGS.
6. Ibid.
7. The Veterans Administration had an extremely unpleasant experience with a delay of just a few days during the Carter administration. The Internal Revenue Service is several months behind on tax refund check as this book goes to press.
8. This is as true in the private sector as in the public sector when systems—such as payroll—are critical.
9. Indeed, many of the firmer estimates for items such as personnel benefits and entitlement programs can be and were taken from the federal agencies' own models.
10. Many of these useful recommendations are probably not original to the Grace Commission's report. It is readily apparent in reading the report that the Commission depended very heavily on the ideas and opinions of current government employees and recent internal government reform efforts to generate such a large number of recommendations.
11. Of course, the victim may well be a heroin dealer or a Baptist minister. The net benefits and costs are almost never easy to calculate ex ante or ex post. But the point is the insensitivity to governmental performance in many such circumstances.
12. Effectiveness is less interesting as a value for reforming government here for reasons that are given below.

REFERENCES

Dole, Robert. In Laurie McGinley, "Touted Report Won't Be Heeded." *The Wall Street Journal*, November 30, 1984, p. 56.

Forbes. "37th Annual Report on American Industry." January 14, 1985.

Salmas, Sandra. "A Budget Cutter Who Won't Quit." *New York Times*, February 24, 1985, p. F8.

Schultze, Charles L. *The Politics and Economics of Public Spending*. Washington, D.C.: Brookings, 1968.

Simon, Herbert A. *The Science of the Artificial*. Cambridge, MA: MIT Press, 1969.

President's Private Sector Survey on Cost Control: A Report to the President (PPSS), Volumes I and II as submitted to the executive committee for consideration at its meeting on January 15, 1984, processed.

APPENDIX A

Selected So-So and Poor Performers Among Contributors to President's Private Sector Survey on Cost Control in the Federal Government

> Those who mistake their good luck for merit are inevitably bound for disaster.
>
> J. CHRISTOPHER HEROLD

This appendix contains data on the performance of 65 of the many contributing corporations listed in Appendix X of the PPSS draft report. The performance data were taken from *Forbes* magazine's "37th Annual Report on American Industry" (January 14, 1985). This is neither a random sample nor a complete set of the PPSS corporations. It is a set of PPSS corporations below the median five-year average return on equity in their industry or segment. The data given from left to right are:

Column 1: *Company* name
Column 2: *Industry* group that is the basis of performance comparison
Column 3: *Rank* of the company in its industry in terms of five-year average return on equity (company position/number of companies in industry group)
Column 4: The *company's five-year average return on equity*
Column 5: The *industry median* five-year average return on equity

In the spirit of the PPSS, which focused almost exclusively on what was wrong with the federal government, this is a biased sample. It is biased in that it does not include data on the performance of all of the corporations affiliated with the Commission.* The sample was constructed by matching the names of corporations listed in Appendix X of the survey report as having been represented on the executive committee or as having contributed to the PPSS effort with the names of corporations below the median levels of performance in their industries (or industry segment for diversified businesses) according to the *Forbes* report. The data do provide a reasonable reading on the performance of the corporations included. The five-year return on equity is widely accepted as at least one very important dimension of the infamous "bottom line" that drive firms to be paragons of efficiency and effectiveness. Using five-year return rather than a single year's return provides some protection from placing too much weight on a "bad year"—all indi-

---

*This would have been a much more formidable data collection effort than the one undertaken because of the difficulty in matching large corporations and in finding performance data on small corporations.

viduals and corporations have those. The comparisons are done within industry as defined by *Forbes* so as to avoid invidious comparisons; noticing that Apple Computer and U.S. Steel have very different performance records over the past five years tells you very little about their relative efficiency and the competence of their managements. There are, of course, many other problems in inferring anything about efficiency and managerial competence from data of this sort, but these inferential problems pale beside the problems with most comparisons of business and government, including those found throughout the survey report.

The data in this appendix reveal nothing about the average quality of the complete set of corporations implicated in the survey. The data also reveal nothing about the quality of the individuals drawn from the corporations to work with the Grace Commission. From casual observation, we note that large, excellent (in terms of performance) organizations have been known to employ some strikingly mediocre, even incompetent people and that less successful organizations have been known to employ extremely able people. But then the individuals participating in the survey are not represented as "average" but as the "best and the brightest," as "the top business and managerial talent in America," and as "individuals who had proven ability to effectively and efficiently manage their own enterprises—whether for-profit or not-for-profit." Since the experience and proven performance in business are the only credentials offered as evidence of managerial competence and as the reason why government should take their managerial advice seriously, it seems reasonable to look at little more closely at the credentials, just as any competent businessman would in considering prospective employees, consultants, and appointments to the board of directors.

The recent performance credentials of many of the Grace Commission contributors are not all that impressive. We found 65 companies with below-median performance. Thirty-seven of the companies in this set finished dead last or next to last in their industry (or one of their industry segments) in terms of five-year return on equity. Most of the companies are far below the best performers in their industries, the "best and the brightest" over the past five years.

Company	Industry	Rank	5-Year Average Return on Equity	Industry Median	Industry High
Aetna Life and Casualty	Insurance/ Diversified	14/18	14.4	18.0	25.8
Allis-Chalmers	Heavy Equipment/ Agricultural	2/4	Deficit	Deficit	8.8
"	Industrial Machinery	48/48	Deficit	13.3	25.8
AMAX	Nonferrous Metals	11/15	3.4	8.6	19.6
American Can	Packaging	24/25	4.4	12.2	54.1

Company	Industry	Rank	5-Year Average Return on Equity	Industry Median	Industry High
American Cyanamid	Chemicals/ Diversified	12/19	11.7	12.3	35.4
"	Health Care/ Drugs	23/24	11.7	19.7	64.1
AMF	Industrial Machinery	42/48	7.2	13.3	25.8
AMF	Recreation	4/4	7.2	12.0	17.4
ARA Services	Services/Food Distributors	13/16	11.0	13.9	27.1
AVCO	Financial Services	7/11	10.9	10.9	35.7
AVCO	Aerospace and Defense	37/43	10.9	15.8	87.1
Bank America	Banks/Multinational	9/11	13.4	15.0	18.4
Beneficial Corporation	Retailers— Specialty, Miscellaneous	7/9	4.7	12.9	65.7
"	Financial Services	10/11	4.7	10.9	35.7
Bethlehem Steel	Steel	22/22	Deficit	6.3	27.7
Boise-Cascade	Packaging	20/25	8.4	12.2	54.1
"	Paper	20/24	8.4	11.2	35.4
"	Lumber	4/6	8.4	8.8	10.9
Burroughs	Computers	17/17	8.2	17.4	113.8
Champion Intl.	Building Materials/ Lumber	5/6	8.3	8.8	10.9
Chase Manhattan	Banks/Multinational	8/11	14.4	15.0	18.4
CIGNA	Insurance/ Diversified	18/18	4.0	18.0	25.8
Cluett, Peabody	Apparel/ Clothing	10/14	10.2	13.8	28.0

Company	Industry	Rank	5-Year Average Return on Equity	Industry Median	Industry High
Continental Corporation	Insurance Property and Casualty	11/11	8.6	16.9	36.3
Continental Illinois	Banks/Multinational	10/11	11.9	15.0	18.4
Crocker National	Banks/West	9/9	10.6	14.5	17.7
CSX	Surface Transp./ Railroads	7/9	11.1	12.6	24.3
Detroit Edison	Electric Utilities/ Midwest	25/25	11.5	14.1	18.0
Diamond Shamrock	Chemicals/ Diversified	13/19	11.3	12.3	35.4
"	Petroleum/ Other	31/36	11.3	19.1	45.2
Dravo	Builders/ Commercial	13/13	3.9	18.2	25.2
Dresser Industries	Oilfield Drillers and Services	19/20	13.1	20.1	33.6
Eaton	Automotive Suppliers/ Parts Makers	26/27	6.5	13.0	35.4
"	Electronics/ Equipment	20/22	6.5	15.7	30.4
First Chicago	Banks/Multinational	11/11	9.6	15.0	18.4
GAF	Building Materials/ Others	26/27	Deficit	11.0	24.2
"	Chemicals/ Specialized	25/26	Deficit	15.6	24.4
B F Goodrich	Automotive Suppliers/ Tire and Rubber	5/7	4.5	6.5	21.0

Company	Industry	Rank	5-Year Average Return on Equity	Industry Median	Industry High
B F Goodrich	Chemicals/ Specialized	22/26	4.5	15.6	24.4
W R Grace	Chemicals/ Specialized	14/26	15.4	15.6	24.4
" "	Diversified Companies/ Conglomerates	13/22	15.4	16.1	35.4
" "	Retailers— Specialty/ Miscellaneous	4/9	15.4	12.9	65.7
" "	Retailers/All	20/36	15.4	16.1	65.7
Gulf and Western	Diversified Companies/ Conglomerates	18/22	10.6	16.1	65.7
" "	Financial Services	8/11	10.6	10.9	35.7
" "	Leisure and Reservation/ Entertainment	8/8	10.6	10.9	28.9
Honeywell	Aerospace and Defense	27/43	14.3	15.8	87.1
" "	Computers	12/17	14.3	17.4	113.8
" "	Electronics/ Equipment	14/22	14.3	15.7	30.3
Hospital Corp.	Hospital Management	5/5	21.6	22.9	38.3
IC Industries	Diversified Companies/ Conglomerates	20/22	7.9	16.1	
"	Food Processors/ Branded Foods	31/35	7.9	16.8	
" "	Surface Transp./ Railroads	8/9	7.9	12.6	
Ingersoll- Rand	Industrial Machinery	41/48	8.1	13.3	25.8

Company	Industry	Rank	5-Year Average Return on Equity	Industry Median	Industry High
ITT	Diversified Companies/ Multicompanies	10/19	13.1	13.1	22.2
"	Insurance/ Diversified	16/18	13.1	18.0	25.8
Kemper	Insurance Diversified	11/18	16.5	18.0	25.8
Koppers	Chemicals/ Specialized	21/26	5.8	15.6	24.4
"	Building Materials/Other	21/27	5.8	11.0	24.2
"	Diversified Companies/ Multicompanies	19/19	5.8	13.1	22.2
Manufacturers' Hanover	Banks/Multinational	7/11	14.6	15.0	18.4
Marine Midland Banks	Banks/ Northeast	17/18	10.5	15.1	23.6
Mellon Bank	Banks/ Northeast	14/18	13.9	15.1	23.6
McGraw- Edison	Electric Equipment	12/14	10.9	17.7	21.8
"	Industrial Machinery	31/48	10.9	13.3	25.8
Mobil	International Oils	5/7	17.5	18.3	33.2
Monsanto	Chemicals/ Diversified	14/19	10.9	12.3	35.4
National Standard	Steel	15/22	1.3	6.3	27.7
NCR	Computers	11/17	15.1	17.4	113.8
Northwestern National	Insurance/ Life & Health	15/16	8.9	13.1	45.2
Olin	Chemicals/ Diversified	18/19	8.6	12.3	35.4
"	Diversified Companies/ Multicompanies	18/19	8.6	13.1	33.2

Company	Industry	Rank	5-Year Average Return on Equity	Industry Median	Industry High
Penn Central	Aerospace— Defense	40/43	9.1	15.8	87.1
" "	Conglomerates	19/22	9.1	16.1	35.4
" "	Petroleum/ Other Oil & Gas	35/36	9.1	19.1	45.2
Pittson	Air Transport/ Freight	4/5	2.6	20.4	37.7
" "	Coal	4/6	2.6	7.8	23.8
Richardson-Vicks	Consumer Products/ Personal Products	14/14	9.2	18.5	26.0
Scott Paper	Consumer Products/ Personal Products	13/14	10.8	18.5	26.0
" "	Paper	14/24	10.8	11.2	35.4
Sears, Roebuck	Financial Services	9/11	10.2	10.9	35.7
" "	Retailers— General/ Department Stores	13/14	10.2	12.6	22.3
Sperry	Aerospace & Defense	35/43	11.2	15.8	87.1
"	Computers	14/17	11.2	17.4	113.8
J.P. Stevens	Textiles	10/11	3.6	9.5	12.4
Stewart-Warner	Industrial Machinery	40/48	8.2	13.3	25.8
Sybron	Health Care	11/11	4.0	19.4	35.7
Tenneco	Natural Gas Utilities/ Products and Pipelines	10/12	16.7	19.8	34.3
"	Petroleum/ Other Gas and Oil	23/36	16.7	19.1	45.2

Company	Industry	Rank	5-Year Average Return on Equity	Industry Median	Industry High
Texas Instruments	Aerospace & Defense	38/43	10.6	15.8	87.1
" "	Electronics/ Semiconductors	8/9	10.6	17.9	33.6
United Airlines	Air Transport/ Passenger	8/14	0.3	1.6	25.8
Union Carbide	Chemicals/ Diversified	16/19	10.6	12.3	35.4
" "	Diversified Companies/ Multicompanies	16/19	10.6	13.1	22.2
U.S. Steel	Steel	17/22	Deficit	6.3	27.7
"	Petroleum/ Other Oil and Gas	36/36	Deficit	19.1	45.2
Warner- Lambert	Health Care/ Drugs	24/24	10.1	19.7	64.1
Williams Companies	Chemicals/ Specialized	20/26	9.7	15.6	24.4
" "	Natural Gas Utilities/ Products & Pipelines	12/12	9.7	19.8	34.3
F. W. Woolworth	Retailers—General/ Discount & Variety	13/15	4.0	14.6	35.6

INDEX

ABOUT THE AUTHORS

GEORGE W. DOWNS is a professor in the Political Science Department and the Graduate School of Administration at the University of California, Davis. He attended Shimer College and received his Ph.D. from the University of Michigan in 1976. He is the author of *Bureaucracy, Innovation, and Public Policy* (1976) and numerous articles on nonmarket decision making. His work has received the American Political Science Association's "Leonard D. White Award" and the Youden Prize from the American Society for Quality Control.

PATRICK D. LARKEY is an associate professor in the Department of Social Sciences and the School of Urban and Public Affairs at Carnegie-Mellon University. He attended Stanford University and received his Ph.D. from the University of Michigan in 1975. He is the author of *Evaluating Public Programs* (1979) which received the National Tax Association–Tax Institute of America's "Best Dissertation in Public Finance Award." He has published numerous articles on governmental budgeting, program evaluation, and government growth.